ENG

TELEVISION NEWS

McGraw-Hill Series in Mass Communication

Consulting Editor
Barry L. Sherman

THIRD EDITION

ENG

TELEVISION NEWS

Charles F. Cremer
West Virginia University

Phillip O. Keirstead
Florida A & M University

Richard D. Yoakam
Indiana University

The McGraw-Hill Companies, Inc.
New York   St. Louis   San Francisco   Auckland   Bogotá   Caracas
Lisbon   London   Madrid   Mexico City   Milan   Montreal
New Delhi   San Juan   Singapore   Sydney   Tokyo   Toronto

ENG: TELEVISION NEWS

This book is printed on acid-free paper.

2 3 4 5 6 7 8 9 0   FGR   FGR   9 0 9 8 7 6

ISBN 0-07-013530-4

This book was set in Cheltenham by ComCom, Inc.
The editors were Hilary Jackson, Fran Marino, and Tom Holton; the production supervisor was Denise L. Puryear.
The cover was designed by Amy Becker.
Quebecor Printing/Fairfield was printer and binder.

Library of Congress Cataloging-in-Publication Data is available.
LC Card #95-36822

About the Authors

Charles F. Cremer is Professor Emeritus of Journalism at West Virginia University, a former associate dean of the school of journalism and head of the school's broadcast journalism sequence.

Professor Cremer received a Ph.D. degree in mass communications from the University of Iowa, a Master of Science degree in journalism from the University of Illinois, and a Bachelor of Arts degree in English from Loras College.

He began his radio-television journalism career as news editor at WILL Radio-TV, Urbana-Champaign, Illinois. His professional journalism experience includes: news director at WREX-TV, Rockford, Illinois; administrator of news and public affairs at WTHI Radio-TV, Terre Haute, Indiana; news director at WSUI Radio, Iowa City, Iowa; and general assignment reporter for the *Terre Haute Tribune.*

Dr. Cremer is a former president of the Wabash Valley Press Club; a former division head of the Radio-Television Journalism Division of the Association for Education in Journalism and Mass Communications; a former secretary of the Iowa Broadcast News Association. He also served as an ex-officio member of the RTNDA Board of Directors, and as a trustee of the Board of Trustees of the Radio-Television News Directors Foundation.

Phillip O. Keirstead is Professor of Journalism and Sequence Coordinator for Broadcast Journalism at Florida A&M University. He received his M.A. in journalism from the University of Iowa and his B.S. in Radio-TV from Boston University. He is completing a Ph.D. in communications policy at the City University in London.

Professor Keirstead began his journalism career at WCCC-AM-FM in Hartford, Connecticut, later becoming a bureau chief, anchor and producer at WFMY-TV in Greensboro, North Carolina, and news director at KFEQ-AM-TV in St. Joseph, Missouri and WHCT-TV in Hartford, Connecticut. He was also a national broadcast editor for the Associated Press in New York and an editor/producer for CBS News in New York.

Professor Keirstead is widely known for his writing on news technology topics and is currently the U.S. correspondent for *International Broadcasting* magazine, published in London. He is also the recorder for the RTNDA Data Transmission Guidelines Committee and has held national offices with the Society of Professional Journalists' Freedom of Information Committee.

 **ichard D. Yoakam** is Professor Emeritus of Journalism and Telecommunications at Indiana University. He received his B.A. and M.A. in journalism from the University of Iowa. He began his career in broadcast journalism as a reporter, editor, newscaster, and sports announcer at WHO, Des Moines, Iowa. He was news director at KCRG, KCRG-TV, Cedar Rapids, Iowa. He has been a newscaster, writer, and editor for NBC in Washington and New York City. For twelve years he served as NBC Indiana election manager for primary and general election research and coverage planning. He has also been a news editorial consultant for ABC News.

Professor Yoakam has served as faculty chairman of the National Press Photographers TV News Workshop and chairman of the NPPA International Flying Shortcourses to Asia and Europe.

Professor Yoakam's research on the production of the 1960 Nixon-Kennedy and 1976 Ford-Carter presidential debates, on broadcast editorializing, and on the news distribution and production practices of European television networks has been published in several books and journals in the United States and abroad.

For those peerless unit managers: Frances, Sonia-Kay, and Mary Bob

On behalf of the Radio-Television News Directors Association it is a pleasure to endorse this third edition of *ENG: Television News.* RTNDA was instrumental in the creation of the first edition and has endorsed this textbook ever since.

By its very nature, electronic journalism is driven by technology. Never before in the relatively short history of our business has the pace of technological change been as great. It is more important than ever before that students of electronic journalism be well grounded in the technology and techniques of their craft.

None of us knows for sure where technology is taking the news business. But we do know that those who gather and report the news for the electronic media in coming decades will require far greater technical skill and versatility than ever before.

Once again, this book promises to be an important resource for a new generation of electronic journalists and the educators who are preparing them for a rapidly changing workplace.

David Bartlett, President
Radio-Television News Directors Association

Contents

Foreword

By Connie Chung*

No reporter ever forgets his or her first story.

In 1969, I was working at WTTG-TV—a small Metromedia station in Washington, D.C.

I had been hired as a copyperson out of college, and on this day was on the assignment desk.

A power failure—electrical, not political—had crippled parts of the city and the assignment editor needed a warm body . . . fast.

My job: to go out with the cameraperson and nail down facts, footage, and interviews in time to make air.

I was scared to death—and thrilled.

Electronic News Gathering—ENG—was a thing of the future. I was covering this story with a *film* cameraperson, Bob Peterson, who was not only a pure professional but an extraordinarily generous and helpful friend.

*A veteran broadcast journalist, Connie Chung has been a correspondent and anchor for CBS News and NBC News.

Bob taught me on day one that a symbiotic relationship in the field is crucial to making words and pictures mesh in the edit room later.

We raced back to the station, I wrote up the story, and just a few hours later, our report made the Ten O'Clock News.

Twenty-five years later, I was fortunate enough to still work with Bob Peterson. But he was by then an *ENG* cameraperson.

ENG technology has given broadcasters a flexibility we never dreamed would have existed in those days.

We can transmit pictures and sound from a telephone line in any hotel room in the world.

Because of the extraordinary satellite capabilities, I could anchor the *CBS Evening News* from virtually any location—and at a moment's notice.

As dazzling as this fast-advancing technology is, it is still only the messenger.

It is the message that has always and will always count.

The single most important tool you must have to be a fine journalist is writing. Good producers, reporters, editors, camerapersons, managers, technicians are good writers.

When you come to work in television, you leave your ego at the door. Collaboration is the key to producing a first-rate television news report.

ENG technology promises to be an even greater partner in that collaboration in the future.

Preface

ENG: Television News is a comprehensive and realistic presentation of the field of television news from a professional and ethical point of view. The authors provide in a single college-level textbook a thorough and systematic treatment of the editorial and technical processes of television news. Their treatment of the subject elaborates two basic themes throughout: (1), a consistent stress on content over technology, and (2), a consistent stress on journalistic ethics and standards of professional conduct. The authors' view is that any journalistic enterprise is content-driven; that the content of the message is more important than the technology used to create it and the delivery system used to disseminate it; and that the issue in contemporary television news is not its technology but control of this technology to achieve editorial excellence. This stress on the journalism and the ethics of the profession is a main feature of this textbook.

The authors hold an integrated view of television news, integrated in the sense that TV news work—field reporting, interviewing, videography, editing, writing, producing, anchoring—involves a team effort. The book stresses teamwork. The reporter must work well with the videographer, the videographer must be responsive to the editor's role, the editor must understand both videography and news writing, the writer must work with pictures and sound as well as with words, the producer must meld these components into a unified whole, the anchor must deliver the product purposefully and convincingly, and those who manage the system must provide the tools and create the rationale, environment, standards and ethic of the enterprise. This comprehensive treatment of integrated editorial and technical functions of TV news is another main feature of this book.

Control of technology requires a solid grasp of the technical aspects of the TV news process. This textbook examines the uses of technology today and in the future to communicate news by television, characteristics of standard electronic news equipment, and the latest technical advances—notably in digital technology and the application of computer technology to the news production process.

To provide unique views of this journalistic and technological mix, the authors called on six gifted television professionals to write personal essays in which they share with the reader something of the ins and outs of television news work, the demands and rewards of the craft, the ups and downs of daily routines, the ethics and responsibilities of professional behavior. These personal essays occur in the Foreword and at the ends of Chapters 1, 3, 6, 7, and 8. These professional essays constitute a unique feature of this textbook.

PREVIOUS EDITIONS OF ENG

The first edition of *ENG* was written by Professors Richard D. Yoakam and Charles F. Cremer. When this textbook was conceived and written—the late 1970s/early 1980s—the television news industry was moving through a period of rapid, industry-wide technological change. Indeed, the first edition of *ENG* was published as a direct response to technical advances in TV news at that time.

Of those technical advances begun in the mid-1970s, one became a symbol (some would say *the* symbol) of the emerging "new order" of the industry. Television news retooled its main news gathering device—from the "chemical/mechanical" technology of 16 millimeter motion picture news*film* to the "electronic/electromagnetic" technology of video*tape*. Early on in this conversion process news gathering by videotape came to be known as *E-N-G*, the buzz phrase for Electronic News Gathering. Professors Yoakam and Cremer intended that their textbook be used by advanced-level college students, working professionals, and student interns, as a bridge over this transition from "chemical/mechanical" to "electronic/electromagnetic." From that point on the technology has continued to change, and so has this textbook.

The most readily apparent changes to the book for this third edition are indicated on its cover—a revised title, and the addition of a third co-author. In the revising, rewriting, editing, and reorganizing of text for this third edition— now titled *ENG: Television News*—Professor Phillip O. Keirstead of Florida A&M University joined the team as a co-author. Professor Keirstead brought to the revision project his extensive knowledge and expertise in the field of new technologies in broadcasting and cable, including his broad background in the incorporation of computers into television newsrooms and the diverse applications of computers to TV news.

For this new edition, Professor Yoakam's role was less concerned with arranging, organizing, and executing the numerous details of text and graphics revision. His attention was directed more toward guidance and overall supervision of the revision process. Besides his diligent reading and notation of manuscript drafts, he offered counsel and constructive criticism (and moral support) to authors Cremer and Keirstead. Professor Yoakam's detached view, coupled with his keen judgment, wide professional knowledge, and enthusiasm, helped steer his co-authors safely around pitfalls in the revision process. He was a main source of steady and invaluable guidance throughout.

Professor Cremer's responsibility was that of senior author for this third edition of *ENG*.

FEATURES OF THE THIRD EDITION

New material dealing with computers in the newsroom, digital editing and other applications of digital technology in electronic equipment have been added to bring the content of the book technologically up to date.

New essays have been added for the third edition. In addition to a new foreword, professional essayists contributed two new chapter essays—one from the point of view of the emergent "information superhighway" including interactive television as it may apply to TV news, the other on television news producing, a specialty of continuing and increasing importance and complexity in the modern television news process.

The adaptation of new technological tools to TV news has resulted in changes in the area of news department personnel. Responding to this facet of change, the authors have included fresh material on job categories and skill requirements, career paths into the various TV news positions, and a wealth of ideas from working professionals about suitable ways for students aspiring to a career in the TV news profession to prepare themselves for the challenges that lie ahead.

In the law chapter, new material has been included on the impact of tabloid television on libel and privacy litigation, access to information, cameras and microphones in courtrooms, and reporter-source confidentiality.

PLAN OF THE BOOK

Chapter 1 examines the contemporary field of television news: its basic tools—cameras, recorders, edit decks, microwave and satellite technology; and its personnel—those who gather, edit, and deliver news; those who operate the electronics; those who direct the production; those who manage the enterprise.

Chapter 2 is devoted to a nontechnical explanation of the technology of ENG. A main goal of this chapter, unchanged from earlier editions, is to provide broadcast journalism students and professionals with information they need to know about the *characteristics* of typical ENG equipment. They also learn to recognize a given unit's *capabilities* and *limitations,* and basic steps in the proper use of ENG equipment to produce electronic journalism.

Chapter 3 concentrates on how television news is communicated, the structural elements of that communication, and how to make the content of news reports clearer. This chapter takes the student through a step-by-step process for shooting video in the field.

Chapters 4, 5, and 6 take up the crafts of editing, scripting, and field reporting. Chapter 4 examines the editing process, both video and sound, in detail; Chapter 5 explores the techniques of television news writing; and Chapter 6 takes a wide-ranging look at reporting in the field. Each chapter presents examples of various techniques of this trio of interlocked crafts, including the intricacies of the separate editing of pictures and sound, with graphics enhancement; writing techniques for coordinating text with pictures and sound; and examples of field reporting, interviews, standups and packages.

Chapter 7 takes the student on a tour of the inside workings of a television newsroom and explains how television newscasts are put together.

Chapter 8 discusses in detail and with real-world examples the techniques, strengths, problems, and pitfalls of live television news reporting.

Chapter 9, contributed by Dr. Dwight L. Teeter, Jr., a legal scholar and recognized expert in mass media law, explores legal issues, cases, and decisions from the special point of view of television news and ENG. This chapter serves to emphasize to the student the need for heightened awareness of the legal problems themselves and the need for vigilance and the exercise of sound and ethical journalistic judgment. The law chapter reinforces a theme permeating the book, namely that ethical sensibilities are crucial to responsible journalism.

In Chapter 10 the authors explore television news industry trends, the constantly changing and evolving technology, and what this means for newsroom personnel, management, organization, and policy.

ACKNOWLEDGMENTS

The authors wish to acknowledge the help of TV news directors, TV and cable news senior executives, technology experts and technicians, and anchors, reporters, videographers, editors, and desk managers who deal with ENG/SNG daily. Their help went well beyond the normal bounds of professional courtesy. We especially acknowledge the contributions of our guest essayists: Connie Chung, Mark Casey, Larry Hatteberg, Lynn Cullen, Valerie Hyman, and John Premack. Special thanks also to Dr. Dwight L Teeter, Jr., co-author of the law chapter in this textbook's original edition but solely responsible for law chapter revisions for this edition.

The authors also gratefully acknowledge the courtesies extended to them by the president of the Radio Television News Directors Association, David Bartlett, and are most appreciative of his statement of endorsement of this edition on behalf of the RTNDA.

The authors wish to thank with deep appreciation the following: Woody Coates, WWBT-TV; Donna R. Danis, Avid Technology; Beth Dolinar, WTAE-TV; Jeff Field, Reuters America, Inc.; Sandy Genelius, CBS News; Dana Grande, WFSB-TV; Carolyn Bailey Lewis, WNPB-TV; Jamie Logue, WBOY-TV; Mel Martin, WINK-TV; John McPherson, KPRC-TV; Jon Petrovich, CNN Headline News; Kathleen Revitte, ABC News; Steve Schwaid, WVIT-TV; Don Shoultz, CNN

Headline News; Roger Sheppard, WTAP-TV; Paul Sisco, Worldwide Television News; Nick Smith, Nick Smith Productions; Deborah Syverson, Conus Communications, Inc.; and Ken Tiven, CNN.

The authors are grateful for services, resources, and facilities provided for this revision project by the West Virginia University School of Journalism, with special thanks to Dean William T. Slater; former dean Emery Sasser; Donna Meadowcroft, accounting I secretary; and Sandra Willard, senior administrative secretary. WVU Law Professor Charles R. DiSalvo provided timely research help. Likewise, at Florida A&M University, the authors received assistance from Gloria Horning, Ernest Jones, and Gloria Woody, for which they are most thankful.

Special thanks also to Dr. James L. Hoyt, University of Wisconsin at Madison, who was mentioned in the preface of both the first and second editions of this textbook and who for this third edition again reviewed the complete manuscript. His thoughtful and constructive criticisms were helpful and most appreciated.

The authors express thanks to Fran Marino, McGraw-Hill College Division associate editor, who introduced them to the McGraw-Hill way of doing things and organized the many details of the revision project to get that project started and then keep the process moving; to Tom Holton, editing supervisor, for his diligence in supervising final preparation of the manuscript and graphics for production; to Carolyn Viola-John, whose editing expertise was gratefully acknowledged in the preface of the first edition of ENG and whose editing of manuscript for this edition was most skillful; and to Carl Leonard, marketing manager, for gathering and organizing data for the marketing effort.

The authors have received much support and encouragement from broadcast and journalism educators who have adopted this book as their television news textbook in colleges and universities nationwide and whose comments and suggestions the authors value and appreciate. For this edition of ENG the authors are once again most grateful to their reviewers: Steve Anderson, Virginia Tech University; John Broholm, University of Kansas; Clay Carter, California Polytechnic State University at San Luis Obispo; Lori Cooke, Marist College; Gloria Horning, Florida A&M University; Kenneth Nagelberg, Southern University; Robert Richards, Pennsylvania State University; Karen Slattery, Marquette University; Gale Wiley, University of Texas at Austin; Evan Wirig, Eastern New Mexico State University; and Stacey Woelfel, University of Missouri at Columbia.

The authors received expert computer assistance from, and are deeply grateful to: Dr. Patrick Conner of West Virginia University and graduate assistant Daiming Liu; and Helen Womack of the University of Tennessee-Knoxville. Additional computer information and advice was provided by Helen Cremer, Jesse Montrose, and Kent Munro.

Charles F. Cremer
Phillip O. Keirstead
Richard D. Yoakam

Impact and Challenge

Technological developments in television news in the last twenty years have been part of a widespread technological explosion in all media. One analyst has called that explosion the most profound development for information media since the coming of the telegraph and telephone. Big concept. And, yes, big changes, now and to come.

Developments in transmitting pictures and sound have brought about the portable microwave, wireless telephones, helicopter-borne homing antennas, mobile satellite transmitting and receiving dishes, CDs, computers, fiber optics, and digital networks, and have made it possible for television news outlets—local, network, all-news cable—to report live from just about anywhere and to cover just about anything that happens.

Adapting these technological tools to TV news has resulted in changes to the organizational, policy, operational, budgetary, and personnel areas of the news department.

Technology continues to provide television news with new and fascinating electronic tools with which to gather and report the news. The basic concept behind the adoption of these technical marvels is the idea that by using these tools skillfully and wisely, we ought to be able to gather, process, and deliver TV news better than ever before.

New technical capabilities also have helped reshape the thinking as well as the duties of those who run TV news. These executives broaden their coverage horizons with a much more wide-angle view of the world to be reported on each day. This broadened scope of news as a part of the overall station/cable channel service to audiences—and its profitability for owners and stockholders—has changed both the role of news executives and their staffs and the news they broadcast.

Figure 1.1. Covering the news with ENG. A typical field reporting team. The reporter is responsible for the facts and the words used to report the story. The videographer is responsible for taping the video and sound elements of the story. Technicians in the van control the equipment and the microwave transmitter that send the video and sound back to the TV station through the microwave antenna on the roof. *(Courtesy of WLWT-Cincinnati. Photo by Jeff Gamblee.)*

ENG—JUST WHAT IS IT?

Electronic News Gathering (ENG) is the basic method of gathering and editing pictures and words. ENG technology is relatively standardized and has three important technical features—helical scanning, portability, and ease in editing—and is related to a much larger family of electronic tools.

First let's look at **helical scanning** technology (see Figure 1–3). The small, lightweight ENG cameras provide picture and sound signals to a small tape recorder. The tape, sealed in a cassette the size of a small notebook or even smaller, travels around the record heads helically—in a spiral. Thus the pictures and sound are put on the tape at a slant—rather than in a horizontal line as earlier tape technology prescribed.

The tape itself comes in various widths—one-inch, three-quarter-inch, half-

Figure 1.2. A professional portable video camera, a basic tool for television news gathering in the field. The unit shown is a 3-CCD Camcorder using the S-VHS format. *(Courtesy of Panasonic Broadcast & Television Systems Company.)*

inch, quarter-inch, 8-millimeter, the trend has always been toward smaller sizes—thus advancing the second technical feature, **portability**. The narrower tape also makes it possible to mount the recorder right in the camera—a feature the home video industry pioneered. The one-piece **camcorder** eliminates the bulky separate videotape recorder with no loss of picture quality.

Cameras are more portable because of important technical breakthroughs, mainly smaller and smaller TV pickup tubes and miniaturized, transistorized internal circuitry. Cameras weighing 10 to 15 pounds, fitting comfortably on the shoulder of the camera operator, are common. The charged-coupled device (**CCD**) camera, which uses solid-state chips in place of pickup tubes, brings even greater portability and reliability.

Editing is fundamental to TV news and here, too, technology continues to evolve. The raw news material gathered in the field can be edited immediately by the use of standard helical record-playback videotape machines linked electronically by an editing controller. A variety of editing functions can be performed by the transfer of selected scenes and sounds from one videotape to another merely by pushing a few buttons. In the simplest technique, selected shots from the raw videotape made in the field are transferred to a blank videotape, one scene at a time. This editing technique is called **linear** editing. The editor moves the raw videotape forward and backward, "shuttling" through unwanted portions picking out only those scenes wanted in the finished product. The editor thus "assembles" the story in its final

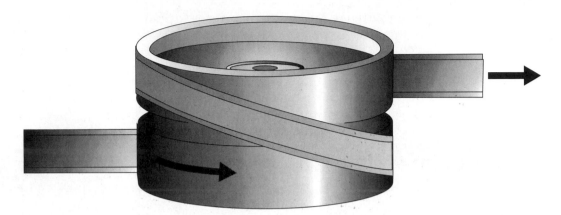

Figure 1.3. How the signals that contain the video and sound are recorded onto videotape using the helical scan principle. The videotape passes around a drum that contains the recording heads as the drum rotates rapidly. Thus the signals are placed on the tape at a slant. This design dramatically reduces the size and weight of the recorder, improving its portability.

order, one scene at a time, by going back and forth through the raw videotape.

Most professional stations use sophisticated equipment which allows for the recording of a **time code**—a visual number that appears in each frame of picture—during the original shooting or later. This code can be used with professional editing equipment to ensure accurate edits. Time code is also used with a computer memory to program edits. The operator types the beginning and ending time codes for a series of scenes into the editing controller. The controller then searches out those "edit points" and makes a series of edits to assemble a whole story, or even a whole program. More advanced systems allow an editor to take pictures, sound, and electronic effects from a wide array of sources and put them all onto one finished videotape in a very short period of time.

Editing by copying from the tape taken out of the camcorder to an "assembly" tape is being replaced by a new approach. This latest editing technology comes from the world of computers.

The material shot by a videographer is **dubbed** (copied) into the hard disk memory of a fast personal computer. (Next we will see camera tape recorders replaced by storage devices which use computer or optical disks. Further along, the pictures will be stored by computer "chips," solid memory devices.)

The editor can view scenes on a color computer monitor, store scenes selected (using a still picture on the screen as a reminder), and then instruct the computer to assemble the finished tape, with effects, from the raw video now stored on the computer hard disk.

This editing method relies on sophisticated **digital compression** technology. It is often called **nonlinear** editing, meaning you do not have to keep moving a tape back and forth in order to copy off, in the desired order, the scenes you are going to use. You view the video, tell the computer which scenes you want to use and in what order, and the computer does the rest.

Supporting the basics of ENG is a whole range of sophisticated **mobile equipment**, including **SNG** (Satellite News Gathering) vehicles, microwave sending and receiving units, satellite dishes, control room digital switching consoles, and electronic special effects that television journalists use to (a) get their raw material, (b) process it, and (c) put it on the air. Looking into the future conjures up images of more machines, more technology, and more opportunities and challenges.

TELEVISION NEWS TODAY

ENG is a lot of things to television news: a technology, a concept, even a philosophy of how to go about covering the news and delivering it to the audience. The basic ENG benefits are deceptively simple.

1. Speed: Videotape and digital disk from ENG equipment are ready to edit immediately after they are recorded.

2. Editing flexibility: The technology allows for quick construction of a basic story *and* the addition of audio and visual effects to that story for emphasis and clarity.

3. Mobility: With helicopter, microwave, and satellite news gathering capability, ENG allows stations and cable channels to reach out faster and farther to provide more breadth and depth to their coverage. It also allows them to go live at the scene of a story.

ENG as a Unifying Force

ENG has had a broad impact on local television news. It has caused changes in station organization, operation, and management. Most of this impact has been unifying.

1. New tasks and skill requirements have evolved that mix technology and journalism in the editorial process.

2. The escape from the confines of the studio and control room to the place in the field where the news is being gathered brings journalists and technicians closer together in situations where the need for "team spirit" is crucial.

3. Taking the entire newscast "on the road" can involve station personnel (such as sales, programming, and promotion people) who never before had any direct contact with the news effort.

Figure 1.4. A television studio set for news at WTAP-TV, Parkersburg, West Virginia. The curved anchor desk has space for news, sports, and weather anchors. The studio features Videssence™, a high-tech and energy-efficient lighting which also helps keep the studio cooler. *(Courtesy of WTAP-TV. Photo by Roger Sheppard.)*

4. As technology becomes more complex, more engineers who work very closely with the news operation on both minute-by-minute and long-range planning are needed. Greater appreciation of editorial and technical problems evolves.

5. The news director and his or her job have moved much closer to top station management. As manager of a huge budget, a large staff, and major daily broadcasts, the news director is now intimately involved with the competition for ratings, overall station strategies, and long-range planning.

PEOPLE

ENG also has had an impact on the way people who hold the key news jobs do their work. Reporters, videographers, editors, assignment desk managers, ENG coordinators, systems managers, and producers all work with the technology almost every moment of the day. If a station's priorities are "Get it first, but first get it right," technology can help get it very fast—getting it *right* requires reporters, editors, and producers to have their news judgment and editing skills working in highest gear.

The Reporter

Television news reporters work with three channels of information: words, pictures, and sound. They have to be attuned to the strengths and limitations of each, and know how to make words, pictures, and sounds work together to tell a story.

In its simplest form the TV story shows the reporter standing at the scene and telling the audience what has happened. This reporter monologue is called a **standup**. Next some videotaped scenes that illustrate what the reporter is talking about, synchronized with the reporter's narration, are added. Then the reporter appears again at the end to wrap up and conclude—another standup.

If you interview a news maker at the scene and edit some of those remarks into the story—these are called **sound bites**—you've added still more information to this report.

It is the judicious mixture of showing the reporter, showing scenes that illustrate what the reporter is talking about, and inserting sound bites to explain what happened that makes a visual story successful.

Compile and edit these elements onto one master videotape and you have what is called a **package**, a self-contained story on videotape or disk with its own beginning, middle, and end.

Reporters frequently work close to program deadlines, which are right up to and into the newscasts themselves. Some reports will be done live from the scene or source. That means reporters must be selective about the informational value and timeliness of the visual material and conscientious about developing the latest angles to the story.

For example, the governor holds a morning news conference and gives out some important information. With ENG's speed the reporter can continue to pursue other angles and reactions to that information throughout the day. Research—check the governor's facts, previous position, political or self-interest. Get reaction—how this will go over with voters, politicians, experts. Then put the story together.

A Midwest news director said of reporters and their responsibilities: "Action news formats, those little packages that purport to tell the whole story in one minute and twenty seconds, are a quick and dirty way of telling the news. They all look the same: Reporter standing before the courthouse telling about a new tax cut announced today; sound bite of the assessor saying a few words while his hand rests on a stack of tax assessment forms; back to the reporter saying something like, 'And so, at least today, your pocketbook got a break; how long it will last only time can tell.' "

"That," he said, "won't do any more. That's because the reporter can get the sound and pictures at the courthouse, and then go on to interview people about the impact of the cut on the individual taxpayer and on the institutions the higher taxes previously supported. He or she can get to the experts so that at 6 P.M. the story can include some reaction as to whether the tax cut is a good or bad idea."

Live Reporting

Live reporting involves the most difficulties for reporters. Reporters must be able to think and talk and sometimes even move all at the same time.

Live reporting is complicated. The news is breaking on the air. The reporter at the end of that microwave or satellite link has to make split-second decisions—reporting what is happening, explaining it, and putting it into perspective.

A Boston news director said, "One of my reporters, coming back after doing her first live report, said, 'That's like patting your head and rubbing your tummy at the same time.' What scares them—and me—is that they are out there running the television station at the end of a high-technology system. What they are saying is going directly to the audience; it's a tremendous responsibility and only some can carry it off."

Any reporter who has to do a lot of live reports must have a strong sense of time and timing.

Unless it is the first report from a major breaking story, any live report has time limits. Within newscasts the live reports are scheduled to fit into a certain spot. Even if the live reports are segments within a live special, producers give them a length assignment and expect reporters to conform.

Satellite live reports are even more strictly timed since satellite time is bought by the minute and often other stations are waiting to use the satellite immediately after the first report is off the air. A major axiom of SNG: "Don't miss your uplink!"

Another major skill requirement—being at ease (or seeming to be at ease) out there in front of your peers, the competition, and the audience—is a natural one. Some have it. Some don't.

The Boston news director: "They've got to blot out the distractions, think about what the camera is showing, and work with it. They have to explain to the audience what they are seeing and try to explain what it means."

Another dimension of "being at ease" is the reporter's ability to proceed with caution. A Milwaukee news director: "Every word is important. The reporter has to think about what she or he is saying and what that has to do with the story . . . and about what the people being interviewed are saying, and what that means. They've got to come up with the pertinent information quickly and then deliver it, ad lib, in a focused way . . . clean, spare . . . stick to what they know . . . don't speculate."

A Washington, D.C., news vice president said speculation is the most dangerous thing to do. During a hostage situation a newsman reporting live had noticed the police moving in a large quantity of boxes. He speculated the boxes contained arms for a SWAT team assault. Actually, the police were delivering food demanded by the hostage takers.

News directors everywhere said they are extremely leery of live interviews because of the lack of editorial control inherent in the situation. They try to direct reporters regarding whom to talk to and what to talk about. They seemingly want reporters to have a sixth sense about an interviewee—what someone is going to say before she or he says it.

A San Francisco news director was blunt: "People can give out wrong information accidentally, or they can do it on purpose. All the reporter can do is try to avoid demagogic material."

"I tell my reporters," she said, " 'Don't interview kooks. You know who they are because they show up at everything ready to talk. Why should we let them run on, live? If you could edit it, you'd cut them out; reporters have got to have their news judgment working in high gear when they're out on a live shot."

Learning the territory is something most news directors wish their reporters would spend more time doing. In a business where there is a lot of moving around from city to city by young reporters on their way up, the nomadic career seeker doesn't put down many roots.

A Detroit news supervisor told the story of a young woman from the West Coast who moved to a network-owned station in Chicago.

"To me what she did is *the* way to get yourself ready for the main tool of local TV news: the live remote," he said. "On her days off she spent a lot of time going around government offices and neighborhoods talking to the people in these places: 'What goes on here? What do you do here? Who are the people who live in this area?' She did this because she has the kind of curiosity you want in a reporter, and because she was getting ready for that next live broadcast. She might end up someplace she had been before, and thus have a little edge because she already knew something about it. You can't ever do enough preparation or talk to enough people to be ready for everything, but you sure can improve the odds."

Another little edge goes to those reporters who have some understanding of human nature, the psychology and sociology of human behavior.

A live broadcast attracts a crowd. Sometimes these people are quiet and friendly and just want to watch. More often some want to get into the picture—these are known as **hi moms**. Sometimes the "hi moms" make rude gestures or want to play tricks on the reporter after they get on the air.

A Milwaukee reporter with a lot of field experience said reporters should take their psychologist hats along with them on a live shot. She was confronted by a group of teenage boys holding soft-drink cups and making motions that clearly indicated they planned to give her an ice shower once she began her broadcast.

"It wasn't a serious story," she said, "just a feature on the day's events at Summerfest. But I knew what they had in mind. So I went over to one of the kids and said, 'What's your name, haven't I interviewed you before?' The kid gave me his name and that took care of any plan to let me have it."

Sometimes the crowd members don't appreciate the efforts of the TV station at all. They can turn surly, especially if they don't like what the reporter is saying or if the spotlight of the news is coming down hard on them, their neighbors, or friends. Here the reporter must have more judgment: The standing rule for most stations is for the reporters and their crews to leave a hostile situation immediately.

Over and over again the people who are running the nation's newsrooms talk about the need for a reporter to be "a higher-quality" person.

In Columbus, Ohio, a news director said, "Old-time, hard-nosed police reporters have a place in any news operation. But they tend to be narrow and parochial in interest. I'm looking for the college-educated, professional person who can handle the tough stories but still represent you in the board rooms."

Renaissance women and men—that's the term a Chicago news producer used to indicate what TV reporters have to be. "I mean by that," he said, "that they've got to be more curious and socially and politically conscious than ever before. They've got to go beyond covering the breaking elements of the story and to begin to think immediately about the impact of that story. That means they've got to be people who read widely about urban government, and economics, and even about the art, culture, and history of the area where they work. If you are going to get reaction to develop the well-rounded story, you've got to know where and how to find the reactors, *and* what to ask them when you find them."

The ENG Videographer

With electronic field equipment, microwave vans, and mobile satellite uplinks, the videographer is a member of a powerful team and the key figure in visual news gathering. The pictures and sounds he or she collects complement the facts and information the reporter digs up. Perhaps even more than the reporter, the videographer in the field is the leader of that team, combining photo professionalism with much involvement in the technology that gets the pictures.and delivers them where they're needed.

What does it take to be a videographer?

As with reporters, ENG has changed the "kinds" of people television stations are looking for to handle the videography.

An ENG coordinator in Los Angeles said there are three qualifications for a videographer: "They've got to have photo skill, but they also have to have news appreciation, and, some electronic training is a plus."

And he said the "types" are changing: "In the old days the crews sat around with their shoes off talking about when the surf would be up . . . The new ENG types are liberal arts, or law, or electrical engineering combinations . . . bright . . . motivated by being in the news."

The Assignment Desk Manager

There is a large flow of raw news material into the television newsroom. Out in the field, reporters and videographers are doing their end of the news coverage. Inside the newsroom the assignment desk manager is supposed to manage their movements, and with the aid of writers, editors, and coordinators, process the raw material.

The assignment desk is supposed to know where everyone is and what they are doing. When there is breaking news the assignment desk manager moves equipment and personnel to respond. When there is a need for more information about a story for those in the field, the desk gets it and passes it on. The system works only as well as the mobile radio and telephone communications linking the station with the field. News coverage is dependent on the ability of the desk crew to plan and react. It is a fragile system that often puts a premium on a few people's ability to make snap decisions that are practical and wise. Practical is much easier to achieve than wise.

Basic news gathering is simple. A reporting crew (but often this is one person) goes to the scene of a story for coverage.

The order of difficulty in managing the coverage increases if the idea is to feed the tape back by **microwave**—a faster delivery system since the station gets the material immediately rather than having to wait for the crew to make its way through traffic back to the station.

Then there is the **live shot**. This takes two forms: **live-tape** coverage and **live-live** coverage.

With live-tape, the crew sets up the cameras and microwave and sends the pictures and sound back as the story unfolds. In the station, the pictures and sound are videotaped as they come in, and each scene is logged for later editing.

Finally, there is the live shot with the reporter at the scene, broadcasting directly.

While any or all of these events are going on, the assignment desk continues to supervise all the other news coverage and plan ahead.

At least two major problems can arise. First, the desk is expected to have logistic, strategic, and tactical roles. That is: The desk is to arrange for the coverage, design how it will be carried out, and follow it as it develops.

The second problem is that with more volume and longer newscasts, planning coverage and supervising it are now much bigger responsibilities.

Solutions to these problems continue to keep pace, and the good news is they all mean more editorial people will be introduced into the system. Also, the organization of the system has become more horizontal—a line of responsibilities that is clearer and more precise.

The ENG Coordinator

One answer has been the development of a whole new set of personnel, often called ENG coordinators. Their job is to work with the reporters, editors, and technicians in liaison with the assignment desk and program producers.

When these jobs started evolving, they seemed to be more technical than journalistic; they required people who spoke the language of the technicians and who would represent the news interests in the organization and operation of equipment. The first ENG coordinator may have been installed in the control room where the video material came in, to report back to the newsroom on its content and length. Or the first ENG coordinator may have been appointed as a referee, to arbitrate the arguments that begin when too many people try to do too many things with too little equipment, all at the same time.

ENG coordinators must be people who know both journalism and its technology. And their jobs are becoming more sharply focused as the need for tighter editorial control over content has become crucial.

In most stations the acquisition of the "outside stuff"—vans, helicopters, bureaus in remote locations—has led to the creation of an "inside stuff" area that looks like the control deck of a nuclear submarine. Many stations incorporate portions of this technology in the news set itself. It is space-age stuff. Here technicians supervise and operate the machines that receive and record the pictures and sound from remote locations. There are walls filled with racks of equipment. Colored lights blink to indicate what is functioning and how it is performing. Scopes glow green and flicker as they report on the technical quality of the signal, the pictures, and the sound. There are dozens of television monitors which show scenes from the remotes. There are panels of lighted buttons which can route pictures and sounds to other control rooms, editing rooms, on the air—wherever they are supposed to go or are wanted.

Always there is a continuous chatter from the communications system. The technicians in the field and those in the station talk to each other by two-way mobile radio, cellphones, and other audio links, lining up antennas, microwave relays, satellite feeds, sending and receiving pictures and sound

Figure 1.5. A video editing bay at WNPB-TV, Morgantown, West Virginia. The set-up is arranged horizontally, with the videotape player unit and its monitor to the left, the recorder and its monitor to the right, and the controller on the desk top. *(Courtesy of WNPB-TV.)*

on cue. On another set of phone and radio channels, the assignment desk manager, editors, and broadcast producers are talking to the journalists in the field, evaluating the story, relaying and updating supporting information.

If those discussions lead to a decision to go live, the activity may shift to a studio and control room, or to a production area in the newsroom itself. Wherever that activity is, the live broadcast is produced and directed just as if it were a regular program. Anchors are brought in to introduce it and to provide the basic information and bridges to and from the reporters in the field. Producers join the control room people to supervise and coach. ENG coordinators provide the liaison between the technicians and the news staff.

In the field, ENG coordinators keep an eye on the crews and on how efficient they are, solve technical and editorial problems, help with production, and generally keep things moving like a staff sergeant on a forced march. They are traffic cop, electronic wizard, coach, and intelligence network all rolled into one.

The Systems Manager

A new TV news professional specialty has emerged out of the advances of technology. More and more news staffs now include someone who helps manage the system by bridging the gap between production and engineering.

Tom Wolzien, a former NBC News Vice President for Special Production

Figure 1.6. Microwave units relay the news. A small microwave unit near the videographer sends pictures of the fire to the news van. From there, other microwave units can relay those pictures back to the TV station through antennas on the helicopter or installed on top of tall buildings or natural terrain.

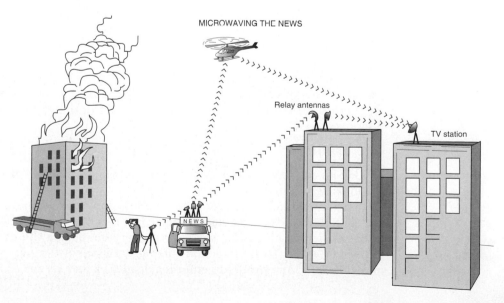

and Design, was the first to spot this trend. He called these people "production systems specialists."

The root of the specialty grew out of pressure from producers, directors, and nontechnical managers for more bridges between the engineer and the producer. Like the ENG/SNG coordinators, people who hold these posts start from a variety of beginnings. One may have first worked between a news director and chief engineer involved in the purchase of millions of dollars worth of equipment. Another may have combined a computer science specialty with an electrical engineering (EE) degree in college, and found her or his way into broadcasting as a consultant. Another may have started out as a producer who got very involved in applying technology to solve coverage problems on a news special, such as election night.

However they got started, what they have in common, Wolzien said, is their approach. They start with the audience or program, not with the hardware. The idea is to decide first what to put on the air, and then figure out what technology, hardware, and people will be needed to make it work.

Around the nation scores of people are now playing this role, and they are becoming more and more important in the news process. They advise networks, syndication companies, cable channels, and their own stations and groups, and help each other as each new technical phase comes along. The key to success in the field is keeping it uppermost in mind that no matter how fancy the gear becomes, the message is still what counts.

Not every station or news organization has defined a need for a sophisticated systems manager, but most stations have someone assigned to look after the newsroom computer system.

The Computer Specialist

This person is frequently someone who likes computers and knows quite a bit about them. Most computer systems companies offer special training to one or more selected staff members, sometimes called super users, so that they may deal with the majority of computer glitches or "crashes" without having to wait for a company specialist to call or visit the newsroom to troubleshoot a problem. These designated "computer gurus" are also responsible for assigning security codes, training new employees, and purging old files.

The Producer

Producers are key newsroom decision makers, **executive producers** being the most senior in authority.

The immediacy of contemporary television news gathering puts a premium on the producer's ability to make fast news and production judgments. Those decisions affect the way almost everyone else in the newsroom does his or her work. Those decisions also greatly affect the overall cost of the news effort. So the producer enforces deadlines and serves as a career advisor, cheerleader, disciplinarian, teacher, and psychiatrist to the staff after the dust of the latest news program has settled.

The producer is at the center of adaptation of the new technology. It is the producer who must control how this technology affects news coverage and content. By inventive and creative use of technology the producer can push for that extra step, direct that extra effort that makes the finished story and newscast more interesting, more complete, and more satisfying to the viewer.

Then there are the production's show-business angles. ENG and the related digital technology provide the producer with a wide array of visual embellishment, **DVE**—Digital Video Effects—that can be shown on a television screen. These effects bring with them a new language:

Squeeze Zoom™—place any portion of the picture into any portion of the screen; move it to any other part of the screen; bring it to full screen or make it disappear entirely.

Multiple Split—a number of pictures put on the screen at the same time in almost any pattern.

Rotary Wipe—an effect that looks like pages are being turned in a book, or pictures rotate or tumble from the sides, top, bottom, background to foreground or vice versa.

Keying—using the color spectrum to insert pictures on top of other pictures electronically.

Unrestricted Keying—multiple layers of pictures placed on top of each other.

Frame Store—graphics, designs, words, and still pictures stored in a memory one frame at a time for instant recall.

Computer Graphics—graphics created entirely by a computer, or existing graphics modified by a computer, using electronic "pens," "pencils," and "painting palette." Can appear to be three dimensional. Can be animated. Can be stored for reuse.

PUP—portable uplink. A small, portable satellite uplink package that can be transported almost anywhere as airline luggage to feed a signal to a satellite transponder.

Window—the time when a satellite transponder becomes available, thus: The window will open at 01:45:30 and will close at 05:45:30.

The producer can order up any combination of this gadgetry. The important point is that the decision to use these "bells and whistles" is a journalistic one: Their use must be aimed at making the story in which they are used more complete and clearer to the audience.

News directors view the producers who work for them as the key people who make ENG and related technology work for the journalism.

Some Conclusions

In our look at the impact of ENG on the way television journalists do their jobs and its impact on the jobs themselves, we have tried to point to a most important relationship—the impact of ENG on the content of television news.

Our premise is that technology is something to be learned and mastered, but that this is no more important than learning any other skill or craft. Artists adopt new media, new tools, new techniques to help them become more creative. Athletes find new ways to train their bodies to gain a split second or other fractional advantage. Doctors and scientists use technology to find new ways to unlock the mysteries of the gene.

Similarly, journalists must look at technology as a means toward a goal. For the journalist that goal is to create messages that are clearer, easier to understand, and more useful to the audience.

The production manager of a Louisville television station said it best: "The technology is like the covers of a book; the important stuff—the content—is on the inside."

In the next chapter we take a more detailed look at technical tools used in television news including some of the standard equipment types, and some of the basics of using these tools for news coverage. But we end this chapter by repeating the basic fact, the technology keeps improving and the equipment keeps changing.

PROFILE

Mark Casey is news director of WTVD-TV, Raleigh-Durham, North Carolina, a Disney-owned Capital Cities-ABC station. Among his responsibilities are editorial supervision, personnel administration, budget management, product development, and talent development for the news operation.

Casey was with Cox stations for ten years as executive producer of news at WPIX-TV, Pittsburgh, Pennsylvania, senior executive producer of news at WSOC-TV, Charlotte, North Carolina, and news director at WHIO-TV, Dayton, Ohio. He also was assignments manager at WKBW-TV, Buffalo, New York, which at that time was a Capital Cities Communications property.

Casey's news experience includes work in front of the camera and microphone but he has spent most of his career behind the scenes. He was a member of a team at WSOC-TV which won the Associated Press National Spot News Coverage award and the Headliners Award for Spot News Coverage in 1989 for coverage of Hurricane Hugo devastation in the Carolinas. He has also produced station coverage of two national political conventions, the visit of Pope John Paul II to Canada in 1984, and the inauguration of President George Bush in 1989. He has worked with news teams in North Carolina and New York which have been named the AP's "Best Newscast" and "Best News Operation" four times.

Casey began his broadcasting career in 1975 as an advertising copy writer and part-time news reporter at WCLG Radio, Morgantown, West Virginia, a job he picked up while pursuing his college degree at West Virginia University. After graduation, he continued his career in radio at small market stations in Georgia and Iowa before landing his first television news position in Minnesota in 1978. Casey has been a nomad in television news, working at various stations in the East and Midwest leading up to his present position in Raleigh-Durham.

The Technojournalist

Mark Casey

Predicting or projecting future trends is risky business. If, as so many predict, our future finds us speeding down the information highway, then the country roads we used to drive are filled with the lost and wandering trend-setters who were supposed to show us the way and never did. But, this essay about television news will take the projection risk because I'm confident that the future will be based on a past and present truth of broadcast news, that is: News Is Now.

To illustrate, I'll share an old war story that was my first on-the-job lesson in broadcast news and its technology, how the journalism and the electronic tools fit together—a lesson that drove home to me the mantra of News Is Now in a way no classroom lesson ever could.

It was late July, 1976, a presidential election year. A few months out of college, I had been hired by a small radio station near Plains, Georgia—home of Democratic presidential candidate Jimmy Carter—and I had also signed on as a stringer for Mutual News. Carter's campaign for the presidency had shifted into high gear. Nearly every day the candidate's staff would create media events to pitch the Carter vision. I would audiotape every word, then return to my station for a long dubbing and editing session. Then I would make the transmission of that day's Carter material to Mutual. The process took me hours.

Mutual Radio, with hourly deadlines and the pressure of a lot of competition, could not wait hours. The network wanted it now. A veteran Mutual correspondent came to Plains to get it, and in the process gave me a basic lesson in the link between electronic news and technology. Compared with today's on-line world, this was very low-tech stuff, but it was a lesson that stuck, the journalism—gathering information, sorting out the relevant material, creating a news story to meet a distant deadline—colliding head-on with the need for immediacy. The lesson came to me through a pair of alligator clips.

What are alligator clips? Two pincer-like pieces of copper—they resemble the jaws of an alligator, hence the name—each pincer connected to a strand of wire, and both joined to a cable with a single plug at the other end. Maintenance engineers use them to test a range of electronic devices which make a TV station work.

I watched the Mutual reporter phone his bureau, unscrew the plastic cover from the speaker end of the telephone receiver, attach the clips to a couple of prongs inside, insert the plug into the audio output of his tape deck, hit the play button, and presto—the Carter material was fed for air down the line and into the Washington headquarters of Mutual. The correspondent followed that feed with two quick voice reports, broke down his clips and tossed them to me.

"Here you go," he said. "No more delays. Get the sound and get it to them quickly. If these break, and they will, call Mutual immediately and have 'em ship you some more." For me, the concept of the quick story turnaround—the demand for immediacy, punctuated with the use of a very simple piece of equipment—had been fixed in my mind.

The career progressed and the learning process continued. Taped voicers (delay) gave way to live phoner reports (immediacy). Radio news skills and alligator clips led to television news opportunities and much more technology. News film cameras were replaced by videotape recorders. Soon we were learning the meaning of immediate all over again—television news by microwave, then microwave live, then satellite, then live satellite. The lesson of the alligator clips plays as well today as it did in the mid-70s: for you and your competition the next newscast is now. Get the story and get it "on." That's the past, and the present, and will be the future. Differences between then, now, and what waits for us all in the future include the definition of "on," the equipment that will get us there, and the expertise of the people doing the work. The alligator clips are getting more sophisticated all the time.

"On" will mean different things for TV/cable outlets; for their news programming; and for reporters, news managers and the individual news stories we cover. Let's examine how the "on" of the next few years may affect each of those areas, and how those of you who may be heading into the profession might find a way to, as the Vulcans would say, "live long and prosper" through it all.

The Television Station

Today, we work in TV stations or cable news outlets with call letters. They televise news programming. In most cases advertisers pay to have their messages included in the programs. Each program comes at a scheduled, specified time. People watch scheduled news primarily to get information: news, weather, sports; and secondarily (on commercial channels) to receive information about products and services. They watch because:

A. they have access to a television set at the preappointed time, or

B. they have a loyalty to that news program.

These two distinctly different dimensions of news viewing are involved in the transition that I see of the television station of the present into the media company of the future—a media company that will create and deliver news and information products on demand. In this scenario, the idea of news being "on" at certain times will change to news being delivered when the viewer is available and ready for it. In this scenario, newscasts and news items are just a part of a range of news and information product lines which will serve the specific, narrowly defined needs of the news consumer.

This sounds a lot like manufacturing. Auto makers manufacture different cars for different tastes, uses, and budgets. Food processors use different recipes for different diets, tastes, and preparation times. Competition drives the process. The same conditions that prompt General Motors to make the Geo and the Cadillac, that prompt Campbell's to create tomato soup and chunky soup, will apply to the making of news products.

Those two distinctly different dimensions of news viewing discussed above lead the media company to do two things: One, create news program products which capitalize on the loyalty of the viewer; and two, acquire the technical means to transmit the program products when the viewer is available to watch.

The programming task is the less complicated half of the puzzle. For many years, good TV stations have created daily news products which viewers make appointments to watch. Evidence that this works lies in increased viewing of local TV news while network news viewing declines.

News-on-demand is the more complicated part of this equation because the people these TV stations serve lead much more complicated lives than ever before. As our society continues to move in the direction of ultramobile, ultrabusy families of two-income earners or single-parent households, it's the practice of appointment viewing that is the catalyst for change.

Watching the news at 5 o'clock, 5:30, or 6 o'clock is difficult when adults in the family are traveling in cars. Dad or Mom may be struggling with a traffic jam on the way home from work. They won't get home until daughters/sons are picked up from after-school activities. The entire family might get together for dinner around seven in the evening and even then that might happen just once or twice a week. Early evening news broadcasts are over at that point. Can they catch the 11 P.M.? Maybe, if they don't have to get up at five the next morning so as to beat the traffic rush. Appointment viewing in America is giving way to new options in an expansion of delivery systems.

Enter the TV station as media company. Make that multimedia company. Missed the early evening news? No problem. Pop on the second cable channel assigned to your favorite station and watch either a repeat of the broadcast or a live presentation of the day's events. Want it quicker? Log on to your PC and view only the portions of the newscast you want to see through your favorite station's on-line service. Want the latest news before going to bed early? Tune in to the one or two other over-the-air stations for which your favorite station produces newscasts and watch the 9 P.M. or 10 P.M. and call it a day. The next morning, download from your PC the printed material compiled by your favorite TV station overnight for a quick review over morning coffee.

Delivery systems vary, information packaging techniques vary, details of any vision of the future vary, but the core product does not vary. It's your favorite TV newscast sliced, diced, wrapped in different labels and sent to you over-the-air, along a cable, and through a variety of other media. The station develops the product, and delivery is dictated by the ability of that same station to create, rent, or contract for outlets. The next newscast isn't only now, it's a product on demand.

The Programs and Stories

The expanded delivery system creates the need for something to deliver. Broadcasting historically has had, has now, and will continue to have, an insatiable appetite for program product. We've seen how your favorite station might satisfy viewers by providing news program products on demand. The definition of "news"—what motivates the selection of an event or topic for production into a news story—will continue to evolve. That evolution, coupled with expanding delivery options, should end an ages old philosophical battle between the supporters and practitioners of two seemingly incompatible news forms—news-as-entertainment v. news-as-public-affairs-watchdog. There's enough room on the delivery spectrum and enough audience appetite to support both.

TV tabloids will be a staple of the viewer menu. They're relatively inexpensive to produce, and they appeal to large numbers of people by focusing not on the broad issues of the day but instead on human interest events with the right mix of sex, violence, and institutional corruption, plenty of fodder for the next day's office gossip, talk radio, or on-line E-mail exchanges. For large numbers of viewers, mass audiences, these will be popular products of daily news budgets.

Does that mean the phasing out of the more serious hard news and public affairs-oriented news items, investigations, in-depth reports, and programs? No way! This is a scenario of viewing options on the increase, not the decrease. It envisions George Will "look-alikes" talking every conceivable position of every conceivable issue. Tune in for a traditional network news show or local newscast. All will be available on demand.

And, as is becoming more and more the case, so-called serious programs and the infotainment tabloids will tackle the same stories, edging ever closer to each other in form and substance. Harding/Kerrigan, sensational allegations swirling around Michael Jackson, People v. Simpson—"story of the century" narratives like these will be spun to fit the program type. Television news in the expanded delivery systems of tomorrow will still be the television news we're all familiar with. That is, the news will have:

- an obsession with crime;

- an obsession with disaster, natural and man-made;

- an obsession with conflict;

- an obsession with hero worship and destruction—that very American love/hate relationship with its celebrities.

As television continues to pursue these staples of programming fare, look for the storytelling techniques to become even more personal than what we are seeing today. The story type is here to stay, the treatment will continue to change both in the tabloid format and in the more serious news programming approaches. Even as entertainment values work their way into the more serious public affairs-based programming, so also will more serious values be reflected in stories with tabloid-style production values.

Another influence that will impact television news programs and stories involves demographic phenomena and sophisticated computer tools to organize, analyze, and extract meaning out of demographic data. Issues heretofore hidden in the data will be unraveled as reporters make computer-assisted journalism of tomorrow as common as the crime beat of today. A population with distinct racial and age divisions creates living trends which are at the root of society's triumphs and tragedies. These diverse populations leave data trails to which reporters will gain access via computer technology. Reporters will be able to organize and analyze new data in new ways to process news stories beyond our grasp before the linking of reporters, computers, and data bases. The growing need for these expanding computer-based skills highlights just one more difference between yesterday's news people, today's news people, and tomorrow's news people.

News people. "People"– the ultimate key to this vision. The reality is, nothing in the vision of the technology and the news product output makes any sense without consideration of the human factor. The notion that people have a crucial role in this confusing "news product on demand" approach is fundamental and will be examined more fully in the closing segment of this essay.

The People

People. Human beings. The least predictable component of this scheme. The most complex machine in the process. That machine is you. You will run the television station turned media company. You will create the programs and products. You will operate the delivery technology. You will put program products "on." Abilities and skills needed to make the system of tomorrow work will differ radically from the skills I've developed to stay employed and progress in my chosen field. We can examine these issues more closely by imagining the role people will play in making the information machine work.

1. The Technojournalist

Take your average photographer (or if you prefer, videographer), tape editor, transmission specialist, and reporter—four positions in all—and fold them into one person I'll call "technojournalist." Technojournalists will emerge and prosper because digital technology will take the equipment functions, all the 80-pound cameras, yards of cable, batteries, tapes, SNVs, transmission dishes, lights, editing gear—all the things we use today in the pursuit of news—and make them all much smaller, much more light weight, much more portable, and much simpler to use. For the first time in the history of broadcast news—going all the way back to the original machine that could record sound onto spools of wire—the equipment won't necessarily have to dominate us and the process of creating stories. Stations won't need four people to get it "on," but they will need one person who is adept at operating this technology. The technojournalist will do it all: shoot, write, edit, voice, and transmit a story live. The implication is plainly visible: Learn all you can about the technology, and be prepared for and accepting of continual technical retraining.

Liberalize your formal education. Television reporting today requires well-educated and widely informed people who are able to gather information, assimilate it, cut it into bite size pieces, and deliver it with a well-written and well-spoken narrative in a manner easily understood by audiences (assuming always, of course, that the electronics function properly). Fundamentally, that won't change. But, the technojournalist will have tools to improve story meaning by improving story context and texture. The technojournalist will bring to the task a knowledge base to better understand how the complexities of society work. They will have to gather this complex information, much of it from secondary sources, and reprocess it in a form that's understandable and informative.

2. The News Manager

The reality of today for this manager: Life was much simpler when all a news manager worried about was getting the newscast on air on deadline. The news manager of tomorrow will still have that responsibility, plus the pressure of constantly leading newsroom personnel through the "C" word—change. Equipment, product, coverage emphasis, marketing, and the competitive environment will be in a constant state of flux. The news manager will be the much clichéd "glue that holds it all together."

The implication for you and your formal education is, again, plain to see: adding to your major a smattering of courses in the humanities, the social sciences, and the natural sciences won't be enough. What will be needed in your program of study is exposure to strategic planning, problem solving, business administration, quantitative research methods, organizational theory, human resources, marketing, advertising, and something to help you acquire the patience of the biblical Job. A news manager will have to bring the product to air—plus promote it, explain its strategic positioning to a skeptical workforce, teach news skills to that same workforce, and bring the product in on deadline and on budget. And, of course, ". . . bring the product to air . . ." will mean "on" as defined by the medium being used and when the viewer orders it.

The constant in this entire guessing game of what the future may hold continues to be the drive for immediacy; for being "on" fast, first, and of course, with the right information. Whether it's alligator clips to feed audio down a phone line, or a satellite relaying an electronic message from earth orbit, being on was the rule of the past, is the rule of the present, and will be the rule of the future. It's literally, just a short trip forward through the time machines that are your PC, or digital camcorder, or portable satellite transmission system. Just make sure you've done all you can to be prepared for what awaits you. See you there.

ENG Technology: A Nontechnical Guide

N o matter what part of the news-gathering process they work in, broadcast journalists today are dealing with cameras, recorders, microphones, lights, and other electronic equipment to get the pictures and sound from the scene of an event to the television station's news and control rooms. And they are working with other machines to edit the pictures and sound into coherent stories. Still other machines will be used to provide graphics, words on the screen, and a large variety of other production elements.

It is not necessary to know the technical *details* of TV news technology to be a broadcast journalist using it. If it were, the journalist might be called upon to understand paragraphs like this:

> The original and still only FCC specification for creating a chromi-nance signal from three R, G, and B signals is represented in the fig. 4.5 matrix unit and modular sections. It stipulates that they shall be combined in separate matrices to form "I" (In Phase) and "Q" (Quad-rature) signals, each of which is then separately amplitude-modulated on commonly generated 3.58 subcarriers which are 90 degrees apart in phase.*

If the broadcast journalist needed to know what that means, college jour-nalism degree requirements would include courses in physics, and there would be fewer students enrolled in the program.

However, electronic journalists using electronic news-gathering equip-ment to report the news do need to know something about how the equip-ment works. More important, they need to understand the capabilities and limitations of the equipment because those define what the journalist can or cannot do.

*G. Robert Paulson et al., *ENG/EFP/EPP Handbook* (New York: Broadband Information Services, 1981), p. 97.

CAMERA-VTR ENSEMBLES

Color pictures and sound are recorded on videotape in the field by the use of the portable camera and videotape recorder or more frequently with a camera which has a videotape recorder built into the camera housing (camcorder).

The camera "sees" the picture it is aimed at through a lens that transmits the picture onto the face of one or more electronic pickup **tubes** or **solid-state** image sensing devices.

These latter devices are members of the ubiquitous "chip" family—silicon chips imprinted with the ability to register a visual image. In the camera application they are called **CCD**s—charged-coupled devices. In a camera CCDs translate the varying light intensities into electronic signals. CCDs are a great improvement in camera technology since they don't retain an image memory and thus avoid the "comet-tail" effect in low-light situations, and the "burn-in" effect produced by aiming the camera pickup tube at bright lights. The chips also last much longer than tubes, are lighter, and use less power.

Think for a moment about something you may have learned in an art class. Or if you've never taken an art class, you probably spent some time in primary school messing with paints and brushes. You discovered that if you mixed all of the colors together you got brown. And you may have experienced a thrill when you mixed yellow and blue to get green.

What you learned there was that any shade (**hue**) and intensity (**saturation**) of color could be made by mixing various amounts of the three primary colors: red, blue, and yellow.

The picture tube you look at when you are viewing color television contains "guns" that send beams of electrons to activate red, green, and blue dots on the face of the tube from behind. The brightness of those dots is controlled by another signal. Your eyes and brain take over and mix (integrate) the primary colors to reproduce the actual shades of the scene on the television screen.

The standard for the color television system in the United States was established by a group of engineers in the mid-1950s at the same time the industry was rushing to get more black-and-white stations on the air. The group was known as the National Television Systems Committee; therefore the U.S. TV standard is known as the **NTSC** standard.

In simple terms what the NTSC did was to decide that the light coming through the lens of the camera would be split—or filtered—through prism-housed **dichroic filters** into its red, green, and blue components. (A dichroic filter is a piece of optical glass that has been coated with a chemical film that lets through all colors except the one which it was created to reflect.) This was a dramatic decision with a lot riding on it. CBS and NBC-RCA were locked in a battle of giants to get approval of their own systems for color signal production and color set manufacture. The CBS design called for a color filter wheel that would rotate in front of the color tubes to do the splitting; NBC-

RCA favored the prism-filter system that was later adopted as the common standard by the **FCC**—the Federal Communications Commission, the federal agency that regulates broadcasting.

The NTSC standard therefore is the one U.S. broadcasters must adhere to when they broadcast their signals under their FCC license.

Until recently, most ENG cameras produced what is called a **composite** video signal to meet NTSC requirements. In this system color and brightness are mixed, in the camera, with all of the other signals needed to produce a picture. The camera delivers the composite video signal to a recorder, or any other place it is needed. But, when that signal is recorded and played back there is always some loss of picture quality.

Coming into use, especially with the newer models of the one-half-inch videotape format, is **component** video. In this system the color and brightness parts of the signal are recorded separately, which provides better band width, less interference in the picture, and therefore better fidelity and detail. However, the two systems thus far are incompatible.

ENG cameras, as they control and process the various electronic signals, also control the color **balance** so that, given the lighting conditions that exist, the image that the camera produces is as truly representative as possible of the scene being shot. Accurate color rendition is achieved by what is called **white balancing**, white being a mixture of all the colors.

White Balancing

In white balancing the red, blue, and green signals are adjusted so that they are exactly equidistant from each other. Actually, only the red and blue signals are adjusted, with green being used as a constant reference. By adjusting the red and blue signals against the green constant the "whitest" white is established, or "balanced." When that is achieved, all of the other colors will be rendered accurately.

Figure 2.1. A simplified diagram of the inside of a video camera shows how the images come through the lens and are converted into a composite video signal. The light passes through the lens (*a*) and strikes the beam splitter (*b*). The prism and dichroic filters in the beam splitter break the light into red, green, and blue components and direct them to the red, green, and blue CCD chips or pickup tubes (*c*). The chips or tubes convert the light waves into electronic signals that are then fed through a series of amplifiers (*d*) and combined with other electronic signals to form the composite video signal.

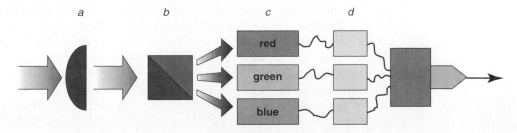

Most cameras have an automated white-balancing system that is activated at the touch of a button, and many of them have memory circuits that remember the white balance and maintain it throughout the shooting done under a particular light condition. Nevertheless, white balance must be adjusted each time the camera location, and thus the light condition, changes. That is why you see a member of an ENG crew holding a sheet of white paper or a white target in front of the camera before they start recording. If this is not done, the colors in the pictures are not true.

The portable ENG camera has many other automated features. With memory circuits and microprocessors the camera can be "set up" to be ready to make good pictures in a few seconds. If all the systems are working properly—if the beam splitting is properly aligned, if the electronic impulses are correct, if the monitoring systems are properly monitoring all functions— then the camera will record pictures that are very close to what the human eye can see.

Exposure

Most portable TV cameras today provide for automatic exposure control with an **auto iris**. The iris in a lens is like the pupil in your eye; it can be opened or closed to allow more or less light to go through the lens. When you look at something that is very bright, the pupil in your eye contracts to reduce the amount of light going to your optic nerve. An auto iris works the same way. A light sensor reads the amount of light coming through the lens and causes a tiny motor to rotate the iris in the lens to the proper setting.

A general characteristic of all cameras with automatic exposure controls is that the sensors that read the light and adjust the lens opening concentrate on the brightest spots in the picture the camera is seeing. If you have a very bright spot in the picture—a ray of sun reflecting from a piece of jewelry, a white plastic coffee cup in the hand of a person wearing dark clothing, the rotating beacon on top of a police car—then the automatic exposure controls adjust the iris to compensate for the bright spot and the rest of the picture goes dark. This can create problems on a news assignment, so most cameras have more switches to allow for *manual* operation of the iris. That, in turn, calls for the photographic skills of the camera operator to adjust the **f-stop** (aperture) by hand so that there is detail (**definition**) in both the brightest and darkest parts of the picture seen in the viewfinder.

The viewfinder, in which the camera operator composes the shots, is a tiny TV monitor that shows a black-and-white picture. As on many single-lens reflex 35mm still cameras, there are indicator lights—light-emitting diodes (**LED**s)—around the edge of the viewfinder. They tell the operator whether there is enough light to make pictures and, if the tape recorder is running, when the battery or tape supply is getting low.

Many cameras also have controls to enhance the picture at low-light levels, giving the whole system a boost in sensitivity. Some of the more expensive cameras have sophisticated exposure adjustment systems that may include such features as a fleshtone indicator, with a switch to be thrown so that skin tones are properly rendered when lighting conditions are difficult.

Lenses

The lens on an ENG camera is very similar to the lens on any still camera you have ever used. The lens controls the amount of light coming to the camera picture tubes or chips, and the sharpness (focus) of the picture. There are some characteristics of lenses that a broadcast journalist needs to understand.

Focal Length

Virtually all ENG cameras use a zoom lens. This is a lens that is built so that its elements can be moved closer to or farther away from each other inside the lens, thus providing everything from a telephoto shot to a wide-angle view. Zoom lenses are very convenient, yet they have the same characteristics as all lenses, properties that affect the pictures you are going to record. These are:

1. Focal length

2. Lens speed

3. Depth of field

4. Magnification

When you **zoom** a zoom lens you are actually changing its focal length from a wide angle of viewing for subjects close to the camera all the way "out" to a closeup of subjects or objects some distance away. When you change the focal length you run into Rule 1:

RULE 1. Different focal lengths produce different effects that actually change the nature of the picture being made.

Zooming to a long focal length tends to distort or foreshorten the depth in the scene. Subjects or objects that are really far away seem to be closer, and items in the background seem to be almost as close as items in the foreground.

You can see good visual examples of this "foreshortening" effect in shots during a major league baseball telecast. In the typical setup, there is a camera located just off the playing field directly behind home plate, and a camera in the centerfield bleachers.

Straight ahead shots from behind the plate show the umpire, catcher, batter, and home plate in the foreground, pitcher and pitching mound in the background (and maybe even second base, and way, way out there, the centerfielder). A lot of space seems to separate home plate and the mound (the distance is actually 60-feet six-inches). Compare that with the straight ahead shot from the centerfield stands. It typically shows the back of the pitcher in the foreground and the batter, catcher, and umpire in the background, but, there appears to be very little distance between them. They all seem a lot closer to each other—the pitcher almost on top of the batter. That's the fore-shortening effect.

One of the most famous scenes in a classic movie, *The Graduate,* shows the hero running to the church to prevent his love from marrying another man. He starts running toward the camera from a great distance away. And he runs, and runs, and runs . . . but he never seems to get any closer or to be making any progress toward the church. The tension builds; it is excruciating as time passes. That scene was shot with an extremely long focal-length lens, so the depth—the distance our hero is from the movie audience—never seems to change, another example of foreshortening.

In a news story about heavy traffic on a freeway, pictures shot at a long focal length will make the cars seem very close together, and their relative motion toward the camera will seem slow. Scenes recorded at shorter focal lengths restore more normal depth relationships in the picture.

The standard lens focal length for ENG cameras is 25mm, which provides a horizontal (side-to-side) viewing angle of about 50 degrees. Pictures shot at even shorter focal lengths can take in a much wider view of the scene, one which is sometimes even wider than the normal human eye can span.

Lens Speed

The speed of a lens—the amount of light it will let through—is determined by the diameter and focal length of that lens. Here we are talking about f-stops. The larger the diameter of the lens, the lower its f-stop. The lower the f-stop—f/1.4 for example—the more light it will transmit. The iris diaphragm inside the lens can be opened or closed to control the amount of light being transmitted. Therefore all lenses are calibrated with f-stops: f/1.4 is "wide open"; at f/16 or f/22 the lens is closed down to a very small aperture.

Depth of Field

TV videographers want almost everything in their pictures to be in focus. So when they are working with a zoom lens they have to be conscious of **depth of field**, the area in the picture from the closest object to the farthest object that is in focus. Two characteristics of lenses affect depth of field: f-stop setting and focal length. They are interrelated.

RULE 2. Depth of Field: (a) **F-stop**: the lower the f-stop, the shorter the depth of field. (b) **Focal length**: the longer the focal length, the shorter the depth of field.

Regarding f-stop: If the light conditions are poor, the auto iris will open up the lens to let in more light. When that happens, the depth of field is made shorter. Further, at any given f-stop, one-third of the area in sharp focus will be in front of the point where the lens is focused, and two-thirds of the area in sharp focus will be behind that point. Finally, the better the light conditions, resulting in closing down the lens, the longer the depth of field.

Regarding focal length: When the zoom lens is zoomed all the way in—to its longest focal length—the depth of field is shortest. When the lens is pulled back to make a wider shot, the focal length is deeper.

Zoom and Focus

Experienced videographers using zoom lenses *always* make one move before doing anything else—they zoom to the tightest shot and then focus on the main subjects in that shot. This is called **rack-focus**. Since depth of field diminishes with focal length, the corollary is also true: All shots wider than the tightest shot will be in focus if the tightest shot is in focus. Yet as the auto iris changes with the amount of light coming through the lens, so does the depth of field. The camera operator thus must be alert to refocus or rack-focus when the subject or scene changes.

A zoom lens is easy to use. You can make any size shot by rotating a ring on the lens, or by pushing a button to activate a motor that moves the lens elements with a gear drive.

The lenses come from various manufacturers in "families" with zoom ranges from about 6 to 1 to 42 to 1—the kind of zoom lens used for sports coverage. Range extenders can be attached to the back of most zoom lenses to increase their magnifying power. Some lenses have separate elements that can be added to the front of the lens body to provide extreme wide-angle and close-to-the-camera focusing. Most also have built-in back focus adjustments so they can be matched precisely to the camera they are installed on. Those zoom lenses used for ENG work are specially made for TV cameras so that their resolution and contrast characteristics match the relatively narrow band width of the TV spectrum.

You have one more thing to worry about. That is Rule 3:

RULE 3. The magnifying elements of the zoom lens or any long lens also magnify all other shooting conditions.

Any unsteadiness of the camera will be magnified and a jiggly picture will result. Camera operators using long focal lengths must use a tripod or steady themselves carefully. Pans and quick movements of the camera are also magnified, as are heat waves, insects at the ballpark, water droplets, or smoke particles in the air.

The Camcorder

Videotape camera-recorder units (camcorders) come in a variety of configurations and formats. The field camcorder is relatively lightweight, less than 10 pounds. With some new technical formats that use metal particle tapes the camcorders produce pictures that are of superior quality. Typically, the field unit operates on battery power or on alternating current (AC) converted to 12-volt direct current (DC).

If the machine is a videocassette recorder (VCR), the videocassette is inserted through a slot or drawer in the recorder's case. Inside the recorder, the tape is "loaded" by a series of automatic mechanical actions: The cassette door is opened, and the tape is pulled out in a loop and wound around the recording heads.

The controls on most VCRs are quite similar to those on an audio tape recorder. Levers, keys, or switches provide forward, fast forward, rewind, record, pause, stop, and eject functions. As on most audio tape recorders, both the forward and record levers must be pressed at the same time to make a recording. The controls on camcorders are integrated with the camera-operating controls.

Other characteristic features are a volume control (**VU**) meter, a battery strength meter, and a display of warning lights that indicate which function the machine is performing, whether the battery is working normally or running low, status of the tape supply, and so on.

Most cameras have a microphone built into the camera housing to pick up sound along with the pictures. In older units, the built-in microphone may have somewhat the same characteristics as the condenser microphone built into an audio tape recorder—that is, not of the highest quality, so that good microphone technique for optimum sound quality is difficult to obtain. But in newer models the built-in mic produces quality sound.

For still better audio quality, external microphones may be plugged into the system, with the sound being monitored through earphones worn by the camera operator or by a sound technician.

Most VCRs have a device to control volume levels automatically, the **automatic gain control** (**AGC**) feature, including the option allowing you to switch to manual control of the sound levels on the two or more audio channels provided. This makes it possible to set the channel levels individually or to **ride gain** (control loudness levels) on them. But if serious sound mixing is desired, a separate mixer must be inserted between the microphones and the VCR audio inputs.

Most VCRs—but not all—provide playback picture and sound monitoring of the recording through the camera viewfinder and the headphones respectively. It is important to check the recorded results in the field so that if there are problems additional material can be shot. And by monitoring pictures and sound on the ride back to the newsroom, you can make some preliminary editorial decisions.

What's Going On in There?

When you are recording on a videotape, four separate signals are being put on the tape: picture and synchronization (**sync**), two separate sound channels, and a **control track**. The last item, the control track, is the most important. You may have the most beautifully composed pictures ever made—you may have the makings of a twenty-first century Francis Ford Coppola—but if you haven't got a control track you haven't got anything.

Why is this? Tracking consists of pulses recorded on the tape, one for each field of the television picture. Tracking pulses are absolutely essential to the editing process because they ensure that the picture will be stable—in sync—on playback. Some VCRs now have a tracking indicator meter to tell you tracking is occurring; others do not.

Most editing control units work by counting the tracking pulses recorded on the tape. The pulses are used by the editing control units to time the pre-roll and rehearse-edit functions, and, of course, to ensure that the edits themselves are made at the correct point. The control track is explained in more detail in the chapters on shooting (Chapter 3) and editing (Chapter 4).

The Mysteries of Helical Scanning

All videocassette recording, regardless of tape format, is done helically. Two tape motions are involved: The tape is transported around a spinning drum that houses the recording heads in a helix—a spiral. The tape is also moving forward horizontally, left to right inside the cassette, from its supply reel to its takeup reel.

Figure 2.2. How control, video, and audio tracks are laid down on the videotape by the recorder. In assemble mode editing, the control track is laid down as the edit is made. In insert mode, tracking is placed along the entire length of the videotape prior to editing. Since this track is already there the machines lock to it even before the edit begins, and the edit will be more stable than an assemble mode edit.

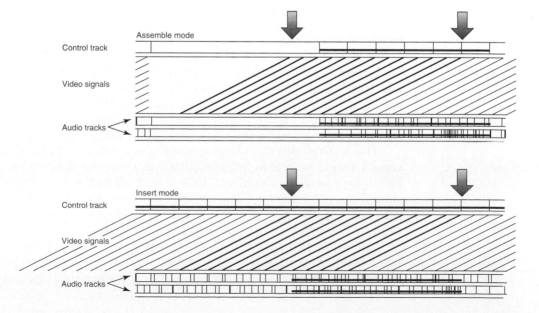

The frequency of these video signals is so high and at the same time covers such a wide range that a high relative head-to-tape speed is needed to record (and reproduce) them. As the head drum spins and the tape passes by it, the video signals are put on the tape in slanted tracks (see Fig. 2–2). Because the control track and the audio tracks are lower in frequency, they are laid down horizontally.

Part of the composite video signal coming from the camera to the recorder is a sync (synchronize) signal that goes on the slanted tracks along with the picture and color burst. All this happens simultaneously. During a recording, the machine is constantly comparing the pulse signal with the sync signal so that the timing of the sync signal corresponds to the start of each slant video track on the tape.

The Servo System

The quality of the performance of any videotape recorder (VTR) and editing system depends mostly on its ability to reproduce exactly the video signal recorded on the tape. The video heads of the playback machines must make a precise tracing of the video signals placed on the tape during recording. This requires what are called **servo systems**—a drum servo and a capstan servo.

The **drum servo** controls the speed of the rotation of the head drum. The **capstan servo** controls the speed of the tape passing the head drum. During playback the machine again constantly compares the sync signal with the pulse signal and feeds this information to the servo systems controlling head drum rotation and tape speed. Such precision controls are essential for editing the recorded tape.

Videotape

Of all the things we use in ENG coverage, the basic medium we record on—videotape—is the most taken for granted, and therefore the most abused, bent, stapled, and folded by those who ought to know better. Perhaps this is because the tape is concealed inside a plastic box, or perhaps because it is so useful: It can be used over and over again, stored temporarily almost anywhere, shipped through the mail. Maybe tape is taken for granted because it is relatively inexpensive and considered to be expendable.

The truth is that the videotape cassette should be handled carefully. It should always be kept in its protective box. It should be stored in a cool, dry place, on end like a book. The tape inside should not be spliced, in fact, should never be touched. The cassette itself should be handled gently: The door that closes over the tape when it is outside a VCR can be bent, and the cassette case itself can be cracked.

Videotape and cassettes have certain characteristics that you need to know about. Videotape is plastic, coated on one side with a metallic layer of material which is bonded onto a polyester backing. This metallic layer captures and holds the electronic signals from the recording and tracking heads. Since the tape moves past the recording heads at a constant speed, the smoothness of the tape surface is an important factor in fidelity of reproduction.

Several things besides human carelessness can damage videotape. Improper functions in the VTR—particularly poor alignment of the tape guides within the recorder and playback machines—can cause the tape to be folded along an edge. Since those essential control track signals are on one edge, this can be disastrous to proper editing.

Improper use of the portable VCR is another danger. If the battery is removed or the power turned off before the recorder is stopped, serious tape damage can occur. This is because when the recorder is stopped in the normal manner, the tape is unwound from the record heads. If power is interrupted with the tape partially or fully loaded, the recorder will hold on to the tape with a death grip. When the eject button is pushed, curls of creased and folded tape come out along with the cassette.

Figure 2.3. The path of the videotape from a videocassette inside the videotape recorder. The tape is in a loop that is pulled out of the cassette and carried around the head drum by the threading arm (*a*). The video erase head (*b*) removes previous signals from the tape before it comes to the video head (*c*) and tracking signal head (*d*). The audio erase and record heads (*e*) are located nearby. The recorded portion of the videotape then continues along the path and is wound onto to the take-up reel in the cassette.

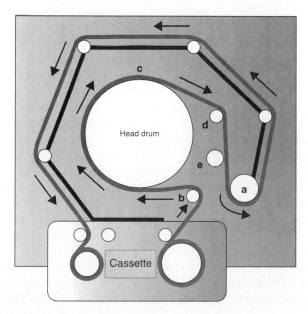

Since the tape moves between two spools inside the cassette—the supply spool and the take-up spool—make sure the tape wind is tight on its spindles. Arrows on the cassette indicate the direction of the tape wind. It is a good precaution to tighten the wind slightly so there are no loose loops inside. But do this gently, since tape can be stretched if force is applied.

Before using a new cassette, you should run it to its end on the fast forward setting, and then rewind it at fast rewind. This will **repack** the tape and thus correct any improper winding or crimping that might have occurred during manufacture and shipping. (When you insert a fully rewound videotape into a recorder, get in the habit of advancing the tape thirty seconds in record before serious recording is begun. When you remove the cassette after recording, promptly label it (they all look alike) with name, date, and content.)

Weather conditions can affect tape and tape recorders. The hot, humid, dirty trunk of a car is not a good place to carry either one. Moving from cold to hot conditions steams up the head drum of a tape recorder just as it does eyeglasses. The tape is very sensitive to moisture; moisture on the head drum can cause the tape to plaster itself to the drum so that both the magnetic coating and the entire plastic backing will "melt" right onto the drum. Drastic temperature changes can also cause the tape to change physical dimension; going from cool to hot conditions will make it swell and stretch.

Each time a videotape is run past the record or playback heads of a tape recorder, it comes into contact with those heads, and a tiny amount of the magnetic recording material is worn off. At the networks and at major-market stations, each cassette is used only once and is then stored in the station's archives. Other stations use the tapes more than once. But the magnetic coating on the tape surface wears off a bit with each use and when the coating is worn down to the tape surface, this will show up in the picture as a **dropout** in the video signal—a visual blank spot. A tape that is held in pause—a frozen frame on the picture screen—is still in contact with the whirling heads. The heads tend to dig a groove into the magnetic coating—another dropout—so leaving the tape in pause/freeze for lengthy periods of time will result in tiny pits being dug out of the recording material. Dust and dirt are perhaps even bigger factors in tape damage. Particles of dust or dirt can get ground into the recording surface and will cause more wear than head contact.

Creased or folded tape cannot be used again. You will never forget the sound a creased tape makes when it runs past the record heads—it is an awful buzzing, hissing sound. The next event will probably be a jamming of the recorder mechanism. And it will happen in a flash. When you hear that sound, stop the machine quickly! A jammed videotape can damage the guide path and the heads and render the recorder useless.

In the event a tape is creased in the field *and* it is absolutely necessary to use that cassette—assuming the machine is not jammed—you can try an emergency remedy. It is possible to advance the tape beyond the creased portion and record on the undamaged portion of the tape. But don't try to rewind back over the creased part.

Now that you know more than you thought you wanted to know about cameras, lenses, tape recorders, and videotape, let's move on to lighting, one of the most poorly done things in all of TV news.

LIGHTING

Lighting is one of the videographer's chores that often gets too little attention. This results in pictures of poor quality both technically and artistically. Let's look first at technical aspects.

Color

Since the video is in color, we have to be concerned with and know something about the natural properties of light in the scenes we want to shoot. These qualities may adversely affect the color in the pictures we are making unless we do something to control them. Light sources may be a mixture of natural and artificial light; there may be too much contrast, or too little. **Saturation** (intensity) and **hues** (shades) can be drastically changed by the quality of the light we have, and to make things even more exciting, the lighting conditions may change constantly—especially on spot news stories.

Scientists define light as visible electromagnetic radiation. The human eye is sensitive to only a small part of the entire electromagnetic spectrum; therefore "light" is that part that can be seen. The wavelengths of visible light range from about 3,500 to about 8,000 angstroms (one angstrom equals one ten-millionth of a millimeter). When light is separated or diffracted by a prism, each wavelength is seen to correspond to a different color.

Color Temperature

The balance of colors in light can be measured in terms of temperature. For this we use the **Kelvin scale**. In the late nineteenth century, William Thompson Kelvin established it as an absolute measure of temperature related to the temperature of a standard "black body" of specified density.

As Kelvin heated this black body, he noted that it changed color from black to red, then blue, then white. He recorded the temperatures at which these changes occurred and thus developed his scale. For our purposes the Kelvin scale can be considered to measure wavelengths of light in terms of temperature, and therefore is a standard comparative measure of colors in light.

But warmer and cooler colors don't work the way we are accustomed to consider them. Red, which we think of as warm, has a lower Kelvin temperature than blue, which we think of as cool. This is because red light has a lower wavelength than blue light. A look at Figure 2-4 shows the temperatures of various sources of light commonly used by ENG crews at news events. All this has a kind of unity: Remember that we adjust the red and blue portions of the video signal (with green as a constant) to reproduce the white parts of the scene as white, and therefore balance all of the other colors. Later in this chapter we will discuss how to manipulate and control the light at a news event to achieve the most natural reproduction possible. For now, let's look at some other characteristics of light from the point of view of news coverage.

Natural Light

The sun is a wonderful source of light, but sunlight can create serious problems for the ENG videographer. It is overhead. It changes color temperature dramatically as it travels through the atmosphere. It is more blue in the middle of the day, more orange or red in the late afternoon. The intensity of sunlight is the same over all of a given scene. Sunlight casts only one sharp-edged shadow, approximately the same width as the subject. The contrast ratios are very high: as much as 7 to 1 between direct sunlight and shadowed areas or the clear sky light above the subject compared to the horizon. Furthermore, people facing direct sunlight tend to squint; if they are wearing sunglasses, you can't see their eyes, or the glasses reflect.

Some of these unwanted effects can be manipulated—for example by using a large mirror-like reflector to bounce some sunlight back into a shadow area, or by using artificial light. But even where such controls are not possible, such as in a spot news situation, you can still develop shooting habits that help minimize direct sunlight conditions. When recording, try to keep the sun behind you or to your side. Be conscious of areas of open shade. Oftentimes you may be able to move to a shooting angle that uses natural shade to good advantage. Experiment. If people are squinting, move slightly left or right; sometimes a small change in angle can make a big difference in light and shadow patterns.

Artificial Light

As Figure 2-4 shows, various kinds of **artificial light** give off different color temperatures and therefore create color balance problems for the ENG videographer.

Artificial light is usually dimmer than natural light, even though it may not appear to be.

Neon or fluorescent lights give off different color temperatures than either natural light or the quartz lights normally used for ENG.

Normal light bulbs—incandescent light—give off a different color temperature than natural light, quartz, neon, or fluorescent.

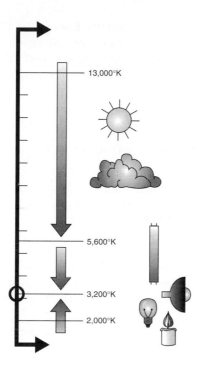

Figure 2.4. The Kelvin scale and the color temperatures associated with various lighting instruments and lighting conditions found at news stories. At the low end of the scale are ordinary (incandescent) bulbs and candlelight, which emit red light waves. Quartz lights provide the 3,200° K standard lighting for indoor TV news shooting. Fluorescent lights provide a wide range of color temperatures. Natural light (no sun) and direct sunlight provide increasingly higher Kelvin temperatures, bluish light waves that must be filtered for optimum recording results.

Mercury-vapor lights (used to light some sports arenas, highways, and parking lots) produce still another different color temperature.

Mixing Natural and Artificial Light

It is difficult to get good overall lighting and color values when you have to mix natural light with artificial light, but since television news videographers usually shoot video stories where people live, work, and play, these conditions must be coped with on a daily basis.

Fortunately professional-quality cameras can overcome some lighting problems. With white balancing, a careful use of filters, the use of lights and reflectors, many of the on-scene lighting problems can be solved—as long as the videographer is conscientious.

Many ENG cameras contain a **filter wheel** mounted inside the camera behind the lens. Some lower cost cameras require that filters be manually installed on the lens. In general the filters are designed to do two things: knock down the intensity of direct sunlight and correct the excessive blueness of daylight on a cloudy (no direct sunlight) day.

Generally the cameras contain:

1. A clear filter for use indoors with quartz lights (3,200° K)

2. A magenta (85B) filter for use in daylight (no sun) (5,600° K) to correct excessive blueness

3. Some combination of magenta and neutral density filters to give an overall reduction of the intensity of full sunlight (as high as 11,000° K to 13,000° K) and correct for blueness

The trick is to use the camera's white-balancing system plus the required filters. In operation indoors, with a mix of fluorescent and incandescent light, the normal thing to do is to place the clear filter in position and then carefully white-balance on faces in the scene to get the best possible picture rendition.

Outdoors the thing to do is to place the proper blueness/intensity filter in position, and then white balance on their faces again if people are in the scene. When the shooting moves from indoors to outdoors or vice versa, the most important thing to remember is to first change to the appropriate filter, then white balance. Failure to do so will result in people in the pictures looking like the Green Monster or the Terror from the Blue Lagoon or a landscape that looks more like a moonscape. You cannot alter the color balance on a recorded tape; your only alternative is to go back and reshoot the scenes with the correct filter in place.

Color Reflects

One final characteristic of light: It reflects from all surfaces within the picture area, and in color. A green wall will reflect green light onto the face and clothing of a subject. A bright red blouse will reflect red on the neck, and under the chin—even on the tip of the nose. Flooding light onto a colored background may reflect an overall hue to the entire picture. Shadows may take on the color reflected into them.

Lighting Equipment

ENG crews carry portable lighting equipment with them at all times and use it routinely. There are times when picture quality must be sacrificed in order to get the story on tape, but these occasions are much rarer than most people think.

The lighting kits used today supply adequate lighting conditions under most circumstances. The kits include lighting instruments, tripod stands on which to mount them, power cords, battery belts to provide power for portable lights, and accessories to help put the light where it is needed and screen it from where it isn't. All units supply a constant source of light at proper color temperatures.

Various companies manufacture different kinds of lights for ENG use. The units themselves are quite similar, but they are used in at least four important ways:

1. **Key Lights**: Here "key" means "main." They light the general area.

2. **Fill Lights**: They "fill in" the shadows created by the key lights.

3. **Back Lights**: They light the back of the *subject* to outline head, hair, and shoulders, and provide separation from the background.

4. **Wash Lights**: They light the background to help reduce high contrast ratios.

Some news events require more lighting than can be provided with a portable light kit or two. This in turn requires careful planning. Almost any scene can be properly lit for television pictures, but a proper lighting setup for large-scale shooting requires considerable time. A famous cinematographer once lit the inside of St. Peter's Basilica in Rome. He was given permission to do so on one condition: The Pope himself would come in to approve the setup before shooting could start, and if the Pope was able to see even one lighting instrument, permission would be revoked. The scores of lights were so carefully placed and hidden that the Pope did not see any of them, and the shooting went ahead.

Battery-Powered Lights

ENG crews carry battery-powered lights for situations where a reliable AC source is not available. Such lights can be mounted directly on the camera or hand held by another person. They can be adjusted to provide either a narrow focus—a **spotlight**—or a somewhat wider pattern—a **floodlight**.

Battery-powered lights require a large amount of power. Thus the length of time they can be used continuously is limited to perhaps thirty minutes before the batteries are completely drained. Other problems with these lights are:

1. When mounted on the camera itself they provide a very high-contrast picture, make sharp-edged shadows, and create shadow problems on the background.

2. They tend to blind people facing them. These lights should be first turned on as they are pointed upward, then tilted down onto the subject. This

Figure 2.5. Lighting instruments typical of an ENG field lighting kit. The two lower lights are floodlights, usually used as fill lights and designed to throw a wide-angle beam of light over a large area. The two lights above are spot lights, usually used as key or back lights, which can be aimed in a narrower beam. *(Courtesy of Will Counts.)*

will give him or her (and your competitors) at least a short period of time to adjust to the glare.

Batteries

Some of the most colorful language ever heard in broadcast journalism has been prompted by and directed at the batteries used to power ENG equipment in the field. Batteries are the lifeblood that keeps the equipment fueled and running, and they should be given careful treatment and care.

ENG equipment (other than lighting) draws very little power—less than 2 amps an hour for the recorder and camera. The rechargeable batteries are given ratings that relate to the number of hours they will deliver a specific amount of direct-current power. For example, a 30-amp-hour battery will deliver fifteen hours of 2-amp current, or three hours of 10-amp current, and so on. Generally, the larger a battery is, the more power it can sustain.

But like your car battery, the batteries used to run ENG equipment respond to the temperature. The colder it is, the less output they will give, and the shorter the life of the charge they contain. On cold days in the field the only answer is to try to keep the equipment as warm as possible and change the batteries frequently.

Batteries are mounted on or housed in the equipment, or are worn on a belt by the camera operator. The most usual charge-holding material inside the battery is an alloy of **nickel and cadmium—Ni-Cad** for short. More recently some manufacturers have come out with **silver-zinc** batteries, which are more efficient and require less space. The trade-off is that they are more expensive and may take longer to charge.

As noted, ENG batteries are rechargeable. In the field they can be recharged on portable recharge units or from an AC power converter. After use they are usually recharged in the news department. Normally this takes about three hours, although high-speed battery chargers can cut that time in half, or to as little as twenty minutes.

The process is relatively simple: The batteries are plugged into a recharger with a built-in protective system to prevent overcharging and LEDs that indicate the status of the charge. Almost all battery belts have rechargers built into them.

How the battery is used and how it is recharged are very important to battery life. Most cameras and recorders shut themselves off when the battery gets low. But a warning light tells the operator when that is about to occur, so there is no need to "play it safe" by automatically changing batteries after "x" amount of time of recording. To change batteries frequently and without regard to their remaining charge reduces their efficiency and shortens their life. All batteries hold a charge better, and last longer, if the pattern of discharge and recharge is regularized. Batteries do lose a little of their charge as they are stored. But "topping them off" with a short charge just before use actually reduces their charge-holding qualities.

Batteries look rugged, but they are not. They do not react well to harsh treatment—dropping them onto a hard surface may make them short out or fail completely.

Lighting in the Field

Sometimes the shooting has to be done so quickly that the lighting setup can be only rudimentary. On breaking stories the pressure to record the events may force you to turn on a battery-powered light, hit the white balance button, and roll the tape with the hope that the auto iris will take care of the problems. In low-light conditions many cameras have a "boost" feature to increase the sensitivity of the pickup tube or tubes.

The basic camera placement and lighting setup for an interview, or any shooting in which the subject or object will not move around, is shown in Figure 2-6. Figures 2-7 and 2-8 show standard lighting setups for a news conference or speech and for shooting reverse-angle questions.

The portable lights and light stands that are part of the standard ENG field kit are quartz lights that provide 600 to 1,000 watts of artificial light at exactly 3,200° Kelvin. Some of them are floodlights, some can be adjusted to be either floods or spots. The stands they are attached to can be raised or lowered as necessary. The lights can also be attached to a spring-jawed clamp that can be clipped to almost any sturdy upright such as a door or window frame. But don't clip them to someone's antique highboy or enameled wood trim without first padding the jaws; you can lose your welcome in a hurry. Also, when the session is over and its time to break down the equipment, be careful to not let lighting units come into contact with room furniture, the wall, the carpet. A lighting unit, just like a toaster or an iron, heats up to the

Figure 2.6. The proper way to set up the lights and the camera for an interview. The reporter and the subject are facing each other. The camera is behind the reporter and aimed over the reporter's shoulder. Key, fill, and back lights are aimed at the subject. The camera zoom lens can be used for any size shot—from a wide angle to include the reporter to a tight closeup of the subject. The subject can relate to the reporter and will seem to be talking to the audience.

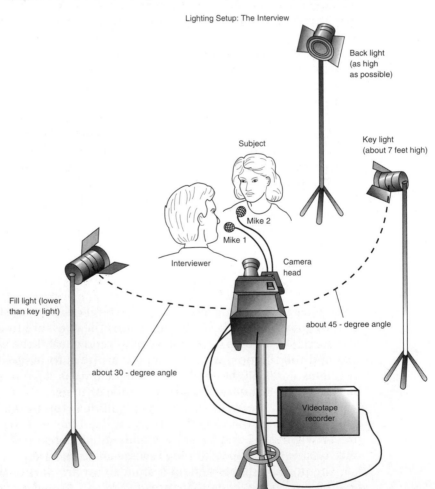

point where it can burn whatever it touches (including you). You must give these units a cool-down period before you dismantle the setup.

A Lighting Formula

The way you position these lights is critically important. The most important of them is the **key light**.

The key light is the main light. It lights the general area and should be placed near the camera, about 45 degrees to one side or the other and aimed at the subject area. It should be *well above* camera level—at least 7 feet from ground level if you can get it that high.

Height is particularly important if you are going to record a videotape of a person wearing eyeglasses. You don't want the key light to bounce off those glasses and right back into the camera lens. The key light should also be close enough to the subject to provide the main light source, but not so close as to blind the subject. This is another reason for getting the light up high.

The **fill light(s)** may fill in the shadows caused by the key light. They should be placed lower and at about 30 degrees to the side of the camera opposite the key light. They should also be placed somewhat closer to the subject because their second function is to light the background. Another way to control background light is to use a reflecting mirror or card, or a lighting umbrella, to bounce light into the background. With this technique you may be able to eliminate one extra lighting unit from the setup.

Lighting the background is *very* important and a little bit tricky. What you want the fill light to do is eliminate the shadows caused by the key light on the subject and on the background. Another function of the fill light is to provide good separation between the subject and the background.

Too many videographers neglect the **back light**. This lights the back of the subject, and is used especially to outline the head, hair, and shoulders of the subject so that she/he (or it) is clearly separated from the background. The back light is placed behind and to the side of the subject or object and as high as you can get it. It should shine down on the subject or object to give a halo effect. Be very careful about the placement. If you place the back light too low and too close, the halo effect is overpowering, and the back light may shine directly into the lens of the camera. This will create flare on the camera lens or wash out portions of the picture.

Note in Figure 2-9*a* and *b* how the key light casts strong shadows under the chin and beside the nose and how adding the fill light reduces those shadows. Figure 2-9*c* shows how adding the back light separates the subject from the background. Back lighting can do more to improve the quality of the picture than any other lighting move you make, and it only takes a few more minutes to do it.

One more light may be useful to overcome problems with the background. The **wash light(s)** may be added on the opposite side of the backlights and aimed entirely at the background. They should "wash across" that background adding more light than it is getting from the fill lights. This is particularly

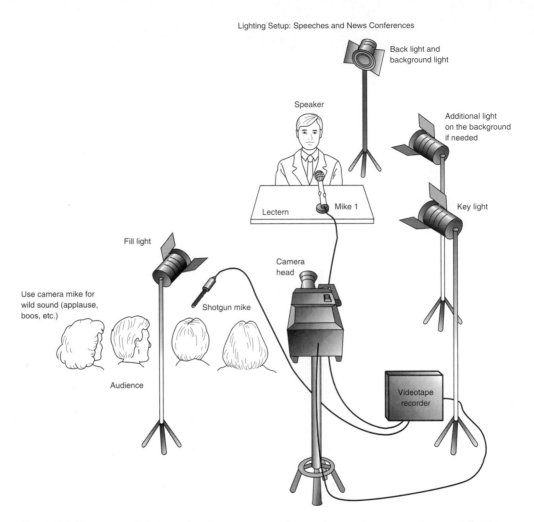

Figure 2.7. The proper lighting setup for coverage of speeches and news conferences. The key and fill lights usually must be augmented with back and background lights to get enough light on the speakers. Also the key and fill lights must be placed so that they provide some lighting on the audience. That way, members of the audience may be videotaped including those asking questions. A shotgun microphone, rather than the camera microphone, should be used to pick up those questions.

important if you have dark backgrounds such as wood paneling or draperies, or if you are lighting a person of dark complexion against a dark background.

This lighting plot sounds complicated. But it isn't and it takes a surprisingly short time to set up. Once it is established you can make small adjustments to fit a particular situation. Very blond persons with very light skin will reflect more light than persons with darker complexions, so you may want to move the lights to compensate. Because the auto iris will adjust for the brightest spot in the picture, you will want to check to make sure no "hot spots"

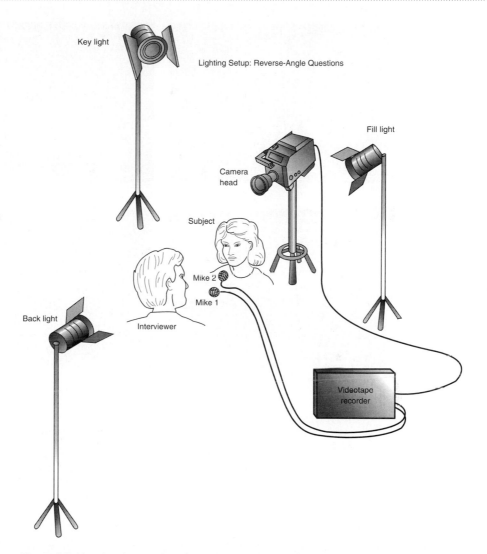

Figure 2.8. How to change the standard interview lighting setup to shoot the reverse-angle questions by the reporter. Only the key light has to be moved. The other two lights are simply rotated on their stands to fill and back light on the reporter. The camera position is moved to get face-on shots of the reporter over the shoulder of the subject.

like glittering jewelry, the face of a clock, or a metal picture frame bounce light back toward the camera. Figure 2-10 shows the effect of a hot spot on the auto iris and the overall exposure of the picture.

Barn Doors, Scrims, and Reflectors

A typical light kit contains a number of accessories.

Barn doors consist of flaps on a ring that fits around the light's lens. The

Figure 2.9. The effects of each of the lights used in the standard light plot (Fig. 2–6). The subject has just the key light on her in (*a*). Note the heavy shadows on the right side of her face and under her nose. Those shadows are softened when the fill light is added (*b*). When the back light is added (*c*), her hair and shoulders are outlined, and she is separated from the background. In (*d*) the subject is ready to answer the first question; the low shadows on the table and background can be further softened by moving the fill light closer, or adding scrims, and will not show at all in medium shots or closeups. *(Courtesy of Will Counts.)*

flaps can be adjusted outward from the sides and above and below the light. By adjusting these barn doors you can control the area illuminated by that instrument; the upper and lower flaps control the light in the vertical, the two side flaps control that light in the horizontal.

Scrims are small round or square pieces of screening or gauze mounted in a frame to fit over the light lens. Strong shadows caused by that light can be softened by using a scrim.

Reflectors are included in many light kits. These may include a matte-finish card or polished metal sheet, folding umbrella, or similar device, that can be used to bounce natural or artificial light toward the subject to fill in or remove strong shadows.

It takes time to get these accessories out and set them up, but the results are worth the time spent. Used properly they help make the subject look natural and get rid of lighting effects that distract the viewer.

a   *b*

Figure 2.10. The effect of a "hot spot" in a picture. Everything is fine (*a*) until she moves her coffee cup into the picture (*b*). When that happens the auto iris in the camera reads the brightness of that spot, closes down the iris, and the exposure on her face is ruined. *(Courtesy of Will Counts.)*

Figure 2.11. A field lighting kit may contain barn doors, scrims, and reflectors to help control where and how the light will fall on the subjects or objects being videotaped. Barn doors can be opened or closed to control where light will fall. Scrims diffuse the intensity of the light and therefore soften shadows. Reflectors provide an overall flat lighting condition and prevent glare on shiny surfaces. *(Courtesy of Will Counts.)*

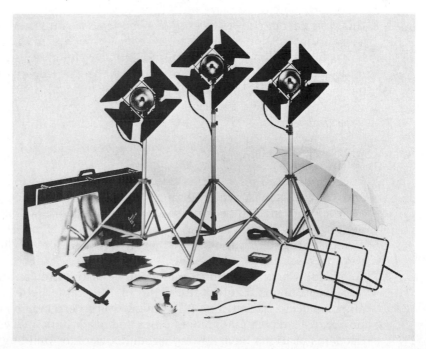

Lighting Ratios

Television itself and the cameras it uses cannot handle sharp differences in lighting contrasts as well as film can. Film systems can handle ratios of as high as 100:1, whereas television systems cannot handle ratios higher than 20:1 to 30:1. Besides this technical limitation, the contrast ratio problem is complicated by the way we view films and television. We see the films in darkened theaters, whereas we view television under all kinds of room light conditions. We are all familiar with the spooky detective thriller on the late movie in which the scenes are so dark and dingy it is hard to tell what is going on. In the theater the dark areas show up in sharper contrast to the bright areas, but on the TV screen they all blend together because room light is reflected off the screen, and the TV set itself provides some illumination.

The dark areas on the TV screen fill up with specks and wiggly things that are called **noise**. It is a good idea to try to minimize noise in the pictures made for news coverage by aiming for setups with overall flat lighting rather than setups with very bright and very dark areas. In other words, keep the bright-to-dark ratios low; try to avoid high-contrast ratios in the pictures.

Check Light Ratios

In a studio, light ratios can be checked carefully with a light meter. But there is no such thing as a light meter for ENG, and usually no time to turn the lights on and off checking their footcandle output.

What you can do more quickly is look at the scene and try to determine that you have achieved *overall flat lighting* by using the key and fill lights. They normally should supply about twice as much light as the back and wash lights, and a 3-to-1 ratio is about as high as you should ever go. The rule always is that there should be *more light on the subject than on the background.* You can learn to see that with your eye and by looking through the viewfinder. Nothing can replace a good, close look at the lighting by the videographer.

Power Supply Problems

There you are, all set up. The subject is ready and eager to tell the world how she won the Nobel Prize in literature. She has agreed to do an exclusive interview for your station because she "just loves" your anchorperson. Then the lights go out. You have tripped the circuit breaker. Embarrassed, you grope around trying to find the breaker box in her home or get the building supervisor to reset the circuit breaker.

In applying the lighting formula you have forgotten another basic: power supply problems. Each of the lights in a portable light kit draws about 6 amperes of electric current. (That number is determined by dividing the watt power of a lamp by 100.) Most homes and other buildings with modern electrical installations have 20-amp circuits, but older buildings may have only

15-amp circuits, making the problem even more serious. So, a little quick mental arithmetic: Three 6-amp lights will draw 18 amps. If a 20-amp circuit is available you are hanging by a thread; if it is only 15 amps, don't even try. With the 20-amp circuit, *if anything else is on that circuit* you run a very good chance of tripping the circuit's breaker.

One reason for the tripped breaker may be that you overloaded the circuit by trying to run all the lights from one floor plug. Furthermore, there is no sure way to figure out how the place where you are shooting is wired. If the electricians ran one circuit all the way around the room and attached several floor plugs to it, no matter where you plug the lights in that room you will have the same problem.

The answer is to try to take power from several circuits, perhaps by running an extension cord to another room or in from the hallway. That's also a quick way to solve the problem after you get the power back on.

There are two things you should do as a matter of routine. First, make sure you have enough extension cords with you (including some two-prong-to-three-prong adapters) and plug units into separate outlets. Second (and more important) think about all this in advance.

Mixing Light

Earlier in this chapter you learned about color temperature and the qualities of various kinds of lighting, mixing light, the problem of reflection. Let's take this information in the field as we continue with the interview with the Nobel Prize winner.

The subject is in her office at the local university. It is a modern building with a dropped ceiling containing light diffusers and fluorescent tubes. When she turns the lights on, the room is flooded with diffused fluorescent light. Over her desk is a cantilever-arm lamp with a bright incandescent light. In addition, there are large windows along one wall admitting natural light. It is an overcast day.

You are confronted with a veritable cafeteria of light qualities. Depending on which light source you use, you will get different color temperatures, and therefore different quality pictures. The fluorescent lights will give you one quality, the natural light coming in through the windows another.

The problem with fluorescent lights is that they emit a wide range of color temperatures, so that there really isn't one filter that can correct for fluorescent light. Fortunately, a camera with a good white-balancing system can help solve the problem. The trick is to be sure that the proper filter is in place and that the white balancing is done on the area of the picture where the subject's face will be. Careful placement of the target—right in the facial zone—will result in a white balance that will render the facial tones accurately and avoid blue or green facial tones, which are more distracting to the viewer than poor rendition of other colors in the background. Adding some quartz light to provide an overall boost in the light level will also help.

You will get some very interesting tonal quality in the picture if you decide to use natural light. But that choice depends quite a bit on the direction of the natural light. If it is behind the subject you cannot use it because you will be shooting into it, and the auto iris will close down, putting the subject in silhouette. Moving furniture around is not a good idea, either. You may end up with the subject out of her normal environment and annoyed with you for rearranging her office. A network camera crew was ordered out of Canada after they moved the Prime Minister's office furniture around to get a "more ministerial" shot.

If you close the window drapes and light the office with your portable light kit, you will make it look like this famous woman only rates an inside office without windows.

So there are a lot of variables to cope with, and the videographer must make choices and trade-offs. Don't brush this off as "too complicated" to spend time worrying about. Improved skill comes with experimenting and experience. The important thing is to make lighting decisions. Once those choices are made, lighting, filtering, and white balancing will complete the process to meet the lighting conditions the decisions created.

Study your light setup. Try to eliminate any distracting shadows that fall on the subject or the background. A background shadow of the subject's head, shoulders, or arms will move as the subject moves. Look also to be sure none of the light stands or cables is casting a shadow or is visible in the picture itself.

Natural Light Situations

In Washington, D.C., a great many interviews with government officials take place out of doors. Many times this occurs because the news crews can catch officials between appointments and they can make use of the natural light for a quick setup with an appropriate background—the steps of the Capitol, the White House, and so on. They also do this because sometimes there is no convenient place for a more formal setup. But it often appears that government officials do not have offices, and that reporters and videographers are not allowed inside the major government buildings—they just lurk around among the trees and gardens, and government officials come outside to visit with them when the officials decide it is convenient.

Sometimes you may have to meet your subject out of doors. When you have no choice because of time pressures, you must make the best of what you've got. When you do have a choice about the location of the interview or story, your first question should be, "Is the place I have chosen appropriate to the story?" The second question is, "What are the lighting problems there?"

If the Nobel laureate is an ardent gardener, choosing to shoot the interview in her beautiful garden on a gorgeous summer day may be just the right thing to do. It will give the viewer some of the flavor of her private life and will put her at ease in an environment she enjoys.

Outdoor lighting setups may look harmless, but can be deceptive. Our subject has a garden full of roses surrounding a small pool with a fountain and with hedges and some trees nearby. You spot a bench near the pool and ask her to sit there for the interview. Roses need plenty of sun, so the chances are the bench and pool are in direct sunlight.

But it may be too sunny. Remember that sunlight comes from almost directly overhead during midday, and from sharp angles early or late in the day. There will be only one shadow, but it will be a strong one. The color temperature changes with the angle of the sun. People in sunlight tend to squint from its brightness or wear sunglasses. Being in direct sunlight is not very comfortable in hot weather.

A better locale would be on another bench beside the hedge and under some trees that provide light shade. There the chances are good that you will have a flat overall lighting situation and one that is easier for you to control. So you suggest that, and your subject is put at ease.

Whether it is sunny or overcast, you will have several things to think about and control.

First, if you have to shoot in sunlight you actually might want to add some light—a battery-powered light held to the side of the camera to fill in the harsh shadows. Or you might want to use a reflector to do the same thing. The reflector is a better idea since it will be reflecting the same light (sunlight) as the main source. Sometimes you can take advantage of a natural reflector, like the white-painted side of the laureate's home or a stone wall to one side. You will have to be very careful, however, because color reflects. If the house is painted green, you will get a green reflection from it.

Second, beware of the water in the pool; it will reflect sunlight like a mirror, and those reflections will move and change if a breeze is rippling the water.

Third, over in the shade the natural light will be flatter. Here, too, you might want to add some light (either battery-powered or reflected), since you want to get more light on the subject than is on the background.

Fourth, you may have "natural hot spot" problems. Sunlight coming through the tree branches will be much brighter than the overall lighting. The auto iris will react to the brightness. Try to eliminate hot spots by positioning the subject carefully. Beware of shooting the subject with the sky in the background. It, too, will be a "hot spot," and you will risk having the subject appear in silhouette against the sky.

In both of the shooting situations discussed above two things are most important to remember. First, the natural light can be useful, but you must look carefully at the picture before you begin recording to be sure you have solved any distracting light problems. Second, the locale should be appropriate—if the subject never touched a clod of earth in her life, portraying her as an avid gardener is telling a visual lie.

SOUND—THE OTHER CHANNEL

The other major information channel of television news is sound. The sounds at a news event—even just the background sounds—are informative. They tell the viewer what it sounded like when the presidential candidate arrived, how the suspect talked, how the crash survivor felt about the experience. Relatively few people live in a soundless environment. Familiar sounds make the place more recognizable. New sounds provide a new experience for the viewer.

Researchers believe that the audience reacts to the way we humans sound when we talk. The voice reflects emotion. A foreign or regional accent is information. Voice and diction may give clues to such things as where the speaker comes from, perhaps their station in life, their background, training, vocation, or profession.

Unfortunately in television news it is often the pictures that get the most attention. The sound is regarded as almost an afterthought, if it is regarded at all. But poor sound quality can be just as distracting, just as aggravating, just as lacking in information as mediocre pictures. Therefore, time spent making the sound of the best quality possible is as important as the time spent making quality pictures.

Microphones

Perhaps you have already had a course in audio production or radio news, where a good bit of attention is paid to the technical properties of microphones and the kinds of sound they will reproduce. At that time you may have wondered why, as a broadcast journalist, you needed to know something so arcane. The answer is that you need to know what the microphones you use can or cannot do, as well as a little bit about how they work.

Microphones contain metal diaphragms that vibrate when sound waves strike them. Those vibrations are converted into electric impulses by backplates or coils. Those impulses can then be amplified and recorded on the videotape audio tracks and stored there for editing along with the pictures. Finally, the impulses are converted back into sound by similar vibrating diaphragms in the television set's loudspeakers.

Two kinds of mics are common for TV news use: **dynamic microphones** and **condenser microphones**. Each has distinctive characteristics affecting the quality of the sound recorded.

Dynamic mics are rugged. They are less sensitive, and therefore can be used in noisy places. Even so, unless dynamic mics are used carefully, "p" and "s" sounds tend to pop and hiss.

Condenser mics are sensitive. They need their own power supply, so most contain tiny batteries like those used in hearing aids. The amount of power needed to run a condenser mic is very small, so these batteries last a long time.

Television field reporting uses four kinds of microphones as basic equipment: the hand-held omnidirectional, the tiny lavalier mic, which can be clipped to the clothing or worn on a neck strap, the transmitter (wireless) mic, and the shotgun mic, in addition to the camera microphone. Each has particular characteristics that dictate its particular use.

The Camera Microphone

The first source of sound is from the microphone built into or attached to the camera housing. Unless something is done to prevent it, that microphone will deliver sound to the videotape recorder, where it will be placed on one of the audio channels—usually channel 2—on the videotape. To prevent the camera mic from operating that way you must unplug it, or plug another microphone or blank mic plug, into channel 2. Most videographers let the camera mic operate whenever they are not using channel 2 for some other purpose so they can record the **ambient** sound (synonyms for *ambient* are: *natural, wild, background*) at the same time they are recording the video at the news event. Ambient sound consists of such things as birds chirping, kids playing, cars and trucks driving by, construction machinery, and so on. News pictures without accompanying ambient sound do not have the sight-sound dimensions that will make the viewers feel as though they are at the news event.

Hand-Held Omnidirectional Microphones

Omni means "all," and these microphones pick up the sound from all around. They come in many shapes and sizes and are adequate for situations where the background sound is low or normal. They work best when pointed directly at and close to the sound source. In situations where the background sound is very loud, an omnidirectional microphone may not discriminate between sounds, and this in turn creates problems in sound recording. Automatic Gain Control (**AGC**) sets volume level according to the loudest sound it receives.

Another disadvantage of the hand-held omnidirectional mic is that it is usually connected by a cable to the recorder thus reducing the maneuverability of the person using it. Then, too, these mics often are visible, and the fact they can be seen complicates editing.

Lavalier Microphones

These very small mics have a pickup pattern much narrower than the hand-held variety and thus also a more limited reception range. Therefore they are attached to the reporter's or subject's clothing at or near the lapel level or are worn around the neck on a cord. They provide very good sound quality for interviews, especially where the background sound is high. Because their pickup pattern is quite narrow, they must be aimed carefully at the sound source they are expected to pick up.

Wireless (Transmitter) Microphones

A wireless microphone (also called a transmitter mic) contains a tiny transmitter that can send the audio signal to a receiver attached to the tape recorder or elsewhere. They are very handy for close-in situations, as Larry Hatteberg explains in his essay at the end of Chapter 3. They may be hand-held, or clip-on. They are useful when the reporter doesn't want to be (or can't be) attached to the tape recorder by a cable. There are no cords to get in the way.

Among the disadvantages: Transmitter mics use radio frequencies that are also used by others, so their receivers often pick up such distracting things as cab calls, or other transmitter mics being used in the same area. Wireless microphones require battery power to operate, and since they use quite a lot of power, the batteries need to be watched more closely. The range of a transmitter mic varies according to the power of its transmitter. Thus the distance they can send their signal is limited.

Shotgun Microphones

Shotgun microphones pick up sound at a considerable distance from the source. They are highly directional and must be aimed right at the sound source. When that is done, however, good sound quality can be obtained from many feet away. Shotgun mics are excellent for picking up reporter questions at a news conference or the remarks of participants at a public hearing. They can get the sounds of individuals in a large group of people; they can single out one person from a panel of speakers, or get the remarks of a news maker moving through a crowd or during a walking interview. They are excellent for getting the questions from the floor at a public meeting or the words of a subject who is surrounded by a crowd. Larger models can be mounted on tripods and can pick up sound from a remarkable distance away. They can also be used to pick up selected parts of ambient sound, or to shield out portions of background sound that are not wanted. A small shotgun mic can be mounted on top of a camera to pick up the sound in the area directly in front of the camera lens.

Camera-mounted shotgun mics should not be used for interviews. The best use of a shotgun is to get specific sound from about 3 to 6 feet away. Shotgun mics look very awkward when they are hand-held by a reporter during an interview. And they bear a startling resemblance to the barrel of a gun. Network crews working in El Salvador with a newly developed shotgun mic found this out the hard way. A sound technician cautiously pointed the mic over a wall. That act drew rifle fire from somewhere nearby within a few seconds.

The shotgun mic does give mobility to both the reporter and the subject of the story. A drawback: Someone in the crew must operate them at the scene if they are to be used effectively.

Microphone Cords

We cannot leave this subject without a mention of mic cords. They are the much-ignored, much-abused but essential link between most microphones and the amplifiers and recorders that process and store sound. They have connectors at each end that come in the form of single or double jacks, multiple-pronged plugs, or locking plugs.

There are two things to understand about these connectors. First, they should be treated with care. A majority of sound problems in the field are a result of broken or damaged connectors. If dirt gets into the connector it will not connect. If a trunk lid or car door is slammed on it, it can be crushed or broken off. Some connectors simply come unscrewed.

Second, since the connectors come in different shapes and sizes, you can find yourself with a connector that won't plug into a socket, or a mic cord extension that won't plug into a mic. The only solution is to make sure you have compatible equipment before you take off for the news site.

The mic cords themselves are easily damaged. A damaged cord can short out, producing either a bad buzz or hum or no sound at all. The lesson is that microphone cords should be handled carefully, and should be coiled neatly after use—no kinks in the coils—and stored in a clean and protected place.

One final warning: Power cables and mic cords don't mix. A mic cord draped over or placed under a power cable will conduct electricity from the power cable. This will result in a bad hum that will accompany the sound you wanted onto the recording.

Audio experts consider the sound work done by TV crews to be quite primitive, and they are right. Using the proper microphones, a news crew can obtain good sound quality. Using them improperly can produce sound that is not clear, not understandable, or so mixed up with the other sounds at the event that no one can really hear what the principal subjects had to say.

Automatic Gain Control

The VCR amplifiers that handle the sound operate with an automatic gain control (AGC) function. That is, the AGC adjusts the loudest and softest sound levels to bring them down (or up) to an average level. Remember the word average because it has a lot to do with the sound quality you will achieve. AGC is convenient and requires no adjustments; you don't have to ride the gain to prevent loud sounds from blasting or raise low-level sounds so that they can be heard.

But this basic function has drawbacks. Because the AGC is always at work trying to average out the sound levels, conditions found at some news events can result in disturbing sound qualities in the recording. If the reporter is standing close to a jet airplane as it taxies away for takeoff, the background sound will be very loud. As the reporter starts to talk the AGC will pull the background level down and his or her words will ride over it. If it is very quiet and the reporter is speaking in spurts rather than in a smooth flow of words, the AGC will crank up the background each time the reporter pauses, and pull it down again when the reporter resumes speaking. This "**pumping**" action between "sound" and "no-sound" is both audible and distracting to the listener.

You can control "pumping" (1) by moving the reporter to a more balanced background sound situation; (2) by changing the type of microphone being used; or (3) by having the reporter move closer to the microphone.

There are two cardinal rules for good sound operation:

1. Proper microphone position is six to eight inches away from the mouth for interviews and speech recording.

2. Use the proper microphone for the job.

You will recall that an ENG field kit can contain four kinds of microphones: a hand-held omnidirectional, the somewhat more directional lavalier mics, and perhaps shotgun and transmitter mics. Now we will see how they can be used to avoid problems and provide good sound quality on the job.

Avoiding the "Ice Cream Cone Lick"

In a single-microphone interview, it is bad practice for the reporter to point the microphone at the subject while he or she talks, then point it back at him- or herself to ask another question. It creates problems.

1. The mic gets into the picture.

2. The reporter becomes a mic stand.

3. The reporter is tied down to the mic cord.

4. The subject is threatened by the mic.

When the microphone is conspicuous, it is distracting. Often the action looks like two people eating one ice cream cone: The reporter takes a lick, then the subject takes a lick, back and forth goes the microphone—usually right in the middle of the picture.

When the reporter holds the microphone at the end of that cord, the subject can simply walk away or move out of range. The worst thing the reporter can do is hand the microphone to the subject. Then the subject is in control of the interview and any chance of maintaining proper mic distance is lost.

It takes only a few seconds to provide the remedy. Use two microphones—hand-held for the reporter, a lavalier clipped on the subject. Or use two lavaliers. Lavaliers are small and inconspicuous. They come with a small "jewelry box" of things that can be used to attach the mic to the speaker: A cord for wearing it around the neck, a clip to fasten it onto a shirt or jacket, and a buttonhole clasp. The lavalier can help eliminate disturbing background sounds if it is the proper distance away from the subject's mouth.

You should take care that the lavalier mic is as inconspicuous as it is designed to be. Drape the mic cord under a jacket or along the subject's side; don't run it across his or her chest so that it looks like a blood transfusion device. The mic should not be placed under clothing since the cloth can muffle the sound or rub against the mic as the subject moves.

With the subject's mic plugged into one audio channel and the reporter's mic into another, you have also provided for further control on each track level during the editing process.

Even the two-mic setup may have problems. The mic cords are still leashing the reporter and subject to the equipment. You cannot attach a lavalier to a fleeing subject and often it is inconvenient to install long mic cord extensions so that the people in the interview can move around freely. These are situations where the other two mics—the transmitter, and the shotgun—may come into play.

Special Sound Problems and Situations

It would be convenient if all news events occurred in a sound recording studio where very sophisticated sound setups are standard. But usually ENG crews and reporters have to be able to cope with a wide variety of conditions in the field.

Other People's Microphones

At news conferences and public appearances by newsmakers, television news crews will often find that the people sponsoring the event have provided their own podium microphone for the speaker and a distribution system for the sound. These are usually called *mult boxes* (or *multi,* for "multiple outlet systems"). They are set up with the idea that there will be one microphone for the news maker to speak into and enough places for the people who want to record that sound to plug into. This avoids the mushroom growth of microphones hiding a speaker and bad shooting angles for the videographer.

But mult boxes have some drawbacks. First, you have to have the right kind of connectors to plug into the central system. Second, you should be sure that whoever is providing the mult feed knows how to run the equipment and has it in good working order. A 25-cent part in a distribution amplifier owned by ABC failed during the first Ford-Carter presidential debate in 1976. All the sound was lost for twenty-seven minutes while the two presidential candidates stood there waiting to complete the debate.

There is no sure answer. One thing is certain, however. Recording the sound while pointing your microphone at a public address system speaker always results in poor sound. Avoid doing that at all costs. If this means carrying 50 feet of microphone cord with you, do it. And take a roll of duct tape (often called "gaffer's tape") with you so you can fasten the mic somewhere within that critical distance—6 to 8 inches from the speaker's mouth.

Other Sound Problems

In the field you can find as many sound problems as places to record sound. Some have to do with:

1. Acoustics

2. The manner in which the subject speaks

3. The environment where the sound is being made

Here are two of the most vexing situations that confront the TV news crew covering a story:

Hard surfaces will bounce sound back toward the microphone.

Soft surfaces will absorb sound.

If the interview is in a room with hard-surface walls you can be sure that the sound will bounce around like a gerbil in its cage. Unless you do something about that, your interview is going to sound like it was done inside the town water tank. So:

1. To control a reverberation, place the mic closer to the subject.

2. Use a unidirectional microphone.

3. Move the site of the interview to a less resonant location.

Conversely, if the surfaces are very soft, they will absorb sound.

1. Again, place the microphone closer.

2. Choose a mic with more omnidirectional characteristics.

When you are confronted with a subject who speaks very softly, you just have to get the mic closer.

People don't live, work, and play in acoustically perfect sound studios, so some of the natural sound "feel" of a location is needed to portray more accurately the location of the story.

It is dangerous—and unprofessional—to proceed with the recording thinking that you will be able to handle sound problems during the editing process. You can adjust sound levels during editing, but remember that raising the level for the speaker also raises the level of all the other sounds recorded on that track.

Background Sounds

Background (ambient, natural, wild) sounds should be checked carefully. They too can be sneaky. In a location interview where you have set up the subject and reporter facing each other (a standard interview setup) you may have placed them in a position where their microphones will gather more background sound than you want. The subject may be standing in front of a very quiet area, but the reporter may be standing in front of an air compressor. Too much of that background sound may come in over the top of the reporter's voice. Even if it doesn't, you will still find a significant difference in ambient sound levels while the reporter is asking the questions and while the subject is answering them.

If you set your microphone on a stand on the subject's desk, right next to a cherished antique clock, you will get the loud ticking of that clock throughout the recording and you won't be able to get rid of it. You should not use a microphone stand in an interview situation if you can avoid it. The microphone on a stand is in a fixed position, but the subject may move, giving you uneven sound levels and disrupting AGC.

Some background sounds will get you no matter what you do. Demonstrations are noisy and may be wildly noisy. Fluorescent lights always hum and if the room gets quiet, the hum seems louder. The dog who has been sleeping soundly at his master's feet will begin to bark when you start the interview. Asking the dog to leave may adversely change your relationship with the subject. The telephone, which hasn't rung since last Tuesday, will ring during the interview. The loud air conditioner will come on. The baby will cry. All you can do is pray that it won't happen, but it will.

Most of the answers to background sound problems come from the same thing that helps to solve visual background problems—the videographer's constant awareness of the environment in which the recording is taking place. You can move the reporter and subject away from the air compressor. You can realize the clock is there and put the microphone somewhere else.

Another background sound problem turns up when the reporter goes into a recording booth to record the **voice-over** (**V/O**) narration written to go along with the illustrative scenes for the story. The material recorded in the field will include ambient, or wild sound. The voice track the reporter records in the studio will have *no* ambient sound. Unless something is done about that, the lack of ambient sound under the **voice-over** (**V/O**) will be very noticeable. Two remedies are possible.

1. As much as possible record the voice-over and standups in the field with the same ambient sound in the background.

2. Mix the sound when the story is edited so that the ambient field sound fills in behind the narration. (It should be noted that some news organizations have internal rules against using anything artificial, including mixed sound. Such rules are usually outlined in a news department policy manual.)

Reporters, field producers, and videographers must always be alert for unwanted sound in the background. Profanity used in a loud argument across the street may wind up on your tape. At the least, using such sound would not be in good taste and might violate FCC rules about the broadcast of profanity.

Special Setups

An assignment that calls for the recording of music or any other special sounds requires special attention to the sound setup and careful planning.

If the story is about an important public hearing on a new wheel tax the city council is proposing, it may call for setting up a variety of microphones. You may have to provide a mic for each of the council members, a shotgun mic to pick up comments from the audience, and others besides. This will require the use of a mixer to control the various mics. Since the VTR has only two channels for sound, the mixer can be used to ride levels on the various mic locations and the mixed sound fed to one of the channels.

Camera/microphone coverage in courtrooms requires special attention and care. Where cameras are allowed, the courts usually have stringent rules about where and how cameras and microphones may be placed and when they may be used. Television journalists want camera access to courts, so the news crews covering those courts must be circumspect and cooperative. At the state level, in those states where courtroom reporting by camera and microphone may be permitted, it is governed by the court and applicable state law.

Music presents special problems for news crews. Although stereo sound for television is commonplace, much TV news sound is not of hi-fi quality. Added to that is the fact that recorders—any recorders—operating on battery power do not run at a speed constant enough to record the wide range of sound frequencies created by a variety of musical instruments. If your assignment is to do a feature on the Fourth of July Pageant, don't just go to the dress rehearsal and point a mic or two at the performers. The chances are good that you will earn the undying hatred of those performers when they hear how they sound on your recording.

You can do some things to improve the sound quality when recording music.

1. Use a converter to run the recorder on alternating current (AC). It will provide a much more consistent machine speed.

Figure 2.12. A small four-channel mixer such as this one is part of the ENG field equipment package. When a number of microphones are needed to pick up sound from a panel of speakers, they can be plugged into an audio mixer. Each microphone's output can be controlled using the "mixing pots" (control knobs). The mixed sound is then fed to an audio input on the videotape recorder. Such mixers can operate on AC or battery power *(Courtesy of Shure.)*

2. Record several of the musical numbers in their entirety with a good-quality audio tape recorder (also operating on AC).

3. Make a very careful microphone plot using good-quality microphones to get the best sound possible.

Then, when it comes time to edit the feature, you may have enough quality sound to mix with pictures to satisfy everyone, even the musicians.

The key to getting good-quality sound to go with the high-quality pictures you shoot is the same as for other operations: Use professional techniques and the right equipment. Think and plan ahead. Anticipate the problems and do something about them. It is not difficult to get good sound if you pay attention to it and believe in the need to get it. We use pictures *and* sound to tell the news.

Preflight Checklist

The following list should become engraved in your mind as soon as possible so that you can perform all the items on it automatically. (Note: Separate camera/recorder units require more steps in the checkoff process than do single-unit camcorders.)

✔ 1. Power up the unit—either battery power or AC converter—and check to make sure the equipment is functioning.

✔ 2. Connect cables/microphones, plug in headphones and check/set the audio levels from the microphone(s).

✔ 3. Lighting: If you are out of doors and the lighting conditions are good, go to 5. If you are indoors or need additional lighting, you should POWER OFF and light the scene now (review pp. 43 to 49, Lighting in the Field).

✔ 4. Set the camera video level. To control exposure manually, look into the viewfinder and adjust the lens diaphragm (f-stop) until clear definition (details) are visible in both the highlights and shadows. Look for washed-out bright spots and shadows with no details. Then adjust the f-stop until you see details in both.

✔ 5. Set the camera filter(s) and white balance the camera. White balancing must be done *before* any shooting, and must be done *each time* the shooting location or lighting conditions change.

Be sure you have chosen the *correct filter* for the lighting conditions you are operating with *before* you white balance.

Put a white target or white paper *directly in front of and close to the subject* you are going to shoot.

Make sure the target is straight up and down, at right angles to the camera lens. If you tilt it upward or downward, or angle it to either side it may not accurately reflect the light back to the camera; thus the white balance will be faulty.

Zoom or otherwise adjust the lens so that the white target *completely* fills the viewfinder screen.

Most modern cameras allow you to set the white balance by flipping a switch. Some cameras have a memory circuit that will maintain the white balance setting for any one shooting location.

✔ 6. Insert a videocassette into the video recorder, and push down *both* the forward and record buttons or levers.

The tape recorder will load the tape around the record heads and cycle into pause.

If you have a new tape you should track it before leaving the office or put color bars on it in the field if the camera you are using provides a color bar signal.

Be sure your tape in the cassette is where you want it—at the beginning if it's a new shooting, after the previously recorded material if you have already shot some scenes on it.

Be sure the *red button* or *knockout tab* is in your cassette. These buttons or tabs can be removed to prevent recording over something you want to save.

✔ 7. For a new (fully rewound) cassette, start the tape recorder and record a minimum of thirty seconds. Then play it back and check the picture and sound by switching the camera ensemble to playback. You should see the picture in the camera viewfinder and hear the sound through the audio monitor system. *Remember to switch back to record mode after checking picture and sound.*

"AND NOW—LIVE FROM THE SCENE . . ."

An Indianapolis television station used to refer to the reporter who did most of the live remote inserts into the station's newscasts as "our live anchor." They changed that to "field anchor" after it was pointed out to them that it sounded as though the anchors in the studio were "dead" anchors.

Live news broadcasts are in many ways the heart of ENG. Let's look at the technology involved, its problems, and its strengths.

Two important developments—lightweight, self-contained camera-recorder and switching units, and miniaturized microwave equipment—are responsible for the growth of local live news coverage. The equipment is expensive; it is easy to spend half a million dollars for a fully equipped remote van including microwave capability, built-in redundancy (extra spare items for emergency use), and the newest electronic gadgetry.

Live remote units need trained technicians to run them; reporters you see doing live reports on the 6 P.M. news have not just raced out there and plugged themselves in. It takes engineers at the TV station to handle the signals coming back from the remote site and to get them on the air. ENG crews can work quickly, and station installations are designed to pull everything together in a few minutes. Yet it does take time to set things up. Travel time is always a factor—it takes so many minutes to reach the scene of the news story. Once there, just how fast the van can be activated depends on how easily the microwave system can be linked to the station.

Microwave

The microwave being discussed here is essentially a wireless transmission system. The basics are simple: High-frequency radio signals carrying the video and audio information are transmitted from one point to another using antennae to send them and "dishes" to catch them. The antennae may be omnidirectional (sending signals in a broadly scattered pattern) or directional (sending signals in a narrowly focused beam). There are no wires or cables connecting the remote site with the TV station.

Gigahertz

Now you learn a wonderful-sounding word: *gigahertz*. It means billions of hertz, just as *megahertz* means millions of hertz. Each of those words denotes a segment of the radio frequency spectrum.

The microwave transmitters in news vans use the 2-, 7-, 13-, and 40-giga-hertz bands for their relatively short-range transmissions. These bands are designated for use by the FCC, and therefore each transmitter must be licensed. Within these bands are a number of separate channels, each of which is wide enough to carry both video and audio signals. Generally speaking, the lower the gigahertz band the less power is needed to transmit signals on it. This is an important consideration in ENG field production since porta-bility of the equipment and the power supply to run it are significant factors. But the less power available, the shorter the distance the signal will travel.

The manufacturers therefore have produced microwave transmitting equipment with as many as ten separate channels available. This equipment allows for switching from channel to channel, or band to band, so that the best signal can be achieved rapidly.

The equipment comes in a variety of packages. Some transmitters can be attached to the side of a portable camera so it can go almost anywhere with-out having to be attached to the van by cable. Somewhat larger units can be mounted on tripods or attached to any stable upright with clamps. If these small units are omnidirectional, the distance they can "throw" the signal may be limited to a few hundred feet. If they are unidirectional, their range may be longer. They usually transmit to a larger van-mounted unit which relays the signal to the TV station.

Covering the News with Microwave

You may know what a TV news van looks like. It has a dish or a rodlike antenna on top that can be raised, tilted, or steered to aim the signal from the van. The microwave transmitter uses these antennas to send the signals to the station.

Because of the very high frequencies used, these transmitters usually require a *line of sight* between the transmitter antenna and the receiving dish at the other end of the link. In many cities line-of-sight between the van and the station's receiving antenna is not possible, so more than one link is required. Therefore many stations mount higher-powered receivers and transmitters atop the tallest building or nearby natural terrain. The signals can go from the van to the high receiver-transmitter, and from there to the receivers at the station.

However, the microwave signals can also be bounced off the side of a tall building or a natural obstacle, so crews get adept at making these "carom shots." Newsroom walls and engineering complexes contain maps showing the locations for the best bounces.

In Chicago, enterprising crews from one TV station actually painted unobtrusive marks on the street near Daley Plaza so they would know exactly where to put the wheels of their microwave van for the best bounce shot to the receiving antennas atop the Sears Tower. In St. Louis one station regularly uses the city's famous arch to bounce signals from its vans down to its station antennas located nearby.

Depending on the terrain and the height of the receiving antenna the vans sometimes can send signals over quite long distances: 50- to 60-mile links have been made in very flat country. The ultimate limit is dictated by the amount of sending power and the distance to the horizon; microwave signals do not bend around the earth.

Besides these major transmission problems having to do with line of-sight characteristics, there are similar smaller-scale problems at the scene of the news event. For example: An interview must be done in an office on the tenth floor of a building. The camera there is connected to a small microwave transmitter—often called a "two-gig"—that is aimed out the window at the news van parked in the street below. Everything will work well until something like a big truck gets between the transmitter and the receiving antenna on the van. Then, suddenly, the picture disappears. Answer: Move the van, move the transmitter, get the big truck to move, or all of the above. All you can do is hope that the news story remains where it is. If it doesn't, you will have to do the whole thing all over again.

If the news story moves then the answer may be a small microwave transmitter attached to the camera. But it can't move very far away, and suffers even more from being blocked by intervening solid obstacles.

The ENG microwave setup involves a lot of technology in even a simple live broadcast. The news van, carrying cameras, tape recorders, perhaps a small switcher and audio mixer, a power generator and the microwave antenna, goes to the news event and is met by reporters, field producers, and videographers. The reporters and some of the videographers go off with camcorders to gather news, while the van crew sets up another camera or cameras for the field anchors to use. Technicians also set up a television monitor so the anchors and reporters can see what is on the air. Using their radio equipment or cellular telephones they establish one or more audio links to provide intercommunication between the station news editors and the field anchors and between the station engineers and the van crew.

For a successful live broadcast the aural communications are as important as the video links, since the field anchors must be able to hear what is on the air and receive instructions and cues. Often the anchors in the studio will want to ask questions of those reporters in the field, and news editors will want to make suggestions about further coverage or provide additional story information they have received from other sources.

If properly equipped, the same news van that provides live coverage can also feed pretaped material back to the station for use later, or to be edited and rolled back into the live report to illustrate what had happened earlier. Or tape made on other portable units at the scene can be edited in the news van for similar insertion into the live report.

Another way to get the signals back is to use a helicopter. If it is properly equipped, it can receive microwave signals from the ground and retransmit them to the TV station. Thus the chopper acts as a floating antenna that can send signals over great distances, depending on how high it is. Such ground-to-air-to-ground links are used frequently when line-of-sight transmission is blocked.

Covering the News by Satellite

The ultimate microwave unit is the one that uses communications satellites in space to deliver television signals from one point to another. Instead of bouncing signals off tall buildings or relaying them from hilltops, the satellite news gathering (SNG) vehicles send signals from the ground to transponders on a satellite 22,300 miles in space. The satellite then sends the signals back to a receiver on earth, and the link is completed. Technological breakthroughs have made the equipment necessary to do this small enough to be mounted on a medium-sized truck. Because of the height of the satellite these trucks can send

Figure 2.13. A helicopter outfitted with microwave equipment. The helicopter can transport ENG crews to and from a news event. It can be used for aerial videography. Also, its microwave receivers/transmitters can be used to originate live broadcasts or to relay video and sound signals from units on the ground to the broadcast station. *(Courtesy of Bell Helicopter.)*

signals back to their stations from anywhere in the United States in one hop. The TV news significance of SNG is examined in greater detail in Chapter 10.

NEWSROOM COMPUTERS

The majority of broadcast and cable newsrooms are using computers or computer systems to manage incoming wire copy, write scripts, keep track of assignments, and produce news broadcasts. Translation: Learn to word process (write) on a basic Apple or IBM-type personal computer. Make learning basic computer skills a top priority.

Whether you learn on an Apple or IBM-type machine is not a critical choice. Your main objective is to become familiar with a personal computer. Once you understand the basics of using a computer, you can adapt to the equipment used by any news organization.

Computers in the Newsroom—Level One

Wire Copy

The most basic use of computers in newsrooms is the reception, sorting, and storage of wire copy. Newsrooms which have no other computers are apt to have replaced the computer printer which used to spew wire service copy on the floor with a personal computer which stores the copy in its memory.

The wire copy is retrieved by reviewing lists or menus which appear on the screen. You can retrieve categories, such as all items from the Florida wire, or all sports items, or you can scroll (move up or down in the menu screen) and select a specific item you wish to see in its entirety. Most menus include brief descriptions of the contents of the items they list.

Once you have found the item you need, you can print a copy to take to your desk.

Assignments

Personal computers are frequently used to keep track of assignments. It is so much easier to enter an assignment into the computer's memory, because it can be changed quickly, and the assignment editor can print out paper copies of the assignment to give to the reporter or videographer. The computer also generates lists of assignments, which is particularly useful in planning the day's coverage.

Archives

Some newsrooms have one computer set aside or dedicated to preserving scripts and information about tapes used on news broadcasts so that they can be retrieved if needed to background a story.

Figure 2.14. Videotape editing area in the newsroom at WTAP-TV, Parkersburg, West Virginia. A reporter or editor can edit video shot in the field in preparation for air. The bay features a playback system with two different player machines for different videotape formats, and, on-screen time-code display. *(Courtesy of WTAP-TV. Photo by Roger Sheppard.)*

Computers in the Newsroom—Level Two

Computer systems for broadcast newsrooms have been available since the late 1970s. Their adoption was slow until the late 1980s. Today you are likely to find a basic newsroom computer system in use at even the smallest small-market station or local cable system.

A newsroom computer system ties several terminals or personal computers together so that information and stories may be shared. There are two ways to accomplish this interconnection. One is by using "dumb" terminals, which have few internal functions, connected to a central computer by a cable network. The other, and the most common method to create a "system," is by "networking" (using one of the widely accepted software programs which allows personal computers to swap and share information).

A reasonably priced newsroom computer system will perform certain basic functions. The system will collect and sort wire copy for reporters and writers, will keep track of assignments for editors, and will prepare rundowns for producers. You may also be able to feed scripts directly to a prompter, provide closed-caption information for the hearing-impaired, and dump the day's scripts and rundowns into an "archives" file.

In the "bells and whistles" department, the computer vendor may also provide software which allows you to process wire service sports scores directly to a character generator, or keep track of election returns and display them on the viewer's screen.

Using the System

Let's find out how a basic newsroom computer system helps get the job done.

You are assigned to cover a news conference put on by a local candidate for the U.S. House of Representatives. Before you go to the news conference, you sit down at your terminal and ask the computer to list all the current wire stories relating to both candidates for the office. You also review the national news budget to see if there is a relevant story coming out of Washington on which you would want the candidate to comment.

If there has been a long-running controversy involving the candidate, you could use your terminal to search the news department's archives for earlier stories about the candidate or controversy. By the time you get to the news conference, you are armed with the reporter's best weapon—knowledge!

When you return to the newsroom, you use your terminal to check the recent wire copy for any relevant updates, and then you begin writing your story. Most newsroom computer systems allow you to split the screen, so you can enter video information on one side as you type the script and insert the sound bites.

Once you have done a "spell check" of your copy and read it carefully for errors, misspellings, and awkward phrases, you "mail" or send the script to the producer.

When the producer is ready, she or he requests your script from the computer and looks it over for possible edits. If the changes are minor, the producer will probably make them. If the producer recommends major changes, the script will be sent back to you to do the necessary rewriting.

Once the script is ready for inclusion in the news broadcast, the producer sends it to the computer's script memory. Information needed for production, such as character generator titles, still store frames, the tape identification, and running time, is automatically incorporated into the producer's rundown and is sorted into lists for members of the production staff who work with these devices. The computer then calculates the effect of adding your story to the rundown and tells the producer how much time still needs to be used to fill the broadcast's "news hole."

Shortly before broadcast time, the producer will instruct the computer system to print out copies of the whole program script. If the news operation has invested in a prompting system, the same copy will show up on the anchor's prompter, thanks to software designed for this particular function.

The decision to include the candidate's news conference in the day's assignments probably resulted from a telephone call the assignment desk received the day before. The assignment editor talked with the candidate's campaign manager, making a few notes about the news conference. As soon as that conversation was ended, the assignment editor typed the basic information on a blank assignment form, which appeared on the computer terminal screen on command.

The computer sorted the new assignment into today's assignment list, and first thing this morning, the assignment editor was able to print out a detailed list of story opportunities. This list was copied and handed out at the "morning meeting" where the department heads worked out the "battle plan" for the day's coverage.

Your news conference is among the items the producers wish to have covered, and that's how you ended up with the assignment.

As the day goes on the assignment editor adds and deletes assignments and information. Several assignment lists may be printed during the day, so that everyone has an idea what is going on.

The assignment desk also monitors incoming wire copy, and sends relevant stories to reporters or producers, using the "mail box" feature of the computer system. When you checked your "mail box" screen on your terminal this morning, you not only found the assignment sheet for the news conference, you found a piece of relevant wire copy, and a note from the business manager reminding you to turn in your expense report for last week! Your telephone messages were also waiting in your mail box.

Many newsrooms set up a special area of the assignment desk computer for emergency situations. Let's say a commuter plane crashes north of the

Figure 2.15. A WTAP-TV A-P News Desk computer. This newsroom unit is used to monitor and store the wire reports of the Associated Press and NBC. *(Courtesy of WTAP-TV. Photo by Roger Sheppard.)*

city. The assignment editor can immediately pull up a list of emergency agencies, with contact names and telephone numbers. Within seconds of receiving word of the plane going down, reporters and interns can be on the phone, beginning to assemble information on the crash. A plan for this type of situation saves valuable minutes and guides the staff to gather information efficiently and helps supervisors and managers direct coverage.

The news director may have additional computer programs installed on his or her terminal. Most of these will not be accessible to staff members because they included confidential information. Typically the news director may have budget information, the equipment inventory, and a scheduling program at his or her fingertips.

There are many other capabilities which may be part of your system, but the ones we have described are typical of smaller, economical newsroom computer systems.

Computers in the Newsroom—Level Three

Some news organizations have extended the reach of their computer systems to provide additional capabilities, such as running production equipment. Add-Ons are the capabilities which can be added to newsroom computer systems: remote terminals, data base connection, CD-ROM playback, production cueing, still video preview, moving video preview, and moving video editing.

Modems and Remote Terminals

Many news operations equip reporters with small "notebook" computers. Field reporters can dial an unlisted number and using a modem, send copy or retrieve information, messages and wire stories. Newsrooms with satellite bureaus sometimes install permanent data lines between the bureau and the newsroom, others rely on unlisted dial-up telephone lines. Security is maintained on these lines by assigning staff members "passwords" which they must type in to complete their connection to the system.

Some news organizations supply data channels or cellular telephone channels to their microwave and satellite vehicles so reporters can use their portable terminals in the field, much as they would be used in the newsroom. These types of data links are important because editors and producers can preview scripts, and instructions and additional information can be sent to the reporter assigned to the mobile unit.

The notebook computer has become a standard part of the field kit for network reporters, who often have to report from locations where they don't have quick access to information about other aspects of a breaking story. The small computers are also popular with political reporters following candidates on the campaign trail. Background data and breaking stories can be retrieved quickly, thus arming the reporters with up-to-date information on which to base their questions to the candidate.

Data Bases

Many sophisticated news operations give their staff access to data bases such as the commercial services Nexus, CompuServe, and America Online, as well as the popular Internet computer network. The on-line data bases contain enormous amounts of information which can be quickly retrieved when a reporter or producer is researching a story. Internet and similar networks make it possible to retrieve data, government reports, and carry on dialog with other subscribers. Many of these services make it possible to send written messages to people, government agencies, and other newsrooms.

CD-ROM

Some news organizations have installed CD-ROM drives in their computer systems. These are particularly useful when a reporter or producer needs to search a large, stable body of data, such as an encyclopedia. Included in the information available on CD-ROM are detailed maps of the United States (right down to the neighborhood level), and nationwide telephone directories which simplify a reporter's search for a person in a distant city.

Production Cueing

In addition to listing character generator titles, tape rolls, and stills on the video side of a script, advanced newsroom computer systems can load, program, and trigger these devices.

Video Viewing

Many newsroom computer systems provide either split-screen or "windows" capability. Split-screen means the terminal screen can be divided into two or four sections with different activities taking place in each section. "Windows" software is commercially available and makes it possible to carry on several activities in different "windows" or screens without having to totally quit other activities. The layout of the screens is determined by the software.

One application of the split-screen or windows approach would permit you to divide your terminal screen into four sections. One would contain wire copy, another would be the work area in which you write, another might show a still picture you retrieved from the still store and the fourth screen might be running video from tape that was shot during the news conference earlier in the day.

Editing

The shift to digital nonlinear editing makes it possible (on some systems) to bring up video on a writer's terminal. The writer can either draw up an "edit decision list" which is then transferred to a floppy disk which is used to con-

Figure 2.16. Avid Technology's *Newscutter*™ digital editor. The newer type computer video editing console compares to the standard videotape edit deck system as a computer word processor does to an electric typewriter. *(Courtesy of Avid Technology, Inc.)*

trol the actual editing in a production room, or the writer can do the editing at his or her desk, rather than having to go to an editing room.

This capability can speed up production, and is enormously helpful at channels like CNN where video is edited several times to match rewrites of ongoing stories. Similar techniques are being used by regional all-news cable channels and by television stations which have expanded the number of news programs they present each day.

This technology also presents a challenge to reporters and writers who may be called on to do part or all of the editing of their stories, rather than relying on the expertise of specialized tape editors.

Automation

The fullest extension of computerization in newsrooms is automation: The newsroom computer system actually runs some of the production equipment used during a news broadcast.

Character Generator

Newsroom computer systems can be made capable of loading (typing in) and playing back character generator images. Instead of relying on a production worker to pick up a list of CGs from a producer, and then enter the new titles and retrieve titles already in the character generator's memory, the CGs which are entered in the script by a reporter or writer are automatically loaded for playback when the director calls for them. The director sees the upcoming CG on a monitor, and the director or technical director simply punches a button, or presses a computer key to put the CG on the air.

Many CGs are the same from day to day, so this type of automation takes advantage of the images already stored by the CG computer. One warning: reporters and writers must make sure the CG is right—right spelling, right title! There's no one else to blame for a mistake.

Still Store

Still pictures can be retrieved the same way as CGs. A still store command is typed into the script when it is written, and the still store's computer retrieves the item on command. The director need only commit the image to air.

Prompters

We've already mentioned that today most prompters receive their data directly from the newsroom computer system, eliminating the need to employ a specialized prompter operator. Most prompter systems can also provide **closed captioning** (CC) for the hearing-impaired. In its simplest form, the closed captioning software translates the script data to images which are hidden within the TV signal. Recipients of the closed caption information have to secure a special "decoder" or "black box" which makes the closed captioning visible on the screen.

This automated service, which is sometimes underwritten by sponsors, is valuable to both the relatively large number of hearing-impaired viewers and to non-English speakers who want to learn to speak English. They can look at the written word as they hear the anchorperson speak it.

Closed captioning varies from simple relay of only the typed script, to a complex system in which trained court stenographers type in live remarks which do not appear in the script. Many network programs are closed captioned under agreements with national organizations which provide this specialized service.

Tape Rolls

If a newsroom computer system with automation software can control character generators and still stores, can it control tape playback?

It certainly can. Many news organizations already use automated playback systems to play cassettes containing commercials, promotional announcements, programs, and news tapes. The newsroom computer system simply instructs the tape library to play news tapes on command.

Automation software can also be used to turn studio lights on and off. Most lighting patterns for news broadcasts are fixed and do not change from day to day, even though they do change from broadcast to broadcast.

Cameras

Many news organizations, such as NBC News and CNN use automated studio cameras for some of their news broadcasts. If you analyze several live news programs you will soon discover that the camera work requires few complex camera moves. Much of the movement is short trucks or dollies (movement across the floor), or pans (moving horizontally) followed by frame-ups of the zoom lens (setting the variable focus lens to show just what you want in the picture).

The companies that developed camera automation systems focused on the pedestal, the device on which the studio camera is mounted. They devised systems to control floor, swivel, and zoom movement through pre-programmed instructions. Some systems use an operator to assist the automation, particularly to make certain the shot is precisely on target. Typically an automated camera unit operator will control four cameras.

Whether or not there is an operator supervising the camera automation system, it can be made to talk to, or interface with, the news computer system. This means camera instructions inserted in the script or on the producer rundown trigger the actual moves during the news broadcast.

Wrap-Up

Television news journalists have always depended heavily on technology, because it is technology which makes the medium possible. Technology surrounds the broadcast journalist. It is there to assist you in doing the best job as a teller of news. Some students shy away from learning how to run the various technical devices which are a part of TV news. This is an unwise course to follow for at least two reasons:

1. The job market in TV news is clearly on the path to "multiskilling." This means that reporters, writers, and producers may be asked to shoot images, write, edit tape or disks, control or "run" broadcasts (we call it "switching" or punching the switcher buttons), and even run the production automation while they anchor the program. (Weather forecasters have been doing this for years.)

Employers realize that few if any newsroom workers will be equally skilled at all these tasks, but many of these operations have been simplified to the point that anyone who pays attention and practices a little should be able to perform the task.

The hard facts of economics say if the number of information channels expands more rapidly than the number of video watchers and video advertisers, then the cost of producing news and information programming must be strictly controlled if employers are to remain solvent. Translated that means doing more tasks with the same number or fewer people so multi-skilled journalists will have greater job security.

2. In some cases, adding technology creates new specialties within broadcast journalism. For example, as newsrooms add more computer terminals and more newsroom functions are automated, the systems need care and supervision. A number of computer-literate (frequently young) journalists have carved niches for themselves by taking over supervision and operation of newsroom computer systems. A large computer company may have over 450 sites to service, so most newsrooms need a computer-literate specialist to keep the system operating properly.

One journalist, who moved from a news director's post in a smaller market to the assistant news director's slot in a larger market at a technically sophisticated station became the supervisor of the computer system largely because he liked computers and took the time to learn more about them. He was promoted to director of the station's entire data and computer operations, and his responsibilities could only grow as computer use spreads. He was also in an excellent position to bargain if he decided to contemplate a job change.

Other specialty areas: sophisticated production and preproduction editing; producing other programs or services using information and images already collected by the news organization (on-line services, news inserts in cable news programs); sophisticated videography; operations management (as systems become more complicated). One news department operations chief became the station's vice-president for operations and engineering. Several news directors have become station general managers.

"ONE MORE TAKE, PLEASE"

In the early 1950s, a group of resolute but nontechnical folks were starting up a TV station in Cedar Rapids, Iowa. Throughout this process there was a lot of determination, and a lot of doubt. Near the date when the station was to make its first broadcast, some wag put up a sign in the control room. It read: GOD NEVER MEANT FOR PICTURES TO GO THROUGH THE AIR. A lot of those folks half believed that. But, the pictures did go through the air all right, and they still do.

In the simpler days of broadcast journalism, it was considered smart to say: "I don't want to know about the technology, because if I do someone will ask me to fix it." Now it is essential that the broadcast journalist understand at least the outlines of the technology.

We are moving ever closer to the day when a TV news reporter takes into the field user friendly equipment which allows her or him to record pictures and sound, feed it back to the station, and go live on the air—even edit a story by portable computer—without anyone else being directly involved.

You may never get a chance to touch many of the buttons, keys, knobs, and dials we've talked about because others may be assigned to do that and because in many cases such use is regulated by union contract. But if you know enough about what that other person does, and what the equipment contributes to making the information you are passing on better and clearer, then you have an advantage. You are controlling the machines rather than letting the machines and technicians control you. And you can do a better job of communicating to your viewers.

Storytelling:
The Structure of
TV News

Before we begin with the application of technology to the daily work of reporters, videographers, editors, and producers, let us look at one overriding concept: structure.

Structure is central to all communication, whether nonverbal or verbal. Music, even the most radically modern or primitive, has structure. All art—painting, ceramics, sculpture, furniture making, stained glass, weaving, whatever form it takes—has structure. Even deconstruction calls for a structured, disciplined approach to the task.

Structure is involved in the way individual television news stories are produced, shot, edited, and aired within the larger framework of the newscast, itself a structured unit. This concept of structure is the single most important idea you will need to grasp because it is central to how journalists communicate with their audiences. For the television journalist, structure is an even more important concept because of the way the communication with the viewers takes place.

Some people believe that what television news should do is transmit a whole event without narration, analysis, or commentary. Some say, for example, that the national political conventions should be telecast gavel to gavel, with cameras fixed on the rostrum and the delegates. There would be no floor reporters or anchorpersons in their skybooths analyzing, explaining, and interpreting what is going on. Those who hold this view say that then the viewers could make up their own minds as to what was important, could decide for themselves the meaning of the event.

A version of this technique is available via cable. When Congress is in session the Cable-Satellite Public Affairs Network services **C-SPAN** and **C-SPAN II** televise the proceedings of the House of Representatives and Senate respectively, as well as selected major political and ceremonial events such as committee hearings, or deliberations by the United Nations. Similarly at the state and local levels, cable outlets may offer on public access or public service channels such events as meetings of state legislatures, local county or city council sessions, county school board meetings, and the like.

The task of journalism is also to explain and interpret the importance and significance of news events. There are reasons why the rhetoric and actions of one person are more important than those of another, why strategies and ideas expressed might or might not work.

These reasons are revealed by interviewing, digging for facts, taping, editing, and writing stories that probe the reasoning, the motives, and the strategies of those involved. These elements are processed into news accounts and provide structure—the "how" and the "why" of the news as well as the "who," "what," "when," and "where." If we left the "how" and "why" out of our reports, the audience would be less well informed.

Editing is fundamental to journalism. News reports are stylized versions of events. To avoid editing would be to avoid journalism and its obligation to present the news in a clear and understandable way and in a context that provides meaning.

With this concept of structure in mind, we look now at some of the ingredients that make up the structure of television news communication. Five distinct aspects are involved: showing and telling, the relationship between the people on the air and the viewers watching their television sets, storytelling, linear clarity, and visual structure.

SHOWING AND TELLING

As local and network television news has expanded and all-news cable channels have developed, the common dialogue today is:

> Did you hear about . . . ?
> Yes, I saw it . . .

The important word here is *saw*. By using it people seem to mean they either "saw" a newscaster telling them about it or, because the technology makes it possible to bring pictures of a news event to people as it is happening, it is also more and more likely that they really did "see" at least some of it. Instant replay and other production techniques also make it possible for the audience to "see it" again and again, to analyze it in slow motion or frame by frame.

Pictures and Words

Television news is more than just pictorial coverage. It "tells" the news with pictures in motion including news sounds, and with words spoken by anchorpersons, reporters, and news makers. The link between the pictures and the words is crucial. At the basic level that wedding of the right words with the right pictures is at once the greatest potential strength and greatest potential weakness of television news. When that link is right the communication may be a whole new experience. When the pictures and words don't work together, when the screen is showing one thing and the words are telling something else—"**cross-scripting**" in the jargon of the craft—confusion quickly results.

THE ANCHOR INGREDIENT

Now add in the second unique ingredient: the fact that the audience is watching anchorpersons and reporters tell the news.

When former NBC News President Reuven Frank said, "Television news is at its best when it provides an experience for the audience," he seemed to be saying that television allows the audience to *go along with* the anchors and reporters to the scene of a news story, either with live coverage or visual coverage on film or tape, and *be there with them* as the action unfolds.

Although anchorpersons are not supposed to become emotionally involved in the news they are telling the audience about, they are human. Occasionally they break out of their shells and indicate by some mannerism, facial expression, or remark, what they think about what they have just watched with the audience. Audiences identify with that.

The "personal" dimension is worth closer examination because it is an integral part of the television news communication process.

Anchors earn huge salaries and are promoted with the ruffles and flourishes befitting heads of state. They are true national or local celebrities. TV reporters also get recognition, more recognition than their print colleagues. People wave at them and call them by their first names as they walk down the street. Tourists are as likely to report they saw a television or cable network news correspondent getting out of a cab in New York or Washington as they are to talk about any other historic event or place they saw on their trip. Viewers develop a personal relationship—an empathy—with the anchors and reporters who are there in their living rooms every day.

Hundreds of research studies have tried to define the dimensions of this relationship and just how it works. Consultants who advise TV stations on how to increase the size of the news audience have earned large sums of money for their work in part because they have concentrated their research on the viewer-anchor relationship. In general a few things stand out:

1. The audience and the anchorperson are involved in an empathic relationship—the audience has personal feelings about the anchor.

2. The audience respects anchors because they deliver an important commodity—the news.

3. The audience imagines personal characteristics about individual anchors; it looks at them closely and reacts to any change in their appearance, dress, or on-air conduct.

4. The audience is forgiving about personal frailties—an occasional flub or a bad performance.

5. The audience is not very forgiving about professional failures—repeated mistakes, repeated poor performance, lack of clarity or precision.

6. The audience likes to get the news from people it likes more than it likes getting the news from people it dislikes.

7. The audience feels that it gets the news more clearly from anchorpersons it likes.

8. When things go wrong, the audience is often more likely to blame the news organization the anchor works for than to blame an anchor it likes.

9. The audience develops a very strong loyalty and viewing habit because of the continued presence of a likable anchor.

In the lore of TV news, there are many stories that illustrate this important personal relationship between viewers and anchorpersons.

Walter Cronkite is the only television news anchor who has ever motioned 18 million people to be quiet. He was anchoring The CBS Evening News the evening word of the death of former President Lyndon Johnson broke.

The newscast had just shown a report from Tom Fenton in Paris on the progress of the Vietnam peace talks. The camera switched to Cronkite, who was seen talking on the phone. (Mr. Johnson's former press aide was on the other end of the line.) Cronkite raised a finger towards the audience in a "wait a minute" gesture while he continued to listen. He then told the audience that former President Lyndon Johnson was dead. He listened to the phone a bit more, then added some more information. He thanked the press aide, and then restated what he had learned. A prerecorded obituary on Johnson was worked into the end of the newscast.

It is easy to imagine what happened when Cronkite raised his finger towards the audience. People grabbed the dog, told the kids to keep quiet, and leaned forward with full attention. Cronkite's action was a simple, human one, something anyone would do when talking to someone else face to face.

Network anchors normally assume a detachment from the news accounts they are presenting or introducing. People use different terms to indicate this phenomenon, terms such as noncommittal, detached, neutral, impartial, non-partisan, objective, and the like.

NBC Nightly News anchor Tom Brokaw's expression is noncommittal about the news he is reporting. But not always. Occasionally, when the camera comes back on Brokaw after a field report, which he obviously has been watching along with the audience, his facial reaction may be very expressive, distinctively Brokaw, especially after a field report when the story has a "human nature" angle, one with poignancy. (Such items are often slotted near the close of the news.)

When Dan Rather replaced Walter Cronkite as the anchor of the CBS Evening News, management experimented with various production details to make Rather's presentation and appearance attractive to the audience. One night Rather showed up wearing a sweater under his jacket. Audience reaction was immediate. *Everyone* talked about the incident for days.

STORYTELLING—A DIALOGUE WITH THE VIEWERS

We have seen that there is a strong audience identification with the personality, the looks, the style of the anchorpersons who tell the audience the news each night. There is also strong evidence that *how* they tell and show the news is also important.

The authors believe what takes place is a dialogue between the anchors and reporters and the audience.

Consider how you would tell a friend the news of a plane crash in a nearby city.

Friend: Well, you've been in the newsroom all day. Tell me what's been going on.

You: There was a terrible plane crash.

Friend: Oh, what happened?

You: A small plane crashed into a passenger plane as it was making an approach to the airport.

Friend: Which airport?

You: The Indianapolis airport. The airliner was coming in and the small plane hit it near the tail, and both went down southwest of Greenfield.

Friend: When?

You: About 3:30.

Friend: How many were hurt?

You: They say that all of the people, about 83 on the airliner, are dead, and so is the pilot of the small plane.

Friend: How could that happen?

You: They don't know yet. The airliner was on final approach, and the other plane either

came from the side, or was under it, and
none of the controllers saw it until it
was too late.

Friend: Don't they have radar?

You: Of course, but they say only the airliner
showed on the screen, and then it disap-
peared. The small plane pilot was a student making a solo. He'd taken lessons for
three years, and would have got his
license next week.

Friend: What did it look like at the crash?

You: It was grim, wreckage and bodies all over
the place. The wreckage almost landed in a
trailer court . . . made a 10-foot hole in
the ground.

Friend: What's going on now?

You: Well, they've set up a morgue and are
bringing the bodies there, and there will
be an investigation about how the planes
got so close; they're bringing the inspec-
tors out from Washington, and they've
found the flight recorder. . . .

The telling and showing of that story on television would involve pictures—probably live pictures—from the scene of the crash, interviews with
airline officials, airport officials, police, firefighters, rescue workers. Perhaps
you would see interviews with relatives of the victims, who, one would hope,
had been approached with hesitancy and asked for permission before being
interviewed. The station might develop some graphics to try to show the
flight paths of the planes. It might even have eyewitness reports from people
who had seen the crash.

The anchors and reporters telling the story would contribute a lot more
facts, identify sources more precisely, give a list of the names of the dead
(one hopes not before close relatives had been notified), interview experts
who might analyze how and perhaps why the crash occurred. The station
would put together a package of information it hoped would be as complete
and clear as possible, a package based on up-to-the-minute information.

Regardless of the visual and word content of the story, there would be a
dialogue going on between the reporters or anchors and the viewers. Those
viewers have tuned in asking to be shown and told about the events of the
day. The news staff at the television station has chosen the plane crash as its
lead story because of its importance, judging it to be the most important

story in that newscast's budget of news. For Indiana viewers, the event happened nearby, and for that reason—proximity—it is more important than a similar story farther away. Viewers count on the broadcast journalist to make that kind of selection—they expect the important news to come first.

But viewers also are participating in the process. Just as your friend asked you questions, the viewer is posing questions to the television set.

What happened?

Who was involved?

When did it happen? And *where?*

How and *why* did it happen?

The above listing is, of course, nothing more than the classic outline of a news story: the hallowed five Ws and H. But because the viewer is being told the news by someone on the screen who is "familiar," and because the information includes motion pictures from the scene of the event, the report has become a visual and personal experience. It is more involving than reading the story in a newspaper, or listening to the voices of reporters coming over a radio. In fact, the dialogue, or conversation, is similar to the face-to-face report between you and one of your friends.

Yet the situations are different. The viewer cannot interrupt the flow of the story. The story must be written and structured so that the important points (answers to the classic news questions) are made clear. Further, these details need to be in the order in which the viewer is asking the questions.

How on earth, you say, is a writer or reporter supposed to know what those viewers out there are asking? As experimentation with interactive television expands, we might see news stories constructed in a much different form. Interactive cable systems do a lot of research trying to find out what kinds of questions users ask, and what those questions mean to the way information may be communicated on those systems.

So far the viewers of over-the-air television news can't talk directly to anchorpersons—a telephone call or fax on the station's viewer hotline is not the same as direct contact. However, with viewers in mind we can imagine from our own lives how a conversation between them and the anchor might go, and then structure news stories to match that kind of experience.

LINEAR NEWS

A fourth structural consideration: Broadcast news is linear. It took the industry a long time to realize this. Most experimentation with developing what is called "broadcast news style" grew out of physical problems. For example, cues indicating where audio or video material is to be inserted into the broadcast must be on the same page with the narration in the script.

For those trying to read the conventional wire service reports on the air, breathing space was lacking. Delivering the long sentences and convoluted paragraphs without taking a breath led to oxygen deprivation. The wire services, particularly United Press International, came up with "broadcast wires" in which the writing was simpler—short sentences, conversational words. It turned out that such a writing style was not only easier to read out loud but also easier for the audience to understand.

Forward Motion

Viewers get the news in a flow of information that is constantly moving forward. The first story is immediately followed by the second, and so on through the entire newscast. A viewer cannot stop the flow to go back and pick up missed points the way a newspaper reader can stop and return to an earlier element or slow down to ponder a confusing paragraph. The viewer cannot speed ahead, or skim, and cannot slow down the newscaster if she or he is talking too fast.

Even within a story the structure is linear. The structure contains:

The beginning—the **lead**

The middle—the development of facts and details

The end—the conclusion

Figure 3.1. The linear structure of broadcast news.

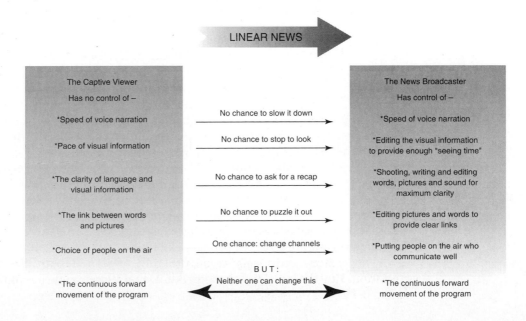

It is natural to want to finish all the parts of Story Element A before moving on to Story Element B. We also know that there is a linear logic to the arrangement of those story elements. What is needed is a logical progression of both aural and visual facts. The audience quickly becomes confused and irritated if we jump back and forth from one element to another in the narration or visual segment. We also know we should keep subjects and verbs close together, avoid too many dependent clauses, and make sure the referents of pronouns are clear, all because the audience can't stop and go back to puzzle it out.

Just as an individual story has linear structure, linear structure runs throughout the newscast. Television news producers spend a large amount of time figuring out where to place stories and how to group stories in the newscast to ensure:

A logical arrangement

A logical progression

Forward movement

This is because the producer wants to maintain the highest level of interest and attention throughout the newscast. Much time is spent determining what the lead story will be, but perhaps as much time is also spent arranging the order of the rest of the items in the news program.

No one would want to arrange the stories in descending order of importance or significance. To do so would be to set up a newscast which loses half of the audience's attention and interest halfway through the newscast.

Total newscast strategies concerning forward flow are developed. A station that has a sixty-minute newscast in competition with another station that joins the network news after thirty minutes works hard to be sure there is something interesting on the screen at the thirty-minute point to keep the audience from switching channels.

Stations that program large blocks of news—the two-and-one-half and three-hour news programs in major markets—use elaborate strategies to keep the audience. These include frequent updates of top stories and a great deal of internal program promotion of items coming later in the newscast. Some plan the format so that regular departments within the news occur at very nearly the same time every day. The audience will, they hope, learn when the features they are most interested in come on.

Purists complain about the loss of news time resulting from the heavy use of "**bumpers**" and "**teasers**." Bumpers are promotional graphics—sometimes with accompanying music—inserted at the end of newscast segments to produce a smooth transition to a commercial or to the next newscast segment; teasers are inserted into a transition point in the newscast just like bumpers, but are more editorial—a headline or other reference to an upcoming news story, purposely vague, titillating, designed to arouse viewer anticipation. But the need for these promotional items comes as much from the basic linear nature of the way people receive broadcast news as it does from the station's promotion pizzazz.

Even commercials affect the linear strategy by which the newscast is organized. It is common practice to allow news producers to decide the precise location of commercial breaks. How many there will be is decided by commercial considerations and station policy. But the producer knows that the commercials represent a break in the news action, that whether or not the viewers watch the commercials, the forward motion of the newscast continues since there will be more news after the spots are played.

Therefore, producers do a great deal of planning to organize the news segments between the commercials. The story order within a segment should follow both logical arrangement and logical progression rules. In Chapter 7 we discuss various strategies producers have developed to achieve a logical flow of items in a newscast, guidelines they follow to help avoid the impression of randomness that comes when the items are reported seemingly without a plan, seemingly following no rules of organization.

About Television News "Guidelines"

Television news professionals have developed many sets of "guidelines"—"rules-of-thumb," "do's and don'ts"—that they apply in virtually every phase of the news process. You will find quite a few such guidelines discussed in this book: videography do's and don'ts, broadcast writing style rules, ending rules-of-thumb, and so forth.

With those many and diverse guidelines in mind, here is a basic principle about formulas to keep in mind: No rule can anticipate every conceivable circumstance that might come up when the rule is being applied in a given situation. What this means is this (we'll call it The Rule About Rules):

> You must apply any guideline creatively, thoughtfully, and purposefully—rather than blindly, rigidly, or by rote.

VISUAL STRUCTURE

The fifth major element of the structure of television news concerns the linear nature of the way the audience receives the news pictures themselves. The scenes of the news event must move forward in an orderly fashion, or randomness will defeat clear communication.

Visual continuity in television news is everyone's responsibility. The videographer and reporter covering a story must be aware that unless they provide the elements for visual continuity in the raw videotape it will be impossible to achieve when the story is edited. Editors and writers must be aware of the rules of visual organization and apply them carefully during the editing and visual-word matching process.

In fact, what the writer does in selecting and arranging the elements of a word story into an orderly sequence strongly parallels what the videographer and video editor do in selecting and arranging the elements of a visual story. The material they gather and process must have the same linear progression as a written story. Compression is essential with both words and pictures. You've heard the expression: "Well, to make a long story short. . . ." Broadcast news stories are that way. An event that may take ninety minutes to unfold may have to be reduced to ninety seconds for a newscast. To do that for television news, the key is to have the scenes necessary to compress the action into a smoothly flowing whole. It is writing with words *and* pictures.

Composition

GENERAL RULE 1. Good visual composition is essential to good visual communication.

In visual reporting, shot composition is an art. Some people just plain have the "eye" to see good visual composition. Some people learn it. Others never do. Composition is much more abstract than some of the other elements of visual structure that we will discuss later. We are talking here about the "feel" and the "look" of the shots as they are produced in the field and edited in the newsroom.

Framing

For the videographer this involves proper framing of the picture. Attention must be paid to the use of the space within the frame, the spatial relationships of subjects or objects in the frame, and the spatial relationships of subjects or objects across a sequence of scenes. For the video editor it involves the same sensitivity to those elements while the raw material is being edited. For both it requires understanding that the elements of visual composition are also journalistic elements that affect the way the pictures will communicate to the audience.

Some pictures look comfortable, others look uncomfortable. When a picture is framed properly, the important visual information fits comfortably within it. Heads that are cut off or that are so low in the frame that it looks like the subject is trying to climb back into the frame, and heads or objects that are cut off on one side or the other are unusable shots. Even if you do not realize how uncomfortable these shots are, members of the audience do, and they are distracted by them.

Shots that are composed with exact symmetry, that is, with the pictorial center of interest in the exact geometric center, are visually less pleasing than shots that are asymmetrical, or slightly off center. Imagine that a TV picture frame is divided into thirds across its horizontal axis. A head shot that places

Figure 3.2. Two scenes from an interview shot to allow "looking room." The interviewer shot is framed to put him in the left two-thirds of the screen. The subject shot is framed to put her in the right two-thirds of the screen. In each shot, the space or "room" is in the direction the person is seen to be looking. When the scenes cut from him to her and back again, each scene shows enough space and each person appears to be facing the other even though each is alone in the scene. *(Courtesy of Will Counts.)*

the head exactly equidistant from the sides of the frame is less visually interesting than one that places the head in either the left or right two-thirds of the frame.

Looking Room

Using "thirds" also gives you the chance to provide looking room. For example, an interview always has a line of action. In a **two shot** the reporter may be on the right side of the frame, while the subject is on the left. Once established, that spatial relationship remains in the viewer's mind even when only one or the other person is on the screen.

Now, dividing the frame into thirds to provide "looking room," the shot of the reporter should put him or her in the right two-thirds of the screen looking into the frame. And the shot of the person being interviewed should put him or her in the left two-thirds of screen, looking into the frame.

When these shots are edited together, the two people are looking toward each other, and both shots leave space on the side where the other person is sitting. By using the rule of thirds, you have created space for the other person to move into when the edit is made.

Natural framing opportunities are everywhere. Examples of some of the more obvious ones are:

An arch that can be used to shoot through to the object of interest, say a park fountain in the distance shooting water plumes into the air.

A traffic control highway sign in the foreground, looking off to the wreckage of a vehicle in the background.

Overhanging branches of a tree through which the shot looks out onto the site of a proposed new industrial park.

Such compositional elements are all around us. Videographers and editors must raise their visual consciousness levels to see and use them, and to avoid making and using shots that contain distracting compositional elements.

Figure 3.3. Framing a shot. The glass lamp seeming perched on the reporter's head (*a*) is a visual gaffe. A slight adjustment to the framing (*b*) corrects the problem. *(Courtesy of James Gustke.)*

Backgrounds

Backgrounds and surroundings can be distracting. The experts say, for example, to watch out for horizontal lines running through the background. It is visually distracting to have a telephone wire seemingly entering a newsmaker's ear on one side and exiting on the other. Similarly, a tower of a build-

Figure 3.4. Shot composition. A partial blocking of a sign (*a*) makes the shot looks sloppy, an unintended or mindless visual arrangement. Getting rid of the blocked off look (*b*) resolves the problem of sloppiness and puts viewer attention on the reporter. *(Courtesy of James Gustke.)*

ing that seems to be resting on top of the head of a newsmaker, thus forming a "hat," is a visual gaffe, and someone in the viewing audience is bound to see it. The videographer must see distracting visual elements in the viewfinder and work to control them.

How Long?

Students of the art of telling a story with motion pictures will ask sooner or later—usually sooner—about the length of things: how long a story should be, how long a sequence should be, how long an individual shot should be. These are good questions and should not be fobbed off with the quick answer: "As long as necessary, as short as possible."

A professor of cinematography, himself a student of those early moviehouse newsreels from which many of our present-day video shooting and editing conventions developed, did a study. With stopwatch and steno pad he timed individual scenes from some *March of Time* newsreels. This was, he admitted, an unscientific approach, but it nonetheless produced interesting data. He found that the average running time of a *March of Time* newsreel scene was seven seconds.

He was careful to note that he was reporting an *average* running time per scene, which of course meant that some scenes were longer than seven seconds, some shorter. And these were *edited* scenes, not raw shots.

When you are recording your video, the minimum length of a shot should be much longer than seven seconds, as much as fifteen seconds longer than needed is a good rule of thumb. As to how much of a shot is needed, a lot depends on the subject of the shot. If it is a sign that reads "Keep Out" the shot needn't roll on at great length. If it is a Civil War Historical Marker giving details of a battle fought there, frame the sign in the viewfinder and read the sign to yourself as you record, and run the shot at least as long as it takes you to read the text. If it's a closeup and your camera aim is not too steady, hold the shot a bit longer so that in editing the editor will have a chance to pick the steadiest part of the shot. Other factors are how "busy" the shot looks, whether there's movement, and so forth.

There's another important reason for getting into the habit of making individual shots fifteen or so seconds longer than needed. This reason is technical. When you finish a series of shots and trigger the camera stop button, the forward motion of the videotape ends. In a series of automatic mechanical functions that are the reverse of the videocassette loading process (Chapter 2, p. 32, and Figure 2.3) the tape is unwound from the recording head. In this process, a portion of the shot you just finished recording is rewound backward onto the videocassette supply spool. The technical term for this is "**roll-back.**" When you start recording your next shot, videotape with some of your previous shot is repositioned around the record head drum and some of your last shot gets erased. Note that roll-back occurs only when the camera is cycled into "stop"; if you go from "record" to "pause," the tape stays where it is, and when you continue recording, the tape continues without roll-back.

When one is recording video, how does one gauge an interval of time, say fifteen seconds? A simple yet remarkably accurate way to measure seconds is by counting as you shoot "one thousand, two thousand, three thousand, four thousand . . ." and so forth. Of course when you are editing, you can time scenes with a stopwatch or counter.

Visual Continuity

The key element of visual structure is visual continuity. Visual continuity compresses the action of a story into a smoothly flowing whole. The word *continuity* means uninterrupted connection, succession, union, or duration over time. The idea of continuity over time makes the word an especially useful one in any discussion of the techniques of telling a story by using motion pictures.

A story occurs over time. It is a narrative with a beginning, a middle, and an end. Just as there are any number of verbal techniques for telling a story with words, so also there are numerous visual techniques for telling a story with motion pictures.

Visual continuity emerged long before ENG developed. Many, perhaps most, of the visual techniques used by videographers are very much like those used in the now largely outmoded newsfilm technology. These conventions, in turn, had been copied from the earlier newsreels that became a staple of motion picture theater fare in the 1920s and the 1930s. Going back even further, the newsreels got their storytelling structure and techniques from feature motion picture production itself.

Long Shot, Medium Shot, Closeup

The newsreel narrative story began by visually establishing the story line in the mind's eye of the viewer. Photographers called this part of the story the **establishing shot**. On seeing this shot first, often the "where" of the story, the viewer was ready to receive other details: a **long shot** (**LS**), a **medium shot** (**MS**), and a **closeup** (**CU**). This trio of shots, first filmed and then edited in a way that achieved a fluidity of continuous motion (and avoided visual interruption) formed the basic construction of the motion picture story. Each time a new idea or fact was introduced into the story line, it was first "established" and then "narrated" by using some combination of the now familiar LS-MS-CU approach. Each such combination was called a **sequence**. Sequences were joined together to make the story move from the beginning through the middle to the end.

This fundamental approach worked then, and it continues to be the most satisfactory way to tell a television news story today using videotape. All of the other visual devices and motion picture skills we apply to make the visual part of the story more unified, more coherent, and more emphatic to the viewing audience have as their starting point one of these three basic elements of visual continuity: the long shot, the medium shot, and the closeup.

So if you became interested in knowing more about the genesis of videography techniques and how today's conventions of the craft came to be, these early feature films and movie theater newsreels would be an excellent place for you to start your research.

You cannot successfully identify an individual shot as LS, MS, or CU when it stands alone. This is because each term gets its meaning by comparison with the two other terms as they are used in a particular story. Thus, what is correctly labeled a long shot in one LS-MS-CU sequence may correctly be called a medium shot in a different LS-MS-CU sequence.

Generally, a long shot shows the object of interest in its surroundings or setting. It doesn't clearly distinguish between the object of interest and its setting because it gives roughly equal space, and consequently comparable emphasis, to both.

Although it looks like there are a lot of details or a lot of elements of the story in a long shot, these are not easily absorbed in the relatively short time the LS scene is on the air. Conversely, the closeup shot greatly reduces or eliminates the surroundings and shifts nearly all the visual space, and thus all the attention, to the object of interest. To return to the analogy of the written mode, the long shot might be compared to a verbal generalization, and the closeup shot to the example or words that provide supporting argument and details about the generalization.

The medium shot falls somewhere between the long shot and the closeup and visually bridges the gap between the two. The point where a long shot ends and a medium shot begins is arbitrary. One idea that you might find helpful in looking for some kind of standard for recognizing a medium shot is the notion of the "full figure shot." The full figure shot shows just what the term implies, the complete object of interest from top to bottom and from side to side.

However, the assumption is that the size and shape of the object of interest have a "normal" spatial relationship with the other shots in the sequence. If the object of interest is a person, a medium shot might show the person's

Figure 3.5. A standard sequence using visual continuity concepts. The LS-MS-CU series begins the sequence, a cutaway bridges the two closeup scenes, and a medium long shot ends it. At that point the story could end, or additional sequences could be added to continue the story.

Scene 1	Scene 2	Scene 3	Scene 4	Scene 5	Scene 6
LS Establishes location and general area of story	MS Moves closer to focal point of the story	CU Gets very close to subjects or objects that are the focal point of the story	Cutaway Avoids jump cut, shows reaction	CU Again, close up on main subjects or objects	MLS Reestablishes locale of story, indicates ending, or beginning of new sequence

a   *b*   *c*

Figure 3.6. Various scenes shot with the traditional LS-MS-CU sequence in mind. The long shot (LS) establishes the locale of the story (*a*), the medium shot (MS) moves the audience closer to it (*b*), and the closeup (CU) picks up the central figure in the story as he moves toward the door (*c*). *(Courtesy of James Gustke.)*

head and shoulders. In that case, a long shot of a person would show that person full figure, head to feet, with some of the surroundings; a closeup would show just the face.

Extreme long shots (**ELS**) are sometimes called "panoramic" shots and they are an extension of the LS. A shot of the Grand Canyon from a mile-high airplane is an ELS. The ELS suggests the idea of grandeur, magnificence, sweep.

At the opposite end of the scale, **extreme closeup shots** (**ECU**), which are sometimes also called **inserts**, are suggestive of the notion of narrow perspective, very specific example, or detailed illustration. Such shots are, of course, extensions of the CU. If a shot of the entire head of a subject is a CU, a shot of just the eyes, nose, and mouth—cutting off the hair and the chin—is an ECU.

The Sequence

You now have three fundamental units of a motion picture sequence: LS-MS-CU, with the ELS the expansion of the LS, and the ECU the compression of the CU. In combination, and almost always in that same LS-MS-CU order, they form a sequence, the basic component of motion picture visual continuity. Sequences are joined together to move the story along smoothly from beginning through climax to conclusion.

The sequence also serves another important function. It moves the viewer closer to the center of action. Think for a moment of what you do when you enter a room full of people. You take a general look (LS), then you pick out the point where the major action is (MS), then you move toward that point and look more closely at it (CU). If that point is very interesting you may walk up even closer and lean over to take a very close look (ECU). The

a   *b*   *c*

Figure 3.7. The relational nature of the terms long shot, medium shot, and closeup. The long shot (LS) begins at a point much closer to the building, but still establishes the locale (*a*). The medium shot (MS) resembles the closeup in the previous sequence (*b*), and the closeup (CU) moves the central figure right to the door (*c*). *(Courtesy of James Gustke.)*

LS-MS-CU-ECU sequence does exactly the same thing for the viewer that your legs do for you.

Taken together, these three basic shots do not seem at first glance to be enough to form the foundation of the mechanics, or grammar and syntax, of motion picture stories. But there are many possibilities for individual variations of their combination and sequencing and many innovations of technique for each basic shot. The possibilities for variety seem to be limited only by the number of people going into the field to record the pictures and the imag-

Figure 3.8. The extensions of scenes that can be made on either end of a sequence. An extreme long shot (ELS) takes in not only the building but part of its environment (*a*). An extreme closeup (ECU) allows the audience to travel right along with the central figure up to and through the door (*b*). *(Courtesy of James Gustke.)*

 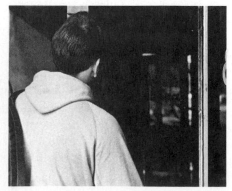

a   *b*

ination of the people using the raw material to construct the finished story. Nevertheless, because the shooting and editing processes of the videotaped raw material are so intertwined, everyone involved in the process must understand and use the same set of basic rules. Application of the rules begins in the field when the scenes are being shot. You need to master them as concepts long before you actually get to the mechanics of shooting and editing.

Jump Cut

A **jump cut** is a visual interruption in the flow of the picture when two scenes in a sequence do not match or fit together. The idea is difficult to express. A student once said, "A jump cut is a lot easier to shoot than it is to describe." The surest way to shoot a jump cut is to record two or more shots of some continuing action from the exact same position without changing the size or angle of the shot. When they are edited together, the action will appear to jump at each point where the scenes join.

For example: The governor is making a speech. You have the subject framed in the viewfinder head and shoulders. In shot 1 the governor's head is tilted to the right. In shot 2 the head is tilted to the left. If those two scenes are edited together by cutting from one to the next, at the edit point the governor's head will "jump" from one side to the other.

Another: You are shooting an interview of a man whose dog has just won best-in-show. In your first shot the man and the dog are shown together, the man talking, the dog drooling happily. Then between shots the dog gets down and goes to investigate some fascinating scent. If you make your second shot

Figure 3.9. A baseline description to help achieve consistency of the designation of a shot in the LS-MS-CU sequence is the "medium-medium," which shows the object of interest "top to bottom," or in "full figure." Thus a building would be shown from ground level to the roof line (*a*), a person from head to foot (*b*). *(Courtesy of James Gustke.)*

a											*b*

the same size and with the same framing, and the two shots are edited together, at the edit point the dog will have magically disappeared.

In each instance an interval of time has elapsed (and thus the content of the action has changed) between shots. However at the edit cut point, the visual movement is not gradual, it is instantaneous. A jump cut calls visual attention to itself thus distracting viewer attention from the story content.

GENERAL RULE 2. Do not shoot jump cuts: After each shot, change the size of the image or the angle of view, or both.

If you follow this rule you will greatly increase your chances of getting shots that satisfy two needs:

1. You will have shots that will help the editor achieve smoothness, fluidity of motion, that sense of continuity in the progression of scenes and sequences which makes the visual story absorbing and viewable.

2. Following the rule is an absolutely foolproof way to avoid shooting what is called a "jump cut."

Various editing techniques have been devised to cope with the jump cut. Replacing a few seconds of video on either side of the cut point with a cut-in (insert) or cutaway (discussed later in this chapter) can avoid the visual jolt. With newer digital editing gear a sophisticated technique that can work well in certain edits is a very short, visually subtle dissolve—almost instantaneous, lasting less than a second—to join two scenes in a smooth, nondistracting way, a sort of visual ellipsis indicating material removed. But back to the videography, you can avoid shooting a jump cut in the first place by following General Rule 2.

If you move either closer to or farther from the object of interest between shots, the size of the image will change. With a zoom lens, changing shot size is very simple: Just zoom the lens to get a closer or wider image. Either way, it should be clear to you that by recording combinations of LS, MS, and CU shots you accomplish the first half of the rule.

The use of different shot **angles** opens the way to following the other half of the rule. One way to approach the idea of angle in shooting motion pictures is to look at it as representing a **point of view**. Let's go back into that room full of people. You look at some things head-on and at eye level. To see other things you must look up or down. To see still other things you must turn sideways, and occasionally you turn all the way around and look behind you. You use a camera the same way: You choose the point of view by choosing where to aim it.

Various Shot Angles

The eye-level shot is called a **flat-angle shot**. These are the kinds of shots which, when viewed in succession, seem routine, dull, boring, visually unimaginative, and uninteresting. Several flat-angle shots in a row tend to become visually tedious. Scenes shot head-on at eye level certainly have their place in the visual story, but different shots from a variety of angles are more interesting and also help move the story along.

As its name indicates, the **high-angle shot** is made by placing the camera above the object of interest and taking the shot looking down at it. If this shot is selected during the editing it tends to create the visual effect of subordinating the object, making it recede, minimizing, or deemphasizing it. It also has the effect of seeming to slow down the action.

Conversely, the **low-angle shot** is made by placing the camera below the object of interest and taking the shot looking up at it. The visual effect of looking up at an object is the opposite of looking down at it. The low-angle shot tends to magnify the object of interest, to make it dominate the shot, and generally to heighten or intensify the feeling and the pace of the action.

Whereas flat-angle and high-angle shots tend to create the visual effect of slowing the pace of the action, the **side-angle shot** has the opposite effect, that of quickening the pace. If you want a graphic demonstration of these contrasting visual effects, try an experiment. Using the same size shot, record some scenes from a moving vehicle, first shooting forward through the front windshield, and then sideways through a side window. You'll notice on playback how leisurely the forward shots seem when compared with the side-angle shots, in which the motion appears accelerated and even exaggerated.

Another kind of shot that has its special uses for television news is the **reverse angle**. For example, visualize a story about a homecoming parade with its floats, marching bands, and homecoming queen and other celebrities. The object of interest is the parade and its participants. Reverse angles will show the spectators, the background of the line of march, what the par-

Figure 3.10. Visual information as well as visual interest may be increased by careful use of angles. The low-angle shot (looking up at the center of interest) tends to emphasize the figure (*a*); the high-angle shot (looking down at the center of interest) tends to deemphasize the figure (*b*). Shots taken head-on at eye level (the flat-angle shot) may be used for visual contrast (*c*). (Courtesy of James Gustke.)

a   *b*   *c*

ticipants see as they look out from their positions in the parade. Reverse angles help the editor give the audience both points of view.

The reverse-angle shot is also frequently used in television news reporting in the interview situation. The subject of interest is the person being interviewed, of course, and the main shots focus on her or him as the center of visual attention.

An interview technique that provides viewer satisfaction and at the same time achieves visual unity and editorial clarity is one in which the picture sequence shows the subject speaking, followed by a CU shot of the reporter asking a question, then cutting back to the subject for the answer. This technique provides pace and visual interest, makes for a smooth flow, and allows for fluid continuity and time compression.

All are achieved by the careful use of reverse-angle shots that have been skillfully composed and framed. The idea of reverse angles brings up the next general rule:

GENERAL RULE 3. Observe screen direction.

Line of Action

This rule is sometimes called the rule of 180 degrees, or the rule of the *line of action.* It applies to any situation where the central action moves along a line, or axis, that is, in any situation where the action is moving at right angles to your camera, either left-to-right or right-to-left.

Figure 3.11. The primary shot in a standard interview setup is the shot of the subject (*a*). The reverse-angle shot—showing the reporter as the center of interest (*b*)—is especially useful in these situations, as it allows for visual variety, time compression, and smoothness of editing. Also, by reshooting the reporter questions in reverse angle, with the subject still present, the reporter gains an additional check on the accuracy of the respoken questions. *(Courtesy of James Gustke.)*

a   *b*

Consider spectators watching a parade as the parade units move along a downtown street. For viewers on one side of the street, the parade is seen as moving left-to-right. For those on the opposite side of the street, the parade is moving right-to-left. The street is the center line or axis of the action, the line along which the parade moves.

Shots of the various units as they move past you convey the visual effect that the parade is moving in a certain direction, either screen right to left, or screen left to right depending on which side of the street you are on (your point of view). Cross the street (thus crossing the center line of action) and shoot from the other side. Now, everything that had been moving from right to left suddenly is shown to be moving from left to right, back in the direction the parade came from.

The screen direction rule recommends that you not cross the center line of the action. To do so, in either the shooting or the editing, results in sequences of pictures in which the line of action is going in one direction mixed with pictures in which it is going in the other direction.

You must observe the screen direction rule in all situations from the simplest interview to the most action-filled sequence. If you cross the line, you must also shoot (and use) transitional scenes which will bring the audience across the line with you and establish a new point of view. The important thing is to establish the center line of action in your own mind as you are shooting and editing. Then when you make the straight-on shots, the reverse angles will conform to that center line of action.

GENERAL RULE 4. You must have cut-ins and cutaways.

Two of the most important shots used to provide visual continuity are the **cut-in** and the **cutaway**. Both can be quite brief, and both are essential to achieving smoothness and flow in the finished product. Editorially, however, the two shots are quite dissimilar.

Cut-Ins and Cutaways

As the name implies, the cut-in is used to cut *into* the central action. The cut-in is also called an *insert*. Consider again the homecoming parade. The central action is the royal float with the homecoming queen waving and smiling to the crowds as the parade moves by. The most logical cut-in would be a full-screen shot of the queen's smiling face.

Or the central action is the varsity marching band stepping smartly down the line of march. In one possibility for a cut-in, the point of view might be down at the pavement level. The camera would be aimed straight across the street, and at right angles to the line of march. What you'll get is a shot of a line of marching feet stepping by in unison, left, right, left. When that shot is edited in between two wider shots of the band marching, it gives a visual accent and allows for compression of time. Cut-ins are usually closeups.

a   *b*   *c*

Figure 3.12. These three shots illustrate a main difference between the "cut-in" (also called an "insert") and the "cutaway" shot. In shot (*a*) the center of interest is the dancing bear and other ballet performers. The cut-in (*b*) looks closer in to the central action; the cutaway (*c*) looks away from the central action to the audience watching the ballet. (*Courtesy of James Gustke.*)

The cutaway, on the other hand, is made by turning *away from* the central action to something that is not part of it although it is directly related. At the parade, a cutaway might be a shot of spectators, a parent with a small child perched on his or her shoulders, a police officer directing the crowd, a man with a "Class of '41" button on his lapel.

A cutaway can also be thought of as a *reaction* shot. In crowds, people look around at other people to see how they are reacting to what is going on. If you are attending a play and something shocking happens, you will very likely look at other people in the audience to see how they are affected by it. If you are listening to a politician making a campaign speech, you might look around to see whether others in the audience seem to be agreeing or disagreeing with what the politician is saying. Television news should provide the audience with as accurate a representation as possible of the human reactions to the news event as well as the action itself. Cutaways will do that if they are shot during (not before or after) the event.

Expert opinion differs as to whether the cut-in or the cutaway is more useful, more logical, more consistent. The real question is whether the cut-in is editorially more consistent and thus preferable. Some believe it is because it stays with the central action, is part of that action, adds detail, and thus is a unifying factor in the sequence. Those who hold this view argue also that the cutaway, no matter how much it is in character with the thrust of the story being developed, looks *away* from the central action and interrupts the continuous flow of the story. Those who disagree say that cutaways provide the reaction to the central focus of the story, giving the viewer a broader look at what happened.

The primary requirement for both cut-ins and cutaways is that they be appropriate to the story. They must be as "true" as possible. The cut-in of a subject's fingers pulling at his mustache may depict nervousness. If the subject was nervous, then the cut-in depicts that reality.

A cutaway at the political rally of a person sleeping under a newspaper while the politician is orating at the rostrum may be appropriate. But if that person is the only one asleep and the rest of the audience is cheering wildly, including that person sleeping shot in the speech sequence would be a form of "editorial comment" and therefore inappropriate. Remember, cut-ins and cutaways must be *related* to the action to be appropriate.

Even with the editorial problems these shots present, there is general agreement that both the cut-in and the cutaway serve a number of very valuable functions. They convey information about an event to the viewing audience. They are visually interesting and add excitement and pace to the story. Most important, they are convenient—and indispensable—editing material for the compression of action.

Take a simple sequence of a school bus coming to a bus stop, loading and unloading passengers, and then continuing on its route. The entire action, from when the bus first comes into view, until it disappears from view down the street after having made the stop, will take five minutes. You want to compress five minutes of action into a twenty-eight-second version. Here is one way to do it using cut-ins and cutaways.

Scene 1
(4 sec.)   LS, school bus coming into view some distance from bus stop.

Scene 2
(2 sec.)   *Cutaway,* MS, four people standing near sign that says BUS STOP.

Scene 3
(8 secs.)   CU, bus bounces to a stop, doors full frame, they swing open, a passenger steps down.

Scene 4
(5 secs.)   CU, reverse angle, group in Scene Two climb on.

Scene 5
(3 secs.)   *Cut-in,* CU, first person of group shows his bus pass.

Scene 6
(6 secs.)   MCU, bus doors close, full frame, bus pulls away, slow pan right to follow shot as bus disappears screen right.

Notice that the cutaway compresses time by getting to the people at the bus stop quickly. The cut-in speeds things up by condensing the business of climbing on and showing the bus pass into one quick shot. By making these shots at the scene the videographer has provided the ingredients with which the twenty-eight-second sequence is accomplished in the editing bay.

Into Frame, Out of Frame

Another pair of shots that are simple to shoot and visually effective in the appropriate circumstances are called *into-frame* and *out-of-frame.* The into-

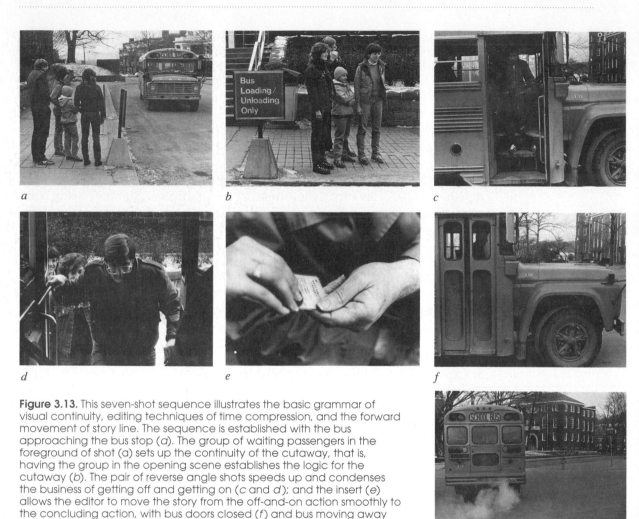

Figure 3.13. This seven-shot sequence illustrates the basic grammar of visual continuity, editing techniques of time compression, and the forward movement of story line. The sequence is established with the bus approaching the bus stop (*a*). The group of waiting passengers in the foreground of shot (*a*) sets up the continuity of the cutaway, that is, having the group in the opening scene establishes the logic for the cutaway (*b*). The pair of reverse angle shots speeds up and condenses the business of getting off and getting on (*c* and *d*); and the insert (*e*) allows the editor to move the story from the off-and-on action smoothly to the concluding action, with bus doors closed (*f*) and bus moving away (*g*). (*Courtesy of James Gustke.*)

frame shot first shows the general location of the subject of interest but without that subject in view. While the tape is rolling and the camera is held steady, the subject of interest comes into frame and is centered, to become the visual center of attention. The out-of-frame technique simply reverses this order, so that the subject is centered up and is the center of attention as the shot begins. As the shot proceeds, and with the camera held steady, the subject moves out of the frame. Note that in both kinds of shots, the camera is held steady in one position while the action and motion are provided by the object of attention.

> GENERAL RULE 5. Action must match direction of action.

When shooting into-frame and out-of-frame the videographer must be careful to make the action in related scenes match the into-frame and out-of-frame scenes so that the viewers don't become confused.

For example: A free tuberculosis patch-test clinic is being offered by a local hospital. The first four shots may show (1) the outside of the hospital (establisher); (2) the front door; (3) a sign, with an arrow, saying CLINIC (cut-in); and (4) the waiting room full of people (reestablisher). Editing those together creates the effect of moving the audience to the center of the action.

Now comes the time for patients to go into the doctor's office. Instead of providing one lengthy medium-shot scene in which a nurse comes into the waiting room with a list on a clipboard and calls out names, the videographer has shot a sequence about one person's being called in.

Shot 5   MS, nurse comes out of door at the back of the waiting room, moving *right to left,* and calls out a name.

Shot 6   MCU, seated person looks up, nurse enters frame from *right* side.

Shot 7   MS, seated person stands, nurse and patient exit screen *right.*

Shot 8   Cutaway LS, waiting room.

Shot 9   MS, door to doctor's office. Patient in Shots 6 and 7 comes out the door, thanks nurse, turns, and exists screen *left.*

By carefully observing the line and direction of the action, the videographer has provided a sequence in which the nurse's and patient's directions of movement relate to each other, to the door of the doctor's office, and to the outside. When the patient leaves screen left, the audience is shown that the action is over—the patient is not going back into the doctor's office.

The purpose of the story is to inform people of the free clinic and to try to encourage them to come in to get the tests by showing them how simple it is. By using the into-frame, out-of-frame technique it is possible to compress otherwise spread-out action and real time, and focus attention on the center of interest.

Tilts and Pans

So far our discussion of shots and their uses in visual continuity and story structure has allowed the subjects or objects of interest to provide the motion.

By purposely moving the camera while the tape is rolling, you can produce other kinds of shots. If the camera is moved horizontally, the motion is called a **pan**. If the camera is moved vertically, the motion is called a **tilt**.

Some beginners—maybe most—seem to have a compulsion to pan. Perhaps that's because we pan and tilt our heads and bodies to look at various objects in sight. On the beginners' tape the pans go left, the pans go right, the pans start left and go right, and then come back left again. The camera is always in motion. It is time to invoke:

> GENERAL RULE 6. Pans, tilts, and zooms must be motivated.

The fact is that a pan is a very useful shot—sometimes. But it often can make things difficult for the editor. The trick is to learn how to pan and when to pan.

The most important reason to pan is, of course, to follow action. In addition, you *may* use the pan to show the spatial relationship between any two related subjects, objects, or pieces of information. Both reasons have a logical motivation. For example, you might make a shot that starts with the beginning point of black skid marks on a street and at right angles to them (high angle, looking down at the pavement). Then you pan in the direction of the skid marks, centering up, ending with a vehicle crumpled against a tree.

The pan is also a useful technique in physically confined spaces, enclosed areas, or places where movement to get another shot is inhibited. A pan may be just the shot needed to show the spatial relationship of various objects of interest in that area.

But the videographer must keep in mind the main reasons editors so dislike pans in the first place. For one thing, a pan is time consuming; once a pan is started it must run its course. Editors hate to interrupt a pan before it ends. For another, a pan is hard on the eyes, and it doesn't take very long for some people watching a succession of them to reach for the seasick pills. Usually it is better to cut from one scene to another during the editing process, but some pans—those which are motivated—are useful and necessary.

You won't run into so many rules about tilts. The slow tilt up or down to relate two objects of interest to each other is often quite useful, particularly in combination with high-angle or low-angle camera placement. But they, too, must be motivated; you must have a storytelling reason for making them and using them.

With both pans and tilts, always hold the beginnings and endings of the shots steady for five to ten seconds—at least five on each end—so that the stationary portions of the shots are usable even if the editor decides to eliminate the pan or tilt movement.

Zooms

Zooming is like panning and tilting in that the motion of the camera becomes a part of the shot. As you will recall, the major purpose of a zoom lens is to provide an infinite number of focal lengths in one lens. With the zoom lens, the size of any shot can be changed at will. This should be the primary use of a zoom lens: to establish the size of the shot, to trim that shot size for more comfortable composition, and to change the size of the shot between takes.

But you might have a good reason for making shots that include a zoom in view. If you want to show the spatial relationship between a subject or object in the foreground to something else in the background, a zoom will sometimes accomplish that. It is useful for following action that moves toward or away from the camera position since the size of the center of attention in the shot can be maintained as the distance changes.

On a spot news story where the action is uncontrolled and fast moving, the zoom is used regularly to frame up the next shot while the tape is rolling. Doing this gives the editor a well-framed shot—with tracking on it—to cut to *after the zoom is finished.*

Beginners seem to like to zoom almost as much as they like to pan. Their tapes are full of shots which move closer to or farther away from the subject while the shot progresses. These scenes are difficult to edit for the same reason pans are difficult to edit (the zoom must be completed before the shot can be cut) and difficult to watch because the motion can distract.

A famous cinematographer at a television news workshop told the students that if they didn't stop zooming, he was going to remove the zoom cranks from their cameras. He said: "Your tape is full of MSTTP shots—My Son the Trombone Player."

MAKING IT ALL TELL A STORY

It's takeoff checklist time.

1. Camera ready?

2. VCR ready?

3. Lighting setup ready?

4. Mics, sound setup ready?

If everything checks out, you can now make pictures and sound. You are ready physically. But hold it. Are you ready mentally? What you accomplish from this point on will be controlled more by that other level of consciousness—the commitment. The equipment is in place. Now it is time to concentrate on making the visual content work toward showing and telling the story in the clearest, most interesting, and most involving way possible.

This brings up a new list of questions. Some of them have already been hinted at. The answers to some of them will create frustration because they will mean you may have to change the physical setup. All of them, whether they deal with mechanics or aesthetics, relate to what you are getting on tape and *how* that will be used in putting the story together.

1. Is the camera location the right one?

2. How will the scenes relate to the subjects and the subject matter?

3. Have I got the proper cover (B-Roll) material, and enough of it?

4. Have I got what is needed to "tell" the story?

5. Have I got what is needed for the editing process?

If you are on a spot news story you must run through this list at break-neck speed. If there is more time you have more time to think your way through it. But the list is there to be applied—always.

Point of View—Visual Awareness

We have already said that point of view is where you are shooting from: the camera location, the angle and size of the shot. Now, let's take point of view a step further—and in an aesthetic direction.

Interviews

Some videographers find shooting interviews a daily chore and a boring one. People complain that there are too many "talking heads" on television news programs. But a talking head that is saying something interesting and significant is an important part of the daily news.

The key to the "talking head" predicament is to have a subject who has something pertinent or important to say, and who is shown in an "interesting" setting while saying it. Part of the job of the videographer is to shoot interviews so that the viewer is allowed to see and hear the subject. Camera location and the placement of the subject in relation to the camera (and the audience) are all-important. (Look again at Figure 2-6, p. 44.)

Note that the reporter is placed so that his back is to the camera, and the camera is shooting over his shoulder. The subject is facing the reporter and therefore is also facing the camera. By keeping the angle of the camera shot as close as possible to straight on, the videographer has the best chance to get a shot in which the subject is speaking directly to the viewer.

Note, too, that this setup gives the videographer several very useful shots. With a long shot (LS) the subject and the reporter are shown together—the picture "says" this is an interview. With a medium shot (MS) the reporter's shoulder or head is included in the extreme edge of the frame—once again relating two subjects to each other. With the tight shot (CU) the reporter is eliminated and the subject speaks in closeup view.

A person being interviewed for television is being asked to do something unnatural. There's the camera, the lights, the other paraphernalia. He or she may be tense or frightened. There's little pretense that it will be a nice, quiet conversation. So the subject will look at the reporter, who plays the role of security blanket, confidant, human receiver. The over-the-shoulder shot emphasizes this subject-reporter relationship and deemphasizes the threat of the camera.

Any variation on this setup that gets the subject and the reporter side by side makes for very awkward shots. In a straight-on two shot the reporter and subject are looking across the screen, and their ears—not their mouths—are aimed at the viewer. There's a hole right in the middle of the scene. If that hole contains a cage with two parakeets or a mobile which is turning slowly in a breeze, no one will watch the subject or listen to anything being said. In a one shot the subject is talking off the side of the screen. Recall, also, remarks earlier in this chapter on backgrounds. Be especially conscious of backgrounds in the interview setup.

The over-the-shoulder setup also helps establish the line of action. Whichever shoulder of the reporter you are shooting over, all of the action shots must remain on that side of the reporter and the subject. You can move the camera around anywhere on that side of the line of action to get cutaways or inserts, but if you cross to the other side you will violate the line of action principle. When the questions asked by the reporter are edited together with the answers from the subject, the subject will not be talking to the reporter. In fact he or she will seem to be talking to the reporter's back.

Reshooting the Questions with Reverse Angle

In an interview done with one camera (in spot news, that's usual) all of the shots have to be made over the shoulder of the reporter. It is a common practice after the interview is finished to shoot the questions over again with the camera pointed at the reporter. These reverse-angle questions give the editor a chance to cut from reporter question to subject answer in a series of scenes that duplicate what actually happened during the interview.

Here are important cautions about the practice of shooting reverse-angle questions after the interview is completed:

1. They *must* be the same questions asked in the first place.

2. You must shoot them in the presence of the subject. You don't want to be accused of mixing answer A in a question that never was asked during the interview.

3. You must shoot them all, since the interview will be edited. The one you didn't shoot may be the only one needed.*

You must take great pains to make sure there is no change in the wording of the question, or in your tone of voice, that might affect and change the meaning or thrust of the question as it was asked the first time.

Make your subject aware of what you are doing. Tell the guest to stay put while the camera is repositioned behind her or him to get shots of you asking

---

*Of course these guidelines assume a station news policy that does not prohibit the use of reverse questions. Some stations do prohibit their use without exception.

the questions a second time. Tell the guest it's an editing technique that will allow your question to be placed in front of their answer. Explain that you are going to ask the question again but for the guest to remain silent (because they've already answered the question). The interviewee—especially one who has never been interviewed for TV news before—may find "reverse question" routine puzzling. So do explain things. You might even go over this *before* the interview starts. Such a discussion might have the additional benefit of helping to establish rapport with the guest.

Locale

If you are shooting a longer feature or a mini-documentary series, the chances are you will make visits to a number of locations in advance of the shooting. You will be looking for the best *locale* to shoot various segments of the feature or mini-doc so that the scenes shot give as true a representation of reality as possible.

For example: If you are shooting a feature about what carnival life is like for those who run the carnival, you will want to find locales that "show it like it is." You want to find places where the people eat, sleep, take a break, wash their laundry. You might want to show the endless drudgery of setting up and tearing down. To get those scenes you might follow the carnival to another town, or meet it before it comes to your city. You will want to shoot some scenes when the carnival is not crowded with customers to show what carnival life is like when the "tip" is not swarming over the rides, playing the games of chance, or eating snacks.

During this kind of exercise, a good videographer's visual awareness is working at top speed. The well-trained eye is looking, always looking, composing shots, "seeing" shot angles, shot sizes, shot sequences. The mind is busy, too: This is the best place to get a cover shot; this is the best place to set up for an interview; over there I can get the carousel operator with the "three-rides-for-a-dollar" sign in the background; from here I can shoot the hamburger cook through the smoke; from this low angle I can shoot over the shoulder of that little girl to get the Alligator Man dozing in that folding chair.

Ernie Crisp, a famous TV newsfilm photographer, had a phrase he shouted frequently at newsfilm beginners: "Get down on your knees, you sinners." Crisp felt that while the tripod was a necessary device to get steady shots, too many TV photojournalists used it improperly. In relating story elements to each other the proper point of view is all-important.

"If," Crisp said, "you are shooting a story about kids in the first grade, the camera should be down at the kid level, not at the level of a standing adult. Kids sit in little chairs, they work at little tables, their world is down there and that's where the camera ought to be . . . If you shoot only from a tripod height you are not in the kids' world, you are in the teacher's world."

Sequencing

The mind's eye must work at all times to insure sequence: Here's the long shot, here's the medium shot, and here's the closeup. Further, any elements or person that is a focal point of the story should be "worked over" carefully.

Instead of just one shot of each basic sequence component, the videographer should make a variety of sequence shots. By changing the angle or location of the camera, by working around, over, or below the subject or object—always observing the line of action—you can get more interesting and informative shots and shot sequences.

For example: Let's say you are shooting the local university's track and field team while they practice for the NCAA indoor meet. You will of course interview the coach and some of the stars. But if that's all you get, you run the risk of a story filled with very dull "talking heads." The coach will inevitably say things like: "The team will have to give 110 percent."; "We're going there to run."; "It depends on the momentum we get from qualifying."

Instead, get the interviews first, and then "work over" the star pole vaulter as he practices. Shoot him full figure. Shoot closeups of his face, hands on the pole, arms cocked, feet and legs ready to make his approach. Keeping screen direction under control, shoot some scenes of him starting out, some more at ground level of his feet going by at full speed. Shoot some closeups of the end of the pole slamming into the vaulting box. Shoot several jumps from the end of the pit. Then shoot several inserts as he clears (or hits) the bar. Finally, shoot medium shots and closeups as he bounces into the landing pit.

Do the same for the best sprinter: her warm-ups, getting her feet set in the starting blocks, kicking cinders from her spikes, a practice surge out of the blocks, and so on.

By working over the two athletes most likely to win you have illustrations for a story on team prospects that will be far more interesting than a couple of interviews.

The Box with the Window in It

Another element of visual awareness that must be considered is somewhat more abstract. The television audience is looking at what some have called a "window to the world." While that sounds dramatic, the concept is important.

The audience is looking at a pane of glass that is one side of a box. The frame around that glass represents the proscenium arch of a conventional stage. In a theater the audience sees the spatial relationship of two or more actors to each other, or one actor to an object on the stage.

The television audience sees the same relationships on the TV screen. And once they are established, the audience will remember the relationships of one subject or object to another, even if one of those subjects or objects is not in subsequent scenes.

If they first see a reporter and an interview subject in an establishing two shot where the reporter is on the left and the subject on the right, they know the reporter is still on the left when they see the subject in a one shot. If a painting and the artist who created it are shown in a shot, the audience knows the painting is still there in the same relationship to the artist when the artist is shown alone in a closeup.

The audience's ability to understand the relationship of two or more subjects or objects to each other in a picture extends to motion. Objects in motion—cars traveling around a circular race track, for example—go right to left if the point of view is from the inside of the track. They go left to right if the point of view is outside the track. The very first action scene establishes that point of view for the audience. It is up to you to keep the point of view in mind so that the audience looking at the box will not become disoriented.

Closeups

Of all the shots a videographer makes when shooting a sequence, the closeup is the most important. People get more information if they can see the visual part of the news clearly. If they are provided with a closeup of the focal point of the story after the long shot and medium shot, they are told visually what that focal point is.

People retain more information from a person speaking on the screen if the speaker is shown in a closeup shot. Medium shots of speakers are just that—medium. Viewers get more involved in a closeup. They relate more closely to the subject. There are some indications they can actually hear better, perhaps because they listen more attentively.

When the focal point of the story is an object, the audience wants to see that object up close. Next time you are in a jewelry store look at how the customers behave. They lean over, or move closer, or put their glasses on to get a better look at the rings, digital watches, silver patterns. Television news can move the viewers closer to give them that better look.

Suppose the subject of the story is the batch of new boa constrictors born at the zoo. The audience will appreciate a closeup look at the babies on the screen, even though they probably would not move closer to the cage if they were actually there for the event.

Closeups, especially extreme closeups, involve some ethical and aesthetic elements that you need to think about while you are shooting them.

Some stations have a policy dictating that blood and gore will not be shown, or shown in graphic, close-up detail, especially during the dinner-hour news or so-called "family" newscasts. Some videographers, because of their ethical standards, are reluctant to shoot the closeup of the wound, the blood, the mangled arm, the head oddly twisted on the neck of the victim. They say that taking these shots reinforces the widely held belief that journalists are ghouls who seek sensation. Others add that since there's a policy against use of such shots, there's no point in shooting them in the first place.

Yet there are those who hold to the position that the videographer's job is to record events—whether a shot is aired is a separate decision and, their thinking goes, an editor cannot edit a shot that has not been recorded. There may be that one rare time when just such a shot is needed to make a vivid visual point. The videotape of the carnage when Egyptian President Anwar Sadat was assassinated in Cairo showed a number of scenes of an Egyptian officer who had only a bloody stump where one of his arms should have been. Those who use such scenes defend the use on the grounds that people must be informed, even about the more violent aspects of life and death. And the argument is revived occasionally still about whether some Pennsylvania TV stations acted responsibly when they broadcast scenes and sounds of a troubled state official who had called a news conference and then at the end, pulled out a gun and shot himself fatally in front of the cameras. During live coverage of that event, no editing decisions were possible. But, in later newscasts stations edited the videotape to stop the video at different points before the shot and some continued to broadcast wild sound of the event beyond the point where the video was stopped.

Extreme closeups of people who are talking are dramatic. Sometimes that extreme closeup tells the story better than any other shot—the exhausted face of the marathon winner, the dejected look of the election loser. But extreme closeups should be tasteful. The extreme closeup of a person who has a large wart on the end of his nose may actually distract the viewer. Because the viewer is looking with rapt attention at the wart and may even be commenting to someone else in the room about it, that viewer may not be paying much attention to the important things the person is saying.

Shooting B-Roll

It is time now to talk about **B-Roll**, the illustrative scenes. Like visual continuity, the term comes to us from the days of film. Today some TV journalists call it "cover material" or "cover video." One of the most useful things about ENG is that the B-Roll can be edited onto the same videocassette along with sound-on-tape scenes.

Let's look at the videographer's in-the-field responsibilities concerning B-Roll. Four main concepts are involved.

1. If you don't shoot the B-Roll scenes, you can't edit them into your story.

2. B-Roll material must follow visual continuity rules in the same way as any other visual sequence.

3. B-Roll material must specifically illustrate what the sound bite or narration is talking about.

4. Production effects are no substitute for good B-Roll material.

The primary purpose of B-Roll is to illustrate and illuminate, to explain things visually. A secondary purpose is to "cover" talking heads or **voice-over**

(V/O) narration. So in shooting B-Roll, the videographer is collecting scenes that will go together to show the audience what the interviewee is talking about, how something is done, what happened at a news event, or provide a closeup look at a process.

Here again visual awareness is the key factor. The videographer on assignment must look for the B-Roll scenes that best illustrate the story and gather them in LS-MS-CU form (and ELS and/or ECU) so they can be edited into sequences. Good B-Roll material can be edited to match with the sync sound on tape (SOT), or to illustrate what the V/O is talking about. Good B-Roll material also should include the natural (ambient) sound (NAT-SOT) that goes with the illustrative pictures. This allows for interesting and creative sound mixes during the editing.

For example: The world's most famous diamond cutter has come to a mall jewelry store in your city to cut a huge diamond into two pieces of the exact same size. He has agreed to allow you to videotape this process. It is both a news story and a feature.

He agrees to spend some time explaining what he is going to do before he does it. You ask him to tell and show what the process is and you video-tape him doing that. You have his voice explaining and you shoot LS MS, and many CUs of his hands, the tools he uses, reverse angles of his face, the diamond, and so on.

Then when the big moment comes you concentrate on it. You are recording well ahead of time and recording the natural sound. It is very quiet now as he steadies himself, makes sure he has the angle of the cutting blade just right—but that silence is also a crucial part of the story. Now . . . he raises the mallet . . . Whack! There they are, two pieces. Keep recording . . . he looks at them, holds them up, smiles, says: "There's really nothing to it if you study carefully, don't drink or smoke, and remain celibate for six months before try-ing it."

Now when the editor puts that raw material together she or he will have all of the necessary sound and B-Roll scenes to make a very interesting and even exciting story.

First the editor would have the establishing scenes to give the audience the locale; V/O narration would tell what was going to happen.

Also, your material has the diamond cutter talking about and showing the action. You have shot B-Roll: LS-MS-CU-ECU. You have observed screen direc-tion rules. You have both closeups and reverse angles of the cutter and the diamond, relating the two to each other.

What evolves is a little package that cuts between the cutter with sync sound and the B-Roll with the cutter's voice continuing while the viewer sees what he is explaining.

Then, when the dramatic moment comes, the scenes of the actual cutting are edited together with the sound. The completed story is something like instant replay in sports. The difference is that you have shown the audience

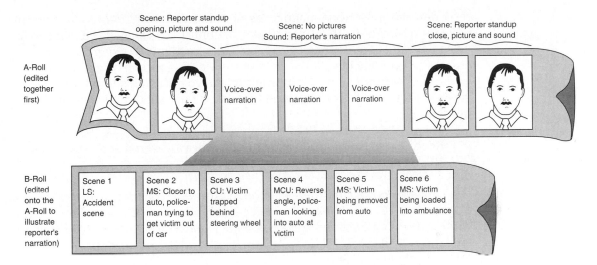

Figure 3.14. How B-Roll material is used to illustrate what a reporter or subject is talking about. Here the standup opening showing the reporter at the news event is the first scene edited onto the air tape. Then the reporter's voice-over narration is laid down, audio only. Next, the selected B-Roll scenes are edited onto the air tape in the space containing the voice-over narration, video only. Finally, the reporter's standup close is added to complete the story. B-Roll material illustrating what an interview subject is discussing is used in the same manner.

what is going to happen and then the real event. The B-Roll gives the viewer a better understanding of the whole story.

We will return to this example story in the chapter on editing and we do this for a very good reason: to emphasize to you the intimate relationship between videography and editing. A truism of the craft is that in order to be able to record good video, you first have to thoroughly understand basic video editing.

Not all stories have such dramatic B-Roll possibilities, nor would you always have so much time to shoot them. But most story locations have some B-Roll elements that can be shot and that, when edited into the sound, will help illustrate the story: There are bulletin boards with announcements, street and traffic signs, relevant objects, the places or things the sound is talking about. With all the fancy graphics we can now create we tend to fall back on them for illustration. Nothing will replace good B-Roll. That comes out of the videographer's eye and mind, not out of a digital brain.

Shooting for Edit

Two major concepts are involved in shooting for edit. One is mechanical, the other organizational.

The first concept has to do with tracking. Since the control track must be there for the edit units to lock together, you have to operate the tape recorder in a prescribed manner. As noted in Chapter 2 *only some* portable videotape recorders have an indicator to confirm tracking. If the one you are using does not include that feature, but the recorder is working normally, you assume proper tracking. If the recorder is working properly and the tracking is normal, there are several important things you can and should do to assure good tracking and to avoid gaps in tracking. These should become automatic operations.

✔ 1. Record at least thirty seconds of throwaway material at the beginning of the cassette.

This is to make sure there is enough tape with tracking on it to allow the editing controller to back up the tape—**preroll**—during the editing process without running onto the trackless leader material on the front end of the tape.

✔ 2. Record at least fifteen seconds of material (*after* the thirty seconds of throwaway material) after the recorder is started and before the beginning of any material you expect to use.

This is to allow the recorder time to stabilize, and to assure you have good tracking *ahead* of the material you want to use so that the preroll can function during the edit.

✔ 3. Continue to record at least ten seconds after any action is completed before pausing the recorder.

This will ensure there is enough tracking *after* the material you want to use so that the rehearse-edit function of the editors will work. It will also ensure that the last few seconds of the tape segment will have tracking.

✔ 4. Keep the recorder running as much as possible. Remember that when you trigger the camera to "stop," roll-back will put fifteen to thirty seconds of your last shot back onto the supply spool of the videocassette.

Except when you are changing the setup or location, or taking a break, it is best not to stop the recorder. This is especially true between shots and on spot-news coverage.

It is better to have the camera movement, the shaky shots, the momentary views of the sky, or the toe of your left foot along with the usable material in one continuous flow on the tape than to have gaps in the tracking caused by stopping and starting the recorder. You can edit around poor visuals, but you cannot edit around a lack of good, stable tracking.

These four mechanical-operational functions should become standard procedures for the videographer. You want to have good tracking on all of

TRACKING INSURANCE

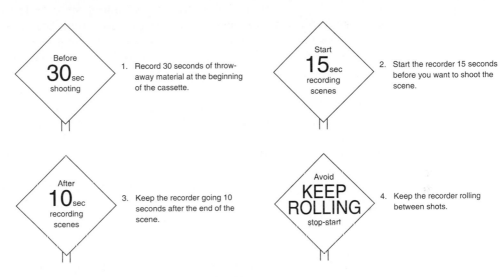

1. Record 30 seconds of throw-away material at the beginning of the cassette.

2. Start the recorder 15 seconds before you want to shoot the scene.

3. Keep the recorder going 10 seconds after the end of the scene.

4. Keep the recorder rolling between shots.

Figure 3.15. The steps to take to assure tracking.

the tape you record, both before and after the scenes you may use in the edited version of the story. If you try to run the recorder the way you would make snapshots with a still camera, that tracking won't be there where you need it.

For example: Your reporter team member is doing his stand-up closer. His last line is, "And that's the story from the XYZ bankruptcy hearing." Then you immediately stop the recorder.

No tracking will be under part of that sentence because the recorder erased the tracking that was on the tape parallel to the pictures of the reporter saying that line, and then put new tracking on a few seconds later. Since that sentence is about four seconds long, it will not have tracking "under" the last word or two because the tape hadn't reached the new track-ing point. Without that tracking you will not be able to smoothly edit the reporter's closing line onto the "air" tape.

The same thing can happen to the front end of a tape segment. If the recorder is stopped when you see someone making a dramatic move or hear him or her start to say something, you have a problem. By the time you get the recorder going you will probably miss the action. Or if you do happen to catch the action, the recorder will not have been recording long enough to stabilize and get good tracking on the tape.

A second recording practice which makes sense in some situations and which is a help to editing: Shoot virtually everything that happens at a news event.

For example, a videographer got pictures of a prominent liberal politician being hit in the face by an egg thrown from the audience. He had stayed on and kept shooting most of the way through a long speech. The politician had some sparkling things to say about the egg-thrower and that person's sense of fairness and decency. Continuous taping allowed the videographer to capture that moment along with the other things the politician had to say.

But that technique is a mixed blessing. Overshooting is rampant. It is so easy to keep running cassettes through the recorder while hoping something interesting will happen that a videographer may lose all sense of discipline. It is annoying to an editor to have to scan through an hour of tape to find the forty-second essence of a story. Some editors refuse to do it. They'll take the first usable forty seconds, and that's it. So, news judgment needs always to be applied firmly.

A more serious fault is random shooting. Sometimes a news event is so interesting visually that a videographer will act like a novice glutton let loose at a groaning buffet table—a bite of this, a nibble of that . . . look over there . . . grab a snack of this, load up the plate with that. World champion eaters don't go about it that way. They organize. They launch a planned and sustained attack on the food and work their way through it with a method.

The videographer should do the same thing. Study the situation, size up the opportunities, and then carry out a methodical program to get all of the necessary and interesting visual material. It helps in the editing crunch if you can get the shots for a LS-MS-CU sequence, the cutaways, the inserts, and the reverse angles somewhere near each other on the tape. That also helps the videographer to remember to be sure the shots were made in the first place.

Pans, tilts, and zooms were discussed earlier in this chapter. We told you about their uses in visual composition and warned you they create problems during the editing process and for the viewer. It is how you shoot them, with the editing and audience in mind, that make them either usable or unusable.

When there is a motivated need to pan from one stationary object or subject to another, you must make the pan as smoothly and as slowly as possible. It is a good idea to practice the movement of the camera, or record the pan several times, to be sure you get the shot you want. You need to decide two things: where the pan will start, and where the pan will end. When you have decided:

1. Place your feet so they are pointing at *the spot where the pan will end.*

2. Rotate your body from the waist to point the camera at *the spot where the pan will begin.* Pan by pivoting from the waist. Do it with a slow and steady motion.

3. Start the camera and let it run ten seconds before beginning the pan. End the pan by stopping and centering up on the object of interest. Again, hold the shot at the end of the pan for longer than seems necessary. If the camera is mounted on a tripod you don't have to pivot your hips but

you still have to pick out the start and end points before you make the shot, and make it slowly.

When you have to pan with a moving subject or object you have three more important things to remember.

4. Try to keep the subject or object comfortably in the frame.

5. If you can, try to keep the subject or object in the left or right two-thirds of the frame *away* from the direction it is moving.

6. At the end of a pan shot that is following a moving subject or object, *stop* the pan and let the subject or object continue on out of the frame.

All six actions will provide a usable shot for the edited story. The smooth pan from point to point will have a beginning and end. The following pan with the two-thirds composition will give the subject or object in the frame "room" to move in the direction of the movement. Stopping the pan to let the subject or object move out of frame will provide an ending to the shot and an opportunity for the editor to pick up the subject or object in any size shot in the next scene, thus avoiding a jump cut.

Tilts do not involve the same problems as pans. But there are three points you should remember: A tilt, too, must have a beginning and an end. Make it very slowly. Be careful that the tilt does not exaggerate the camera angle at the end of the shot so much that the view of the center of attention becomes wildly distorted, for example, as when a huge face looms over the scene like a vulture.

For zooms the same things apply. If you need to trim the size of a shot in view (the audience sees the trim) you can do it easily with the zoom. But do it very slowly, so slowly that it is almost imperceptible to the eye. Zoom to change the size of a shot of a subject, but do it *during the reporter's off-camera question.* This gives the editor a different-size shot to cut to when condensing the interview. During fast action on a spot news story, zoom to frame up the next shot while the tape is rolling. This gives the editor a well-framed shot to cut to *after the zoom is finished.*

Lastly—to remind you again—the one zoom you should always make is the one that moves in to the tightest shot and focuses there. That will insure that all shots wider than that will be in focus.

Just One More Shot, Please

ENG has had a great impact on the picture content of television news. It has made it possible to be almost anywhere and to get visual coverage of almost anything. And, some think, it is now too easy—so easy that it has dulled our sense of responsibility to the journalism involved.

You won't think it's easy when you are just starting out to do all of the things described in this section on making pictures. The complexities of running the equipment can be very daunting, but you must get past this point as rapidly as possible. Then you can join what is a rather distinguished group of men and women who work in visual journalism. You will share with them great satisfaction from knowing that what you did today gave the television audience a clear, honest, disciplined, and artful look at what happened in their world.

COMMITMENT

We began this chapter by discussing structure for a very good reason: It is an essential to one final concept, what the professionals call "commitment." They have a special meaning in mind when they use this fundamental—you might even say philosophical—word to describe how they go about their work. The concept is mentioned briefly elsewhere in this chapter and in other chapters as well. It's an important characteristic.

The process of commitment begins with the news assignment. Experience is the television journalist's guide just as imagination is her or his tool.

For the videographer and reporter the basic questions are: How am I going to cover and shoot this story? What will its outstanding ingredients be? What photographic opportunities might this story present? What hazards or obstacles is it likely to impose? How will I overcome these obstacles, and how will I take advantage of the opportunities? How can I get the maximum there is out of this story? What is this story *really* about?

For the writer, the editor, and the producer the basic questions are: How can I put this story together so it will flow in a logical way? How can I tell it so the audience will understand it? How can I be sure that the important and significant information is there? How will it work with the rest of the stories in today's news?

Finding the answers to those and other questions is part of the everyday business of television journalism. When the answers come, the professionals make their commitment and get to work. But they will do a better job in all of their reporting, shooting, editing, and writing activities if the commitment is made against a background of understanding how television news is structured and delivered to the audience, and how that audience receives and uses it.

PROFILE

Larry Hatteberg has been chief photographer, anchor, executive news director, editor, writer, you name it, at KAKE-TV, Wichita, Kansas, where he has worked for more than thirty-one years. In that time he has covered every possible kind of story in every corner of Kansas and the world, including China, Hong Kong, New Zealand, the Mideast, and Europe, including Russia.

Competing with photojournalists from all U.S. television stations, as well as the major networks and their foreign bureaus, Larry is one of a handful of photojournalists to twice win the coveted National Press Photographers Association News Cameraman of the Year Award. He is the long-time cochairman of the NPPA Television News Workshop at the University of Oklahoma. He has been a judge for the White House News Photographers Association and is a past president of NPPA. He has also done photo consulting work for over forty television stations.

Larry is nationally known as a photojournalist who cares about people. His "Hatteberg's People" series is widely recognized for bringing out the personalities of individuals in very human terms. He has produced two books based on his "Hatteberg's People" television series; the first book was a regional best seller.

Telling the Story Visually

Larry Hatteberg

Every day some technological advance gives us a new gadget that is supposed to help us do our jobs better. Some of them work; some of them don't. The cold world of the computer, microchips, and satellite technology has transformed us all from the chemical-mechanical world of film to that of videotape and "live shots" that just a few years ago were only dreams.

But even with all this technology, it still all boils down to one thing. Photojournalists, and the reporters who work alongside them, are storytellers. The revolution brought by technology has moved television a long way—technically.

We don't need more technicians. We don't need "shooters"; shooters kill things. We do need the very best photojournalists that we can find. We need people who understand how to tell a story visually and at the same time understand that it is journalism.

What kind of training and thinking will help us change? In broadcast journalism courses across the country there is emphasis on writing—students are told how to gather facts and how to put those facts into proper form. And there are courses in photojournalism where mechanics, composition, and pictures are given strong emphasis. What we need on top of that is to develop, for reporters and photojournalists alike, the ability to "think visually," and to "see visually."

Types Of TV Video Story-Telling

In the early days of television there were two basic types of video stories: illustrative and sequential.

Illustrative photography can be used effectively when time is important. It does not require matched action or great amounts of editing time to produce a story of this type. It communicates very simply what the viewer needs to know. You see it used most often on network newscasts when they are putting down the last edit just before the story airs.

Sequential news photography is best used when the photojournalist has some degree of control over the subject. Wide shots, medium shots, and closeup shots in sequence with matching action shots are usually the trademark of sequential photography.

Sequential photography requires a high degree of skill in both the photojournalist and the editor. It is the closest to "Hollywood" shooting that most photojournalists will ever come. Almost anyone can shoot illustrative video, but mastering the art of sequential photography requires an artistic mind, an ability to sense the story and find the pictures that will portray that sense, a feeling for the human equation, and great discipline.

While illustrative and sequential shooting and editing serve as the basis for TV story-telling, there are new ways creative people are using to create visually interesting story-telling.

Sound-Sensitive Story-telling

CBS's "48 Hours" popularized the concept of "Sound-Sensitive Story-telling." At first look, the video scenes appear to be nothing but jump cuts, moving camera shots and shaky and sometimes intentionally blurred video. Actually it's meant to give the viewer a "reality-based" feeling. Viewers feel that they are there *experiencing* the story at the same time the reporter is. Instead of narrative track, the story relies on natural sounds to tell the story. In many cases, their video will actually be secondary to the requirement for good audio. The reporter asks the same question viewers would ask if they were on the scene. The reporter becomes the viewer's advocate.

This type of story-telling requires skilled video editors and producers all working within a single concept.

While it may look like it is easy to shoot as a photojournalist, it is actually incredibly demanding physically. This type of video art works well for long-form documentary work. But inside a newscast, it can become confusing if not well-planned and executed.

Another sound-sensitive concept was pioneered by Ray Farkas, a network producer and photojournalist who uses sound and unusual camera framing to tell his sound-sensitive video stories.

Farkas places his camera well away from the subject, uses wireless mikes, and then waits for the subject to talk. In the foreground may be objects that help put the rest of the frame in context and help tell the story. His method works well but requires massive amounts of tape and time usually not available to the typical reporter and photojournalist on a daily basis.

Working with People

If it were possible for television photojournalists or photojournalism students to be invisible, our work would be much easier. Since we are not, each of us must develop our own techniques in working with people. It is easy to get so involved with the technology that you forget you're working with a human equation—you and the subject. How you and he or she communicate will mean the difference between a successful story and one with little meaning.

It begins with attitude. Always treat people the way you would like to be treated. Because you work for a television station or a network doesn't give you any special dispensation where manners are concerned. Most of the time you will be in someone's home or on their property.

Respect the property of others. Doing things like putting gaffer tape on expensive wallpaper and then pulling the tape and the wallpaper off at the same time will not endear you to those you are trying to cover. Don't put heavy metallic objects on top of expensive furniture, thus running the risk of scratching it. Don't move furniture around unless you ask permission; you wouldn't do that if you were visiting in someone's living room, and you are a visitor no matter how much "glamour" goes with your job. You can be sure that if the personal property of your story's subject is damaged by your carelessness, the rift between you and your subject will become as large as the Grand Canyon.

If damage does occur, offer to compensate the person for the damage. To ignore it will continue to foster the notion that those of us in television are high handed, arrogant, and disrespectful.

Attitude is involved in any kind of story, whether it is a fire, natural disaster, news conference, or some other spot or general news story that makes up the bread and butter of the newscast.

In these cases you will most likely be on a secondary relationship level with most of your subjects. What that means is you, as a photojournalist, will only be dealing with that person for a moment or two before moving on to another shot.

For example: At a fire you are taping three firemen holding a hose and pouring water into a burning building. Your three- to six-shot sequence will include a wide shot, a medium shot, and a closeup shot. While taping that sequence you may or may not have had conversations with the firemen. It may have been just a short sentence: "Hey, guys, tell me if I'm in your way."

By saying, "Tell me if I'm in your way," you have acknowledged their importance and are saying that you, as a photojournalist, are willing to work with them. By saying nothing a subconscious rift develops between you and the firemen. They may tell you to move before you get the shots you need. By working with them, you may even get shots you hadn't planned on.

Perhaps the most difficult and most criticized situation for a photojournalist is taping someone who has just lost their home or a loved one, or who has been an eyewitness to a tragedy. The question is: How do you do it and still retain your integrity as a human being?

The first rule is to avoid putting the camera and microphone into someone's face without asking their permission. I don't think this rule applies to most other situations, but it surely does on those stories where emotions are running high and the individual to be photographed is not a public figure. Instead it is someone who, through no action of his or her own, has been caught up in the event.

The first thing the photojournalist should do is to put the camera down and walk up to the subject to be photographed. Tell that person who you are and spend some time with them so that condolences can be expressed about the loss or the fearful experience they've had. The secret here is that the photojournalist must be genuinely concerned or supportive. You can't fool people—you must feel the way you speak. Then, after words of condolence or support, tell the individual that you know this is a difficult time for them, but it might help someone else if he or she could tell the viewers what happened.

If you approach the story that way, several things will happen. Because you have stopped to talk with the person for a moment to express your feelings to them, you don't come off as some insensitive and bloodthirsty newsperson who's only in it for the gore. You do show that you are a sensitive person who is just doing his or her job. Then, by telling the subject that his or her version of the incident may help someone else who might have to face similar problems, you are saying that there may be a positive side to this tragedy after all—and you are only trying to help.

Ethical Attitude

Each of you must decide for yourself what your limits are in covering a story—the scope of your photojournalistic ethics. In a recent motion picture about the news business, a newspaper editor says: "I know how to write the facts and I know how not to hurt people. But I don't know how to do both at the same time." It is a dilemma that we, the photojournalists who are among the first on the scene, face every day.

Is it tasteful to show a woman screaming with anguish as they pull the body of her son out of the water? Do you tape someone who's been burned in an explosion and show them in closeup detail? Do you show an uncovered body on the air? Only judgment by reasonable and experienced journalists based on a specific situation should prevail.

At emotional crime scenes and violent events no good is served if you lose your head along with everyone else. It will work against you to talk back to law officers while they're doing their jobs, even if you think they are acting improperly.

If you believe you've been wronged, then discuss it rationally later, either with the officers or with their superior. Don't create a scene unless you believe your life to be in danger because of some officer's action. You are there to record on tape the factual events of life. When someone interferes with your job, it is only natural to want to blow up and recall all of your First Amendment rights.

But those rights don't automatically admit you to crime scenes or allow you to disobey any law enforcement officer. In truth, you have the same rights as any other member of the general public. No more, no less.

Feature Stories

My favorite area of working with people is the feature story. There is sort of a universal feeling among photojournalists that they have "arrived" when the assignment desk gives them time to go out and do a nice feature piece. The problem is too many reporters and photographers botch the job even before the tape has been recorded. There are several possible causes for this.

Many reporters and photographers worry more about their equipment than about the person they are about to tape. Photojournalists must know their equipment as well and as intimately as they know their spouse.

The mechanics of the camera must become second nature to the photojournalist. In fact, you shouldn't even have to think about the equipment as you are taping. Your entire thinking process should be directed toward the subject. How is what you are shooting relating to what the subject is saying? How can you make this person relax? Are you getting the shots you need to tell the story? Those are the kinds of thoughts you ought to be having, not whether the exposure is correct, the right buttons have been pushed, or the tape is rolling.

When you meet your feature subject for the first time leave the equipment in the car or van. In most cases your subjects aren't interested in your equipment—in fact, they are terrified by it. Without your gear you will be free to talk with the subjects and get to know them.

At first, talk with them about what *they* are interested in. Talk about their garden, their kids, their stamp collection, their nice furniture—anything but why you are there. They already know that, and so do you, so what's the point of discussing it? In the time you spend talking with your subjects you are, in effect, becoming friends with them.

Again, you have to be genuinely interested in people; you can't fake that and shouldn't want to. Probably one of the reasons you decided to become a photojournalist is that you are interested in people. Most people you will work with can spot a phony smile a mile away.

Whether you take five minutes or an hour to get to know your subject it will be the most valuable time you spend on that assignment. Why? Because the more you give of yourself to your subject the more your subject will give back to you on the tape. People find it much easier to talk to friends than to strangers. You will remain a stranger unless you take the minutes we've been discussing to get to know your subject as a human being.

Don't make a big deal about your equipment. It's scary stuff to outsiders. When you have finished getting to know your subject and it's time to bring in the gear, do so carefully. Keep the conversation going and continue to reassure the person that there is really nothing to what's going to happen next, and that they'll do well.

Humane Lighting

Light the scene as simply as possible. Be professional about it but don't go into complicated lighting setups. As quietly as you can, try to figure out how to plug in the lights so that you don't end up blacking out the entire area with a blown fuse. Don't get into a big discussion of this with the subject either. He or she will be nervous enough already. There will be enough cords and lights and other paraphernalia to worry about anyway, so keep it as simple as you can.

Humane Sound

One of the most valuable tools you can use with your subject is a wireless microphone. It's important for several reasons. Once a wireless mic has been placed on your subject, he or she will be more likely to forget about it than if you have the mic cord running from them to the tape recorder like a heart monitor cable. Further, with a wireless microphone there is nothing tying you to the subject. You can move around much more freely without disturbing him or her. And because people tend to forget they're wearing the mic, they usually say things in a more natural way. When the subject feels more at ease you get a truer representation of what the person is really like.

Absolutely the worst thing you or the reporter can do in a personality story is to hold a microphone in front of the person while doing the interview. Nobody likes to talk into a microphone stuck in his or her face. It looks horrible in the picture, it makes the subject uneasy, and it makes editing difficult.

Lavalier mics are better. The wires are still there but lavalier mics are somewhat less conspicuous to subjects so they forget their voices are being recorded.

The Reporter Equation

About the reporter's role in all this: In personality stories you and the reporter must remember that the subject is the most important person in the story, not the reporter. In these stories the reporter should be heard and not seen. I know that this goes against many station policies, but so be it. Television journalists must understand that people want to see real people, not reporters. Reporters are not real people. The person who is being interviewed is the real person.

Also, the whole story should be more than an interview. You don't interview people in personality stories, you have conversations with them.

What do I mean by conversations? Let's say you are doing a story about someone who carves lifelike figures of birds out of wood. What many reporters do is to have the cameraperson tape a brief sequence of the person carving the birds. It is the standard long shot—medium shot—closeup sequence that is basic to television news.

That's fine, but then what do they do? They have the person stop carving so they can do an interview. This takes the subject out of context and puts him or her in front of the TV camera to answer questions. What has happened is that the subject has been moved from a natural environment to a foreign one and is now expected to perform for the camera.

That is all wrong. The result may be a sound bite, but seldom will it be memorable. The subject usually makes one of those "I carve birds because it makes me feel good" answers—not exciting stuff, not natural, not personal.

Instead, why not let the subject continue to carve the birds, but don't ask questions, just have a conversation.

You or the reporter might say, "I'm impressed that you have the patience to do this painstaking work."

They might reply, "It's not patience that lets me do this, it's an inner peace I get when I make with my hands one of God's beautiful creatures. If they bring a smile to someone then it doesn't matter how long it takes; a simple smile makes all the work worth it."

Now there's a nice sound bite and you haven't even asked a question. The reporter must introduce topics to discuss and then lead the subject towards his or her natural way of saying things that will make the sound bite memorable. The reporter should let the subject do most of the talking. The editing will organize the story and make it clear to the viewer.

Another benefit of taping someone as they are actually doing their work is that it is photographically easier to edit. If the sequence leading up to the sound bite has been of the subject carving the bird, then the sound bite scene shows the carving continuing; it makes the whole piece flow more smoothly and keeps the tempo and pace moving.

It is important to try to keep the people whose personalities you are trying to capture as comfortable as possible in their own environment. Have them do a variety of normal things if there is no real central visual focus to the story. Talk to them while they are getting into the car, or walking, or going through the refrigerator, or feeding the cat. People talk when they are doing those things in real life. There is no reason for them to be still and posed in front of the camera to be able to speak. It is important to remember what you are trying to do—show that person the way he or she lives, works, thinks, talks.

Personality and feature stories are the most difficult to do well. However, if you, as a photojournalist, will remember to befriend the subject before you start the taping, keep the equipment out of the way and as unobtrusive as possible when it is there, take advantage of the natural surroundings to put the person at ease, and let the subject be the star of the piece, you will find these stories rewarding to you, to the subject, and to the audience.

The job of a photojournalist has never been more important than it is today. Over the past thirty-five years we have all learned to deal with an infant that has grown into a giant, global telecommunications industry. Television and the computer have carried us all into a communications revolution. They have given us ways to communicate that we never thought were possible.

But with all the technology comes pressure. We, as photojournalists, must continue to understand that our job is storytelling. More than ever before, our industry is crying out for communicators—people who can tell stories about others visually. We don't need more shooters or more photographers who only understand focus and f-stop.

The greatest compliment we can receive as photojournalists is that we are good storytellers. Give me a person who can *visually tell a story* and I'll show you a photojournalist who can communicate with the world.

Editing

In all forms of journalism there is underlying tension between those who gather the raw material and fashion it into stories and those who take all of the material aimed at an edition of a newspaper, or magazine, or television news program and produce a finished product.

The news gatherers like to boast that the program would be nothing without their persistent digging, organized minds, and glittering writing talents. They see themselves as the front line, the shock troops, the wide receivers, the soloists who make things happen.

Those who shape the news material into the finished product, called editors and producers in television, see themselves as sages who make sense out of nonsense, the bastions of accuracy and judgment, the guides and mentors of the somewhat overbred, high-strung, frivolous reporters.

Every profession has its own mythology. It gives its practitioners a sense of mystery and dedication. It is mostly bunk, but it has a nice ring to it.

Editing is essential. It is perhaps more essential to *clear communication* of thoughts, ideas, and information than the news gathering function. All journalists must have excellent news judgment; editors simply need the most. All journalists must be able to focus, clarify, condense, synthesize, and analyze huge amounts of raw material. Those skills are central to the editor's job.

In addition, editors are packagers. They bring the story, segment, and program together to make an understandable and coherent whole. To do this well editors must be the guardians of the concepts of structure and linearity. Close attention to these two basic concepts is the key factor in:

1. Eliminating randomness

2. Giving focus to the significant and interesting elements of the news

3. Providing pace, mood, and tone

4. Assuring a logical progression through stories, segments, and entire programs

Finally, editors provide guidance—a second or third mind to give meaning, clarity, direction, and form. No matter what job in television news you aspire to, you must understand the editing process because (1) it affects all those other jobs, and (2) it is essential to clear communication.

THE EDITING PROCESS

The first idea to keep in mind is that the editing process begins at the moment stories are chosen for coverage.

Just the choice itself means that one story has been selected over another because the journalists think it is more interesting, significant, or important. And having made the choice, the journalists begin to think about the possible content, shape, and focus of that story, how it can best be told, what illustrative elements will be needed, how it will weigh in importance with the other stories chosen for the newscast.

Second, the editing process never stops, because everyone has to think about it all the time. Reporters, videographers, crew members, and technicians working in the field must have news judgment. They are, after all, making the first editorial decisions on what is important and significant about the story they are covering. They gather the raw material, weed out the extraneous, and try to get all of the facts (and pictures and sound) that may be needed to tell the story.

Third, the editing process, like the reporting process, begins with an absolutely essential question: What is this story *really* about?

A famous documentary producer once said one of the most important things he does at the beginning of the editing process is to give the program a title. That, he said, forces him to think about most of the other priorities such as structure, focus, and direction. The title may be honed and polished—edited to get it succinct and accurate—a primary editorial decision. Naming a program is akin to answering the question, What is this story *really* about?

In television news, the word *editor* applies to two different jobs. One editor is a person who proofreads and corrects copy written by reporters and writers. This position tends to be filled only in network and large market newsrooms. Generally producers perform editing duties as part of their preparation of stories for the news broadcast.

The second type of editor is a person who operates the equipment used to select and assemble raw field videotape scenes and sounds into polished news stories. The videotape editor follows an outline or script prepared by the reporter or producer, pulling out portions of the field tape that are needed for a story. These portions are then copied in order and combined with other videotape (called B-Roll) with recorded and/or live audio and perhaps other production elements, to create a final story, which is then often referred to as a **package**.

Videotape editing is an art. A skilled editor knows precisely when to begin or end a scene. He or she must combine several channels of video and audio into a precisely timed, aesthetically pleasing, logical explanation of an issue or event in the news. This high level of creativity is accomplished under tremendous stress created by deadline pressure.

In this chapter, you will be introduced to the steps required to edit videotape into coherent news stories. It is important that you achieve an understanding of the editing process. The majority of entry-level broadcast journalists have to edit their own, or other people's news stories. Even if you do little "hands-on" editing, you need to know how editing is done and be able to discern the difference between good and bad editing. There is a very good chance you will have to work with, instruct, or supervise editors, and your most effective defense against being embarrassed by someone's carelessness is to know how to edit.

EDITING VIDEOTAPE

The first step in the process of editing videotape is concrete and important.

Logging

With the raw videotaped material in hand, the first step is to make a careful log of its content. That is, the videocassette is played back and a list of all the shots is made. It must include every shot—even those that may be out of focus, poorly framed, shaky, or otherwise obviously useless—along with each shot's exact location on the tape (counter number, time code number).

Time spent in careful logging is time saved later, so logs should be as accurate and complete as possible. And while logging, the editor can begin to make some judgments about which shots will work best and the linear order of the story. If someone else is going to operate the editing machines, the log becomes his or her record of where the material to be used is located on the videocassettes. The **cut sheet** or **scene list**—the list and order of the scenes to be used—grows out of the log.

In electronic news gathering some logging and preliminary editing decisions don't even have to wait until the raw material is in the newsroom. Reporters and/or field producers can view material just shot, log it, and dictate editing suggestions on their two-way radios. Or they can view the material as they are riding or flying back to the television station and make notes and decisions as to which scenes will be used and in what order. It is also standard procedure to log all video and sound as it is being received from the microwave back at the station during a live shot. More editing is being done right in the field. ENG and SNG vans equipped with edit packs, and even compact production switchers can handle packaging of stories with all but the most elaborate effects.

Audio and Video

When videotape is shot the pictures and two channels of sound are recorded on the tape at exactly the same instant during the recording. Even in the most simple video edits, the editing controllers can perform a number of functions at the same time. With a controller you can edit video and sound together, or video or sound separately. With a controller you can add other sound to either of the **audio tracks**, or (using a sound mixer) combine additional sound with the sound already on one or both of the audio tracks.

Various options are possible:

1. The story can be edited with the sound on tape just by transferring scenes from the original tape to the edited tape.

2. The story can include reporter narration over scenes plus sound bites from interviews.

3. The story can include a reporter standup joined with illustrative scenes edited into the story while the reporter continues with narration.

4. Music and other sound elements can be edited into and mixed with the natural sound.

The final version created comes out on one videotape cassette, ready to be played back into the news program with the touch of one button.

The Editing Bay

An editing console can be simple or complex. The basics are two servo-controlled videotape machines—one to play wanted portions of the raw videotape, the other to record these wanted portions on a new videocassette—the two machines linked to each other by an editing controller. Remember the control track emphasized earlier? That track—that is, the pulses on it—locks the two machines together so that precise edits are possible. Pictures and/or sounds from the raw material in the player machine are electronically transferred to the videocassette in the record machine, one scene at a time, to build the edited story. Some definitions:

Cut—excerpt from a videotape

Cuts only—attaching excerpts without manipulating the picture to create transitions

Fade-out, fade-in, dissolve—picture goes from clear to dim (fade-out) or dim to clear (fade-in), or overlaps with one picture becoming less clear as the next picture establishes itself (dissolve)

Wipe—picture is gradually changed right to left or left to right across the video screen

If it is a "cuts only" system, the editing that can be done with the audio or video in a cuts only system is relatively unsophisticated compared to the elaborate things that can be done in post-production using an entire control room full of sophisticated mixers, switchers, and effects generators. But it is fast and efficient, and for news work that is important. Furthermore, in most television stations more complex production equipment is just a step away. Also portable production switchers and effects generators are standard in many field-editing packages.

How an Editing Bay Works

The specific tasks that are performed before and during an editing session are not difficult to understand.

1. The original material is played back in the player machine, and each shot is located and timed. This is called "logging."

2. Scene selection and order are decided and a list made. This is called a **scene list**, or, **cut sheet**.

3. **Edit points** are established by moving the videotapes backward and forward to find the desired start and end points of each scene.

4. The machines **preroll**. Each machine—play and record—backs its video-tape from its precise edit point as they both count the pulses together.

5. Each machine stops at the exact preroll point.

6. Both roll forward—the player in "play"—locked together in sync down to the edit point. At the precise edit point, the "record" machine automatically starts its record function, and the material being played is recorded from that precise point.

7. *Note that steps 4, 5, and 6 happen as one continuous movement.*

8. The operator ends the edit by the touch of a button, or the machines stop automatically and wait for the next command.

9. Subsequent edits are made the same way by establishing an edit point on each machine's videotape, and then commanding them to perform again, one scene at a time, until the story is finished.

Finding the Edit Point

All VTR-editing-controller combinations allow for manual movement of the tape forward or backward at a variety of speeds from fast to one frame at a time. TV pictures are actually still pictures transmitted frequently enough to fool the eye into believing there is motion. Thus, the operator can search for the exact frame desired by listening to the sound and watching the video monitor as the tape moves. When that frame is found, different machines han-

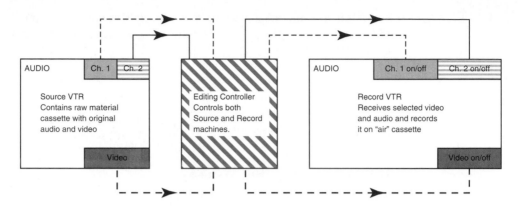

Figure 4.1. The units of a videotape editing station and their basic functions. The editing bay contains two videotape (VTR) machines—the source machine on the left to play wanted portions of the recorded material, the record machine on the right to record these selected portions. Both "play" and "record" machines are connected to and controlled by an editing controller. Audio and video signals are fed from the source (play) machine to the record machine through the controller. The controller is used to select edit points, preroll both machines, and perform the edits. Switches on the record machine control whether the edits contain video and audio, video only, or audio only, and which audio channel will be used.

dle it in different ways. The simpler editing controllers freeze the frame and use it as a reference point. More sophisticated controllers display the exact frame count on a screen or on a read-out counter, and a memory keeps track of it. Editing controllers with such memory units and keyboards will perform search functions and can be programmed to perform a series of edits.

Rehearsing the Edit

One of the nicest things about videotape editing is that the VTR-editing-controller system lets you **preview** the edit before actual editing. A button or switch commands the machines to back up, pause, go forward, and show the edit on the monitor—except that the actual edit is not performed. The machines then return to the edit point. The editor can decide whether to perform that edit or to make changes in it by moving the edit point or points. Some controllers have keypads that permit the editor to add or subtract individual frames of picture and sound by typing this information into the digital memory. When the edit is previewed again, the alterations are made automatically.

Insert and Assemble Functions

You can edit material from one VTR to another in either of two ways: **assemble mode editing** and **insert mode editing**. The difference has to do with the way the control tracks are used.

In assemble mode editing, the "play" machine sends all the elements of

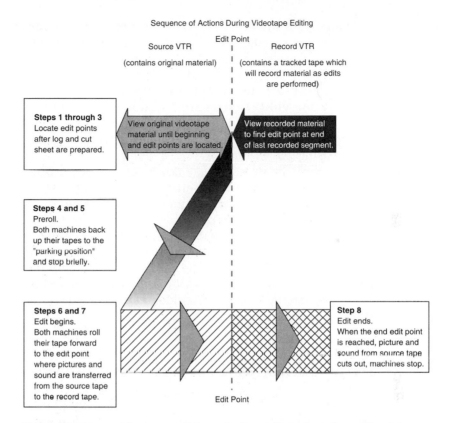

Figure 4.2. How a videotape edit is made. The editor selects the edit points on each VTR by moving the videotapes backward and forward to the appropriate video frame on each videotape. Then the edit controller takes over to back up both tapes, stops at the parking position, and then rolls both tapes forward through the edit point and to the end of the edit.

the picture to the "record" machine. The record machine erases all other material on its tape while laying down the new material coming from the source machine—including a new control track.

Using insert mode to edit requires that the tape in the record machine be "tracked" in advance of its use. Sync pulse and black video or color bars are fed to the record machine and are recorded over the full length of the tape needed for the edit. There are two reasons for this:

1. In insert mode, the new track put on the record tape in advance will be used to control the capstan servo—the mechanism that controls tape speed exactly on both machines, thus making a very precise edit.

2. Putting new video and tracking signals onto the record tape avoids **dropouts**—magnetic "holes"—in the tracking in the material that was pre-

viously on the tape. The tape is given a clean coating of tracking and video signals, and old audio signals are erased. Almost all edits are made in insert mode.

A brand-new videocassette cannot be used to do insert mode edits until tracking and video signals are laid down on it. (In the field the portable recorder will put tracking and video signal on a new blank tape as the recording is being made. But even so, it is standard practice to track a videotape before using it in the field.)

Assemble mode edits may not be as clean and precise as insert mode edits because the way the control pulse and video signals are recorded on the videotape makes assemble mode edits less smooth. Look again at Figure 2–2 (p. 33) to see the difference between the track patterns in assemble and insert mode edits. Note that important gap between the control track and video track at the beginning and end of the assemble edit. That represents a "hole" in the track where the machines will temporarily not be locked together. Assemble mode edits are used mainly to do what the word implies, *assemble* material from the raw videotape or tapes onto the record tape, or to dub (make a copy of) a tape.

Audio Only/Video Only

Even the simplest editing setups have the ability to separate the audio and video editing functions. It is possible to edit the pictures only, or the sound only, or just one of the two sound channels. It is also possible to lay down sound on either or both of the sound channels from another audio source. When you do this you flip switches to tell the machines which channels you want new material put on. Thus the original video or audio remains on the source tape. Only the new video or audio is added to the record tape.

This is another significant characteristic of these video editing systems. The original video and audio material is always available on the source tape. Unless by some freak accident someone has managed to erase the original material, you can always go back to it if you want to re-edit your story.

Time Code, Time Base

Most video editing bays in TV news departments will contain two VTRs, a controller, an audio mixer, and a time base corrector. Many editing machines also have components that allow the use of time code in locating taped material and in editing.

Time coding is a simple idea that grew out of the space age. The idea is to have a machine that generates a continuous standard code—in most cases the exact hour, minute, second, and video frame at the time the tape was being recorded. It shows up at some location in the picture when that material is played back on video screens (see Fig. 4–3). The National Aeronautics and Space Administration (**NASA**) began putting time code on all of its video

Figure 4.3. Time code on a video frame. The numbers indicate the hour, minute, second, and frame number at the time that frame was recorded. Time code is used in videotape editing to locate edit points, to program a series of edits, or to program the entire editing of an entire story. *(Courtesy of Will Counts.)*

and data tapes during the Apollo and Gemini space programs. Thousands of miles of various kinds of video and data tape are made during every space mission. In order to be able to find a batch of pictures and data relating to a single event, NASA inserted Greenwich Mean Time (**GMT**) in hours, minutes, seconds, and frame) on all the tapes. Then if something broke down at 14:22:05:16, all of the material on tape—telemetry, computer data, video, audio, data streams, and so on—that was recorded at that time could be located quickly by using the code. NASA uses it as a filing system with time as a universal index.

Small time code generators were developed so that they could be attached to or built into cameras and recorders. These then put time code on video tape as it is being recorded.

Time code is seen on video monitors because a time code reader picks it up off the videotape and inserts it separately into the monitor picture. It is not seen by the viewer at home because it is not inserted into the video signal at any time during the recording or editing process.

Editing with time code is even easier than without it. Scenes can be selected by marking down the time code as the logging procedure is carried out. An editing controller with microprocessor (computer) that reads the code can then be used during the editing process to locate edit points quickly. And since microprocessing involves memory units, the editing controllers with these features can be programmed to perform a series of edits or even an entire story.

Time code can also be used as a standard reference point. Most stations use the precise local time as their time standard. Those reporters in the field and those in the newsroom can simply note the exact time something important happened during coverage of a story and then use that time to locate the important material quickly during the editing.

More important to news operations, time code can be used to lock together the various units of the editing system more precisely than pulse count. Therefore edits are cleaner and tapes more stable on the air.

The Vertical Interval

The most useful place to put time code is in the vertical interval in the video picture. Without getting too technical about it, the vertical interval is that area of the television picture between the frames that normally is not seen at all on a television set. Lines of information are put there as the picture is being made to stabilize the horizontal and vertical timing of the picture, among other things, in order to bring it up to FCC standards. But that unseen segment contains unused lines, so it is possible to put the time code signal into those lines and therefore *include* it in the video signal but not in that part the viewer sees. Time code inserted this way is much more dependable, and can be used in various ways to add stability to other functions such as switching and programmable editing from a variety of video sources.

Time Base Correcting

A frame of television picture is much like a frame of film: one complete picture. But two television **fields** make up that one complete frame containing (in the United States) 525 scanning lines of resolution. Each recording head on the spinning head drum puts one field on the tape, therefore, each head lays down 262.5 lines alternately on odd and even lines.

Obviously it is important to get those lines exactly where they ought to be for stable broadcast performance. Since helical scan recording equipment has not always performed as precisely as desired, another operation—time base correcting (**TBC**)—was developed to bring the pictures up to FCC standards.

Before we tell you about time base correcting, we must introduce a new concept called **digital** signals. We use the word *signal* to mean any form of information whether it is video, audio, or data, which is moving from one point to another. The movement can be by wire, fiber-optic cable, or through the air.

The electronic signal which has been used since the first days of radio is called an **analog** signal. An analog signal is continuous, like the flow of electricity which lights a desk lamp, or water flowing through a garden hose. Interrupt the flow, the signal stops.

Ever since the invention of the computer, electronic science has been moving toward using digital signals. Digital technology takes its theory from the binary systems of computers in which combinations of zeros (0) and ones (1) are used to create computer commands. In digital audio or video, pictures or sounds are "scanned" and are captured as little "dots." (It's like the dots used to print a picture in a book or magazine. Try looking at a book or magazine picture through a strong magnifier, you will see the little dots which the eye takes in as a single "picture.")

In digital technology information from a picture or sound is stored in tiny impulses or "dots," which can be transmitted in unconnected batches and reassembled later.

It's like substituting fine sand for water and letting sand drop down a suspended garden hose. The sand will come out at the bottom, in a random pile. In digital technology, those "grains" or dots of information can be reassembled to be the same picture or sound which was introduced at the beginning of the circuit (or top of the hose).

Digital electronics allows us to do many exciting tasks. **Compact disks (CDs)** use digital technology to play back music with astonishing clarity using tiny players and disks. Compact disks hold notebooks worth of information, and digital TV equipment can store pictures and sound on compact disks.

Time base correcting relies on digital electronics. Going into great detail about how TBCs work is beyond the scope of this book but briefly: A TBC (Time Base Corrector) is a "black box" that converts the video signal coming to it into digital information. Once the information has been digitized all sorts of signal processing can be done using standard computer circuitry. In essence what the TBC does is make sure that each line of the picture occurs at a uniform interval. As each line of picture comes to the TBC from the tape being played back, the TBC corrects its timing, stores it, and then retrieves it and sends it on its way at a uniform interval. This not only straightens up the picture, but it also corrects all timing elements using sync as a standard referent. Of course, this happens in microseconds.

The result is a picture that meets government standards and is stable when seen on the home receiver. A patient engineer friend once told one of the authors who was struggling to understand the TBC: "These pictures jiggle, so the TBC gets them and everything else to jiggle all together."

The TBC has a second function that allows use of more sophisticated production elements in ENG editing. We have already said that most standard ENG editing functions are "cuts only." Adding fades or dissolves and inserting words or graphics during the editing process can be done with the use of a TBC and a switcher. The TBC serves to stabilize and lock the signals coming through it from the source machine to the switcher. It will also process material from any other video source coming through the switcher, such as a character generator putting name identifications on the bottom of the screen. The TBC is used to help combine the video effects from various sources together onto the recorded tape in the record unit.

When pictures coming from the field on helical scan machines are being played over a microwave or satellite relay system, TBCs are used to lock them to the other in-station signals so that they can be broadcast.

In addition to the TBC a station's control room contains a lot of other electronic wonders that are designed to improve picture stability: field and frame synchronizers and picture enhancers, to name two. One thing seems certain: The broadcast journalist will always find strangely named gadgets are a part of the jargon of the workplace.

Standard Editing Procedures

Editor-controller equipment packages operate somewhat differently depending on the way the manufacturers lay out the various functions. You will have to learn the specifics of the ones you are working with. Furthermore, most stations have their own peculiar ways of doing things. Most have standard procedures designed to cut down on errors and poor-quality results. Most of those have to do with the potential pitfalls of tracking.

Let's suppose that you are sitting at a typical editing console, log and cut sheet in hand, about to use a widely accepted standard procedure. In front of you are two record-playback videotape machines with TV monitors that show you the pictures and sound from each machine. You will have an editing controller, an audiotape record-playback, a mixer, and perhaps a time base corrector and character generator. Figure 4–4 shows a typical editing console setup.

All editor-controller consoles are conformed left to right, or top to bottom. That is, the "play" machine is on the left or on top; the "record" machine is on the right or on the bottom. Each machine has its own monitor. The editing controller is located either between or to the side of these VTRs. All of the other units you will use should be within arm's reach.

Virtually all edits today are made in insert mode. Therefore:

Step 1. Put a fresh videocassette in the record machine and lay down a control track on it.

Do this in the following manner: Feed color bars or black to the machine; some sort of routing switcher or internal system will do this at the touch of a button. Record the color bars or black on the videotape cassette in the record machine. Many stations routinely "track" all cassettes daily. The first

Figure 4.4. A production editing suite. This Matrox™ computer-based edit system at WTAP-TV is used mostly to create commercials and special programs. *(Courtesy of WTAP-TV. Photo by Roger Sheppard.)*

time you find someone slipped up and didn't do that will be the last time you will trust that it *has* been done. A cassette without track on the tape will not edit.

Make sure that you have tracked a space on the cassette tape that is *much longer* than your edited story is going to be since you don't want to run out of track before the story ends. One final pre-edit preparation: Rewind the record tape to the beginning, roll it forward fifteen seconds, and edit a **countdown leader** onto it.

A countdown leader is just what it sounds like. Ten seconds are displayed on the tape, counting down from ten to two. No number one is displayed, so that one second of black will be on the tape just ahead of the first pictures. By dubbing this onto the beginning of your story tape, you provide a simple way to cue the tape for playback and a visual countdown for the director as the tape is rolled into the newscast.

Step 2. Put together your A-Roll.

The A-Roll, or basic edited story, may contain several things. If you are editing an interview, the log and shot list will show what portions of the interview you have chosen as well as the in cues and out cues.

In editing an interview or speech excerpts, simply lay down those sync sound bites (SOT)—both video and audio—in the order you have chosen after laying down whatever opening scenes you have selected. You can

> **A-Roll**—a holdover from news film, meaning the basic audio and video of a story, which can consist of the reporter on camera, the reporter narrating over pictures, or an interviewee or speaker (audio and video)
>
> **B-Roll**—another holdover from news film, meaning pictures inserted to cover or replace existing video on the A-Roll. Scenes of a fire shown while a victim describes the event would combine an A-Roll interview with B-Roll video.
>
> **Sound bite**—interviewee, speaker, or video and sound of an event
>
> **Jump cut**—an abrupt change of scene creating an awkward visual "jump" effect at the point of the change.
>
> **Cutaway**—a short video scene inserted to bridge two similar sound bites or a reporter's question on the audio. Typical cutaways include video of spectators at a fire, or the audience at a city council meeting.

edit the sound bites together without worrying too much about things like jump cuts and other distracting visual material because you are going to cover those with cutaways and inserts from your B-Roll material later (see Figures 4–5 and 4–6).

If you have voice-over narration to be illustrated with B-Roll pictures, lay down the narration sound first (see Figure 4–7). The narration should be recorded in advance by the reporter and will have been delivered to you on an audio cassette or CART (audio cartridge) along with the videocassettes.

Remember that these machines will edit both video and audio, or video

Figure 4.5. The steps involved in editing a story containing sound bites from an interview and a standup close. After the first seven edits create the A-Roll, the B-Roll material is laid over the V/O narration, and the cutaway is inserted between sound bites one and two to cover a jump cut.

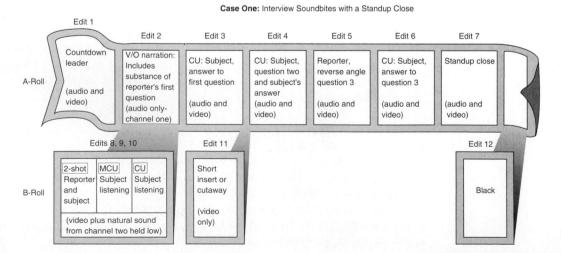

Case One: Interview Soundbites with a Standup Close

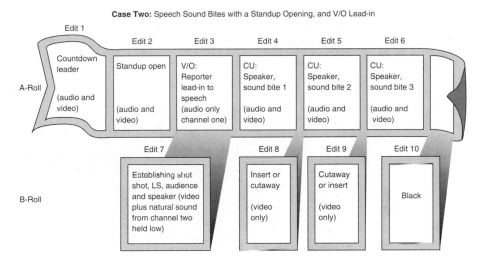

Case Two: Speech Sound Bites with a Standup Opening, and V/O Lead-in

Figure 4.6. The editing of a story in which a news maker is delivering a speech. The first six edits create the A-Roll with sound bites. The last four edits insert an LS establishing shot of the speaker and audience over the V/O lead-in. Inserts and cutaways are placed between the sound bites to avoid jump cuts.

only, or audio only. The appropriate switches on the record machine control these functions.

To lay down narration set the record machine switches so that you are recording *audio only, on channel 1.* (You may want to use the camera mic sound on channel 2 for ambient sound.) You have timed the narration and know exactly how long it is, and exactly how long you want each scene of the B-Roll video that will illustrate the narration.

Step 3. Insert the appropriate video.

In the first A-Roll situation (Case One) you have your voice-over narration and interview excerpts edited on the sound. You must now go back and insert, *video only,* the B-Roll scenes for the narration and the cutaways and inserts that will cover the jump cuts. What cutaways and inserts? The ones you, or your videographer, were so careful to shoot in the field.

Case Two presents a similar situation; you have to lay down the standup open and then three sound bites. Again, inserts or cutaways must be inserted between the sound bites to avoid jump cuts.

In Case Three, containing voice-over narration, you now go back and insert, *video only,* those B-Roll scenes you have chosen to illustrate what the narration is talking about.

If you have a standup open and close, or bridges, you will, of course, lay down the open right after the countdown leader and the close as the last scene of the story.

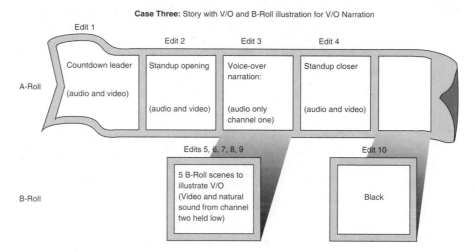

Figure 4.7. The editing of a story with standup open and close and narrated V/O scenes from the news event. The first four edits lay down the countdown leader, standup open, V/O narration, and standup close. Then five more edits insert the B-Roll scenes over the V/O narration.

You have just edited a video story with video and sound. But you still have one more thing left to do.

> Step 4. Record black immediately after the end of the story.

To do this, rewind the edited tape to about fifteen seconds from the end of the story. Feed black to the record machine. Play the edited tape. Punch the record *and* edit buttons at the exact instant the story or standup close ends. Record plenty of black. This will prevent extraneous video or audio from getting on the air if the control room director is slow on the next take. A little black on the screen is preferable to random scenes from last week's news that were on the cassette before you edited this story.

The three editing procedures outlined above are very basic. They do include, however, all the moves you must learn to make with the editing equipment.

Some Audio Procedures

Most editing bays contain equipment designed to allow you to edit in sound other than that which is on the raw material cassettes. This may include an audio mixer fed directly to the "record" machine or a separate audio console with audio cassette, CART (cartridge), compact disk, and reel-to-reel playback units, and disc turntables. Many stations seem to prefer a setup that connects audio cassette and/or audio CART playback units through a relatively simple four-channel audio mixer.

If more elaborate audio mixes are needed they can be prepared elsewhere and dubbed onto audio cassettes or CARTS for insertion onto the videotape during the editing process. (The reproduction quality of CARTS is generally better than the reproduction quality of audio cassettes.)

Even a simple four-channel mixer with a reel-to-reel or audio CART record/playback unit is quite flexible. And it can be used to balance between channels when you want to incorporate wild, or ambient, sound under voice-over narration.

Recording Separate Audio

To feed audio from another source—such as the voice-over narration in Case Three—to the video editing ensemble, you must first set the sound levels. Most audio mixers will include a button or switch that will provide a 1,000-cycle tone—a reference tone that can be used to establish levels.

Note that most videotape recorder-playback units have audio limiters on them. Turn them off when you are setting levels and be sure to turn them back on when you have finished doing so. If you don't do this, it is possible to misadjust the levels in such a way that the videotape machines will raise the background noise to a very high level during periods of low or no audio. This can be very distracting to the listener and can destroy the effect you wanted to create.

Now, with the limiters off:

✔ 1. Turn on the tone on the mixer and set the level on the mixer volume unit (VU) meter at zero VU (100 percent modulation). Put the needle right at the beginning of the red. It will stay there, since the tone is constant.

✔ 2. Place the record videotape machine in record mode.

✔ 3. Adjust the audio level controls on the record videotape machine to show zero VU (100 percent modulation) on the channel one or channel two VU meters, or both.

✔ 4. Turn the limiters back on.

What you have done will assure that the same level that comes out of the mixer is being recorded on the videotape. This also lets you do all of your mixing and balancing with the mixer rather than with the VTR controls. This is preferable because you are dealing with only one "mixing pot" (control knob or slider)—you have already established the level by feeding the 1,000-cycle tone from the audio recorder and matching it on the record machine. Adjustments can now be made easily with the mixer pot.

Once you have set the levels on the record videotape machine correctly, you are ready to begin more sophisticated audio work. Most of the situations you will encounter will fall into one of these two categories:

1. Using the mixer to balance between two channels of the videotape.

2. Using the mixer to add narration, music, or wild sound to the tape.

Balancing between Two Channels

In some circumstances it may be necessary to reduce the level of one channel on the videotape relative to the other during editing. For instance, you may have sync sound (SOT) recorded at the scene of the news event with wild sound recorded at the same time on the other channel of the videotape. In this case the wild sound would probably be on channel 2 (from the camera mic) and the narration on channel 1. If the wild sound from the camera mic has to be reduced, you can use the audio mixer to do it.

First, use the mixer tone to set the level on the record videotape machine. The mixer usually can be set up so that it carries sound from the "play" machine to the "record" machine, so you will want to connect one of the pots on the mixer to channel 1 on the "play" machine, and another to channel 2 on the *same* machine. You will play back the sound from "play" to "record" during the edit, and control the levels through the mixer.

At this point you must use your good judgment:

✔ 1. Play the tape on the "play" machine and set the levels to achieve the balance you want.

✔ 2. *Listen* to those levels; get the balance the way you want it to sound. (The meters don't tell you everything.)

Finally, simply recue the "play" and "record" videotapes and make a normal edit with the controller. The sound will be balanced the way you want it.

Laying Down Narration on Part of a Video Story

Frequently you will find you want to put voice-over narration on a part of a video story. This occurs when you want to use some prerecorded voice-over narration and some sync-sound (SOT) interview material. Or you may have a standup open and close, prerecorded voice-over narration, and sync-sound interview.

The two most common situations you will encounter are:

1. Putting down narration before the video has been laid down.

2. Putting down narration along with the video.

Again, the first move is to establish the proper levels. In both situations, it is wiser and easier to use the editing controller to make the edits since it is much more precise.

In the first instance, cue the "play" machine to any arbitrary point on the videotape in it and let the automatic functions of the editing controller make the actual edit while you roll the prerecorded narration at the edit point.

In the second situation, cue the "play" machine to the exact edit point you want and insert both video and narration at the same time. Here's how to do this. When you have both videotape machines cued, and the prerecorded narration connected to the proper audio channel on the "record" machine, start the edit. When the machines complete the preroll and rundown and begin the edit, the "record" machine insert or record light will come on. When that light comes on, start the audio cassette or CART with the narration on it; the narration will be recorded on the "record" videotape. The editor will do the precision work while you roll the cassette or CART when the insert or record light comes on.

Mixing Narration with Wild Sound

Mixing means blending sound from two different audio sources. There are many times when doing this will help make the "main sound" clearer while you still retain the other sound on the other audio channel of the videotape.

Assume now that the narration is prerecorded on an audio cassette or CART, and that wild sound is on channel two of the videotape in the "play" machine. For instance, the videotape of last night's important basketball game has been edited to present the highlights of the game. On the videotape is the sound of the crowd cheering as the home team won the game with a flying fast break. Your sports reporter has written narration describing the action and has recorded it on an audio cassette or CART. You are going to mix the narration with the cheering.

Connect the audio cassette player through the mixer to channel one on the "record" machine. Connect channel 2 from the "play" machine through the mixer to channel 2 on the "record" machine. Roll them and set the levels where you want them. Recue the audio cassette or CART machine and both videotape machines. Make the edit as you normally would. When the red insert or record light comes on, start the audio cassette machine to add the narration to edited pictures of the game along with the cheering.

Backtiming Narrative Inserts

If you have prerecorded narration, wild sound, and sync sound, you can, of course, edit the narration and wild sound as we have just described. Then you would make another edit to add on the sync-sound interview or other story material that is to follow the narration. But that can cause a video or audio jump, or both.

Instead, let's **backtime** the narrative inserts, and insert them in the proper length of time ahead of the place where the interview or other sync sound begins. Since you won't have edit where the two join, you won't have a jump, either.

To do this, use the time counting features found on most editing controllers. You will have noticed that as you move the videotapes in the "play" and "record" machines the counters, or readouts, have been timing the tapes in minutes, seconds, and frames. If the editing controller contains a memory unit, you can use these readouts to tell the controller where to start and stop

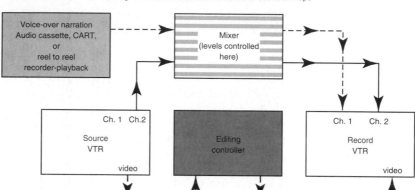

Figure 4.8. Mixing two sources of sound during a video edit. In this case prerecorded voice-over narration has been cued up on an audio playback machine and run through the mixer to channel 1 on the record VTR. The natural sound on tape (NAT-SOT) picked up by the camera mic is on channel 2 of the videocassette in the source VTR. It is fed through another mixer pot to channel 2 on the record VTR. Thus the levels of the two channels of sound can be adjusted to hold the NAT-SOT at a low level while the V/O narration is allowed to come through at full level. The video scenes are transferred from the source to the record videotape through the editing controller.

the edits. If not, these readouts can also be used as stopwatches to tell you the length of each scene, the length of each sound bite, and the length of the finished story.

Suppose you are trying to hold the interview subject's audio or other sync sound as a low sound bed under the prerecorded narration, and then bring it up to full level at the proper time.

✔ 1. Time the narrative insert *exactly*.

✔ 2. Set up for editing through the audio mixer, just as if you were going to mix narration with wild sound.

✔ 3. Roll the audiotaped narration and set the proper level. Recue the taped narration.

✔ 4. Roll the "play" videotape and set the proper level for the videotape sound. *Make a mental note of the position of the audio mixer pot controlling the videotape sound and turn it down so only a very low level of that sound will get through.*

✔ 5. Recue the "play" videotape, and note the exact tape time.

✔ 6. Back up the "play" machine videotape one-half to one second more than the length of your narrative insert. For example, if the narrative insert is

Figure 4.9. An editing controller with LED readouts. The numbers in the rectangles at the top of the machine report the hour, minute, second, and frame count from the videotape being viewed. These numbers can be used to locate exact edit points and to subtract or add frames following the preview of an edit. If the editing controller has memory circuits, the numbers can be used to program a series of edits or an entire story. *(Courtesy of Sony Corporation of America.)*

exactly eighteen seconds long, back up the "play" videotape until the timer shows you are eighteen and one-half to nineteen seconds *before* the point you want the sync sound to begin.

✔ 7. Enter this point as your "play" videotape edit point. (The extra one-half to one second is to allow for your reaction time in starting the audiotape machine, and raising the interview audio or sync sound at the end of the narration.)

✔ 8. Cue the "record" machine videotape to the proper point and perform the edit with the controller as you normally would.

✔ 9. When the red insert or record light comes on, play the narration on the audiotape machine.

✔ 10. At the end of the narration, make two quick level changes. First, raise the level of the "play" videotape sound to the proper level using the pot on the audio mixer. Then pot down the audiotape level.

If all has gone well, you should have brought up the sound level of the interview or sync sound at exactly the proper time, and you will have a very smooth transition with no jump in either the video or audio continuity.

The "Lip Flap" Problem

When you use any video that shows a person talking, the audience expects to be able to hear those words. When you use those pictures without the sound, you automatically create a **lip flap** problem. The mouth is moving, but the words are not coming through. This problem usually develops when you try to use a medium or closeup shot of an interview subject, without the sound, as an establishing shot. The subject is talking with the reporter, but the audience can't hear what he or she is saying.

A simple sequence will solve this problem:

✔ 1. MLS two shot, subject and reporter chatting.

✔ 2. CU, subject, listening to reporter.

✔ 3. MS, over the shoulder of the reporter, subject listening.

With these three scenes you establish the reporter-subject interview relationship, establish the subject's face, and set up for the answer to the first question.

Of course, there are different combinations and different shot angles that can provide variety to these kinds of establishing sequences. But if you consistently do it this way and insist that the videographer give you these shots, "lip flap" will disappear from television news.

Live Narration

Of course it is possible to have someone in a recording booth or studio do live narration, but we would like to discourage you from doing this. First, it is difficult to cue a live narration with the precision that is needed to prevent jumping in either too soon or too late. Second, by putting the narration on tape you don't tie up that person or the studio for long periods of time while you try to get a "keeper."

On the other hand, there are occasions where the live narration involves description of a complicated series of scenes on the videotape and needs to be carefully paced to those events. In this case putting the narration on the videotape as the narrator watches the scenes may be the most practical solution.

Editing B-Roll

We have already introduced you to the concept of B-Roll from the point of view of the videographer working in the field. We said the whole procedure starts with getting good B-Roll material at the scene. That procedure continues and comes to its logical conclusion in the editing of the raw material. Doing it well at both ends of the production process is one of the most creative elements of television news.

Remember the rules:

✔ 1. B-Roll must be illustrative.

✔ 2. B-Roll must have sequence.

✔ 3. Special effects are no substitute for good, illustrative B-Roll.

In the logging process the editor is looking for B-Roll scenes that will illustrate, explain, and illuminate what the speakers are talking about.

If the story is a feature showing someone doing something unique—such as the diamond cutter illustration in Chapter 3—it is the B-Roll material that will tell the story. All of the "talking heads" in the world, no matter how fascinating they are, cannot substitute for good B-Roll that *shows* the audience what is happening.

If it is a simple interview, or even a spot news story, there are still scenes that are needed in editing to illustrate the tenor and circumstances of the interview or the details of what happened at the spot news story.

That brings us to the second rule. A B-Roll segment must have sequence just as an entire story must have sequence. It must have a beginning, middle, and end. It must match words and pictures just as carefully. The scenes in a B-Roll sequence are really a small visual story within the larger visual story. Too many times we see B-Rolls that seem to have been put together in a haphazard, random manner.

Since you are trying to illustrate what the narration or the subject is talking about, all of the rules of visual continuity come into play. You want to carry the audience into that illustration using long shots, medium shots, and many closeups. You want the B-Roll to flow and move forward.

Let's go back to the story of the diamond cutter. You have an interview with the diamond cutter telling how he cuts a diamond into two equal pieces. And you have B-Roll material showing him doing it. Edit the first part of the interview as sync sound (SOT), and go back and put in cutaways and inserts to cover the jump cuts.

Then edit the part where he describes what he is going to do, again just cutting it on the sound. Here you don't have to worry about the jump cuts because you are going to cover all of that with the B-Roll pictures.

Look carefully at the raw material from which you will construct the B-Roll, and select those scenes which are most illustrative of what he is saying. Then arrange those scenes in a sequence. See Figure 4-10.

Notice that several B-Roll segments are intercut with the sync sound. The B-Roll has been edited to fit the diamond cutter's narration and has shown the audience the process with closeups, just as if they were there leaning over the cutter's shoulder. When the sync sound is being used the diamond cutter is seen speaking, and when the B-Roll scenes are shown they are matched to what he is saying.

The B-Roll scenes also give visual continuity. You move from a medium

Sound	Scene
"The first thing to do is to be sure the diamond is tightly fastened to the dop with lead and plaster."	MS: Diamond cutter's hands holding diamond in the dop. CU: Diamond in dop. ECU: Same as above.
"Then, we mark the grain line so that we are sure the cut will follow the crystalline structure of this particular diamond. . .and so divide it into two equal parts. . ." (SOT)	Insert ECU: Diamond cutter's eyes looking down. Insert CU: Hands marking the line.
"This takes a lot of study. Every diamond is different, so there is a lot of time spent and a lot of skill involved in figuring out just where the grain lines are, and how they can be used to make the cut. I'm sure I have it right. . .we will see."	MCU: Diamond cutter.
(Reporter narration, V/O: "Now Darrell Drake, making the actual cut. . .") (SOT)	MS: Diamond cutter, intense concentration.
(No sound from him; just the ambient sound since he's not talking.)	MS: Another angle, he picks up mallet, places cutting knife on diamond, replaces it. CU: Knife on diamond.
(SOT) "Now. . ."	ECU: Same as above. CU: Mallet taps knife three times, then comes down hard, making the cut.
(SOT) "There, another success. . ."	ECU: Diamond in two pieces. MS: Diamond cutter, holds up the two pieces. Smiles. CU: Cutter's hand holding the two pieces.
(SOT) SOT continues as the diamond cutter says he wasn't worried, etc.	MCU: Cutter.

Figure 4.10. Raw material ingredients of a feature story—video, natural sound, narration—and how the various elements are combined in editing to complete the final product.

shot to very tight shots of his hands at work, the diamond, and the results. Several times you have cut back to scenes with the diamond cutter in them to help reestablish the relationship between the medium shots and the closeups.

Notice that this story has two time sequences: the first during the demonstration, the second during the actual cutting. A short reporter narration V/O was inserted to tell the audience that from there on they are going to watch the real event.

When you get to that moment you and the audience are grateful that it is shot close up—that's what we came for. Let the ambient sound carry the load. This is not the time for words.

End the story by using the sync sound of the diamond cutter expressing his relief and satisfaction. If you were to end the story with the shot of the two parts in the diamond cutter's hand it might be adequate, but the audience really wants to hear how he feels and probably needs help in coming down from the tension of the high moment before moving on to the next news event.

Problems

In the edited story above, it is obvious that you have all of the shots needed to take maximum advantage of the B-Roll possibilities. The videographer has been careful to shoot all of the scenes from the same side of the line of action, so you don't have screen-direction problems. And there are many good closeups to use to bring the audience close to the focal point of the story.

The sound, particularly the ambient sound, is very useful. The diamond cutter has "talked you through" the process and demonstrated what he is going to do. You can then cut the demonstration scenes to fit his "play-by-play" narration and to prepare the audience for what they are about to see.

If you had not had that sound—if, for example, he is reticent in telling about his exotic profession—the reporter would have had to write and record voice-over narration. But it should be very loose. If the narration filled all of the scenes with words, much of the tension of the climactic moment would be lost.

As we noted in Chapter 3, you will find very few set rules about scene length. The two major ones to keep in mind are:

✔ 1. A scene should be long enough to let the viewers get a good look and absorb what they are looking at.

✔ 2. If you have a scene where you want the audience to absorb a great deal of visual and aural material it must run longer than a scene with minimum complexity.

Yet scene length has dramatic possibilities. As you get closer to the big moment, you may want to shorten the scenes, particularly those inserts that cut between the hands at work and the face of the diamond cutter expressing concentration. Then, when you get to the actual cutting of the diamond, you may want to start that as early as possible so that you have a scene that says to the audience, "Now—hold your breath." And you surely would not want many fast-paced cuts in the video to destroy the tension.

The best guideline to follow in editing a story like this is to ask that key question: "What is this story *really* about?" The answer is not "about a man cutting the world's largest diamond." The real answer is "about a man *actually* cutting the world's largest diamond." Adding that one word gives focus to the story. You are going to show the audience something it has never seen before. The early part of the story explains what is going to happen, and, even though the diamond cutter uses some technical terms, the audience can see generally what he is talking about. Then the audio and video carry the audience up to and through the critical act—*actually*—and through to the end where everyone can breathe a sigh of relief.

Other B-Roll Applications

You won't have such good B-Roll material most of the time. The only thing that would have made the story more dramatic is if the diamond cutter had goofed and broken the gem into a million pieces.

Other more common situations usually do not include such good B-Roll possibilities. Yet almost any story is improved with the insertion of B-Roll that is illustrative of what is being said.

Take a more prosaic story, one about people working their way up through a line to get their unemployment checks. This can be shot and edited in a very routine manner. It will look routine when it is aired. Or it can be shot with some attention to the B-Roll possibilities, which can be used in the editing to show and tell the story more effectively.

If all you have to work with is a series of medium shots of people standing in line and of the people behind the counter handing out the checks, the visual material will not show the audience what it's like to have to go to the unemployment office to get the weekly allowance.

A run of medium shots is like looking at someone's snapshots after they get them back from the drugstore. You know that if you have made snapshots of an event that itself had a beginning, middle, and end, you often arrange those snapshots in that order. While you show them to someone else you sometimes provide a "narration" that may sound like: "This is before he was going to jump into the lake; there he is, ready to jump; there's the splash—I didn't shoot fast enough—and there he is all wet after he got out." You constructed a sequence even though all of the snaps were medium shots. Of course, there isn't a lot of detail in the shots, and there are no closeups, so the "story" you've shown and told isn't very interesting.

But the story of the unemployment check line can be made more interesting, and more meaningful if B-Roll scenes can be edited into the story to help focus it. The videographer should do the following:

✔ 1. Concentrate on one or two individuals in the line after shooting some scenes of the mass of people.

✔ 2. Record closeups of the individuals and the actions they had to take to get their checks.

Among these scene possibilities are:

MS and CUs of the individuals

CUs of their faces

CUs of their hands as they receive the checks

CUs of the face of the clerk handing out the checks

CUs of the clerk's hands

CUs of the hands of the applicant signing for the check

MS and CUs from both sides of the counter but on the same line of action, from the applicant's point of view as he or she gets closer, and from the clerk's point of view as he or she does business with the applicants

With those scenes to work with you can edit the story for voice over narration so that it shows:

Scene 1. LS: "A large number of people showed up today to get their checks."

Scene 2. MS: "The lines were long but things went efficiently and the applicants were patient," or "It was a mess and the applicants got impatient."

Then, with the B-Roll material showing one person going through the process, it might look like this:

Scene 3. MS: Person third from front of the line

Scene 4. CU: Face of same person, now second from front of the line

Scene 5. CU: Clerk looking at same person

Scene 6. MS: From behind the counter, looking over the shoulder of the clerk

Scene 7. MCU: Person receiving check from clerk

Scene 8. CU: Person's hands signing for check

Scene 9. MS: Person thanks clerk, turns and walks away out of the frame

This sequence could be edited in as the narration is telling the audience the average amount each person received, how many are getting close to the end of their allotment, and so forth. It is much better than a series of medium shots showing people's backs because it personalizes the activity and allows the audience to identify with the individual who is going through it. It also shows that the process is easy; or that the process is long and boring; or that you'd better get there early, or whatever.

In interview situations, the opportunities for B-Roll material are often limited, so acquiring good B-Roll shots requires imagination. Perhaps the subject has something she or he wants to show the reporter, or wants to conduct a simple demonstration connected with what is being discussed. Even if the story is about something as simple as the new tourist brochure the chamber of commerce is going to publish, you have chances for shots of hands holding the brochure, opening it up, closeups of the cover, the inside pages, the pictures it contains, or hands stuffing brochures into envelopes.

It may be difficult to shoot those scenes while the interview is going on, but they can be shot after the interview is completed. The effort should be to show the brochure as well as talk about it. Remember, the audience will quite naturally want to see it.

Don't limit B-Roll shooting to the interview site. Sometimes illustrative B-Roll can be shot somewhere else in town, such as the airport, or at a tourist attraction.

DEALING WITH SPECIAL SCENE PROBLEMS

Cutaways and Inserts

The editor should always keep in mind the differences between cutaways and inserts and their appropriate use.

Cutaways should be suited to the action. Like those standard shots of the reporter listening to the subject, they are used to cover jump cuts and to establish and reestablish the relationship between the subject and the reporter. A cutaway, like a shot of the collection of miniature elephants on the subject's desk, may or may not be appropriate. If the subject is the state Republican chairman those elephants become a part of the story. If the subject is the head of the local Planned Parenthood chapter and the story is about a new series of lectures about contraception, the elephants are a visual non sequitur.

Inserts should take the viewer closer to the action. They are used to emphasize and illustrate what the subject is talking about. Even when they are used to cover jump cuts they often work better than cutaways because they provide emphasis and focus on the objects or actions the subject is discussing with the reporter.

Zooms, Pans, and Tilts as Editing Problems

Some years ago the faculty of the National Press Photographers Association (NPPA) Television News Workshop came up with four very unofficial but graphic names for various kinds of zooms.

Zoom—a gradual transition in the picture from distant to close using a variable focal lens

Mooz—the reverse of a zoom, the transition being from close to distant

Zoof—a zoom that ends up out of focus

Moof—a mooz that ends up out of focus

Add to these four two other basic motions:

Pan—horizontal motion of the camera, side to side. A pan should be executed slowly and *in one direction only*.

Tilt—vertical motion of the camera, up or down

Of course, zoofs and moofs are unusable and tell you something important about the skill of the videographer who shot them.

Shots that include a zoom or a mooz are useful in editing only if they are *motivated*. That is, they must purposefully take the audience closer to an object or subject to provide a closeup look or pull back from a closeup to show the relationship of the object or subject to something else relevant to the story. A zoom shot should not be executed too rapidly.

For example, a zoom starts from a two shot showing the back of the reporter's head in the foreground, then moves to a MCU of the subject. It might be very useful if the reporter's V/O narration tells about the question asked of the subject. It shows the audience the relationship between the two people and allows the viewer to "lean closer" to hear the answer—it is motivated.

A mooz that starts with a tight closeup of an object and then pulls back to reveal that the object is part of an exhibit in a store window is also motivated. It catches the interest of the audience and then shows the object's relationship to other objects and its location.

Each of these shots and all of their counterparts can be put to good use by an editor. But they take up precious time. Once the zoom or mooz is started, it must be allowed to continue until it is completed; you should not cut on a zoom or mooz. These shots might be appropriate for the beginning and ending scenes of a story. Nevertheless, it is almost always better to cut between the scenes within a story rather than waste the time letting the zoom or mooz carry the viewer from one size shot to another.

Further, except in very special circumstances—such as using the motion of zooms and moozes to create an effect—you should studiously avoid cutting from zoom to zoom, or mooz to mooz, or any other combination: The audience will become disoriented. And you should avoid frequent use of zooms and moozes; they rapidly become visual clichés.

Finally, zooms and moozes are almost never a substitute for the LS-MS-CU sequence of scenes cut to appropriate length. It may seem that the zoom encompasses the long establishing shot, the medium shot that comes next, and ends up in the closeup that should follow. Lazy editors use them because it means they don't have to make three edits to get to the closeup. But the zoom used that way takes a relatively longer time to move the visual story forward. Editing the LS-MS-CU into a sequence may not be quicker in the editing room, but the sequence that results is usually more forceful in getting the story started or beginning a new segment within the story.

Moozes that focus tightly on an interesting object and then pull back to reveal its setting and relationship to other objects or subjects in the scene have dramatic possibilities. Sometimes it is a good idea to use such a shot at the beginning of a sequence as an attention getter. You show the viewers a closeup of something interesting, maybe something they cannot figure out. Then you let the shot pull back to show how that object relates to the story they are looking at.

For example: A tight closeup of a Super Bowl Championship ring on the finger of a hand, then a mooz back and tilt up to a medium shot showing that the person wearing the ring is the new quarterback that the local NFL team has hired today is an interesting way to start the story of the announcement news conference.

Or a shot might begin on the hands of an artisan performing some delicate work on a strange-looking object, then pulls back to show the artisan and the object. It turns out the person makes flower holders out of old auto engine valves. The visual story shows how she does that. The audience doesn't recognize that the object is a valve in the first shot but finds out what it is as the story develops. The main thing to remember is to use these shots in editing where they are appropriate. Use them sparingly. They often are not a good substitute for a series of cuts which will focus on the center of action more quickly.

USING SPECIAL EFFECTS

Many ENG editing complexes, TV station control rooms, and post-production suites contain stunning arrays of computer-based machines that can create special video effects. These range from simple machines that generate and insert words on the screen to electronic palettes on which an artist can add features to already existing pictures or create entirely new pictures with an almost infinite range of colors, lines, and brushstroke widths.

Some image manipulators can shrink an image to a pinpoint, then send it spiraling across the screen leaving a trail of afterimages as it goes. Others can turn an image around like a revolving bank thermometer sign and reveal a different image on the other "side." Images can tumble, roll, cartwheel, and zoom off to infinity.

You can get quite a bit of heat out of a confrontation between those who say the image manipulators are a danger to television journalism and those who say audiences are becoming more visually sophisticated all the time—and therefore desire graphics and understand them.

One side says it is possible to re-create with graphics scenes of events that could not possibly have been covered with videotape or live equipment. These graphics can be made to look remarkably real, as a visit to any video games parlor will prove. If, the proponents say, the information used to create the graphics is absolutely accurate, then the renderings will be absolutely accurate.

Opponents point out that no graphic representation can be the real thing, and they worry that the false portrayal—no matter how lifelike—can be too easily mistaken for that real event. "You are showing people something that never happened," they say. Further they worry that if the graphic creating is done by people less responsible than journalists, the door is opened to hoaxes of catastrophic consequence.

It is easy for an editor to get caught up with these technological wonders—and the argument that surrounds their use. Clearly when that use creates appropriate and useful visual information that use is positive. When graphics are used to cover up the obvious fact that good video, especially good B-Roll and appropriate illustrative material, is missing, they are just crutches. Let's look at some of these special effects and some practical applications.

Character Generators

These machines, referred to as *CG*'s, *Chyrons*™ or *fonts* (after Videfont™), create a few words, a few lines, or even a screenful of words that can then be inserted in, or edited onto, other video. The word *Chyron*™ is the commercial name for one brand of character generator, just as *font* is short for Videfont™, another brand.

The most common insert is a lower-third super, that is, a line or two of words placed in the bottom third of the picture frame to identify the person speaking. Some stations' procedures call for lower thirds to be put on the videotape at the time it is edited. Most insert them live during the broadcast.

Such inserts perform the important function of identifying the speaker by name and title visually. Even though that speaker may be identified in the voice-over narration or by the anchorperson reading the script in the studio, lower thirds should always be used and inserted as quickly as possible after the picture of the subject appears.

Figure 4.11. Character generators, graphics generators, and frame stores can be used to add a wide variety of information to the video frame. Here characters have been developed as special effects to add to a bumper about the regatta. The action within the video frame could be frozen, or the racing boat could speed on out to the frame as the videotape rolls on through. *(Courtesy of Laird Telemedia, Inc.)*

You probably don't have to use a lower third to identify the president or a handful of other readily recognizable people in the world, but you should use them on all unknowns, and always if there is the slightest possibility the audience won't recognize the subject.

If the audio portion of the story contains the voice of someone who has not been identified visually, a lower third that reads "Voice of _____ " should be inserted while that voice is being heard to help further with identification.

It is common practice to use a lower third only the first time a subject appears in the story. However, if that person appears again much later in a long story, and if reidentification is important to the clarity of the story, use it again. And to repeat, even when there is a lower-third super on the screen, it is a good idea to also identify the person on the screen in the script audio.

A major problem with lower-third supers, especially ones that are two or three lines long, is that they cover the mouth of the speaker in a closeup. CBS News solved the problem several years ago by moving the lower third to the lower left-hand edge of the screen. The alternative is to look for a shot of the

Figure 4.12. One frame from a videotape showing a lower-third super used to identify the subject who is speaking. These words are created by a character generator and are inserted onto the tape or are superimposed during a broadcast through the control room switcher. *(Courtesy of Will Counts.)*

subject that is loose enough for the lower third to appear below the subject's chin and then cut to a tighter shot as soon as possible.

Depending on how sophisticated (and expensive) they are, character generators can do many other things to add visual interest and clarity. Most provide either upper- and lower-case or all upper-case letters. Some provide different typefaces, some have drop-shadow letters that have three-dimensional characteristics. Some provide for a border around the edge of the letters to make them stand out more clearly. Many allow for the letters to be colored, or color can be added through a switcher, or the letters or words can be made to blink on and off. All of these functions can be called up with the touch of a button or two.

Besides providing the lower-third supers, character generators can be used to position words and symbols almost anywhere on the screen, to make lists and scroll them up or down, or to make words move horizontally across the screen. With a character generator that has memory capacity, lower thirds or symbols such as the station's logo can be filed and then retrieved when needed. CGs are also widely used to present and update sports scores, election results, and other tabular information.

An editor has to think carefully about the possibilities for using the character generator to provide additional information on the screen, about the design and layout of the material, and about the appropriateness of it.

Words and other symbols added to the television picture call attention to themselves and sometimes distract the viewers' attention.

You have probably seen the weather warning march across the bottom of the TV screen just at the high moment of drama in the movie you were watching. Certainly the weather warning is important and in this situation the distraction is part of a valuable service. But watch out if you are going to include a lower third, the station's logo, and "Skycam 2" over some very interesting video shot from the helicopter. You are likely to have so many layers of video on the air that the audience is forced to look through this visual picket fence and is so distracted it loses everything.

The editor must also try to keep the words to a minimum. The TV screen is small. People read at different speeds. A whole screenful of words must remain there long enough for the audience to read it all the way through *twice*. If the message is an important one—perhaps the numbers to look for on cans of food being withdrawn from sale for health reasons—you would probably want to have the narrator read the words as they appear on the screen. That way you would be more certain that the message got through.

If the words are a list of three or four important points from a new government report, the narration and the words on the screen should be synchronized. Merely putting words on the screen, hoping the audience will read them, usually is not very effective communication.

Frame Stores and Frame Manipulators

Digital computer-driven video storage devices can be used to generate words and pictures, store them, and bring them up onto a TV screen in almost any form. They are limited only by the amount of memory capacity of the device and by the imagination of the people who program them.

Frame stores, sometimes called **still stores**, can take one frame of video, hold it in memory, and return it to the screen on command. These frames can contain almost any visual material—one frame of picture from a slide, photo, videotape, chart, table, a piece of graphic art, or anything else.

At one time, networks and stations reporting election returns had to construct massive scoreboards in their studios. Today the precise and speedy vote totals and the graphic frames they appear in come from computers.

Graphic frames for election results are created by artists and then stored in a computer. The vote totals are also fed to the computer. With the touch of a few buttons the totals are electronically inserted into the frame and brought up on the video screen. With other computer programs sampling the vote and providing projections, the hopeful candidates get the good or bad news just as they are lowering themselves into their favorite chairs for the election night ritual.

Frame stores and frame manipulators have many uses in television news editing. The frame store is like a huge filing cabinet for visuals of all kinds. Hundreds of video frames can be kept in the memory for instant retrieval.

Thousands more can be stored on videotape or computer disk for retrieval within a few minutes. New frames can be created using camera shots of still pictures or drawings, computer-generated effects, a frame from a videotape, and other switcher-generated effects.

An editor confronted with a story—for instance, about the local or state economic conditions—often needs to combine the video, interviews, and voice-over narration provided by the reporter with graphic material created during the editing process. The videotape shot in the field can provide topical scenes. Then words, phrases, lists, numbers, percentages, or dollar amounts can be added using the character generator (CG) and special effects.

The special effects usually come through a switcher, where a variety of sources of still or moving video can be mixed by keying, splitting the screen into segments, wiping, scrolling, dissolving, or superimposing one video image over another. With the touch of a button, the screen can be cut up into halves, quadrants, or almost any type of segmentation, and different video can be inserted into those segments.

Suppose you want to show the cover of the latest city government report on one side of the screen and a list of the four major points made in the report on the other. The report is set up in front of a studio or graphics camera, and the camera is positioned so that the report fills the left side of the screen. Then the list of four major points is entered into the CG and positioned on the right side of the screen. The CG is also programmed to scroll those four points upward on command. Color can be added behind the scrolled material. Voice-over narration to "read along" with the list has already been laid down on the videotape that will contain this segment of the story. Then the switcher effects are set to split the screen into two halves, so that the camera shot of the report fills the left half and the main points the right half. All video signals are fed to the videotape recorder, and the TV screen will show the report and its major points while the narration gives emphasis to them by repeating them. The graphic can just as easily be programmed to add the points on the screen one at a time as the narration proceeds.

Switchers can also be set up to provide circles and rectangles that are brighter than other portions of the screen. And the more sophisticated ones will make the edges of those circles, ovals, or rectangles hard or soft. Thus, you can "vignette" the edges as a photographic portrait studio would, or highlight a line, sentence, or sentence fragment from a page in a document. Again, the narration might repeat those words as the audience views them.

Then you have the ultimate special effects, devices with names such as Squeeze Zoom™, CBG-2, Chyron 4, ADO, ADDA, Quantel™. These and other electronic effects systems provide the ability to zoom into any part of a video frame and to insert that portion of that frame into any portion of any other video frame.

Sports events producers have made startling use of the Squeeze Zoom™. The pictures of an event's action can be moved to a small portion of the screen with results, averages, and other tabular material added while the action continues. Or an interview with a star player can be inserted while the player continues to perform. Almost any combination of split-screen and frame-insert effects and continuing live action pictures can be created.

But such uses don't have to be limited to live sports coverage. An editor can use this equipment to create all sorts of graphic and video combinations to be edited into videotaped stories.

Keys, Windows, and Pictorial Graphics

Almost all newscasts make use of some kind of on-set graphics. This is another producer responsibility. One familiar graphic is the traditional "window" behind and to either side of the anchors. Sometimes the set contains one window centered so that the anchors can sit on either side of it and it can be seen by the audience to the left or right of whichever anchor is speaking. The effect is called chromakeying. The window is not a window at all. It is a part of the set wall with a frame around it. In that frame is an opaque area painted or lighted green, or blue, or almost any color. When the control room

Figure 4.13. The key window. At WSAZ-TV, Huntington, West Virginia, the anchors report in front of a Chromakey™ window that is isolated at the back of the set. Any video source can be inserted into this window space electronically so that it is combined with the picture of the news anchor, as the air monitor on the left shows. Other set designs incorporate the window into the set wall. *(Courtesy of WSAZ-TV.)*

switcher is set up to use the selected color for the **Chromakey**™, any other video signal can be electronically inserted into the broadcast picture in that space.

It's the electronic equivalent of taking a pair of scissors and cutting out a rectangular hole over the anchor's shoulder and then inserting another picture in that hole.

The additional video signal can come from a number of sources. It can be from a slide projector in the control room. It can be moving video from a tape, or live video from a remote source. Or it can be one frame of video from a frame storer or a computer-generated graphic.

On the air the two video sources—the studio shot of the anchors in their set and the stills, frames, or video keyed into the window area—come together as one picture. To the audience it looks like the keyed material is actually in the window. In the studio all that is seen is the painted or lighted blank wall. Anchors see the combined picture by looking at a monitor placed strategically in their view but not visible to the home viewer.

More elaborate electronics can get rid of the window entirely. Control-

Figure 4.14. The key window. On a news set at KPRC-TV, Houston, Texas, the Chromakey™ window is to the rear of the anchors. Note the laptop computers on the anchors' desk. On election night anchors can access computers at the state and local elections returns offices via modem. Anchors (and viewers) thus can get election returns numbers virtually at the same instant the numbers are released at the county courthouse or state election office. *(Courtesy of KPRC-TV. Photo by John McPherson.)*

room switchers containing these special effects can insert any video signal into the studio picture without the Chromakey™ target.

Although the mechanics of all of this is very much a part of the technical operation, the use of such effects for news is a journalistic decision. The graphics represent an opportunity to provide additional information to the viewer. Thus, the producer makes the decisions whether to use such effects.

Many stations subscribe to special services that provide generic graphics. By generic graphics we mean vertical or horizontal artwork, perhaps including words, that can be used in the window to accompany stories. They are things like slides, stored video frames, drawings, or other artwork that shows flames along with the word *Fire,* or a picture of a "Saturday night special" pistol, with the words *Gun Control* or the word *Crime.* The all-time favorite must be the drawing of a Capitol dome, which is used everywhere to depict "The Government" or "The Legislature." There are map services that sell graphics depicting various news-related areas of the world, like the Middle East, the city of Sarajevo, San Salvador, China, and so on. Network affiliate feeds send graphics packages for stations to insert with their own graphics equipment.

Many stations call on their own art departments to prepare their own generic graphics or specific ones as the need develops. Thus, the producer has at his or her command a file of these graphics which can be called up from slide files, frame storers, or computer-driven graphics generators.

Whatever the source, the producer must think about the proper use of graphics. The important thing to remember is that they present more information on the screen. If they serve as cues for the audience as to what the story is about, or provide details about the exact location of the story, or show the face of the newsmaker in the story, graphics relate to the story in a positive way. If they are inappropriate because they are difficult to figure out, or don't really fit the subject matter of the story, graphics can have a negative impact because they are distracting. The test is whether the graphics add information, help focus the story, and make it easier to understand.

Artwork

Every station has an art department. The graphics specialists who work there create material for commercials, programs, promotions, and news broadcasts. A good graphic artist can be a great aid to an editor looking for ways to illustrate complex stories. Simple line or bar graphs can be created and then shot with a studio, ENG, or graphics camera and then sent to the frame store for insertion into the news. Stations which have sophisticated computer graphic capabilities can do animation onto videotape for editing with voice-over narration or other B-Roll applications.

One of the most exciting innovations in computer graphics has been the development of machines to display the weather. Even an amateur can create animated computer graphics sequences from symbols and maps already stored in the computer's memory. These can then be mixed with weather satellite pictures and other materials to show what the weather has been, is now, and will be. So far, these machines have been used mostly by meteorologists, but there is no reason other applications cannot be made to help illustrate other stories in a newscast.

The Editor's Choice

We started this section with you sitting in front of an editing console ready to do some simple editing. It has ended up with you in a big control room filled with machines that can do all sorts of wonderful things.

Everyone in television news these days is, or should be, visually conscious. After all, we work in a visual medium. The important thing to remember is to use the capabilities of the equipment to provide more information and to do so with clarity. Editors must avoid sensory overload for the viewer. Too many things that blink, wipe, dissolve, scroll, and read all at the same time can lead to confusion. The viewer may be dazzled but may also mumble: "What was *that* all about?" You should keep your visual story simple and make sure that what you are creating adds focus and clarity to what you are trying to communicate.

NONLINEAR EDITING

Over the next few years many newsrooms will be using a new technology called **nonlinear editing** to edit videotape.

The traditional technology, linear or tape editing, requires the editor to move back and forth through a tape cassette (or several cassettes), picking out desired scenes and then copying them to the production tape in the desired order. With tape editing any transitions have to be built in as the parts are assembled.

It is also difficult to make significant changes in linear editing. "Shuttling," moving back and forth, is time-consuming and confusing unless the reporter or producer has had most of the desired tape shot in the order in which it will eventually appear on the air.

With Nonlinear, random-access, digital editing, however, the producer, reporter, or editor determines the order in which the logged material is to be used and then instructs a computer to assemble the final product. The computer does the equivalent of "shuttling," but much faster. Transitions can be added later, and changes are easy to make.

Most nonlinear editing is disk-based. The material shot on tape is logged and transferred to optical or computer disks. In many cases the actual editing is done using a personal computer, rather than using a specialized controller with its distinct operating panel. Current technology permits the editor to see sample frames from the video, and to listen to audio. Since this is not as help-

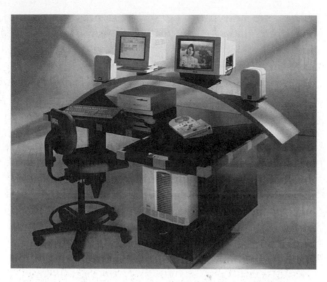

Figure 4.15. VideoCube™, a disk-based digital nonlinear video post-production work station. The work station is an example of an array of new products on the market for computer processing of video and audio using digital nonlinear technology. *(Courtesy of ImMIX Company. Photo by Bill Santos.)*

ful as being able to view all of the video, a careful job of logging the source material is required.

One of the earliest applications of nonlinear editing was in the off-line studios of post-production houses which did editing for commercials and TV programs. The producer would record editing decisions on a computer floppy disk from a regular PC keyboard. The editor assigned to do the actual assembly would insert the computer disk in the editing computer, selecting the needed scenes from videotape loaded in traditional playback machines. The assembly editor would do the finishing touches, such as fades and wipes.

When it became possible to record several minutes of video onto disk-based media through compression, it also became possible for the person making the choice of scenes to record the choices in a computer memory, and then proceed to edit the finished product. The trend has been to play back nonlinear stories from their disk-storage medium, rather than go through the additional and time-consuming step of dubbing the finished product back to tape.

Then there are digital recording units which attach to cameras. The advantage to these is that the audio and video shot in the camcorder does not have to be dubbed (copied) before an editor begins to work on it. The computer disk is simply taken out of the camcorder and loaded into the nonlinear editor.

Computer-based editing of material recorded on a digital disk speeds up one of the most routine, and yet most important jobs in the newsroom: taking the feed of stories from the network (sometimes called the syndication feed). With digital editing technology, stories can be pulled from the feed for use on the air while the digital disk recorder is still recording the feed.

You can see where all this is heading. It is necessary today for anyone in television journalism to be comfortable with a computer.

There are many nonlinear systems available. Each combines hardware and software in a slightly different manner. You simply have to adapt to the system in use in your newsroom.

The Editing Process

Nonlinear editing usually follows these steps:

1. The source material is logged to select the portions to edit. Currently the analog tape has to be converted to digital format by dubbing the tape to a high-speed magnetic disk. Gradually this dubbing step will disappear as more video and audio is recorded on digital medium in the field.

2. Play and edit the material you have "captured" from the disk. This gives you an opportunity to trim transitions between shots to create overlap cuts, or move transitions forward or backward in the story. With the touch of a button, scenes can be captured in any order and moved to any location within the story.

3. If time, equipment and skill permit, graphic effects can be added at this point. These might include dissolves, wipes, or DVEs (digital video effects). Multiple tracks of audio can also be edited. Graphics can be created or imported from another device and "keyed" (as in Chromakey™) over video.

4. There are several output options. A digital cut can be recorded which can be transferred to tape or broadcast directly from the disk or another disk-driven playback device.

Terms

The terms used by developers of nonlinear editing systems may vary. With the permission and cooperation of Avid Technology, Inc.,* here are some terms used in reference to one of the popular nonlinear editing systems:

Media file—the computer creates a *media file* for each track of audio and video dubbed from analog tape. (If you record a video section with two tracks of audio, three separate media files are created.)

---

*The authors express their thanks to Avid Technology, Inc. of Tewksbury, Massachusetts, for permitting access to user guide documents, which in some instances, were paraphrased.

Master clip—This is your material. The clip does not contain the audio or video data, it simply points to the appropriate media files when you request that media files be played. A *master clip* is created for each shot captured.

Subclip—Master clips can be broken into smaller units called *subclips* by marking IN and OUT points and then saving the frames between the marks.

Story—The piece you are editing. You create a *story* by editing clips together. It is possible to create a generic *story* and then create several versions. This allows you to experiment. More important, you can make different versions of your *story* for the 6 o'clock, 11 P.M., and 7 A.M. newscasts. This attribute of computer-based digital editing is tremendously helpful for organizations like the Cable News Network which are constantly re-editing audio and video from stories to fit different time periods and types of programs.

Bin—One manufacturer's name for a *file* where information about master clips, subclips, and stories is kept. This bin file is a database of information about each clip. It contains the name, start time code, end time code, tracks, and can deliver representative frames of the video to your terminal.

The typical nonlinear editing system uses *icons* or symbols to designate certain files and activities. If you have used an Apple™ computer or one of the DOS-based "windows" computer programs you probably have used icons. Many systems use the familiar computer mouse to point to icons. Some computer graphics people use the terms "drag and drop" for the process whereby you point the mouse arrow at an icon and move something to the screen.

Brave New World

Digital audio/video editing is considerably different from the traditional techniques of videotape editing. If you have to move from tape editing to disk editing, the transition may be easier than you think. Any experience you have had with a computer, especially one utilizing Macintosh™ or Microsoft Windows™ software will ease your transition to nonlinear editing. Prior editing experience, no matter what equipment you used, will help if you have learned to know when and where to edit. And, all of the rules of visual continuity, editorial control, sequence development, screen direction, and visual and aural clarity, will still apply.

You will help yourself a great deal if you will try to develop your skill at "visualizing" a story so you aren't bogged down trying to figure out how to use your video and audio. You will also benefit from developing good organizational skills, such as good tape-logging techniques.

Writing: The Leavening Agent

PRINCIPLES

Experienced broadcast news writers refer to various principles that are guides to good radio-TV news writing. Their principles usually include the following ideas:

1. Broadcast news involves a group in a team effort. Therefore a standardized and uniform set of rules for the preparation of copy is a must.

2. Broadcast news lacks permanence. The listener or viewer has no chance to go back over parts of a story not clearly understood. Thus simplicity and ease of understanding are primary news copy requirements.

3. Nearly all the written portions of broadcast news programs are presented orally, that is, the sender speaks the text and the receiver hears it. Thus the writing style approaches ordinary conversation.

This last item, a conversational writing style, is often recommended as the number-one standard of broadcast news writing: "You should write the way people talk."

WRITING WITH WORDS, PICTURES, AND SOUND

A main focus of this chapter is on how to combine good voice-over (V/O) writing and video pictures. The idea is to combine words and pictures into a story in which the words and pictures are purposely created and edited to synchronize with and complement each other.

This kind of writing is challenging. Often other ingredients besides text and pictures are folded into the story mix to make the story more interesting and informative, to give it impact and realism. These may include natural sound, standups, sound bites, graphics, and other visual embellishments.

The focus of this chapter is on the craft of **keying**, making text and visuals mesh. Skill at the fundamentals of broadcast news writing is crucial. And that is where we now turn.

BROADCAST NEWS WRITING: A REVIEW OF THE BASICS

Simplicity—In a Conversational Style

Broadcast news copy should be written with an eye and an ear for simplicity and in a writing style that is conversational. A lot of basic advice is available about these two fundamentals.

1. Write Short, Direct, Simple, Declarative Sentences

The short sentence is the bread-and-butter writing tool for broadcasting. But experienced writers know that news stories consisting entirely of short sentences tend to sound choppy and singsong when read aloud. Conversely, long sentences are not bad just because they are long. Long sentences with dangling phrases, clauses, and attributions make the story difficult to read aloud and difficult to grasp. Here are some examples:

Weaker: For the first time since the spaceship *Challenger* exploded January 28, 1986, killing all seven crew members, electricity surged into the shuttle *Discovery* on Monday as NASA began readying the ship for the first post-Challenger flight, an official said.

Stronger: Space officials at NASA have turned on the electricity in the shuttle *Discovery* for the first time.

Weaker: The civilian unemployment rate was down to a decade low of 16 percent in July, the government said Friday in a report released by the Bureau of Labor Statistics.

Stronger: A government report released today shows the unemployment rate last month at 16 percent, the lowest rate in ten years.

Weaker: The annual Pro Football Hall of Fame Festival in Canton, Ohio—birthplace of the National Football League—will take place July 22–30 and will feature an Air Force band concert and fireworks show, a grand parade expected to attract 200,000 spectators, the Hall of Fame exhibition game, and the induction ceremony itself.

Stronger: The annual Pro Football Hall of Fame Festival begins this Friday evening in Canton, Ohio. An Air Force band concert and fireworks show will start a week of celebrations leading up to the ceremony to enshrine six of yesterday's gridiron heroes.

2. Use the Active Voice

Because of the conversational nature of broadcast news, because of the immediacy of broadcasting, and perhaps especially because of the "personal" dimension of the delivery system, news writers show a preference for the active voice over the passive. As you will recall from your English composition class, in the active voice the subject of the sentence *takes* the action, for example: President Clinton signed the crime bill into law.

In the passive voice, the subject of the sentence *receives* the action, for example: The crime bill was signed into law by President Clinton.

3. Read It Aloud

But remember, we're talking here about *preference*. No newscast is or should be constructed entirely in the active voice, it is only the more basic of the two forms. The true test of the conversational quality of a piece of news copy comes when the text is read aloud. The proof is in the listening. If it *sounds* fine to you, chances are it will sound that way to the listener. Therefore it is very important that you get into the habit of reading your copy *out loud*. Read it aloud as you keyboard it. Try it out. If it sounds stiff when you read it, it will sound worse when the listener tries to understand it.

4. Avoid Abbreviations and Symbols

Abbreviations are rarely used in broadcast news copy; symbols in place of words, almost never. For example:

Weaker: The accident, which occurred at the intersection of So. Jones Ave. and W. Adams Blvd., caused a 90-minute traffic jam-up in the So. Hills area.

Stronger: The accident happened at the intersection of South Jones Avenue and West Adams Boulevard. Traffic was tied up in the South Hills area for about 90 minutes.

Weaker: B & D Coal Co. Pres. James Black says 3rd qtr. profits are going to be 7.5% higher this year as compared to last year's figure.

Stronger: B and D Coal Company third-quarter profits are up. Company President James Black says the increase over last year's third-quarter figure is seven-point-five percent.

Exceptions to the abbreviation rule are *Mr.* and *Mrs.* when used together, *Dr.* for Doctor, and abbreviations that are supposed to be read aloud—F-B-I, T-N-T, C-I-A, U-S-A. Note that these are typed in capital letters and hyphenated. The hyphen tells the anchor person to speak each letter individually. Acronyms, where the first letter of words combined to make a word, are keyboarded in caps without hyphens. Examples: NASA, NATO. They are expressions so familiar that they are easily recognized by all the audience.

5. Use Contractions

Well-placed contractions will help make your story sound more conversational when read aloud by giving it a sense of ease, cadence, and flow. We use contractions freely in our conversation, but not all of them. Some contractions sound awkward, and we rarely speak them because they don't sound right. An example is the contraction *it'll* for *it will*. Contractions brighten everyday conversation. They are to broadcast news copy what seasonings are to food: small amounts in tasteful combinations are great, but use carefully—don't mix anise and sage. Here are some examples:

> **More formal:** Bauer says he is certain he will be a candidate for student body president.

> **Less formal:** Bauer says he's certain he'll be a candidate for student body president.

> **More formal:** The Environmental Protection Agency says it will announce new standards for clean water today.

> **Not improved by contraction:** The Environmental Protection Agency says it'll announce new standards for clean water today.

> **More formal:** Council members say the money is not available.

> **Not improved by contraction:** Council members say the money's not available.

> **More acceptable:** Council members say the money isn't available.

> **A variation:** Next, a vacation idea that definitely is *not* for the timid.

> **Comment:** If you want to emphasize the negative, don't (do *not*) use the contraction.

6. Be Extra Careful with Names

The general rule for names is to notify the audience that the name is coming by putting some alerting words or sentences ahead of it.

People listen to and watch news amid distractions—the kids want in, the dog wants out, and so on—and they are likely to miss the first few words of a story. Until they hear those first few words, they don't even know whether they're going to be interested in the story. Thus writers avoid beginning a report with any crucial information such as a person's name or indeed with any proper noun. This is why we hear an item begin with a statement, which is then followed by its attribution: "A government cost accountant has revealed a plan to overcharge the Pentagon for aircraft parts. Accountant David Jones says . . ." Another writing device to prepare the audience for the story is to write an introductory phrase—in this case, the attribution—ahead of the main point: "Harrisburg police say the body of a missing teenage girl . . ."

Most authorities recommend a person's middle initial be dropped unless very particular identification is needed. A person's age is also frequently left out. When age is used, it comes before the name. Omit the names of obscure persons and places if they are not meaningful to the story.

When you use a name for the first time in a story, use the full name; in subsequent references the last name is enough. A title normally precedes the name, although this is varied for ease of listening; if the title is long and unwieldy, it should be shortened or perhaps written as a separate sentence.

Weaker: Bill Jones, 16, son of Dr. Thomas L. Jones, chemistry department chairman of research and graduate studies, was presented the Governor's Heroism Medal this morning for saving a life while on duty as a guard at the city swimming pool.

Stronger: The son of Chemistry Department Chairman Dr. Thomas Jones—16-year-old Bill Jones—has received the Governor's Heroism Medal for preventing a tragedy at the city swimming pool.

7. Use Phonetics

Words that are difficult to speak aloud—the spelling doesn't indicate how the word is supposed to be spoken—must be given special handling. First, of course, you must learn the correct pronunciation. Then type a phonetic into the script. This should be done each time that word occurs in the text. For example:

Weaker: A teenager seeking to learn the fate of Lebanon's lost Shiite Moslem leader hijacked a Lebanese airliner today.

Stronger: A teenager seeking to learn the fate of Lebanon's lost Shiite (SHEE'-ITE) Moslem leader has hijacked a Lebanese airliner.

If two words in a row need the phonetic, keep these words together in the original and in the phonetic version:

Wrong: The program featured the famous pantomimist Marcel (MAR-SELL') Marceau (MAR-SOH').

Right: The program featured the famous pantomimist Marcel Marceau (MAR-SELL' MAR-SOH').

8. Be Wary of Numbers

Numbers are especially difficult for the viewer to grasp. The general rule is to round off a number unless the exact number is significant. Some helpful rounding terms are:

about

just over (or under)

nearly

slightly more (or less) than

Another technique is to write the number into the text twice, first as an approximation (rounded), then as the exact figure. You would do this where the *exact* figure is important.

Exact figure not vital: The tax increase will raise property owners' tax bills by three percent this year.

Exact figure stronger: The three mill tax increase will cost the owner of a house valued at 75-thousand dollars an extra eight dollars on this year's taxes.

For very large numbers (any number over a thousand), the standard technique is to use a hyphenated combination of figures and spelled-out words, for example, "50-thousand," "six-billion."

Weaker: The legislature has approved an emergency money bill of $3,497,800 for relief work in tornado-stricken . . .

Stronger: The legislature has approved an emergency money bill of just under three-point-five million dollars for tornado-ravaged . . .

NOTE: Numbers like three-point-five are "journalese," invented for the benefit of wire services and newspapers. Viewers would better understand "three and one-half million." However, some TV stations find they need to stick to the wire style (three-point-five) to accommodate the limitations of prompters, whose large letters make it difficult for anchors to read long strings of words or numerals. The prompter may even show three-point-five as "3.5" to save space. Thus, the correct style for numbers becomes a newsroom policy decision, and everyone should be consistent as to the form used.

Weaker: Foreigners last year were granted 31,476 patents, or 46% of all U.S. patents, and Americans got 38,124, or 54% of the total of 70,600 patents issued, U.S. Patent Office officials announced today.

Stronger: The Patent Office reports that last year foreigners received more than 31-thousand U-S patents.

The rest—a little more than 38-thousand, or 54-percent of the total—went to Americans.

Fractions are written as words and hyphenated.

> **Weaker:** The mayor says 3/4 of the money has been spent.

> **Stronger:** The mayor says three-fourths of the money has been spent.

Some newsrooms prefer that numbers from 1 (one) through 12 (twelve) be spelled out, and numbers 13-999 be written as numerals. Thus $878 would be 878-dollars, and $1,300 would be one-thousand-300 dollars, or, 13-hundred dollars.

9. Use Standard Punctuation

Follow traditional punctuation rules for the most part. Here are a few additional things to consider about various punctuation marks.

1. The question mark is rarely used in broadcast news. A news story should answer questions, not pose them.

2. The dash and the ellipsis (a row of three periods) seem okay (either one, but be consistent) where a pause in the delivery is wanted for emphasis or dramatic purpose.

3. The comma can be overused and misused. If you rely on short, declarative sentences as your basic style you won't need a great amount of punctuation. Commas are also warning signs. A single comma in a sentence frequently warns us that we have put the grammatical cart before the horse, as in: "Seeing the need to slow the rate of inflation, the Federal Reserve has ordered an increase in the prime interest rate charged major banks." A better way to write this is: "The Federal Reserve has ordered an increase in the prime interest rate charged major banks in an effort to slow inflation."
   Two commas within a sentence usually indicate the presence of less important supplementary information. For example: "A political opponent has taken Governor Ellen Smith, who is running for reelection, to task for using state aircraft for campaign trips." A better way to write this is: "A political opponent is criticizing Governor Ellen Smith for using state aircraft to make campaign trips. Smith is running for reelection. Her aides say . . ."

10. Spell Correctly

If you're not certain, look it up. Bad spelling invites problems at the microphone. Simplified spellings—*nite, frate, tuff, kwik*—do not work well in broadcasting. Avoid them.

11. Direct Quotes Need Special Handling

The scripting of a direct quotation is another sticky area for the writer. Experts generally agree that the direct quotation should be short—a few words, a line at most—and right to the news point. The words quote and unquote are used rarely, and then only when it is crucial for the audience to hear the exact words spoken—the words amounting to an extra precaution. In broadcast news the best direct quote is a good sound bite.

TV NEWS WRITING—A COMBINATION OF SKILLS

Use All the Tools

Television news writing is more than words. It is a mixture of words and sounds, voices, faces, scenes, lighting, background, color, motion, editing, combining, mixing, sequencing, and producing. Bob Dotson, NBC News:

> If you show me a good television writer, I'll show you a guy or a girl who is also a good television director, who is also a good television producer, who is also a passable lighting person, who also knows something about audio. We have to tell these stories with all the tools we have.

Former CBS-TV News President Fred Friendly making just about the same points:

> We are all writers: the editor . . . the guy who writes the copy, who plans the broadcast, they are all writers. Writing is really only the final act of what people do . . . If you do your work well, most of the writing is done by the people in the program—and by the sequence of scenes.

With that concept in mind, that "writing" for television news is a complex combination of jobs—gathering the facts, choosing the story focus, selecting visual material and words, and putting it all together into a package that is going to go into a program with other stories in a planned arrangement—let's look to some of the researchers to see what they have found out about the better ways to proceed.

WHAT RESEARCHERS SAY

John Robinson and Mark Levy of the University of Maryland published a book that focuses on the research that has been done about television news in the

United States and other countries.* Their book summarized the theories and findings of mass-communication scholars from a variety of fields and reported on their own research into how much people understand of what they see on television news. They challenged a lot of propositions, suppositions, myths, and warmly held beliefs. Among these myths are:

1. Television news programs are the main source of news for a majority of people.

2. Because that is true and a lot of research shows people remember only one-quarter to one-third of what they watch on television news, the world is in terrible shape.

3. Journalists know best when it comes to selecting what is news and preparing it for broadcast.

Robinson and Levy said that a lot of the data alleging that myth one is true come from asking the wrong questions in the wrong way. Myth two is in question, they said, because it calls for human perceptions—which are often misleading and distorted. Myth three fails, they said, when those journalists fail to take enough account of how people receive and process information from television.

These researchers said that if television news is not the main source of people's information and is not as influential as some say, it could be if journalists would make the news as understandable as they can. Because television news is transitory, quick, and a mass of complex aural and visual messages, they said, the final test is not how much information is acquired, but how much of it is understood.

One Day's News—One Week's News

Robinson and Levy asked real viewers about real newscasts they had watched in normal (in-home) viewing situations in the United States and Great Britain. They asked people what they could remember from newscasts they had just watched (recalled) and then asked them what the main point or gist of the stories was (understood).

One study covered a week of network newscasts. The results agreed with other studies that have shown low recall. But since they probed more deeply, the Robinson-Levy data showed higher numbers. About 62 percent of the viewers remembered something about the stories, but less than half of the week's most important news was understood by those viewers.

In another study of one day's network newscasts, about one-third of the

*John P. Robinson and Mark R. Levy, with Dennis K. Davis, *The Main Source: Learning from Television News* (Beverly Hills, Calif.: Sage Publications, 1986).

viewers in the United States and Great Britain understood the stories in that day's news.

Those results clearly show that there is a serious problem in getting the news to the viewers. There are a number of factors that Robinson and Levy believe do help recall and understanding.

1. Prior knowledge. People who had previous information about the stories, either about the stories themselves or about the area or issue the story focused on, did better on recall and understanding.

2. Education level. Better-educated people also did better. Better-educated people also read more (and more serious) newspapers, listened to more informational radio, and felt they were better able to understand TV newscasts in general.

3. Attention. Those who paid close attention got more out of the newscasts. (But only one-third of the American viewers said they were able to watch without being interrupted.)

Content and Structure

W. Gill Woodall, professor of speech communications at the University of New Mexico, summarized experimental and observational research and related it to the journalistic guidelines we often use to structure news content.* Woodall pointed to studies from Sweden that showed that the five W's and H so dear to us (Who, What, Where, When, Why, and How) may not work as well for television as we think they do. First, he said they are not equally important, and not all stories include all these "criteria." Second, he said that the "why angle" is the one most often left out, and it is the one that increases comprehension the most.

Woodall said that repetition and redundancy help people remember and understand. If the pictures and sound material in a story repeats and backs up person (who) and place (where) elements, viewers will remember those elements better.

But these researchers also said it is the cause-and-effect element (why) that helps the most in understanding. Woodall agreed that this creates a problem for journalists, since the why angle of stories is often the most difficult to determine, and speculation on why could hurt journalistic credibility and objectivity, especially if the speculation turns out to be wrong. Yet cause-and-effect elements are so important that we need to make every effort to get them into our stories.

*Robinson and Levy, pp. 133–158.

Words

How about vocabulary? Over and over again researchers have found that we need to be more sensitive to the fact that we, as journalists, know a lot more about the news than the viewers do. And we are verbal chameleons: We pick up and use the technical terms and the vocabulary of experts. Such expressions as "bilateral agreement," "leading economic indicators," and "economic embargoes" get into scripts and roll off the tongue with great ease. Sound bites from experts are filled with similar terms. Few viewers understand them, and researchers urge us to explain them or use alternative language that helps the viewer comprehend.

Pictures

How about the visual material? Experiments reveal three factors that most help people understand visual material. Woodall said they are:

1. Vividness: compels attention and starts powerful mental images to work on understanding.

2. Concreteness: provides details and specifics about people and what happened.

3. Linking: the connection between the visual information and news content.

Robinson and Dennis Davis, a professor of speech communication at Southern Illinois University, said that further analysis of the British and American TV newscast surveys showed that vivid and concrete pictures that were loosely linked to story content hurt comprehension, but that vivid, concrete pictures that were tightly linked to story content helped people retain and understand the news.* This was especially true when those links dealt with cause-and-effect elements.

A warning about "vivid": Some evidence indicates that pictures that are too vivid actually hurt comprehension, apparently because they create such strong mental images at the time they are seen—and drive everything else from the viewer's mind. But they may be remembered for a long time.

Story Types and Newscast Structure

What does the research tell us about what kinds of stories people understand best and the effects of where they are placed in the newscast?

Robinson and Davis said that the first stories and the last stories were

*Robinson and Levy, pp. 196–197.

usually well understood. But lead stories that contain a lot of extraneous and unrelated angles, words, pictures, and graphics could be poorly comprehended. Closing stories were always understood better, perhaps because they are often quite visual and high in human interest elements. Good comprehension of stories in the middle of the newscasts seemed to be connected to how much personal relevance the stories had—oil and gasoline prices, a truck drivers' strike that blocked major roads, and changes in national health insurance policies, for example. Or the audience understood and remembered stories better if they contained famous individuals doing something unique—the pope in Poland—or were about unique situations such as a plane crash.

Here are a couple of lists of helpful and less-helpful story characteristics that may hold some surprises for journalists and their news judgment traditions.

Helped Understanding

1. Length: longer stories are always understood better—includes stories with longer anchor on-camera time.

2. Human interest.

3. Personalization.

4. Excitement.

5. Unusual story structure.

6. Surprise: a large number of unusual elements.

(While research may point in the direction of longer stories led by longer anchor on-camera time, there is a segment of the industry that prefers the opposite approach. This segment favors short on-camera time for anchors and brief items with a number of rapidly-paced scenes.)

Not so Helpful to Understanding

1. Conflict.

2. Proximity.

3. Relevance of the story to society.

4. Relationship to viewer's own group or culture.

5. Prominence.

Notice some of those words, such as *conflict, proximity,* and *prominence.* A lot of research remains to be done—and the researchers emphasize that all the time—but it may be that some of our most strongly held beliefs are not as potent as we think.

And a note about grouping stories: Producers often group stories about similar topics, or the same topic in different locales, within the same program segments.

The Woodall report referred to findings of Barrie Gunter in a series of British experimental studies that concern what the researchers call "pro-active interference."* That is: When viewers see and hear a series of stories that contain many of the same elements, they may have trouble remembering most of the stories after the first one. So grouping a series of stories under some generic theme such as "Local Crime Today" may result in a blur of stories and a real chance the audience will transpose the details from one story to another.

Gunter said a way to prevent this is to use production techniques: changing the format from tape with V/O for one story to anchor on-camera narration for another similar story or including other aural and visual elements that make it clear to the viewer where the story is going.

Gunter's research suggests that the audience may have a hard time following stories that are grouped together, and that such visual crutches as file tape and generic graphics may confuse more than they illuminate.

How Can We Help?

Levy, Davis, and Robinson recommended that journalists work harder at anticipating future events and prepare to explain them better. It might be a good idea, they said, to try to find out how much prior knowledge people have about future subject "x" and begin to build a common body of knowledge about it.

They recommended that we stop assuming the audience knows as much as we do about the news. They complained that journalists are too much concerned with the latest details and not concerned enough with the background. Updating is fine, but if the audience has little prior knowledge, you can't update a vacuum.

Specifically they recommended:

✔ 1. More repetition and redundancy. But they don't mean just repeating things. They mean that every story should be organized around a main point, that the story should build up to the main point, and that all elements should contribute to the main point and its various implications.

✔ 2. Emphasize why the story is important.

✔ 3. "Slow down" the news with tighter, better-structured reporting and more demanding and reflective writing. Highlight the historical context as well as the latest angles.

*Robinson and Levy, pp. 221–228.

✔ 4. Be explicit; don't expect the audience to get hidden, implicit messages.

✔ 5. Separate similar stories from one another. Avoid having the stories melt together.

✔ 6. Make extensive use of graphics to handle statistics and other quantitative information.

✔ 7. Tell the story in human terms whenever possible.

✔ 8. Explain technical or specialized terms. Avoid jargon.

Robinson and Levy's report and recommendations offer a good example of a scholarly approach to the problem of how to improve the way we communicate news stories. Often they've "got data to prove it." And we need all the help we can get.

TV NEWS COPY: THE MECHANICS

A page of television news script is typed in what is called the "split-page" format (Figure 5-1). (We refer here to typing on paper to help you visualize what the copy looks like. Most TV news copy is keyboarded on a computer terminal. After editing, it is transferred to the prompter's memory, and backup paper copy is printed.) The two kinds of information in the script are (1) video and audio cues and (2) words to be read aloud.

The video-audio descriptions (cues) are located in the space to the left and the material to be read aloud (text) is typically located on the right, which splits the page vertically. There is no one standard way to divide the page into right side and left side. At some stations the dividing line is exactly in the middle; in others the text is typed across nearly the whole page, and cues are squeezed down the left margin, or the text is squeezed down the right third of the page. In some newsrooms all cues are printed in caps and all text in "down style" (upper and lower case). In other newsrooms this is reversed. You should follow the format your organization is using. The important thing is to be consistent.

Because the production of a television newscast requires so many people and such a high degree of coordination among them, multiple copies of the script are necessary.

TV News Copy: Adapting It to Video

Because the words and the pictures must work together to tell the story, writing text for a voice-over requires that the writer have not only a solid grasp of the fundamentals of television news writing but also a solid understanding of how a picture story is put together, the role of narration, and how the picture, word, and sound portions of a story depend on each other. The work of the

```
                                    (GENE)

                                    FORMER GOVERNOR, NOW
                                    SENATE CANDIDATE, DOUG
                                    WILDER IS JOINING FORCES
                                    WITH THE CITY OF RICHMOND
                                    WHEN IT COMES TO FIGHTING
                                    CRIME . . .

ROLL BETA VO                        WILDER MET WITH
##TODAY                             RICHMOND MAYOR LEONIDAS
##RICHMOND                          YOUNG TODAY TO SPEAK OUT
                                    IN FAVOR OF THE CITY'S
                                    CRIME PLAN THAT WILL BE
                                    ANNOUNCED TONIGHT . . .

                                    WILDER SAYS THE CITY
                                    NEEDS TO WORK WITH
                                    BOTH STATE AND FEDERAL
                                    OFFICIALS IN ORDER TO GET
                                    ALL AVAILABLE HELP TO
                                    COMBAT VIOLENT
                                    CRIMINALS . . .
                                    - - - - - - - - - - - - - - - - - -
(4:5Ø:31)                           "i do applaud the
##DOUGLAS WILDER                    efforts of the city
##SENATE CANDIDATE                  programs in terms of
                                    making sure we combat
                                    violent crime."
                                    - - - - - - - - - - - - - - - - - -
                                    WILDER SPOKE NOT
                                    ONLY OF TOUGHER ACTION
                                    AGAINST CRIMINALS BUT ALSO
                                    OF PREVENTION PROGRAMS
                                    THAT NEED ATTENTION . . .

                                    WITHOUT REACHING THE
                                    YOUNGER GENERATION, WILDER
                                    SAYS, THE PROBLEM WILL GO
                                    UNSOLVED. . .
```

Figure 5.1. A page of script from a WWBT, Richmond, Virginia, newscast. It is organized in the so-called "split-page" format. Text to be read aloud appears on the right side of the page. Most production and other identifying information is on the left. Production cues— for the insertion of graphics, roll cues for videotapes, etc.—are located opposite the same line in the text where the production is to take place. *(Courtesy of WWBT.)*

writer and the videotape editor must be coordinated so that the visual and aural ingredients are unified and fitted together to become the complete story.

Which Comes First?

This brings us to another question: Should the pictures be edited first and then the narration written to fit? Or should the text be written first and then the pictures edited to fit?

One stock answer is that television is a visual medium, and therefore the word is subordinate to the picture. Furthermore, you have all the words of the English language at your disposal, but only a limited number of videotape shots to work with. By that theory and reasoning at least, the visual part should be edited first to tell the story visually. Then the text can be written to coordinate with and complement the picture part, to add details needed to understand the pictures, to round out and finish off the story. As you might have guessed, the answer is not that simple, and there are other, contrasting views to consider.

Recall the discussion of the idea of structure in Chapter 3. A news story requires structure. Television is not just a visual medium; it is a *narrative* medium. And in any narrative, words provide structure for the story. NBC's Bob Dotson on the question:

> This is not the classic argument between "Is it the reporter who is more important, or should the pictures tell the story?" The point is that everything is of equal importance going into an assignment.
>
> If you have tremendous pictures . . . well of course you don't put any copy in there. But on some other stories the copy may become more important.
>
> So it's more than just that classic argument, "Which is more important?" The point is that the reporters and the camera people in the field ought to be aware of all the tools and not just rely on this wonderful technology we have back in the studio to flip-flop scenes when we get the wrong screen direction—if you worry about screen direction at all—and all the things that technology has been able to backstop us with.

So another view is that the answer to the "edit or write first?" question depends on variables of each story: What is the main news in this item, what pictures do I have, what natural sounds do I have, what facts do I have—even the very practical variable, how much time do I have to finish the story? Those who take this approach seem to be saying: Whichever way you do it, have a reason for your choice.

Voice-Over

As you get down to the business of starting a text for a V/O story, you will need two sets of facts: (1) facts about the news event, the five Ws and H of conventional on-camera news reports; and (2) facts about the edited version of the video part of the story. Armed with this information, you are ready to begin the task.

Story Facts

Television news writers sometimes refer to the facts related to the news event—all the facts that they have—as the **dope sheet** or "poop sheet." The dope sheet consists of information about the event and can include such things as the reporter's notes from direct observation, notes on interviews with eyewitnesses or participants or others at the scene, newspaper clips, magazine articles, background research culled from reference works and computer data bases, a printed program, a public relations handout, faxes, or packages of information—just about anything that will shed light on the story.

Visual Facts

As for the facts describing the video material, the profession has no accepted uniform or standard set of terms to describe the various elements of the video. Nevertheless you will need a shorthand description of each scene of the picture story and its running time in seconds. In order for us to consider this further, however, some agreement on terms is essential.

The smallest visual unit of videotape is called a frame. A series of frames with the same content makes up a **scene**, or variously a **shot**, or **take**. Let's stick with *shot*.

When a videotape recorded at a news event is ready for editing into a story, the first thing that happens is that someone, perhaps the writer, reporter, or video editor, logs each shot, as discussed in Chapter 4. Now sometimes in the real world no log is made; shots are screened and so forth, but nobody actually makes a log. Why? For one thing, logging can be tedious. And a bother. (Nobody ever said television news was easy, or lacking in tedium.) But skipping the step of logging can be a mistake, perhaps a big mistake. Bob Dotson again:

> I really don't ever write the final draft until I have personally logged every shot. And I do a double log. And you can do this sometimes on a general news story. It doesn't take that much longer. Try doing this sometime: You log your shots. You also log your natural sound. So that when you get to the writing side of it, and you say, "Well, I've got to say this, because this is an important part of the story." Then, you suddenly realize that, "Hey, Joe Blow already said that."
>
> For not just the sound bites but the natural sound, you know there was back here a cat crying, and at the point where the cat is important, why don't I just let the cat cry instead of me saying, "A cat cried tonight"?
>
> So if you do a dual log—I'm talking general news, obviously on spot

news you don't have time for this—if you do this dual-logging system, it's a lot easier to write, because you do know what you've got hidden there. Sometimes things will pass through that you weren't aware of because you were busy getting information, or writing, or whatever when you were on location.

Okay, so you do your log. You've got to know what the video contains. Using the log, the videotape editor, the writer, or the reporter may now decide how much of which shots will go into the edited version of the visual side of the story and in what order. In making the edited version, the editor might rearrange the sequence of the shots, shorten their running time, break a shot into shorter segments and intersperse these among other shots, and use other editing techniques to turn the raw videotape into an edited story. One with continuity (flow), we hope.

Now we need another term, this one to describe an edited segment. Remember, we're calling unedited segments *shots*. We'll call an edited segment a **scene**. If a log is compiled by listing in sequence the content and running time of each shot on the unedited tape, then a scene list is a listing, in sequence, of the content and running time of each scene in the edited version. Some newsrooms refer to these scene lists as "cut sheets." Armed with the cut sheet and the dope sheet, you are now ready to write the V/O text.

Writing voice-over narration—text to go with motion pictures—has a certain element of precision about it. The running time of the picture story clearly limits the number of words that can be fitted into that time, and what the pictures show (content) and the order in which they show it (sequence) clearly force a parallel development of the accompanying text. Bob Dotson again:

> I walk into a story, and I do it the same way every time. I do the "fly-on-the-wall," you know, do the "Columbo," I just kinda sit around and eavesdrop on the situation.
>
> And then I start thinking of it in terms of building blocks. Where is the camera? Where is the sound? What have I got to say?
>
> I write constantly. I don't take notes; I write constantly. I try to write what I call "the corners of the picture," things that I know the camera can't show, things that people tell me that aren't in the sound. I'm constantly writing it down.

Word-Picture Match

A very basic need in this kind of writing is to make the words and the pictures work together to tell the story. For example, suppose the story is about local reaction to a new drug-paraphernalia law passed by the state legislature. The scene shows a store countertop with items on display—packages of cigarette wrapping papers, snuff boxes, and so forth. It might start like this:

VIDEO	AUDIO
Merchandise 7 secs.	Customers find in these shops all sorts of merchandise related to the use of drugs—from cigarette wrapper papers to snuff boxes.

The writing here is backward—sometimes called "cross-scripting"—a text that is not well linked with the visual. The words and the pictures are not working together. The audience is looking at "merchandise," but the text is talking about "customers." Clearly the pictures cannot be changed (unless shots of customers are available), but the matter can be resolved rather easily by recasting the sentence so that merchandise is the subject of the sentence. You could change the sentence to read:

VIDEO	AUDIO
Merchandise 7 secs.	All sorts of merchandise related to the use of drugs—from cigarette-wrapper papers to snuff boxes—is for sale in these shops.

Getting the words and the pictures in sync takes time and thought, and a lot of practice, until you get a feel for the techniques involved. Remember the advice earlier in this chapter about reading your script aloud as you write it? Now we have a new problem—writing, reading the script aloud, *and* keeping one eye on the pictures that will go with the words. Of course, where the pictures are compelling, keep the writing out of their way; where the pictures do not give their own meaning, then the writing must play an entirely different role.

Keying: Keys to Word-Picture Fit

Writing to the Picture

If you write a text that is directly related to what is being looked at while the text is being listened to, you are using a technique called "writing to the picture," or **direct narrative**. This is what you do when you write text so that the name of a person in the story comes up in the narration just slightly ahead of or at about the same time that face of that person appears on the screen. This technique is also called "keying." An accomplished writer can deftly weave details into the narration in such a way that at key points all along the story the scenes being looked at and the words being listened to match and mesh with each other perfectly.

```
                              CUT SHEET

BANK ROBBERY
Scene                                      Scene Time/Cumulative Time
```

Scene	Scene Time/Cumulative Time
MS, Exterior of bank	:04/:04
MS, Money on bank lobby floor	:06/:10
MCU, Money on floor	:04/:14
CU, Hand holding $50 bill	:04/:18
MS, Police talking to Mrs. Louis	:04/:22
MCU, FBI taking fingerprints	:05/:27
MS, Police talking to newsmen	:04/:31
MCU, FBI questioning Hayes	:06/:37
MS, Police examining holdup car	:07/:44

Take, for example, some standard videotape coverage of a story of a branch bank robbery. The robbery is routine except for one thing. The robber was so nervous he dropped part of the loot on the floor of the bank lobby as he was leaving, and a customer in the bank ran after him to tell him about his loss. The pictures show a crowd of people standing around looking at the money on the floor and closeups of the money. Later there is an interview with the "good Samaritan" who tried to be helpful.

In editing the tape, those pictures of the money and the interview with the "good Samaritan" are included. The pictures of the money, in fact, are scenes 2, 3, and 4 in the cut version. Therefore, the writer has to figure out how to explain why the money is on the floor and the significance of those scenes as they are viewed. Obviously, those scenes and the explanation should come before the interview. This structuring of the visual part of the story is logical and dictates the way the story is written even before the first word goes on paper.

Writing away from the Picture

If, on the other hand, your text covers aspects of the story that cannot be shown, your text at those points is said to be written "away from the picture." Another term for this approach is **indirect narrative**.

While the pictures are unfolding the visual part of the story, the text may be covering *why* the event happened, or *how,* or it may give perspective by telling how what is being looked at relates to what can't be shown. For example, a story showing the president visiting a poor family that does not have health care insurance may relate more to the unpopularity in Congress of the president's health care proposals than it does to the visit itself. So while the pictures are showing one aspect of this political fact, the text is adding context. In another example, pictures show rescuers in icy lake water pulling a child out. Narration adds facts that the pictures cannot show, for example, the temperature of the freezing water, how long the boy was in the water, and so on.

The skillful writer may use this in-and-out (direct and indirect) weaving pattern, synchronizing the narration to the pictures at some points and adding background and additional nonvisualized facts at others. In other words, the text is written to complement the pictures, to flesh them out, fill in blank spots, to give added meaning, context, understanding, clarity—writing the corners of the pictures, as Dotson says. Of course in any one of these examples you may have good reason for deciding to write the text first. You would then go back over the log to pick out the shots that best illustrate or illuminate the text, and match the video to the words.

Avoid Visual Reference

It is important to link the text and the pictures firmly at those points where words are needed to explain to the viewer what's going on. But there are weaker and stronger ways to firm up the linkage. Keep in mind that while you want the words and pictures to go together, you also want the text to be independent of the pictures, or as it is sometimes put, you do not want to *stop* the pictures with the words. The text should not duplicate the picture by telling viewers what they can plainly see. Also the text should avoid direct visual reference. Expressions such as, "The president, *seen here getting out of his car . . .*" or "*. . . seen here driving off the number one tee . . .*" are usually unnecessary and are considered unprofessional and amateurish. The same holds true for the expressions "As you can see," "Shown here on the left," and similar visual references.

However, remember the phrase, "Apply the rules thoughtfully and carefully." A picture shows two men handcuffed together, walking toward the camera on the sidewalk outside the Criminal Court Building, both dressed similarly. Nothing stands out there, but the story is that the detective is returning a convicted murderer to his jail cell. Direct reference to which person—"the one on the right (or left)"—is the detective, and which is the criminal, is not only permissible, it is *mandatory*.

Timing

Beginners in the art of voice-over text writing have no clear notion of how much text will "fit" a given scene in the scene count. Here is a formula that has proved helpful and allows the beginner to gain some "feel" for the quantities involved:

Guideline: Three Words Maximum Per Running Second of Video

Counting words is tedious, however, so there are script formats that provide other guidelines: On paper, with the split-page space for text and cues evenly divided, and a standard pica typeface, a thirty-five-character line of copy will take about two seconds to read, a forty-five-character line about three seconds to read. Thus in a five-second scene, a writer will have about two and one-half lines of script space, or about fifteen words to "fit" the narration to the scene. Ten seconds of picture will use up five lines, or thirty words, and so on. Line count is a less exact way of estimating text length, but is much quicker. On the computer, most computer scripting software includes timing indicators in the screen margins or borders.

Script formulas are merely starting points and must be adjusted for a variety of individual variables, for example how rapidly or slowly an individual anchor reads, or whether the story pace is quick or slow. If line counting is being used, variables such as line length and the size of the typeface come into play.

Overwriting

The single most frequently occurring weakness in beginner-written voice-over scripts is overwriting. The problem is not only that the text spills over the running time of the video, but also that the viewer drowns in the words and isn't given a chance to correlate the pictures and words into one unified entity. Keep in mind that the pictures are giving visual information, and the text is filling in the gaps, providing information needed to better understand what the pictures are showing. This is a case where watching is primary, listening secondary. Similarly if the report contained "natural sound" (the background or ambient sound at the news event) that was compelling, natural sound could be primary and text secondary at key points in the story. At those points any words would get in the way, and you would need to "write silence" into the script (no words, just letting the pictures and sound tell the story).

Careful Pencil Editing

Voice-over writing technique calls for economy of words and compression of style. A handy trick students have found useful in helping them achieve leaner voice-over text is to write the first draft of their script to just about the exact count of the videotape running time. Thus if the video runs 60 seconds, the text will run to 180 words; for 90 seconds of video it would be 270 words, and so forth. After drafting the text, the trick then is to edit (remove) about 10 percent of the words. For example, in a 180-word text draft, you should cut 15 to 20 words; in a 270-word text, 25 to 30 words, and so forth. Many students are amazed to discover that this can be done with no damage to the content, clarity, or meaning of the text. Often such editing actually improves clarity by getting some of the wordiness out without taking away any significant information.

Another adjustment to the formula may be needed because of the mood of the news event itself. Some stories are exciting, happy, fast moving. Others are languid, soft, slow. Still others are sad, emotional, shocking. Each requires a different approach in writing narrative for it and in each case, the formula must be adjusted to fit the mood.

Voice-Over with Sound Bites

A special writing problem is created when the voice-over story also includes an actuality or sound bite, a sound-on-tape statement from a news maker. The scenes will have been edited to build up to that point in the story, and so will your text. The word-count or line-count formula should help you avoid having too few words—**underleading** (or *undercutting*) the sound or too many words—**overleading** (or *upcutting*) the sound.

On the air you can recognize underleading when the narrator reads the text right up to the end of the lead-in line, right to the sound bite, and then you hear an awkward silence while the narrator (and the audience) waits for the last part of the scene to run up to where the sound bite begins. Overleading, just the opposite problem, results when the final words of lead-in text spoken by the narrator override the first words of the sound bite.

Each of these problems is easily avoided, but you do have to take care to count accurately. For example, if the visual material for voice-over narration is 20 seconds long, at which point the sound bite begins, the voice-over text should be a maximum of 60 words (the 3-words-per-second formula) and then pencil-edited to adjust, probably by removing five words or so (10 percent of the copy) to allow breathing room. An out-loud rehearsal allows the anchor to get the feel of the copy, and final adjustments can be edited then.

A variation on this kind of voice-over report is the story with a V/O introduction, a sound bite, and a V/O tag. Figure 5-2 is an example.

The anchor reads the story lead, the first 12 seconds, on camera. Then the story visual cuts to silent videotape while 12 seconds of narration is delivered "voice over." An "upper thirds super" is shown during this portion of the story. Then comes a 32-second sound-on-tape bite, and during this portion of the story, the name of the person talking is supered over her image. At the end of the sound bite, silent video scenes continue and the anchor reads the 7-second tag.

To script this story the writer wrote a 12-second on-camera lead (36 wds.); then another 12-seconds (34 wds.) of text voice-over to lead into the sound bite; then a story-ending 7-seconds (20 words) of voice-over text.

The scripting problem here was to have the right amount of copy fitted to the silent videotape leading into the sound bite, and the right amount of copy to go with the silent videotape coming out of the sound bite. Those were the mechanics of the writing.

As to content, the writer was striving to create not only the right amount of text but also an informative lead, a lead-in tied to the content of the sound bite, and a suitable story close.

Slug: FGH Preview   TOMORROW MORNING, NEGOTIATIONS
Date: 10-21   WILL GET UNDERWAY ONCE AGAIN IN
Writer: Hertrick   THE FAIRMONT GENERAL HOSPITAL
                                                     STRIKE. SINCE THE STRIKE BEGAN
                                                     AUGUST 31ST, THE HOSPITAL HAS HIRED
                                                     82 REPLACEMENTS FOR STRIKING
                                                     NURSES.
                                                     THOSE REPLACEMENTS HAVE BEEN
                                                     PROMISED PERMANENT EMPLOYMENT.
vo/sot/vo tag. . . . . .BUT LOCAL 11-99 SAYS THE
:00 Upper/Fairmont   REPLACEMENT ISSUE IS THE KEY
                                                     STUMBLING BLOCK TO RESOLVING THE
                                                     STRIKE.
                                                     THE UNION SAYS THE HOSPITAL MUST
                                                     AGREE TO KEEP ALL STRIKERS BEFORE
                                                     AN AGREEMENT CAN BE REACHED.

                    sot. . . . .

                                                     _____

:16   super/Vickie Tennant
                    cue/". . .problem with that."   :32

                                                     _____

v/o tag   HOSPITAL ADMINISTRATOR ROBERT
                                                     PTOMEY SAYS HE HOPES ALL ISSUES
                                                     AND CONCERNS OF THE UNION WILL BE
                                                     RAISED DURING TALKS TOMORROW.

total rt/1:05

Figure 5.2. A page of script from a WBOY-TV, Clarksburg, West Virginia, newscast. The television news industry does not follow and has not developed one standard form or format for organizing a news story script. Some script abbreviations are standard—SOT for sound-on-tape, V/O for voice-over, etc.—but scripts vary from station to station. *(Courtesy of WBOY-TV.)*

Lead-Ins

An important problem concerns the *content* of the text and especially the lead-in to the sound bite, the sentence that introduces the news maker's statement. First of all, the news maker's statement is an important part of the story because it gives the audience not only the content of what the speaker said, using his or her own words, but also the richness and dramatic effect of the speaker's speech, tone of voice, facial expression, perhaps gesture, and all the other things that combine to convey the meaning of the words spoken. An actuality incorporated skillfully into an ENG field report is an example of using the unique tools of television news to their fullest.

Your challenge in working up this report is to capitalize on this unique opportunity with introductory words that focus audience attention on the speaker and on what he or she had to say. You want your text and sound bite lead-in to be better than merely "good."

A key to "great" is to know exactly what the speaker said in the sound bite. Armed with this knowledge, you are ready to create a text and a lead-in to the actuality that highlight this element of the story, to guide audience attention toward the speaker and the speaker's message, thereby making the meaning of the story clearer to the audience.

The lead-in to the sound bite should establish clearly who is speaking, and it should set up the content of the sound bite. Your text might establish the significance of the news maker's statement or the effect it is likely to have, or your lead-in might paraphrase that content. Often the text before the lead-in to a sound bite will explain where and under what circumstances the statement was made. The important thing is to make clear (1) who this person is, (2) the context in which his or her statement was made, and (3) the point of the statement.

The Echo Effect

Watch out for the **echo effect**, also called **parroting**, in which the text lead-in uses the respondent's exact words. For example, the story may be about a judge's ruling in a custody case.

Weaker:

```
(Text Lead-In)          The judge said this case was
                        unusual and that therefore he would
                        take exceptional cautions for the
                        children's safety.

SOT Sound In—Cue:       "This court will take exceptional
                        cautions for the children's
                        safety . . ."
```

The combination of the narrated lead-in followed by sound bite having the exact wording of key words in the judge's comments on the tape illustrates the echo effect. Do not use the speaker's exact key words in the text lead-in.

Stronger:

```
(Text Lead-In)          The judge said the main thing he
                        wanted to do in this case was to
                        protect the children.
```

```
SOT Sound In—Cue:        "This court will take exceptional
                         cautions for the children's
                         safety . . ."
```

Reinforce the Sound Bite Content

Whatever your script for the text lead-in, check that the text refers to the issue the news maker is discussing. Make sure you understand the sound bite and then paraphrase, summarize, outline, digest, and condense, as long as your lead-in avoids the exact words of the sound bite.

Be Specific

A specific lead-in is better than a vague one:

Weaker:

```
(Text Lead-In)           When asked what he thought about
                         the president's reinstatement of
                         registration for the draft, Herrick
                         had this to say:

SOT Sound In—Cue:        "It's probably the worst
                         decision . . ."
```

Stronger:

```
(Text Lead-In)           Herrick was especially critical of
                         the president's decision to once
                         again require 18-year-olds to
                         register for the draft:

SOT Sound In—Cue:        "It's probably the worst
                         decision . . ."
```

The first lead-in is weak because it is wordy and doesn't give a hint as to what Herrick said in the sound bite. It stops the story's information flow, stops the forward movement of the story in its tracks. The second example not only avoids the awkward and wordy text ("When asked" and "had this to say," both of which state the obvious), but also reinforces Herrick's statement by alerting the viewer to the thrust of what he said.

Here are other examples:

Weaker:

```
(Text Lead-In)           Defensive end Delbert Fowler has
                         played under both coaches. And
                         Fowler talked about some of the
```

	changes the new coach has begun to make.
SOT Sound In—Cue:	"Now, you'd better be on time or you're in trouble . . ."

Stronger:

(Text Lead-In)	Defensive end Delbert Fowler has played under both coaches. Fowler says a big difference is the discipline.
SOT Sound In—Cue:	"Now, you'd better be on time or you're in trouble . . ."

Weaker:

(Text Lead-In)	Wilson told W-X-X-X News about the main idea behind the Jaycees:
SOT Sound In—Cue:	"The whole purpose of this thing is, we want the members to . . ."

Stronger:

(Text Lead-In)	Wilson says the focus of the Jaycees is to promote the self-development of its members:
SOT Sound In—Cue:	"The whole purpose of this thing is . . ."

So construct lead-ins with the content of the sound bite in mind and with a goal of helping the audience understand the news maker's statement by reinforcing it in the lead-in.

In today's television news, the function of the news anchor is often one of introducing the story covered by the reporter. The text the anchor reads to introduce the reporter/story is called an **anchor lead**. (Anchor leads are discussed in Chapter 6, p. 221.) Frequently, the anchor lead text is written by the field reporter who covered the story. From that point on, the entire story, including the lead and story introduction, the voice-over narration, and other story elements (on-the-scene interviews, standuppers, transitions, closer) is recorded in one complete **package** onto the "air" videotape.

For example, the reporter and crew may go to the scene of a news event and begin the coverage in what might be called the "normal" way, with the videographer gathering the visual material with natural sound and the reporter gathering factual information and doing interviews with eyewitnesses or others directly involved in the story. Then, choosing a key location at the scene of the event (often one showing the "where" of the story) the reporter may do an on-camera standup introduction to the story, a standup transition, or closer, any combination of these, or even all of them.

Editing the Package

Back at the station, the reporter may sit down with the videotape editor and pick out the sound bites—the wanted portions of the interviews—plus the best version of the standup open, transition, and/or close, all of which are going to be used in the packaged report.

Next, the reporter may write the voice-over text to fit between these various sound-on-tape elements. Then the reporter may take this script to a sound recording booth to record it on an audio cassette, CART, or reel, or the narration may be recorded directly onto videotape, depending on the newsroom's technical setup.

Then the videotape editor is ready to cut the story and piece it together. Onto the master videocassette goes audio and video from the standups and interview sound bites and the recorded V/O narration that bridges those sections. The editor then returns to the raw videotapes to select B-Roll scenes where appropriate and perhaps the natural sounds that go with them. These are then edited onto the master tape *over* the voice-over narration that goes between the picture-plus-sound bites laid down earlier.

One advantage of doing the editing this way is that it is efficient and saves reporter and writer time; it is an economical way to edit a field report.

The Snapshot Effect

But the technique is not without its problems, at least one of which is pretty severe. In the process of looking for B-Roll scenes or shots that appropriately "cover" the voice-over narration, the editor risks losing the sense of visual story line, the continuity, the visual "flow"—the ingredient that converts a series of scenes into a story. The danger is that the shots may end up looking like a bunch of unrelated snapshots in a photo album, scenes chosen just to "cover" the narration rather than to establish and advance a visual story line. The fundamental weakness of this technique—and you're likely to see this any night of the week on your local television newscast—is that the visual has been made secondary and subordinate to the writing and the writing has gone off on its own without taking into account what shots are there to go with the words.

File Tape Sins

This book refers several times to observations Reuven Frank, former NBC News Division president, has made about television news. He spoke about many issues over his long and distinguished career. In a keynote address to an annual convention of the Radio-Television News Directors Association Frank chided his colleagues:

> Satellites and portable cameras and miniaturized tape have put us within instant range of everything happening everywhere. That is what we used to long for. But the result has been a kind of bulletin service that provides information no different in essential nature from what comes by other media, radio or print. Because we can bring all the news, we therefore must. It is rare, however, that the information is other than the words, or that the value is other than the speed of dissemination.
>
> What television does uniquely, the transmission of experience— what was it like?—is a rare and accidental accomplishment. Pictures, when they are available, are matched to words. The words come first—not pictures. I dare say there are people in this room who have never seen pictures put together to tell a story and then words fitted into them, as needed, to fill in, to underscore, to bridge gaps. Almost nobody writes silence any more.

Eyewash

Frank was especially critical of two visual techniques that are fairly widespread in television news. One is the use of file footage and library shots to visually "cover" the text of a story; the other is the use of electronically generated graphics and other production elements to "dress up" the visuals over the narration. Of these two practices Frank said:

> We keep files of pictures to show when there is nothing else to show, truck shots down the aisles of supermarkets, wheat pouring into a boxcar, a slow zoom into the Capitol dome. I understand you have a word for this—eyewash—pictures that can go with any words . . . And then there are the graphics. Television is a visual medium, so there must be graphics, devices that give forth numbers and letters, and split screens, and zooms and starbursts, and insets and flipovers.
>
> I will give you a rule: A device can only enhance, and if there is nothing there in the first place, you can't enhance it.

SUMMARY

✔ 1. Double-space all text using the split-page format and all caps or lower-case form as dictated by newsroom policy. (On computer, scriptwriting software may do this and other formatting automatically.)

✔ 2. Each scene in the videotape and its running time must be typed into the video column on the same line of the text where it occurs (comes on the screen) and matches the narration.

✔ 3. Do not overwrite the text. The formula "three words per second" is a maximum and should be adjusted downward as the individual circumstances of your story and the situation dictate.

✔ 4. Sentences should be short, but vary the length for better audience comprehension and copy "flow." Avoid long, involved sentences with many words separating subject and verb, dangling modifiers, puzzling pronouns-antecedents, dependent clauses, compound constructions, and the like. Short words are better than long words.

✔ 5. Where "keying" is necessary, match the words to the pictures very carefully by counting words or timing them to the running time of the scenes, so that identification and descriptions of action match the visual material. You want the on-air person to be talking about what the audience is watching.

✔ 6. Do not state the obvious. The audience can see what the pictures are showing. Tell the audience what the visual material means, not what it shows.

✔ 7. Do not stop the picture flow with words ("shown here on the left"). Avoid visual references unless it is absolutely essential to understanding or identification.

✔ 8. The text should complement the visual, but it also should be capable of standing by itself.

✔ 9. When the pictures (or sounds) are especially compelling, especially exciting, or especially dramatic, write so that the text anticipates this highlight by explaining its impact or significance, or by following it with a similar explanation—with silence (no text) artfully used to let the picture (or sound) speak for itself.

✔ 10. When the visual or sound material is especially strong, do not try to jam too many words on top of it. The audience will be concentrating on the interesting visual material, and you will not be able to punch a lot of facts through that concentration.

✔ 11. Read your text aloud as you type it. The style of the writing should approach the conversational. Write the way people talk. Avoid jargon and stuffy wording; use action verbs and descriptive adjectives and adverbs. Try to match the mood, pace, and tone of the visual material; avoid words that are stronger than the visual.

✔ 12. Keep the text lean and loose. Give the audience time to see *and* listen.

Reporting

A REVIEW OF THE BASICS

Reporters are the shock troops, the nerve ganglia, the heart of the news-gathering system in any journalistic enterprise. Reporters go out and gather the facts and process them into news stories. They usually do the initial writing, editing, and narrating of those stories. Without reporters, there would be no news.

Television reporters also go on the air. They are seen doing their work in the field and in the studio. The audience knows and respects them. Most reporters are proud of their profession and wouldn't want to be doing anything else.

"Reporter" is a romantic title, and we create specific connotations when we put an adjective in front of it, such as investigative reporter (though all reporters investigate), economics reporter, field reporter, general assignment reporter, and so on. A reporter might covet only one title more: correspondent. That title is even more romantic, especially at the national network level, where the aura of the term gives it a connotation that is very heady for the person who has the title.

In this chapter we are going to look at how television news reporters use ENG technology to report and process news stories. We'll look at some examples of basic story types such as the field reporting assignment, spot news, and live coverage from the field. We'll consider techniques of ENG field coverage, various problems that crop up to challenge the field-reporting team, and what field reporters come up with to solve those problems.

But first let's check the basics of news reporting that beginning journalists (and unseasoned students just starting out) must know about.

RESEARCH: LOCATING INFORMATION AND SOURCES

Reporters have several ways of gathering facts and information, the background and the raw materials of their news accounts. On-line computer services such as CompuServe® and Internet® are fundamental to a reporter's research, and anyone who cannot search and use computer sources effectively and efficiently is at a competitive disadvantage today. Reporters also must know how to search and research through such records and documents as police blotters, courtroom transcripts, courthouse files, and so forth. And they often have to look at and interpret other written or recorded information: everything from meeting minutes to PR handouts, from annual reports to printed programs.

Many newsrooms maintain disk-stored computer and library files, videotape and scripts of their local coverage, and reference works. Reporters who have beat assignments routinely keep their own such files concerning major elements of that beat and the personalities on it, materials that may include newspaper and magazine article clips by subject and other background information about a topic, the reporter's notebooks, and lists of public, private, and unlisted phone numbers.

When the name Lee Harvey Oswald surfaced after President Kennedy was assassinated, a reporter scored a worldwide scoop by digging into her files to get out her notes from an interview she had had with Oswald in Moscow many years before. A Chicago radio reporter got early details on the death of a mayor by quickly locating the number of a pay phone in a bar where he knew a key contact made a regular stop for a drink no matter what was happening. Whatever the sources, you must know how to use them in order to

Figure 6.1. A reporter's newsroom work area at WTAP-TV, Parkersburg, West Virginia. The newsroom is also used as a set for live updates. The newsroom location gives the staff ready access to computers, edit booths, NBC News Channel record system, an extensive video library and archive of local news video, the main studio, and ENG staging area. *(Courtesy of WTAP-TV. Photo by Roger Sheppard.)*

take good advantage of them and avoid wasting precious time hunting through them, trying to figure out what kinds of information they contain, and how it is organized and indexed. Time is usually critical, and you need to be able to find things quickly.

FIRST-HAND REPORTING

At Events

Reporters also witness things. They watch critically, and listen carefully at events as observers and eyewitnesses. They learn to keep their eyes and ears open. They teach themselves to be attentive, to record what they see and hear. They become skillful at techniques of fact gathering. Most reporters master the art of taking notes, and they devise their own system of abbreviations and other "shorthand" notations and symbols to keep track of what they witness. Also popular with reporters are portable and hand-held electronic devices such as notebooks, laptops, and pen devices. With the pen unit, you use a stylus to write directly onto the computer screen. The device converts your handwriting to print and stores it in conventional computer document form.

Covering Beats

Television news organization staff structures vary. Some stations assign reporters to "beats"; others have reporter "specialists" who specialize in a general area such as health, business, politics, religion, and so on.

The beat system is a traditional journalistic structure that was set up to assure that someone on the staff was covering important news-producing spots such as City Hall, the courts, the sheriff's office—society's points of record. The idea of "specialist" implies the reporter has special knowledge or training about a field (like economics), a profession (like medicine), or an institution (like government).

However, if you are going to be a TV reporter, whatever the staff structure, a number of common and unique things can help hone your competitive edge.

✔ 1. Learn the territory. If a lot of your coverage responsibility is going to be within the confines of a building or headquarters, you must become as knowledgeable of the layout and functions in that building as the oldest denizen of the place.

It is too easy to fall into bad habits about this. The regular trip from the parking lot through the same door to the same space every day leaves you unprepared to find your way when something unusual happens. Learn to think like a reporter. Take time to explore and learn the history of the place. Especially learn the location of telephones, computer-access points, electric outlets, stairways, windows where your crew might run a cable or a microwave dish, the best place to park a truck. Imagine the day you'll go live, and plan for it—when that moment comes you won't have much time to search out the building superintendent.

✔ 2. Know the people. Get to know the little people as well as the big ones. One truism says that an army is really run by its sergeants. The same idea is true about most other institutions.

It may be useful and ego boosting to hobnob with the mayor or have the governor or senator call you by your first name, but if you always have to explain who you are to those in outside offices, reception desks, gates, and security checks, you're going to be slowed down when it counts. Besides, if you make friends with them, these people can be extremely valuable sources of inside information—not the quotable kind but the fill-in-the-blanks kind—and they don't give out those kinds of goodies to strangers.

✔ 3. Know the rules of the game. All public institutions, professions, businesses, and private social and cultural institutions operate under a set of regulations. These may be statutory laws, common laws, ordinances, legal contracts, articles of incorporation, mandatory or informal codes of ethics and practice, or even teachings and customs that have, over time, become rules of conduct for those who subscribe.

A good reporter will learn what the rules and resources are. You can't cover the courts well without understanding what the law says about how the criminal justice system should work or how lawyers can operate and what the rights of the accused are. You can't cover the school board or the city or county council without knowing about what the laws let those institutions do. You can't cover science and scientists without understanding how and why they are dedicated to the scientific method. Once you know them, you have to be able to explain all these "regulations" to your viewers in language they can understand.

✔ 4. Know the subject matter. You never stop being a student or having to do your homework.

You must continue to study—with special attention now to the world of the people and institutions you are covering. You need to know the nomenclature, the culture, the issues, the major debates, and the history and background of that world. That means reading everything you can get your hands on, discussing this world with the people who live in it, and being forever curious about it. And again you have to figure out just how to explain it in ways the viewers can comprehend.

INTERVIEWING

The Reporter as Interviewer

Of all the things a reporter does to gather information for a story, the most basic is interviewing. The interview is the one main way a reporter gets both background and facts on which to build a story. Interviewing is the backbone of the reporting process, and interview results are the backbone of a news story. We now take an in-depth and detailed look at the art and science of the news interview that is planned and scheduled.

Plan It

Here is the main key to doing a good interview, the main advice all the experts give: preparation. Interviewers are performers and interviews are their performances. All accomplished performers prepare. A good interview does not just happen; it requires careful and detailed planning, and preparation. Skillful interviewers do both.

So let's assume that your interview has been scheduled, and that you are determined to start cultivating the habits of the professional approach to interviewing. The process begins with planning, and you should start your planning with a little analysis. What is the goal of this interview?

For purposes of analysis, interviews can be classified according to their objective. What kind of information, basically, are you after in this interview? Is the main purpose of it to elicit facts, such as the cost of the project, the amount of the contract, the results of the vote, or the terms of the agreement? Or is the basic purpose to get opinions, for example, the reason for the loss, the seriousness of the situation, the meaning of the decision, or what the political candidate sees as the main issue of the campaign? Still another possible purpose is to reveal to the audience aspects and dimensions of the personality and life-style of the interviewee, whether that person be a beauty contestant, sports hero, Oscar nominee, or lottery winner. Asked another way, is the fundamental thrust of the interview to get facts, to get opinions, or to explore the personality of the guest?

Of course, no interview satisfies just one objective exclusively. Facts and opinions get intermixed, and the manner in which someone answers a question can override the words themselves. Sometimes *how* a question is answered reveals more than what the person said.

But frequently one objective is the main goal of the interview and it helps to think this through ahead of time. Such an analysis will help you to clarify your basic purpose, focus your preparation more sharply, and help you think more clearly about planning.

Research It

Having spent time thinking about what you want this interview to accomplish, you will want to learn something about the background, talents, expertise, and past activities of the person to be interviewed.

We've already looked at some of the many sources of facts and information you can turn to, but let's go over them again. Some of these sources are obvious, others not so obvious.

First, that expanding universe of computer data banks: Sharpen your abil-

ity to search and travel on the information highway, that storehouse of com-
puter-accessed data with its expanding menu of home pages and their links,
and users and their exchanges.

There are basic on-line services like Prodigy® and CompuServe®, yes, but
also more specialized and sophisticated ones, a good example of which would
be Dialog®, a high-end content-rich (and pricey) service leader—that put a
world of information at your fingertips. File scripts/tapes of newscasts, newspaper and magazine article clips, news releases and PR handouts, printed programs, reference works, transcripts of speeches, Who's Whos, compendiums,
almanacs, books, some bibliographies and biographies, can help a lot.

The city directory (as distinct from the telephone book) lists a wealth of
information about residents of a community. On campus the faculty-admin-
istration-student-staff directory is usually packed with all sorts of background
and current information about the university community. (A word of caution:
Publishers of compiled facts and other information do not guarantee the complete accuracy of the material nor is there any mechanism on the Internet
addressing the question of the accuracy of the information posted on it, so
keep alert and make a habit of cross-checking information you glean.) The
library adds literally hundreds (no, make it thousands) of sources to the pool.
Practice searching through stored information; the more skillful you become
at it, the better.

Don't overlook the telephone as an information-gathering tool. You can
contact many sources, cover a lot of ground, and gather information quickly
with a telephone. As with any other skill, you need to study telephone interviewing technique, you need to carefully prepare for such an interview, and
you need to practice telephone interviewing to improve your skill. Here are
some pointers. This is one instance where a printout of your exact questions
is helpful. Write the exact questions, get them in their right order for the interview, and edit the wording. Your script should include the exact name and
title of the person you are calling, and the telephone number. Your script may
even include your own name and your station's call letters (or the name of
your college, or the name of your journalism professor and the class for
which you are doing this assignment). You include your name on your script
because when you get your party on the line it saves everybody's time to get
these basics out right away so that you can move quickly to your questions. If
you are taping the conversation, make that point clearly, up front. Having the
tape rolling at this time has the advantage of "memorializing" on tape your
request to tape and your respondent's answer.

With your preparations complete, conduct the call in a businesslike manner. When the other party gets on the line, the very first thing is to make sure
you have the right person. Get the exact spelling of the person's name, and
her or his exact title. Identify yourself fully. Tell the purpose of your call. You
might at this point "confirm" your guest's participation with "I need three
minutes of your time to ask you several questions about . . . is now a good
time for you?" or similar statement. But however you begin, get right to your

questions. The other person's time is valuable. Your call is an interruption. Because you are being businesslike, you will be creating the impression of being a person who is organized, who is prepared, who is specific, and who will keep this interruption to an absolute minimum.

For the face-to-face interview, investing productive time getting background on both the guest and her or his "area" is another investment that will pay you dividends. You will be able to approach the interview more confidently. Again, your preparation will show, it will be apparent to the guest, and it will say, in effect, "Look, I care about this interview and I care enough about you to have done my homework, and to have looked into your background a little bit." That will come across as a compliment to your guest, will put the person a little bit at ease maybe, and (assuming you are sincere and not blowing smoke) will help create the climate and proper atmosphere for a productive interview. So first of all, get background yourself. All good interviewers do.

Write It Out

Then get serious about the questions. Think up questions. Lots of questions. As many questions as you possibly can. Sometimes other staffers may join in the thinking process. That is a form of something called "brainstorming." In brainstorming you all think of as many questions as you can, and someone writes them down. You make big lists of questions. Try to keep the viewer in mind because the viewer is the ultimate target for the answers.

Don't worry about the exact wording of the questions. That comes later. Avoid making judgments about them. That comes later, too. In one news shop, a particular reporter had a habit of criticizing questions being suggested by other staffers with comments such as, "Nobody cares about that." or "That's a dumb question." Finally in exasperation during a brainstorming session a staffer blurted out, "Look, friend, either think up or shut up!"

Organize It

With a full set of questions you are ready for the next step in the process, organizing. One part of organizing is to group the questions into categories so that they're not jumping around all over the place and going back and forth in random fashion. You should try to avoid having to say in an interview, "While we were on the subject of 'X' I should have asked you . . ." or words to that effect. Occasionally you will have a good reason to go back to something touched on earlier in an interview, but generally it is preferable that the interview move forward, not backward.

Another part of organizing is to rank the questions according to their importance. Frequently you'll be able to sequence a progression of questions that leads step by step to the more important ones. You'll have your main questions, of course, and you'll want to have some secondary questions as well. And then, just to be safe, have some back-up questions.

During this time of sifting, sorting, and organizing your questions, you should weed out those which have little or nothing to do with your topic, those which are mundane, those whose answers are already well known or could be easily learned just by doing a little research.

Having done your research, you'll recognize questions that fit the "don't use" category. Also, don't be too intent on fitting every last question into some category. Some questions will not fit no matter what scheme of categorizing you use—they just seem unrelated to any others in the pile.

As you organize the questions also start working on their wording. Try to hear how the questions sound, and try to hear them as your guest is likely to hear them. Don't be so ready to accept the first phrasing that comes to mind. Rather, be critical of the rough draft wording. Edit the question to sharpen it. Is this question clear? Can it be interpreted in more than one way? Does it have words with fuzzy meanings in it? Nothing will slow down the forward motion of an interview more quickly than a puzzled guest saying, "I'm not sure I understand the question," or "What do you mean by . . . ?"

Does the wording make the question an open-end or a closed-end one? An open-end question is just what the label implies. It lets the respondent take the answer in any direction he or she wishes. "How do you feel about . . ." and "What do you think of . . ." are examples of open-end wording. Some experts believe an open-end question is a good way to get an interview started because it helps to create a more relaxed atmosphere, allows the guest to hear the sound of her or his own voice, allows a release of built-up nervous tension and anxiety, and generally makes for a smooth and easy start to the conversation.

A closed-end question focuses the answer by reducing the guest's options for an answer. "Will you vote for or against the motion?" is a closed-end question because it narrows the range of possible answers. Of course, the guest might reply, "I haven't decided yet," or "I plan to abstain," so just how "closed" a closed-end question is depends not only on exactly how it is worded but also how the respondent chooses to reply.

During this evaluation of the phrasing and editing, you will want to look carefully too at whether your question might be a "yes-no" question. Q.—Do you play the piano? A.—Yes, I do. Q.—Do you enjoy that? A.—Yes, I do. Q.—Do you play any other instrument? A.—No. Those are "yes-no" type wordings. Q.—What do you enjoy most about playing the piano? That wording pretty well rules out a "yes-no" answer.

If you take the time to say aloud each of your proposed questions, trying to hear it as your interviewee is likely to hear it, and trying to anticipate what the answer might be, you'll avoid some of the more common pitfalls of interviewing. Mostly it's a matter of deciding what you want to know and then making the wording clear, precise, and specific. Keep asking yourself, "What, exactly, do I want to know?" and "Will this question ask for that information?"

Should you script the final versions of your questions? Some beginners find that this helps overcome their anxiety; it gives them a sense of confidence to know that if their mind goes blank, they can fall back on a written list. However, most seasoned reporters seem to agree you should not read questions to your guest. Mike Wallace, widely recognized for a lifetime of superior news interviewing skill, writes out all his questions. And then rewrites them. And then again . . . until he gets them the way he wants them. As a matter of fact, reworking and rewording questions is an excellent way to become so familiar with them you won't need any notes. In most situations probably the best technique is what is sometimes called "the rehearsed ad-lib" approach. You know exactly what you want to ask, but, you let the exact wording and phrasing of the question occur spontaneously as you ask it—not winging it, not ad lib (no preparation), not memorized (scripted), but prepared and rehearsed.

Schedule It

Many interview appointments are arranged over the phone. If you are the one to contact the interviewee to schedule the interview, plan the phone approach part of it as well. Review the guidelines in this chapter.

When you set up the interview, be businesslike. Be polite of course, but don't waste time: Be organized, be direct, be specific. Identify yourself fully and clearly. Make sure the guest understands the interview is going to be videotaped—make sure of this up front! Tell the purpose of the interview and give the guest a general idea of the area you want to ask about, the general line of the questioning.

If the guest asks "Well, what do you want to know about that?" be ready to respond. Perhaps something like "Well, that is what I want to talk with you about. Shall we make it for 10:30 or would 11 o'clock be better for you?" may work. (Note, your question is closed-end. Either choice is OK for you!) Confirm the details before you hang up: "OK, I'll see you tomorrow at 10:30 in the morning, in your office." Adhere strictly to these arrangements.

During guest/reporter chatting just before the interview, should you tell your guest the exact questions you are going to ask? Journalists are pretty uniformly agreed you should not. The risk is that the answers may sound canned, rehearsed, and lacking in animation and spontaneity, or hesitant and tentative. When the guest is told exact questions before the interview what often happens is that he or she gives an answer in practice and then, when the light goes on, gropes to re-create that exact answer.

On the other hand, it is standard procedure to tell the guest what areas you want to cover so that the questions don't come pouring down out of the blue, catching the guest by surprise, breaking concentration, and making him or her less able to deal with the question effectively. A reminder, during this pre-interview chatting may be the ideal time to explain the how and why of the reverse question technique. We'll go over the "how" of reverse questions later in this chapter.

Execute It

At the interview, start communicating immediately. The fact that you are on time does exactly that. So does your attire. Be a lady. Be a gentleman. And dress appropriately.

Your equipment should be set up quickly and efficiently. It should have been tested and checked out before leaving the shop. This is no time to fiddle with the gear. Many people find recording equipment disturbing, even frightening, and you need to help ease that tension, or at the very least not make it worse by calling undue attention to the paraphernalia.

The Special Role of Listening

Researchers estimate that we humans spend about 80 percent of our waking hours communicating—reading, writing, speaking, and listening. That's eight minutes out of every ten we're awake, forty-eight minutes out of every hour.

Another fact, according to the experts, is that just a little more than half this communicating time, 55 percent, is spent in a combination of reading, writing, and speaking. In other words, we spend 45 percent of our communicating time in listening. A big problem is that, without realizing it, we often listen quite badly.

For example, most of us know from our own experience that when we're listening to a joke, story, or the details of some adventure, we're not totally listening at all; no, we're impatiently awaiting our turn to respond with a similar story of our own in a sort of "Can you top this?" contest.

The act of listening seemingly does not come naturally, and it certainly does not come easily. We can, however, analyze this activity and our own listening habits and then teach ourselves to become much better at it. The very first step in that process is to become aware of the importance of listening, to become conscious of how well or how badly we do it, and what difference that makes.

A student intern who was doing television interviews with county extension folks on homemaking topics reported in one of her progress reports that she felt the best interviews from her point of view were those that went smoothly. She meant those in which the guests were very articulate and talkative, people who would respond readily, people who would answer a question almost before the question was asked, indeed, people who would talk even without questions being asked. The student's point was that all she had to do to conduct the interview was to get the person started and then sit back and relax and take it easy.

That's a widely shared view about what makes a good interview, and it's a wrong view, a misconception about the nature of face-to-face communication. Good communicating requires effort from both the speaker and the listener. Good listening is crucial to the process. Good listening is not passive; you just don't sit back and let the speaker speak on. Good listening is a much more active process than that. The listener shares half the responsibility for a good exchange of ideas.

The listener must listen to the words being spoken, of course, but it is much more involved than that. Another thing the experts tell us, for example, is that in the typical face-to-face communication situation, the words being spoken (the verbal part of the message) carry a startlingly small part of the meaning of the message, considerably less than half of it.

What we listeners get as the meaning of another's message comes from such other things as the speaker's rate and pattern of pauses and silences, intonations (the up-and-down pattern of voice inflection), facial expression, posture, hand and finger movements, gestures, and other nonverbal cues. Even how the speaker is dressed influences the meaning we get out of a message. Not only that, we're told that message meaning is subtly influenced by such things as room lighting, wall coloring, furnishings, ambient sound, and a variety of other factors in the interview setting.

To be a good listener, you must first of all focus your complete attention on the speaker and keep it there. Second, you must studiously avoid sending the speaker nonverbal signs of impatience, boredom, and inattention. Signs of inattention (while the respondent is answering) include checking your notes, staring off into space, looking around at what is going on in the background, tapping the fingers or the foot, glancing at your watch, sitting on the very edge of your chair, straightening your trousers or tie, brushing back your hair, adjusting your skirt, and so forth. These nervous mannerisms are guaranteed to make your guest ill at ease and convert a creative tension of heightened awareness that should exist between yourself and your guest into a destructive tension of distraction and dismay. Your inattention will ruin the atmosphere of the interview.

To be an active listener you should watch the speaker and pay attention to the words being spoken and to the guest's nonverbal cues. Your job is first to integrate and then to interpret all this information so as to be able to understand what the speaker *means* rather than just what the speaker *says*.

Often when the process doesn't seem to be working well, you can help straighten out the situation and clarify the meaning with a statement or question such as, "It sounds like you're saying . . ." or, "As I understand it, your point is that . . ." or, "Am I correct in hearing you say . . . ?"

Lastly, as with any other skill, you can practice good listening, and you can get better at it with practice. Here is a game you can play with a friend to get yourself started. First, you both have to agree on the rules of the game, and the only rules of this game are: Let your friend start a conversation by telling you something to which you must respond. However, before you are permitted to respond, you must tell the other person what she or he said. When your friend agrees that you got the message right, and only then, may you respond. Then, before your friend is allowed to reply to your response, she or he must tell you what you said, to the point where you agree they got it right. A little exercise of this kind will go a long way toward raising your awareness of the hazards of communication and the importance of careful, active, critical listening to the process.

To review:

✔ 1. Two-way communication is an active process for both the speaker and the listener.

✔ 2. The nonverbal part of a speaker's message is as important as the words being spoken.

✔ 3. Look at and listen to the speaker. Your actions are as much a part of the message as the speaker's words and actions.

✔ 4. Practice your listening skills to improve your listening skill.

Practical Pointers—Do's . . . and Don'ts . . .

• Don't ask "obvious" questions . . . that is, questions that have answers that are already common knowledge or easily learned

• Ask straightforward questions . . . don't assume and presume

• Avoid the "echo effect" . . . don't parrot every answer back to the guest before asking the next question

• Resist interjecting meaningless comments into the interview, comments such as "I see" and "Uh huh" and the like

• Don't monopolize the interview . . . if your questions take longer than their answers, something is definitely wrong somewhere

• Ask one (1) question at a time, avoid asking multiple questions

• Don't answer guest questions, skirt them and continue your questioning

Before You Depart

Don't make any promises about the use of the interview, when it is going to be on the air, that sort of thing. You don't even know whether it is going to be used, let alone when, so just say you hope it will be on a newscast later that day or whatever.

Lastly, say "Thank you." And mean it. It is seemingly a small enough thing to do. And yet, "small" is deceptive. If you get in the habit of showing courtesy, you will be amazed at the dividends your thoughtfulness will return to you.

With all that interview advice to ponder, let's take a look at an excerpt from a television documentary hosted by Harry Reasoner, a first-rate interviewer who achieved great success as a network television news reporter/anchor.

Reasoner: Dr. N._____ is recognized as one of the world's authorities on languages. He's a professor at N._____ University and the author of a lot of books. Just looking at languages as an expert, which, uh, which is the best, would you say?

< **This question is short, concise, direct, and clear.**

Guest: English is very practical, very flexible, extremely usable, concise. It is by no means the most, uh, euphonious language in the world. It has some pretty tough sounds to the ears. I remember when I first came to this country, some of the people on the boat said that English sounded like cats meowing.

R: Which would you pick for beauty?

< **And so is this one, smoothly linked with the first answer.**

G: Well, I'm prejudiced, but I suppose my native tongue would be my preference.

< **Reasoner is listening to this answer, doesn't fully understand it, and instead of just plunging on to the next question, stops to**

< **clarify matters.**

R: Italian?

G: Yes. Well, it's the most musical language. Certainly it is the best language for singing.

< **Notice the logical arrangement and progression of the questions, first "practical," later "impractical."**

R: Speaking again from the standpoint of practicality and flexibility, what's the worst major language you can think of?

G: Well, the one that I have some slight familiarity with that impressed me as being the most difficult, the one that I've had the toughest time really learning, is Vietnamese.

R: Vietnamese?

G: Uh-huh.

R: Because of the tonal quality?   < **Follow-up.**

G: Yes, the tones, and the glottal
stops.

R: What are the shortcomings of En-   < **Open-ended.**
glish? Are there things that you worry
about in it?

G: The, uh, worst shortcoming of English is the tremendous spread between
the pronunciation and the spelling. Or
to put it another way, the fact that
the spelling is awfully, awfully
archaic.

R: What are the particular strengths   < **Now a "reverse-**
of English? Now you mentioned flexi-   **angle" look at it.**
bility, are their others?   **Reasoner continues to**
                                                 listen to the guest
G: Ah, the flexibility, conciseness,   **and here again is**
the fact that you can say what you   **proof.**
are out to say in probably the small-
est number of words and with the
greatest directness. A business letter in English, for example, will
occupy a certain space. Now, you try
translating that same business letter, with all the nuances, into
French, or Spanish, or Italian, and
you'll get almost twice as long a
letter.

R: How many words altogether are there   < **Notice how short**
in the English language?   **and concise the ques-**
                                                 tions are and how
G: I would say that a fair guess right   **they focus attention**
now would be about a million words, of   **on the guest and his**
which no man knows more than about a   **answers.**
hundred thousand.

R: Is that so?

G: You know one word out of ten in your language.

R: What about the influence of television and radio on usage and on phonetics?

< **Another open-end question, and again, short, concise, direct.**

G: The influence of, uh, television and radio on language and phonetics is tremendous, overwhelming. It is the biggest force that has ever operated in the world. Ah, it reaches everybody, and every person is a potential willing and unwitting imitator of what he hears. In other words, your television, especially the television but also the spoken movies and the radio, are in the process of obliterating local dialects in all languages.

Now, Let's Hear from the Interviewee

Interviews with various kinds of experts who are visitors to the community are fairly common story assignments for television reporters. The guest usually is prominent at least in his or her own field, and sometimes, of course, will be famous and well known to the general public.

The point is that such assignments happen so often that unless the reporter does something about it, they all start sounding and looking pretty much alike—dull and shallow. At best they have predictable questions and standardized answers.

Two Chicago professors and free-lance writers, Connie Fletcher and Jon Ziomek, did a study of just this issue.*

They joined forces to research—by interview—prominent people who had been guests on various TV interviews to see what celebrities had to say about their experiences with reporters. The celebrities' strongest complaints included:

*"How to Catch a Star," *The Quill,* December 1986, pp. 32–36.

1. Reporters who show up unprepared and say so

2. Reporters who show up with one or two preconceived notions and ignore everything else

3. Reporters who talk more about themselves than about the celebrity

4. Reporters who act bored or distracted by other things so they don't listen carefully

Fletcher and Ziomek said that research is the key to getting good results from an interview and that what the researching reporter should look for is the question that is brand new or seldom asked. They advised: "Research your subject like a prosecutor who wants to win every time. Look for clues as to what the celebrity wants to say but hasn't, or what the celebrity stopped saying ten years ago, or what the celebrity shies away from, or what has been buried under piles of standard questions and angles for years."

They also offered a number of tips on how to get the most out of the interview once the cue light goes on:

✔ 1. Reinforce everything they say. "That really helps me, this is really interesting."

✔ 2. Let them talk about what they're doing in town. That's their reward for doing this for the twenty-fourth time.

✔ 3. Give them a compelling reason to keep talking—the provocative, unusual, and sensitive questions may bring them to actually enjoy the interview. Most celebrities have larger-than-average egos.

✔ 4. Get them out of the "usual quotes" rut by responding more positively to the unusual or to the sidelights and unexplored territory.

✔ 5. Use *reflective listening techniques,* that is, play back a summary of what they have said: "That made you angry?" "Why did he say it wasn't your best?" "What was it about that situation that made it work so well?"

✔ 6. Let them ramble, but don't be afraid to redirect the interview to where you want it to go: "This is really interesting, and I want to get back to it, but right now I'd like to ask you about . . ."

✔ 7. Never denigrate or put down the subject by giving or showing your personal reaction to what they have said.

✔ 8. Try to get what you want and need from the interview, but don't be so stiff you refuse to follow into new and interesting areas if the celebrity heads in that direction.

Interviewing is the main way broadcast journalists do a couple of important things—gather background information from people, and obtain the recorded material needed for sound bites. We have given you some prescriptions for how to prepare yourself, some techniques to try, and some standard approaches.

Alternate Approaches

Even though these lists of do's and don'ts (and there are many other such lists) cover the basics of interviewing, you can do interviews in other ways as well.

In Larry Hatteberg's essay in Chapter 3, he describes one of the ways he goes about "interviewing" when he is profiling a person, a technique that comes out looking more like a friendly conversation than a Q. & A. session (p. 129). Bob Dotson uses what he calls the "Columbo technique" (Chapter 5, p. 190).

In the introduction to *The John McPhee Reader,** the editor of the book, William L. Howarth, tells us how the famous author goes about the interviewing he does for his extremely successful nonfiction books and articles. Howarth says that when McPhee does an interview, he tries to keep his mind as blank as possible: "He has found that imagining he knows a subject is a disadvantage [because] that will limit his freedom to ask, to learn, to be surprised by unfolding evidence." He says McPhee believes an interviewer doesn't need to pretend ignorance because most stories are full of surprises, and the reporter should resist the temptation to "bluff with a show of knowledge."

Howarth admits that this sometimes makes McPhee seem dull-witted. He repeats answers and even garbles up what the subject has said so that the subject has to provide a new answer. That gets the subject to elaborate and perhaps amplify and simplify until McPhee has virtually everything the subject knows about the topic. For McPhee, the ideal interview is one in which he listens without interrupting.

The things he learns in one interview lead to other interviews and also tell him what things he needs to research. (He does not use a recorder because he thinks they inhibit people.) When McPhee hears the same stories the third time, he stops interviewing and begins the writing job.

That job includes first transcribing his notes. He says that process is like the way a magnet attracts iron filings—as they take shape, he gets ideas about how the story will be structured. Then McPhee reads the notes over and over, producing more notes and more impressions of how the story will develop.

A lot of things in this description of how McPhee works are not suited to broadcast reporting. Clearly we have to have sound and **actualities**. We usually don't have as much time as he has. And none of us is a world-famous author. But think of the parallels to what Bob Dotson and Larry Hatteberg say in their excerpts in this book.

*William L. Howarth, ed., *The John McPhee Reader* (New York: Vintage Books, 1978), pp. 7–33.

Follow It Up

Carl Hartman, a veteran AP correspondent with considerable experience covering international economics from Washington, has said that reporters need to guard against being just transmission belts for the obtuse and sometimes misleading language used by bureaucrats and public relations people. He said, for example, that "no comment" and denials should be handled with more precision, either with follow-up questions or copy that focuses sharply on just exactly what was said.

When you get a "no comment," Hartman said it may be that your question was improper and what your source is really saying with the no comment is, "You're asking me a question that you know it would be wrong of me to answer." He suggested that your reply to "no comment" in such a situation could be a polite: "I didn't ask for comment; I asked for facts." And Hartman said, reporters should be precise about just what was asked that produced the no comment answer.

Evasions also need follow-ups.

Statement:	"The subject wasn't discussed at the meeting."
Follow-up:	"What was discussed?"
Statement:	"To my knowledge, that didn't come up."
Follow-up:	"How complete is your knowledge?"
Statement:	"I won't discuss anything so silly."
Follow-up:	"What is silly about it?"
Statement:	"We never discuss personnel matters."
Follow-up:	Hartman said that it is perfectly legitimate for the reporter to point out other times when personnel matters were discussed.

Denials are somewhat more complicated because they have the reputation of the person or the institution behind them. Hartman said that reporters should look carefully at exactly what is being denied. As an example he pointed to former national security advisor Robert McFarlane who "categorically denied" in November of 1986 that he had been in Iran "last month." McFarlane had visited Iran, but in May, not October.

It is important that the reporter be professional about such jousting. Hartman said reporters should:

✔ 1. Report statements by officials as precisely as possible (a good reason to play the tape and save the sound bite for later use).

✔ 2. Avoid implying your own conclusions. (The facts may prove you wrong next week.)

✔ 3. Not be afraid to point out what a statement does or does not include or where other facts point elsewhere. (Part of your job is to give the audience the facts so it can make its own decision about who is telling the truth.)

FIELD REPORTING: GENERAL STORY ELEMENTS

Having reviewed the basic tools of reporting—(1) research, (2) first-hand information gathering, and (3) interviewing of various kinds—we now turn to the matter of putting these and other skills to work on ENG assignments in the field.

There is a good deal of argument about which part of a television news field report is the most important. Some experts discuss whether it is the opening or the closing. Others say the crucial part of a story is the middle, its development and progression, its "story line." But these are differences of degree, not of kind. Everyone agrees that the open and the close are both vital to the ultimate success of the package. So it simply makes good sense to give special attention to all elements in the story.

The Opening Segment

The story lead may be either "hard" or "soft." A soft lead is somewhat non-specific and rather generalized. It flows naturally from the story's **anchor lead**, read live by the anchor in the studio, to introduce the report. In contrast, a hard lead is much more direct and specific, a sentence or so zeroing in on the most newsworthy element of the story, and thus, a lead that stands by itself. Let's look first at the hard-lead technique.

HARD NEWS FEATURE WITH HARD LEAD

VIDEO	AUDIO
ANCHOR, ON CAM	Next in the news, a dream come true for Yourtown Mayor George Arfield. Our man Stanley was there, and filed this report.
VTR STANLEY	SOT (hard lead) Mayor George Arfield officiated at ground-breaking ceremonies this morning

```
                        for the city's proposed new domed
                        stadium. Under sunny skies . . .
```

With a hard lead, the basic newsworthy facts are laid out in a direct, declarative sentence. The story's lead sentence captures the essential point of the event. The anchor lead—the story intro read by the anchor—acts as an introduction to the report, but these two elements are different in tone and thrust. The anchor lead doesn't get to the essential news point of the story, but the reporter's story lead gets right to the news point.

When the story is written with a soft lead, the linkage between the anchor lead and the story lead becomes much more direct. The anchor lead again introduces the report. But in this case the story lead picks right up on the tone and theme of the anchor lead without interrupting the flow. The soft approach makes for a smoother transition from the studio anchor to the field report. The field reporter picks up right where the anchor left off.

```
               HARD NEWS FEATURE WITH SOFT LEAD


VIDEO                   AUDIO


ANCHOR, ON CAM          Next in the news, a dream come true for
                        Yourtown Mayor George Arfield. Our man
                        Stanley was there, and filed this
                        report.

VTR STANLEY             SOT (soft lead)
                        It had been the mayor's pet project for
                        years . . . going back even to his days
                        on the city council. This morning under
                        sunny skies he was beaming as he . . .
```

Notice how with a soft story lead the reporter doesn't get right to the news point, but rather starts the story with a look back at how (or when or where or even why) this occasion began.

Many television news people prefer the soft lead approach because of its smooth transition from anchor desk intro to field report. Of course, the approach is varied from story to story, one, because no two stories are alike, and two, because a newscast with a large number of either kind of lead becomes predictable and begins to sound too repetitive.

Story content should be a main factor in your decision as to which kind of lead to use. On a breaking story with some stunning development—the mayor unexpectedly and dramatically announces his resignation, effective immediately—you certainly would not want to keep the audience in suspense with a soft lead, something roundabout like, "The mayor summoned reporters to his office this morning with what everyone assumed was going to be some sort of routine announcement, so you can imagine our surprise when he . . ." In this situation the story fairly shouts for your lead to get to the point immediately—a hard lead.

With either technique, though, you must keep in mind the fact that the audience needs to be stimulated to watch. It is as though the audience is asking, "Why should I even be interested in this?" Your opening should address that question even before the audience gets a chance to think about it. The opening should be a "grabber."

It is true that you cannot communicate effectively with an audience until you have its attention. But remember that it is not just a matter of getting attention. You should get the audience focused on your report in a way that is relevant to and consistent with your material.

The opening must be related to the content of the story; the purpose of the opening is not just to get attention, but to lead the viewers into an understanding of the meaning of the story. You want an opening with a point.

When a speaker begins a speech by telling a joke, and it turns out that the joke was just for laughs and had nothing at all to do with the speaker's message, the audience feels cheated. A good joke with a point that illustrates a speaker's message is much better for two reasons. One, it avoids the audience's having that let-down feeling, and two, it helps the speaker get the message across by focusing audience attention on that message, by reinforcing the message.

Actuality: Interviewing in the Field

An actuality report is one of those basic ingredients in broadcast news that sets the medium apart from other news media. Television news people are well aware of this special capability, the special value and special appeal of using the faces and the voices of people in the news. Watching and listening to the comments of an official is quite a bit different from watching and listening to an anchor quoting the official, and it is vastly different from reading the direct quotes off the printed page of a newspaper.

The human face and voice have impact, they convey special excitement and realism. For the viewer, watching the official and listening to what she or he says is the next best thing to being there in person. Actuality is one of the greatest assets of broadcast news. Actuality can be and has been overused, misused, and abused. But when done skillfully and used purposefully, the sound bite is a broadcast news ingredient no other medium can match.

The actuality thus is a staple of many field reports. Here is where the reporter gets to combine skills: Techniques of interviewing—discussed earlier in this chapter—and techniques of camera positioning and shot framing, and perhaps the technique of reverse questions, as explained in Chapter 3.

The goal in this situation is to get short, concise answers that are clear, informative, and to the point. But you also have to keep in mind what it is that you do not want if it can be avoided, and that is either a yes-no answer or a nonstop answer. It is easy to blame the subject when you get either a yes-no response or a long-winded talker. But the truth is that much of the reason for the clipped or windy response may go back to the question that was asked and/or to nonverbal cues you sent out.

For example, some reporters "jump" on answers, that is, they fire their next question even as the last syllables of the previous reply are being spoken. This not only makes the editing of the tape more difficult, but it also may be sending a message of impatience to the person answering the question, a nonverbal "Hurry up, now!"

Controlling for Time

If you get a long-winded answer, you might narrow the question or sharpen the focus of it and ask it again. You can also control for time by keeping your questions short. The goal of the interview is to let the other person do the talking and in his or her own words.

Throughout your childhood, people probably told you, "Don't interrupt." But you may have to if the speaker is rambling on and on. You can interrupt strongly or gently. If you crash in and override the subject, not only are you being impolite, but you also risk frightening your subject and destroying their train of thought. However, you can interrupt more gently. Listen closely, then say something like, "Pardon me, that's very interesting, let's go back over it," or "Just a second—can you explain this point for me?" However you phrase the break, try to put the blame for it on yourself without sounding foolish. Members of the audience want to get the subject's ideas, and they will appreciate your efforts to steer the guest and help him or her understand.

People who are used to being interviewed for TV know they should keep their answers short. And, experienced interviewers have expressions to make time constraints clear. A good way to learn techniques experienced reporters use to control an interview for time is to watch television programs where live interviews are being conducted. Some examples: Live TV news interviews were pioneered on "The MacNeil/Lehrer NewsHour,"® including interviews involving a complicated technical set-up where some guests are in the main studio (New York or Washington) and others are at remote locations. ABC's "Nightline"® with host Ted Koppel is another program famous for use of this technique. The hosts of the commercial networks morning programs also do this sort of live interviewing via satellite with regularity. You can learn a great deal about ways to control an interview for time and wrap it up on time by watching these reporter-interviewers and morning show hosts conduct these interviews. They control time with expressions such as "To sum up now in the thirty seconds we have left . . ." or "Can you answer in just a few words, we have just fifteen seconds . . ." or "We're going to lose our satellite link in exactly twenty seconds . . .," and so on.

For recorded interviews remember that your interview is going to be edited before it gets on the air. You should leave a pause between the end of an answer and the beginning of the next question or at the points of interruptions so there is room for the edits to be made cleanly. The point made previously in this section is that it is not a good idea to jump right on top of a subject's answer with a new question. It is much easier to remove "dead air" during an edit than it is to try to find a tiny edit space in that split second between the last word of an answer and the first word of your next question.

Editing your actuality tape will go a lot more smoothly if you have reverse-angle questions, a technique discussed in detail in Chapter 3. To review the main points from that section:

✔ 1. The re-recorded questions must be the same questions you asked the first time, the exact wording voiced in the same tone with the same inflection.

✔ 2. You must re-record the questions in the presence of the subject. This is an external check on the accuracy of your phrasing and voicing of the question: You don't want to be accused of recording the subject's answer to a question and then putting a different question in front of that answer in the editing process.

✔ 3. You must re-record all the questions you asked in the interview, since the interview will be edited. The one you didn't re-record may turn out to be just the one needed.

Standups

Another standard feature of many field report packages is the standup, or standupper. The standup is a short monologue delivered into the camera by the reporter. The reporter needn't be standing, by the way. Some standups are delivered while the reporter is seated, some are done while she or he is walking, usually toward the camera, less frequently, away from it or parallel to it in a side-by-side motion.

A standup may be used in the middle of a report as a bridge between two segments, or at the end to conclude it, or at the beginning of the report to open it. That third one, the standup open, is frowned on as a matter of principle by some professionals, who say the standup open focuses attention on the reporter rather than the story.

For your standup, look right at the viewers. Imagine they are the lens of the camera and talk with them through that lens. You want to appear relaxed but disciplined. A standup is no place for slouched posture, groping hesitations, or fumbling for what you want to say.

A term borrowed from the legitimate theater, **quick study** refers to a performer who memorizes lines quickly and effortlessly. Of course, memorizing words and delivering them well are two different things. Many fine actresses and actors agonize endlessly to commit lines to memory; others might have a script firmly in mind after only a couple of readings even though they are in fact pedestrian performers.

For the TV reporter, the main problem with the technique of memorizing is that the delivery is very likely to look and sound stilted and mechanical. It may lack spontaneity even when it's done without a mistake. Furthermore, total disaster (or an endless succession of retakes) lurks in the background waiting for the reporter who loses the train of thought while pouring out the memorized lines or keeps flubbing that one particular word in the canned version.

But speaking impromptu—that is, with no preparation or advance thought as to what exactly you are going to say—usually doesn't lead to the kind of precision you want in a standup. The drawbacks of (a) memorizing or (b) extemporizing leads us to a third method: the rehearsed ad lib. (That expression is an oxymoron, but if you just keep in mind that your preparation is the key to your standup, what the method is called won't matter so much.) In this method, you memorize your key points in their correct order, but not your lines of delivery. In this method, you have a better chance of avoiding the stiffness of delivery from memory and the looseness of meaning that pure ad-libbing can cause.

We've already touched on this recommended method; we covered it in the section on interviewing where we discussed the best way to prepare the final version of your questions, rehearsed but not memorized.

- First, you get the main points of the standup and the order in which they come firmly fixed in your mind.

- Next, you run through the delivery a couple of times to set the pattern in your mind. You may—in fact you undoubtedly will—use different words and expressions each time you run through the standup. Only the main points and their sequence remain unchanged.

- Then when you do the "take" you let the exact wording come out spontaneously.

The Body Language of Tension

For some of us, just the thought of being in front of the camera makes for a case of the jitters. The palms sweat, the throat constricts, the mouth goes dry, and the words just will not come out, at least not in any way near normal.

In order to cope with nervousness we need to understand something about what is going on. Anxiety is a normal condition when we're in a performing situation. Of course we want to do well in front of others. But will we? Ah, that is the question. If we do well, fine, but if we don't, then others may think less of us. Thus one aspect of anxiety is that performance poses a threat to our self-esteem, which creates tension.

But tension is also latent energy. It is the body's way of getting ready to exert. Our senses become acute, our muscles tighten, and other biochemical changes occur. We're thus poised to have all our energy—mental, physical—channeled to the task at hand. The problem occurs when the tension gets so great that we are unable to control it. So the need is to control this nervous energy, to discharge the build-up in a constructive way, to make it work *for* us rather than *against* us.

Try a few deep breaths. Take them in through the nose, and let them out in a slow and controlled exhale through the mouth. A sip of water might help. Clear the throat and then speak out loud (*mi-mi-mi, la-la-la,* get the jaw, throat, mouth muscles working).

And about as important as any of the foregoing, permit yourself to be less than perfect.

By that we mean set your personal goals high, but not impossibly high. High personal standards encourage maximum effort and lead to improvement and to excellence. But impossibly high goals are unrealistic, become self-defeating, and lead to frustration and failure.

So give up the notion of a "perfect" performance. Prepare as best you are able; do the best you can; learn from your mistakes; keep improving. In time you will know where your talents are, what you are good at, what you do best, what you like most, and what you want out of yourself. Don't be impatient. These things take time. A sense of humor sure helps keep things in perspective.

Try to avoid nervous mannerisms that tend to be distracting to an audience. If you're using a hand-held microphone, hold it firmly, but try not to "white knuckle" it. Don't open and close your fist around the mic in a nervous rhythm with your delivery. If you wear a ring, don't hold the mic with the ring hand; you will get a clicking sound on the audio track. Keep the mic clear of all objects and clothing so that taps, rubbing sounds, and clankings don't drown out what you are saying.

Distribute your weight evenly on your feet, get into a comfortable position, and stay there. Some reporters like to stand with one foot in front of the other at an angle because it is virtually impossible to rock in such a stance. If you rock from side to side or back and forth during the shot, the camera will try to follow you and you will look as nervous as you probably are. Keep your head steady and avoid nodding repeatedly to punctuate your phrases.

About appropriate dress: It sometimes seems that the first thing anyone does on getting a job as a reporter is to buy a trench coat. Nothing is really wrong with that except that it has become a fashion cliché. Dress so that you look presentable, professional, and businesslike. Avoid attire that calls undue attention to yourself: Save the trendy, high-fashion stuff for your leisure time. If all your subjects are wearing rodeo outfits, it's probably because that's what the story is about. It may be appropriate to wear casual clothes on some assignments, but you will look as silly in a big hat and a flowered shirt on the rodeo assignment as you would wearing a plumed helmet to interview the Queen's Household Cavalry captain. Of course, sloppy attire is never justified. How you dress in private is your business; how you dress on the air is another matter.

Watch Your Language

Be professional in the way you talk off as well as on the air. Badmouthing, flippant remarks, and profanities may entertain your videographer/crew, but such behavior is also ill-mannered and adolescent. Around cameras and microphones, horseplay and loose talk are not only bad habits, they're dangerous habits. If something like that gets on tape or especially on the air, it can get you fired or hunting for a good lawyer. A good rule is: When a microphone or camera is present, assume it is "on" and behave accordingly.

VOICE AND DICTION

"Delivering" versus "Speaking"

Here's a quotation from Shakespeare's "Hamlet" (Act 3, Scene 2), from a passage literary scholars refer to as Hamlet's advice to the players: "Speak the speech, I pray you, as I pronounc'd it to you, trippingly on the tongue; but if you mouth it, as many of your players do, I had as lief the towncrier spoke my lines."

"Trippingly" means nimbly. To "mouth" is to mumble. We'll revisit Hamlet's advice to the players in a moment. For now, let us take up mechanics of good oral style: articulation, pronunciation, rate, and pitch.

Articulation

Articulation (or enunciation) refers to the precision and clarity of speech. A common speech problem is slurring, skipping some syllables and running others together—"Juh'eet jet? No d'ju? No, skuhweet."—Translation: "Did you eat yet? No, did you? No, let's go eat."

The accomplished actor Jack Lemmon, whose many fine performances include several portraying a drunk, was once asked by an interviewer whether his real life struggles with alcohol helped him in his successful portrayals of these parts. Lemmon's answer is instructive. He said that the key to playing a drunk is simple: "Don't slur!" Shades of Shakespeare's Hamlet!

Less frequently, delivery might suffer from the opposite problem, a presentation that is overly precise. But this is rare. The more common delivery problem is occasional lapses into sloppy articulation.

Pronunciation

Whereas articulation is about speaking distinctly, pronunciation is about speaking correctly: (a) vowel sounds, consonant sounds, also combinations of them; (b) the emphasis or accentuation of words; and (c) the accuracy (as distinct from the clarity) of these sounds. "Correctly" in this case means pronunciation that is commonly used and accepted by the generality of people.

Pronunciation of the names of persons and the names of places in the news is especially important for the broadcast journalist. Just like reporters in print journalism, broadcasters must get the spelling correct. But in broadcasting, the words also have to be spoken. Smith, Smyth and Smythe are not necessarily pronounced the same way. If the story is about Cairo, Egypt, it's KEYE-roh, or you might see it spelled phonetically as KI'-RO—that same name Cairo in the southern Illinois town near the confluence of the Ohio and Mississippi Rivers is KAIR-oh. Local variations such as these abound. Every state in the United States has place-names in which you cannot get the correct pronunciation from the spelling. Handle (and speak) names with care.

Rate

Rate has two basic components: duration, and pause. Duration is the amount of time given to saying each word (its individual syllables), and pause is the amount of time given to the spaces between words. Duration and pause are linked, and taken together they give your speaking its sense of pace. For example, you would not narrate a story about a homecoming parade and a story about the death of a prominent local citizen at the same rate. One is set in a mood of happiness, the other in a mood of sorrow. The variation in the rate of the presentation is part of the way in which these distinctions in meaning are conveyed to the audience. Usually, by the way, by slowing down the rate of your delivery you can improve other mechanics, such as diction or intonation.

Pitch

Pitch is also called intonation, inflection, or vocal variety. And again, the fault can be either too little, or too much. We label too little inflection "monotone" which means not enough vocal variety (the up-and-down of the voice) in the presentation. Monotone creates an impression of a lack of enthusiasm; to an audience this equates with newscaster "boredom."

About as disturbing is the effect of "sing-song," where the pattern of the ups and downs of the voice is regularized, exaggerated, or random, in any case seemingly unrelated to the words being spoken, unrelated to the meaning of the words and sentences. Try this as an experiment: Find a passage of text that you just plain do not understand, and try delivering it aloud with meaningful vocal variety. That's tough. To be unsure of the meaning is to be unsure of the proper inflection.

Practice

There are two kinds of practice for you to consider. One is practice on your own, away from work, and the other kind is the practice done just before recording.

Using leisure time to practice reading aloud takes much dedication and determination to be sure, but it is just this sort of discipline that propels one ahead of the competition. Certainly reading aloud will strengthen your voice muscles and vocal technique. What should you read aloud? Almost anything will do, fiction or nonfiction, poetry or prose. A professional announcer visiting the campus told the class he was fond of reading aloud the poetry of Poe, not only because he liked Poe's works, but also, he said, because he was impressed with Poe's vocabulary and felt this helped increase his own storehouse of words. Some people do in fact prefer to practice by reading poetry aloud. Also a good course in oral interpretation has been a favorite elective of more than just a few broadcast news majors.

The other kind of practice is the kind reporters do just before recording the V/O or standup, in other words, the rehearsal. The point is, you should get in the habit of doing a complete read-through *aloud* before recording.

Concentration

Concentration is one factor that affects virtually all performers in all forums and at all levels. Performance requires concentration. Concentration does not come naturally and it does not come easily; the human mind wanders, and it is difficult for us to keep our attention fixed on any one thing for very long. Yet, keeping focused is a key—some say *the* key—to a smooth narration.

Lack of concentration is not just a matter of inexperience—it can and does afflict anyone, seasoned professional as well as novice. In broadcasting distractions are everywhere. Focusing requires effort and practice.

Speaking for Edit

We've already talked about the editing problem that results when you leave less than a split second of space between the last word of one answer and the first word of your next question. The same principle applies to your standup.

When you get your cue that the recorder is rolling and up to speed, remain silent and still for a few seconds (a good way is to count silently to five) and then begin. When you get to the end, stand motionless and remain silent for a few seconds (again, a silent five count).

This procedure will put a little editing space on either end of your standup, which provides the videotape editor with editing space. If you begin right at the cue, there may not be room to make the edit at that point. At the end of the take, if you immediately break and ask "How was that?" there'll be little space in which to cue the end of the edit. The edit may either lose the last syllable of the last word of the take or include the first syllable of the first word following the end of the take. Either way is very sloppy, but hardly the editor's fault.

When you are recording voice-over narration try to keep your energy level and your concentration up so that you are projecting and relating to the audience just as much as when you are doing your on-camera standup.

Many stations ask their reporters to "label" their standup or V/O takes, for example:

Sports Ace, standup open, take one

Enterprising Reporter, transition, take two

Some station procedures call for the reporters to count down audibly at the beginning of each take, for example: "Sports Ace, standup open, take one . . . in five, four, three, two . . ." (Pause silently for one beat, then go.)

If something like this is standard procedure in your case, be sure to make the silent count in the same rhythm as the spoken ones. Nothing is quite as frustrating to an editor as a countdown that leaves no space after the final audible count, or leaves four or five beats before the narration begins.

If you have trouble getting a satisfactory version in three takes, one of two things may be happening. You may not be mentally ready and well enough prepared to begin with, or you're just having one of those days. What the takes amount to, then, is rehearsal, something you should have done before recording. Or, maybe you are striving to be perfect. We've already gone over that.

Ending It

The closing of your story is at least as important as the opening, maybe even more important. You've aimed your opening squarely on the mark, and you've gathered actuality to develop the news point. Now you should tie it all together with flair. Whether you close with a standup or with V/O narration, the important thing is to make the content of the close relevant to the news point of the story. If you are going to sum up or restate or recap the two or three important points of the story, make sure that what you say in the closing grows out of what has gone before.

Content-analysis studies in which researchers try to determine if the reporting was fair and balanced sometimes show that bias can occur more frequently in lead-ins, openings, and closings, than in other parts of the story. As reporters try to focus the story on the news point, they need to be extra careful of words that connote an opinion. For example, the anchor lead-in to a story might be something like this:

VIDEO	AUDIO
ANCHOR, ON CAM	It was a bad day for state Democrats: statehouse reporter Doug Huber has the story . . . (VTR HUBER)

Huber's story must provide the evidence to support that lead-in assertion. Or if Huber makes the assertion in his standup opening, the support for it must be in the packaged story content.

Huber could use the same idea in his closing instead:

```
VIDEO                    AUDIO


VTR HUBER                So it was a bad day for the state
                         Democrats, as they lost another round
                         in the courts. . . .
```

The story should already have provided evidence that Democratic Party interests were damaged by the court action.

Nothing is intrinsically wrong with such a lead-in, opening, or close if the evidence is clear. But reporters are reporters, not editorial writers. It is just as wrong for reporters to insert their own opinions, characterizations, or judgments into stories as it is to insert conclusions that are not clearly supported by the facts simply for the sake of a nice, tight ending or a clever turn of phrase. Prepare the closing carefully. Rehearse it enough to be sure that you get the result you want and that it is a proper, sensible, clear conclusion to the story.

You Are a Member of a Team

The relationship of the reporter, beginner or professional, and the crew is a very important element in field reporting. The relationship must be a positive one if the team is to be effective. Perhaps it is not absolutely necessary that crew members like each other personally, but it is essential that they get along well professionally. Without this professional compatibility, it will be very difficult to get the raw materials needed to make the story jell. On the other hand, when all crew members are working together, they complement one another's efforts, and a more complete story is likely to be the result.

When differences arise—and they're bound to—the differences must be faced and worked out. Out in the field is no place for "the silent treatment." This point is so important and so basic that Frank Kearns, a veteran CBS News foreign correspondent who capped his professional career with a dozen years as a college teacher and distinguished professor of journalism, frequently devoted an entire class and lecture to this. He emphasized to his students that everyone in a field reporting crew simply had to be on the same wavelength. As Kearns put it, "You've got to talk these things over and keep talking them out until you do come to an understanding."

As the team reporter you must also respect the equipment and the problems the other members of the crew may have in operating it. That is one rea-

Figure 6.2. In the field the reporter and the videographer work together to gather the facts, visual information, interviews, and eyewitness accounts. This raw material will be combined and edited to make the finished story. *(Michael D. Sullivan.)*

son why we've put so much emphasis on learning the limits of the technology. You cannot detach yourself from the need to protect the gear so that it will continue to work properly. As the reporter you will often be cast in the role of team leader, so your attitude toward the operational and environmental problems you find at the scene of a spot news story may be reflected in how other team members go about their work. If you don't take care to protect equipment when you're working in the rain, it sends a wrong message to the crew.

We covered this previously but it bears restating: Keep the words *please* and *thank you* in your vocabulary. Television news brings together you and the other members of your team, and then you are all in contact with members of the general public. So the need to say *please* or *thank you* will come up. You can express these sentiments in many ways, and a little courtesy goes a long way toward assuring cooperation both from the team and from the public. Of course, it must be sincere. If you do not feel it, better that you say nothing. But a well-placed and well-timed expression of thanks costs you nothing, and you may be amazed at the dividends such simple courtesy can return.

COVERING SPOT NEWS

Spot-news stories are breaking events, usually fast-moving, spontaneous, and chaotic. They include such things as fires, explosions, vehicle accidents, hijackings, shootings, floods, and other events of violence and disaster—of natural or human cause—that come under the umbrella of what some people call "down-side news."

Television news departments (the more progressive ones, at least) have "disaster plan" policies and procedures. Similarly street reporters (at least the more skillful ones) have professional habits that help them prepare for their coverage of spot news as thoroughly as possible in the shortest amount of time. It is partly a competitive and winning attitude. These reporters play "What if" games—"What if, right now, I had to fly out of here and cover a furnace explosion at P.S. 105?" "What if the phone rang right now and the word was that the mayor had just collapsed and died of a heart attack?" The goal is always the same, staying on top of the news in a highly competitive field, not only being first but, more important, being right.

So being mentally prepared and mentally flexible for the unpredictability of spot news is a good start toward being ready when spot news breaks. And when it does, you will either be between assignments or already out in the field working on something else. If you are between assignments, gather yourself up, get as much briefing as can be crammed into a few minutes, and get to the scene with your crew as fast as you can. If you are in the field, rapidly conclude the coverage you and your crew are on, pack up the equipment, and move quickly to the new location.

Experienced reporters will tell you that this shifting of mental gears is one of the more difficult things about television news field reporting. You have all your attention and mental energies focused on the original assignment, and then in midstride you must break off that story and turn to an entirely new and unrelated event. Often it is an event filled with confusion, chaos, and perhaps even danger to yourself and your crew.

Hazard Training

Let's pause for a minute to think about safety. Here we want to distinguish between the professional and the student.

Occasionally television news field reporting may involve risks to the crew. News directors and the crews themselves worry about these dangers and the odds. It is stupid to drive to the scene so fast that you have an auto accident before you get there. Helicopter pilots and reporting crews can recognize a dangerous situation; they follow preflight checks and flight rules scrupulously. And even with all the precautions and safeguards, accidents do happen; news people are injured, and some are killed, while on assignment.

At the scene, professional crews are alert to dangerous situations and try to stay out of them. Being aware of risks means that when news people take risks, they do it in a calculated way and not thoughtlessly.

It is never too soon for you, the student, to practice common sense, to sharpen your instincts, and to protect yourself and your crew from danger. Remember this: Your professor does not want you endangering yourself or your crew, no matter what the class assignment is. On the contrary, your professor's first concern is that you stay well away from such harm. At a construction site with heavy equipment in operation, stay well out from under moving cranes; keep well back from bulldozers, earth movers, and other machines. Stay away from exposed electrical power lines. Avoid leaning out of a tenth-floor dormitory window to get that great high angle shot that's "going to earn you an A." Don't set up in the middle of the superhighway for that great into-frame-out-of-frame sequence. Don't set up the tripod on loose, shifting ground. If you are carrying the camera and recorder, watch where you are stepping and be aware of what's to the side of and behind you. Look in the viewfinder to see what's in front of you, and when you see something coming toward you, don't just assume that whatever it is will miss you. At some point (sooner rather than later) take your eye away from the viewfinder to see if your position is safe. Don't run a drop cord from the house to poolside to run the equipment from AC power, then get into the pool, mic and all, to do that "innovative standup." As in all other phases of this work, your good judgment is always needed.

Problems of Spot News Reporting

Throughout this book we deal with the various elements of covering a spot news story for television. At the end of this chapter is an essay by Lynn Cullen, a veteran television news reporter. Her essay is filled with detailed tips from the reporter's point of view. For now we will look at some of the general problems.

1. Time pressures and fact gathering

2. Sources

3. Shaping the story

4. Clarity of expression

1. Time Pressures and Fact Gathering

Start out by assuming that you won't have enough time to get yourself fully ready to go on the air. You are the vanguard person at the story. You must learn to capture the basic framework of the story as rapidly as possible: the who, what, when, where, and the how and why. It may seem that those are so basic they don't need to be mentioned again, that "it goes without saying."

But it is worth repeating the basics. The first four—who, what, when, and where—are usually easier to get than the last two, how and why. In fact the how and the why may not be determined for hours or days after the event, if then. You don't want to leave them out of any story, but you must be on guard against speculating in the early phases of coverage.

You will be under other kinds of time pressures. The goal is to get as much information as you can and get on the air as fast as you can. You may already have been given time limits: The next newscast is going on the air in thirty minutes; you are going into it live for two minutes, thirty seconds. Or a newscast is already on the air, and the station needs facts for a bulletin. Or it's forty-five minutes to air time, and you are expected to deliver a story before the newscast is over. Whatever the situation, the clock is ticking like a time bomb, and it is up to you to meet the deadline. When they explain the procedures for using the oxygen masks on airplanes, they always say, "Breathe normally." Whether that's possible is a good question, but of course you should try. Plunging into a spot news story requires as much level-headed thinking and acting, as much "normal breathing" as you can muster.

So you race around to find out what you can. If you stick to the key story elements (who, what, when, where, how, why) you have a better chance of getting what you need than if you go about it in random fashion without plan and without purpose. But those basics will not come in any set order. You may get the what before you get the who. The when may not be exactly clear. You know where you are, but in reporting the where you need to be precise, exactly where. There might be some facts that point to the how and why. You need these, but you also need to be cautious in assessing what you know or think you know about this event. You may not be able to get all these basics in your first sweep of fact gathering, but you must try to be as complete as you can be.

You also need to begin to think about interviews and eyewitnesses as soon as you can.

2. Sources

A cardinal rule for any reporter is: "Be sure of your source." At a spot news event you frequently can't be certain. But here are some things to think about:

✔ 1. Who's in charge here?

✔ 2. Where is the official source?

✔ 3. Where and from whom is the information coming?

✔ 4. Who is here whom I know?

✔ 5. Does this story have "sides"?

✔ 6. If yes, who are the spokesmen or women?

✔ 7. Is what I'm hearing different from what I'm seeing?

✔ 8. Have I seen something others have not seen?

✔ 9. What can (should) I do about that?

✔ 10. Do some people here, including official spokespersons, have a vested interest in what has happened?

✔ 11. What can (should) I do about that?

Clearly many of the answers to those and other questions like them depend on your ability to evaluate the information you are getting in the confusion of the moment. Some of the sources will give you basic facts; others will give you opinions based on the little knowledge they may have at the moment. Some will try to get their version on the air for self-serving reasons. Part of your evaluation will come from comparing what you are seeing with what you are hearing and from comparing what you are hearing from one source with what you are hearing from another. Part of making sense of all this will come from your own common sense and gut instincts. Does what you are hearing make sense? Is it logical? Is it a reasonable explanation for what is happening? Does the demeanor of the source—whether the person looks directly at you, his or her facial expression, posture, and so on—convey an impression of sincerity? Does the information you're getting come from more than one source? If not, can you verify it, or have you checked it with other sources? Is this source in a position to know—firsthand, secondhand, or even less directly? If the source quotes someone else or starts saying, "I was told," or "I heard," or "Someone said," you know right away you'd better talk with that someone for confirmation. Is this information official, unofficial, or rumor? You never report a rumor. You do check out a rumor.

What you must try to do in the time available is come as close to the truth as you can. Many things may be unknown. There's a good chance that some of the facts you gather from your sources will turn out later to be wrong or incomplete. In the heat of the moment, people can and do simply misstate something or misunderstand what you want. It is unfortunate that errors get into spot news stories. They should not. But when you feel sure you've done your best under the circumstances, errors should be few and far between. And you should work as diligently as you can to see that any errors are corrected just as quickly as possible.

3. Shaping the Story

At a spot news event, time to think is the most precious time of all because there is so little of it. But you must take enough time to put shape to your story. Seasoned live reporters say that the trick is to stick to the basics and keep it simple both in language and in structure. If you are on the air live, tell what you know. Don't speculate. Be willing to admit what you don't know.

Remember two essential ingredients of news judgment: what is important and what is significant.

You are trying to reconstruct for the audience the main elements of the event. Often keeping a chronological outline in your head or in your notes will serve as a good guide to how you ought to tell the story. Keep it straightforward and simple. You might begin by saying, "To take it from the top . . ." or "Here is what happened, and what we know so far . . ." and then outline the important and interesting facts. Develop and finish one element of the story before you go on to the next. Avoid jumping back and forth between elements whether you are dictating a bulletin or doing a tape report or a live insert. If you have a little time to write something out, keep the direction of the story going forward. Organize it. A simple, tight report of the known facts in some sort of logical sequence is preferable to something that meanders around. And, of course, almost anything is better than a random, ad-lib delivery of unevaluated facts, rumors, speculations, or what "somebody said."

As in the hard news feature reporting situation, the way you end the story is crucial to the impression the audience takes away from your report. Here is where you and your audience will come together on the point of this story, on its meaning. An excellent technique for ending is to summarize the main news points that you have just made in your report, but briefly. This is usually much better than trying to do a "mood" ending or offering your opinions about how grim, stark, humbling, terrifying, or whatever it all has been.

In fact, be wary about waxing eloquent in any segment of your report. The classic piece of press lore on this is: A reporter covering the great Johnstown Flood of 1889 got carried away and wired his lead, something like: "High atop a mountain peak, God viewed nature's awful destruction below . . ." The reporter's more down-to-earth editor at the other end wired back, "Forget flood! Get interview with God!"

4. Clarity of Expression

Let us restate a main point from the writing chapter: All the rules of simple, tight, easy-to-understand writing that apply to the presentation of a script also apply to the material you ad lib or rehearse and deliver in a spot news situation. In fact, the guidelines should be applied with even more discipline in the field. It is very difficult to maintain proper syntax and grammar if you allow yourself to get involved with a lot of compound or compound-complex sentences. You wouldn't do that in your scriptwriting; you shouldn't do it in the field, either. You should always try to:

✔ 1. Use declarative sentences.

✔ 2. Keep the sentence subject and verb close together.

✔ 3. Keep all verbs in the same tense throughout the story.

✔ 4. Be wary of pronoun references; if you have any doubt, substitute the proper noun for the pronoun. To write (or say), "An unidentified assailant shot the police officer through the shoulder with his own gun last night" leaves the meaning of "his" dangling.

If you use big, colorful words, you run the risk of conveying a wrong meaning or impression or overdramatizing. If you use a simile or metaphor, take care to make sure the reference is apt. Sometimes just the right phrase will come to you. You get a thrill out of that, and your audience gets a wonderful insight. But be wary—forcing it, you may find yourself standing there with egg on your face.

SUMMARY

Field reporting with or without electronic news-gathering equipment calls upon the reporter to use all of his or her ability to gather facts and background, to organize and edit, and to tell the story in a logical and clear manner. Interviewing is both art and science, and preparation is a key to good interviewing. Good listening skill is essential.

In the hard news feature the aim is to make the story as complete as possible. In the spot news story the reporter strives for reportorial completeness, but time often cuts this process short. The aim, therefore, is for the best available version of the facts at the moment of coverage.

Because time restrictions do not permit you to tell everything you've learned about a story during the gathering stage, your ability to make news judgments is crucial. Deciding what is the main point of the story is the single most important choice you have to make.

PROFILE

Lynn Cullen is a native of Green Bay, Wisconsin. She studied at Northwestern University and earned a journalism degree from the University of Wisconsin at Madison. After graduation she spent seven years as a reporter, anchor, and talk-show host at WISC-TV, Madison.

In 1981 Cullen moved to WTAE-TV Pittsburgh, where she became the "Offbeat" reporter, producer of "specials," and half-time reporter for Pittsburgh Steeler football telecasts. During this time she won numerous honors including a 1992 Emmy Award for feature reporting, of which she is justifiably proud; four Pittsburgh Press Club Awards; numerous Associated Press Broadcasters awards; and a national Women in Communications award for a series about sexual harassment.

Cullen's more recent broadcasting assignments have included being an on-air host in a variety of formats including a talk-radio program, a public television quiz show called "The Pennsylvania Game," and a prime-time hour-long live talk show on a Pittsburgh public television channel, WQEX-TV.

Reporting Live, Being Live
Lynn Cullen

Rumor has it that when opportunities for dodging bullets are in short supply in television news, war correspondents like to keep in professional shape by doing live inserts for the six o'clock news. Perhaps that's a myth, but it is not a surprising substitution. Both jobs offer the adventuresome reporter the same kind of thrills, if not the same ultimate risks.

Done correctly, a live report can be television news at its best, providing the viewer with eyewitness immediacy, information, and drama. Done incorrectly, it can be uproariously and unintentionally funny to the viewer, while the reporter who ends up DOA—Dead On the Air—seldom considers it amusing. That is why live-shot reporters, like war correspondents, must possess the best in reportorial skills and a more than casual knowledge of basic survival training.

Of course, few live reports are as risky as facing enemy fire in a war zone, although a few do come close to that. But first, let's take a look at the gentlest of the genre: the planned live event that happens during a newscast. It could be a testimonial dinner for a local civic leader or a rank-and-file union vote on a tentative contract agreement that, if accepted, would end a bitter, month-long strike. Perhaps the governor is coming to town for a closed-door briefing with county officials regarding the proposed location of a hazardous-waste dump in the far corner of their bailiwick.

Because the meeting itself is planned, the producer and the reporter will have the luxury of planning their coverage. They will know, for instance, that a group of angry and frightened citizens who live near the proposed site is planning a noisy greeting for the governor. And they will know his arrival is scheduled for five o'clock, one hour before air time. It's a perfect opportunity for what is sometimes referred to as a wraparound, or more inventively, as a "Sony Sandwich"—a taped and edited package, coupled with a live introduction and tag from the reporter at the scene.

Since the meeting between the governor and the county officials will be occurring behind closed doors during the newscast, it is their comments beforehand that you will want to tape and package. And because the demonstrators will be waving their signs and hollering before, during, and after the meeting (fully aware, of course, that the news will be on the air and they will be on the news), their protest will provide both a dramatic backdrop for the live report and a spokesperson for a live interview.

How do you, the reporter, approach this assignment? Chances are you will be given no more than two and a half to three minutes to tell the story. That includes the live introduction, package, interview, and tag. Organization then becomes the key factor, and that should begin in the truck on your way to the scene. Simply shelve the small talk and instead talk shop with the crew. After all, you are all in this together.

Their concerns will be with logistics such as finding a place to park the remote unit and figuring out how to get the signal (and consequently your report) from the scene to the station. If, as is possible, they must operate from a location a few blocks away from the action because an uncooperative building or hill is blocking their transmission, that fact will have an impact on how you can perform your job.

But let's assume the best—that the truck can park and operate well at the scene, and that you've arrived a comfortable thirty minutes before the scheduled five o'clock appearance of the governor and county commissioners. Even though they may not yet be in attendance, it's a safe bet your competition is, so you need to get to work.

Go straight to the demonstrators and like that mythical Martian ask one of them to take you to their leader. Then, while you are talking to the group's spokesperson, you should be doing two things: getting the spokesperson's concerns and what he/she plans to do about them down on paper; and gauging how good an interview that person is likely to give on camera. If you find someone who is distractingly nervous or inarticulate before the fact, imagine how tongue-tied he or she may become with the camera on and thousands watching. So, say thanks for the valuable information, ask him or her to point out some other protesters you should question, and then go quickly to find someone who *can* talk.

What you are looking for, ideally, is a person who can respond intelligently to the politicians' statements and can do it in terse twenty- to thirty-second "bites." That niggling time allotment may seem preposterous at first glance. But if you remember that the producer has given you just two and a half to three minutes to do the entire report, it begins to appear almost generous.

At any rate, line the person up. Make certain he or she will be at your truck ten or fifteen minutes before air time. And don't forget the correct pronunciation and spelling of his or her name, and any title he or she may claim. You will need to radio that information back to the producer so that it can be "supered" on the screen during the live shot.

It's probably getting close to five o'clock, so your photojournalist should already be videotaping some B-roll video for the package: shots of the protesters, their signs, any visible security precautions taken by the police, establishing shots of the scene. If you have a minute—and try to work so that you do—you now need to organize your thoughts on how best to tell this story and to figure out what questions are likely to elicit the most newsworthy responses from the governor and the county representatives. You're going to have to work very fast and hard in the next sixty minutes, so efficiency is one of those things "devoutly to be wished" to paraphrase a certain melancholy Dane. You might wish you'd done a little spring training with the local football team, because if the governor's not in a particularly talkative mood, you might find yourself in one of those car-to-door press stampedes where you'll need your microphone, a good bit of moxie, and the muscle of a middle linebacker.

Let's assume you survive the governor's arrival, even manage to grab a good, tight sound bite from him, and that you also have a less strenuous opportunity to interview one of the more articulate commissioners. It's 5:10 and you have the lead story, but a major portion of it is not yet written, fed back to the station, or edited.

Unless you have an unusually well-honed memory or were wise enough to carry a small audio tape recorder during your interviews, you'll need to review the scenes that have been shot on the truck's monitor while the engineer transmits the raw video back to the station and into the hands of an increasingly impatient editor. Your concern now is to pick out the parts of the governor's and commissioner's interviews you want to incorporate into the package, and to write down their verbal in cues and out cues so that you can radio them back to the producer.

Once that is done you've got to get the script for your package written. It is, of course, wise to bear in mind that the editor will need a minimum of fifteen minutes to put it all together in time for the six o'clock program open. It is, however, paralyzing to dwell on this disquieting fact. Just bear it in mind, and keep your package simple and straightforward.

Quickly outline the major points you'll make during the live opening standup. Only rough it out, though, and get on to the edited report, because that has top priority. It should run no longer than a minute and a half, and its end should be scripted to allow for a smooth transition into the live interview with the protester. For example, if the package concludes with the governor's promise that all interested parties and points of view will be heard before any decision is made, you'll be in gravy when the camera returns to you and the protesters are chanting in the background, hoping the governor will hear them through the closed doors of the meeting room. You could, of course, make reference to that very point and then move effortlessly to the live interview.

But meanwhile, you're still in the remote truck, and ready now to record your voice-over narration track and transmit it back to the station. When that's done you can get on the two-way radio and give the producer specific instructions about the package, the in cues and out cues, and any names or locations that should be inserted over the video. Maybe you'll want to down a few Rolaids about now, but don't waste time because you've still got to construct carefully the live portions of your report. It is not wise, however, to script these segments verbatim. You're not going to have a TelePrompTer™ from which to read the words; nor should you lose all eye contact with the audience by having your nose firmly planted in your scribbled copy. Memorizing the script also presents problems for most reporters. There's always the danger of forgetting the lines, or perhaps worse, reciting them in an unnatural, stilted manner. Have some faith in your ability to tell the story simply, as if you were talking to a friend. Help yourself by jotting down key words, phrases, or statistics that will help if you should lose your train of thought. It's a good idea to write down the name of the person you'll be interviewing live. It's one of those things you can forget, and that's embarrassing.

After having said all that, let me suggest that it would be wise, nonetheless, to have a very good idea of what your opening and concluding statements will be. No good reporter wants to stumble into a report or mumble out of it. You are the only person who knows where this live presentation should start and where it should end.

I'm guessing it's now about ten minutes to air time, which means you'd better comb your hair, join your photojournalist, and turn your attention to the subject, who is more than likely suffering from cold feet, clammy hands, and a dry mouth. If you're smart you'll try to calm him or her down. It's in your own interest to make the subject feel as relaxed and comfortable as possible under the rather unrelaxed circumstances. By all means tell him or her exactly what's going to happen. Tell him or her to look at you, not at the camera, during the interview, and to try to keep their responses short and to the point. Be as reassuring and calm as you can, given the fact you may well be a nervous wreck yourself. It's not improbable that the feeling most reporters get before their first live shot is very much like that of the novice parachutist before the first jump. The only difference seems to be prepositional in nature—one will be *on* the air and the other *in* it. Both are living somewhat dangerously.

Before we take the plunge, though, let's get a better idea of where we are. I suggested earlier that the protest would make an ideal backdrop for the live report. But will it? The last thing a reporter needs in the background is a crowd of mugging yahoos—people who wave wildly and inexplicably scream, "Hi, Mom!" That can be distracting and should be avoided whenever possible. But if the demonstration or crowd is relatively civilized, peopled with folks who will continue to do whatever it was they were doing before your camera arrived, then the more the merrier. Their presence will give life and immediacy to the report much more readily than the letters L-I-V-E superimposed on the screen ever can. And if you're especially lucky, your mobile truck will be outfitted with a rooftop platform where a camera can be placed to photograph over the heads of any rowdy troublemakers, yet still give the viewers a clear picture of the scene.

It's time now to lend me your ears because one of them must be fitted with a contraption called an IFB, which stands for *interrupted feedback*. It is an earpiece connected to a small receiver that clips on a belt or can be hidden in a pocket, and it's your personal lifeline to the support crew back at the station. Through it you will be able to hear program audio and the director's instructions. If he or she is good at the job and reassuring by nature, you'll get a countdown to the report just like Mission Control: "About five minutes till we come to you . . . How about another mic check? . . . Two minutes, Lynn . . . ten, nine, eight . . . and you're on the air." If you are going to take your cue from the anchor introducing you, you'll hear the anchor's words (program audio) over the IFB (mix-minus audio). In this way, when you finish your report, if the anchor asks you a question, you'll be able to respond smoothly.

It was Ringo Starr who said, "All you gotta do is act naturally." It's a deceptively simple suggestion, but it's a good one. The live shot reporter is certainly not in anything approaching a "natural" situation, although the good reporters will appear not to have noticed that. So when air time comes and the photojournalist's finger points in your direction, here are some tips on assuming the natural look:

> Try to speak in a normal tone of voice and in a normal cadence. Eyeball the camera lens as if it were an old friend and tell your story with as much feeling and enthusiasm as you can muster. Whenever possible, make reference to the scene and include the viewers: "These demonstrators, as you can hear, seem to have their doubts about that . . . This so-called briefing is going on right now behind those locked doors. . . ." Don't worry if you have to refer to your outline. It looks perfectly normal, and in some instances can underline for the audience just how quickly your cameras have brought them to the scene—so quickly you're speaking from scribbled notes!

Back to our hypothetical live shot and some potential wrinkles that can develop. For instance, it's possible that you'll be leading effortlessly into the taped package when the director's voice breaks into your thoughts with the order to "stretch." What that means is that there is some sort of a problem on the other end with getting the package on line and you'll have to stall. The direction to "stretch" is as unwelcome to a reporter as the suggestion to "tread water" is to a drowning man. A seasoned, unflappable reporter, however, would use the occasion without batting an eyelash to tell the viewers all those little details she'd had to jettison because the two and a half to three minutes wasn't enough time to tell it all. In this situation a good gift of gab comes in very handy.

Eventually, the director will give you either the good news that the tape is ready or the unwelcome information that it's not going to play at all. If it is a no go, you'll have to ad lib a summary of the report as best you can, do the interview with the protester, throw it back to the studio, and then count to ten between clenched teeth. Technical difficulties, you see, are one of the pitfalls of live reporting and continually remind us how relatively new all this electronic gadgetry is.

If the package is there as scripted—and it usually will be—you should use the ninety seconds in which it is playing to reassure the subject and to remind him or her in a pleasant way that nice, short answers are best. If, despite this, the subject begins to ramble when the moment of truth arrives, don't be afraid to jump in at the first punctuation mark and redirect the conversation. This is not an easy thing to do, but it should now be apparent that good live reporting as a whole is not an easy thing to do.

At a spot news event the reporter often must go live with very little information and within minutes of arriving on the scene. Here television has a tremendous advantage over newspapers, and if you're lucky, you'll beat out your competition, too. But some of the examples that spring to mind here also raise serious questions about journalistic responsibility in volatile situations. To illustrate, here is another hypothetical situation: An armed man has taken hostages in a downtown office building. Some shots apparently have been fired. You and your cameras have just arrived on the scene. One thing that you must remember at all times is: Don't get in the way of the police. It's your job to report the story and bring the viewers as close to the action as possible, but it is certainly not your place to get involved or to alter the situation in any way. Unfortunately, some reporters and producers have made questionable and potentially catastrophic decisions in situations like this one.

For instance, showing the location of police sharpshooters on the roofs of adjacent buildings during your live report could be helpful to the hostage takers, if they have a television set available—and they easily could have access to one. Showing police crawling toward the getaway car they've agreed in the negotiations to provide, but then continuing to show them letting the air out of the tires might be wonderful video for your purposes, but also could cause a nervous TV-watching gunman to explode. At night, simply turning on your bright television lights could spook a cornered gunman, or transform an unruly crowd into a rock-throwing mob.

There's another type of remote report. It is one to which the adjective "gratuitous" easily applies. I know you've seen them, many of them, as a matter of fact.

The poor reporter stands, microphone in hand, at the now-deserted scene of some story that happened hours before and ended long ago. Why is the reporter still there? Probably because station management thinks its viewers are still struck by the sheer wonder of this new technology and because station management is still struck by the cost of it.

For the reporter, though, the gratuitous remote presents a bit of a problem. What to do? My advice is to try your best not to look foolish or furious, keep the introduction short, get right to the package since there's nothing going on where you are, do a quick live tag, and then head right for the nearest watering hole.

Going live merely for the sake of going live is still a problem in many markets, and unfortunately, such indiscriminate use of television's live capabilities only serves to minimize the impact of on-the-spot coverage in those situations where it is truly warranted.

Here are some more helpful hints.

1. The live interview puts the reporter in an exceedingly vulnerable position.

First of all, it's quite possible that despite your most earnest efforts, the subject will be a dud. He or she will either talk too much and say too little or, worse, answer your questions in monosyllabic yeses and nos. In such cases the smart reporter will have an alternate line of questions in reserve, just as well-applied assertiveness training may help when you are confronted with the nonstop talker. Also, you will get only one shot at each live report, so you must be concerned with the quality and coherence of your questions. In a taped interview the reporter can even be lazily conversational if that approach will get the desired responses. If the question sounds foolish, it can be reworded and asked again or simply edited out of the piece. But no such escape routes are available to the live shot reporter. A stupid question asked is a stupid question aired. Most live shot reporters would have a comfortable nest egg set aside if they could collect a dollar for every word, phrase, or question they wish they'd never uttered.

2. In certain live situations, some say ideal ones, a picture is truly worth a thousand words.

When confronted with such a situation the reporter (who is never, incidentally, paid by the word) might want to remember that fact and keep quiet, letting the natural sound and video do the job for a while. A spectacular fire or a parade are two disparate examples of possible opportunities for this kind of reportorial restraint. Although many reporters would never think of it, there are times when they should get out of the way and let the camera take center stage without superfluous commentary.

3. Contacts are your master weapon.

If it's a big story (let's say the decision in a spectacular criminal trial), all the stations in town will be going live at the same time and all will want the same people live—the district attorney, the defense attorney, perhaps the defendant. If a reporter is to stand any chance of getting a commitment from any of the principal players to talk to him or her first, the calls, the contacts, the professional relationships that have been established before the fact will be the decisive factor.

4. The IFB as friend and foe.

Those earpieces (IFBs) I mentioned earlier that feed you the director's instructions and program audio are wonderful when you are feeling alone and vulnerable. But if you are trying to ad lib a cogent paragraph or two about the story you're covering, it can be very distracting to have to listen to, "Wrap it up, please," or, "Twenty seconds, Lynn," or, "Throw it back to Don." To take all that in, keep your delivery smooth, get out on time, and never let the viewers know you're suffering sensory overload, amounts to nothing less than a mental juggling act. Don't worry if you should drop the ball occasionally. It happens to the best.

5. Wind is always unwelcome at a live shot.

This is especially true for female reporters who sport longer hairdos than most of their male colleagues. Trying to do a serious report while looking like an English sheepdog is not a comfortable situation. Combs and hairspray are unisex, barrettes or headbands can be indispensable for female reporters and should always be taken along just in case, the same as foam wind protectors for the microphones.

6. How you look on the air is important to your credibility.

This may not be a popular idea to raise. But the reality of the business is that television reporters are supposed to look neat and attractive on the air. Some pancake makeup, a hairbrush, and just plain good grooming between times will prevent the way you look from distracting the audience. Of course, your first priority is to get the story, but you are also expected to look presentable when delivering it.

7. Always dress for the weather (advice your mother would give you if she only knew).

If it's wintertime and your station is not located in a tropical zone, always dress warmly. If it's snowing, blowing, and cold, lined boots, gloves—you can't take notes wearing mittens—and a hat are essential. I once found myself stuck outside during an interminable hostage situation. The temperature was well below freezing and I had a flimsy coat that was not up to the job, open-toed, high-heeled shoes, and no hat. My mouth actually froze that night, so when I went on the air I could not shape my lips to pronounce certain consonants. Needless to say, I was as embarrassed as I was cold.

8. A prop can be apropos.

A prop or visual aid can be very useful, especially if video is difficult to come by.

Let's say a pipe in a huge natural gas tank has sprung a leak and five thousand people have been forced from their homes because of the danger of an explosion. It's a big story, and you are in big trouble, because the police are keeping you far away from the dangerous tank and far away from the pictures you need. Even though you have video of the evacuees leaving and video of the emergency crews arriving, you still have no video of the very thing that is causing all this chaos. What do you do?

The reporter who actually found herself in this difficult position employed three tools at her disposal: her reporting skills, her inventiveness, and her can of hairspray. Using her reporting skills she learned the leaking pipe was no more than six inches in circumference, about the same size as the can of hairspray in her purse. So on her live tag she simply traced her finger around the base of the hairspray can, illustrating in a very visual way the irony of such a small object creating such a big problem. It was very effective.

9. Show some leg; or, take a walk.

Since these are called *live* shots, it is not a bad idea to look alive during them. Nowhere is it written that a reporter must stand stock still, cemented to one spot.

Try starting a report off screen and then walking into the establishing shot. Or if you're reporting on a drop in automobile sales, for instance, start the report by getting out of a car and then move through the dealer's showroom until you encounter the salesperson who is to be your interview subject. To enhance and lend immediacy to a spot news report, you could retrace the steps an armed robber took leaving the scene of the crime.

The idea here is to be creative. But please be careful! I once started a live shot in an elevator, pushing the "open" button so as to reveal myself as I began my intro. It was very dramatic. The only problem was, the doors shut on me while I was still talking.

10. Be prepared.

If the director has told you you'll be on in a minute or so, get yourself in position *immediately* and stay put. That "minute or so" could become seconds if something unforeseen happens. Nothing looks more unprofessional than getting caught off guard when the anchor introduces you.

And on the other end, when you've finished your report and thrown it back to the studio, always stay put and maintain eye contact with the camera until the director gives you the all clear. You don't want the camera to catch you dropping your mic and leaving as if you had more important things to do.

So that's the advice from the trenches. Live reporting is probably one of the most difficult jobs television can offer to a journalist. Not all reporters can do on-the-spot reporting well, and few excel at it. But this much should be apparent from what you've read here: Only the thick of skin, the fleet of foot, and the quick of tongue need apply.

Producing the News

Television news involves a group of people in a team effort. No matter how large or small the staff may be, the jobs of those who gather the news and those who bring it together and put it on the air are intimately linked. Television news is no place for loners. Of all forms of journalism, putting together a newscast is the most team oriented. Whether it is a one-minute update, a local insert in the morning network news programs, or a complete regularly scheduled newscast, the way the teamwork goes determines how successful the news programming will be.

Editorial control is important. At a conference on press responsibility conducted by the Gannett organization, then ABC News White House correspondent and veteran Washington reporter Ann Compton gave an insight into the world of television news on two different levels—local and national. She said:

> When I started out in Roanoke, Virginia—back in the Third World of television news . . . I often thought up the story, drove myself there [and] on rare occasions picked up the silent camera and shot the cover footage myself.
>
> I screened the film, often did the splicing myself, wrote the lead-in for the anchorman and then went back and rewrote the whole process for the 11 P.M. news later that night. . . . I never felt more creativity than I did back in those days; it is far less creative at the network level. . . . Where I had real impact and felt the greatest sense of responsibility was reporting for a local station covering half the state of Virginia.*

Correspondent Compton said it is much different at the network level.

> . . . When I do a minute-and-fifteen-second spot on "ABC World News Tonight," consider the cast of characters that goes into putting that

---

*Quoted in "Editing in the 80's," Part V, *The Gannetteer*, March 1982.

Figure 7.1. Ann Compton, ABC News Correspondent. *(Courtesy Donna Svennevik/ABC News.)*

spot together. There are three network correspondents for ABC, NBC, and CBS working at the White House each day; there are two full camera crews and a lighting technician. There is a research staff back in our [bureau] with computer access to a myriad of clippings and resources that we need in putting together, for instance, a spot on the unrest in Poland.*

And other members of the team are at work.

There is at least one producer back in the shop who does nothing all day but screen all the video that might go into my spot, be it from our library files in New York, be it stuff that we've shot today and have sent back to the office, or be it things sent in from our affiliates or our bureaus across the country.

There is one senior producer in Washington who not only screens my script but coordinates to make sure that I do not step on the toes of any other correspondent.

*Ibid.

There is one desk editor who does nothing but read the wires and concentrate on the other news sources that are commenting on Poland so I can have access to all the information I should on the story.

There is one videotape editor who puts my pictures together so they don't look like a patchwork quilt but instead flow from one scene to another.

There are two senior editors who review my script and fit it in with the total lineup of "World News Tonight."

And there is an anchorman who more often than not writes his own lead-in to my script. . . . The strength of that lead-in often enhances the value or quality of the spot.*

Ann Compton's account of her team vividly shows the difference in staff size and responsibility between small market stations and a network. It is obvious that there is an economy of scale at work. In the small market station—the kind of station where Compton began—there are fewer levels of responsibility; a staffer may perform any combination of jobs such as reporter, videographer, editor, writer, and even anchor. As Compton's account indicates, in the small market situation editorial and content control was firmly placed on her shoulders. At ABC News that all changed, she became part of a team of a large number of people helping her and supervising her coverage.

THE NEWSROOM: ORGANIZING STAFF, PLANNING COVERAGE

A television station's staff is a complex organization. Just in the newsroom part of the operation alone, such people as the news director (and assistant news directors), assignment desk manager and editors, producers, technicians and technical coordinators, studio and control room personnel, videotape editors, writers, researchers, reporters, videographers, interns (keep that in mind) and others all combine their talents to "manufacture" the product. Organizational details vary from station to station, of course, but one standard feature is that the organization is hierarchical. There's an explicit chain of command.

At the top is the news director, sometimes the title is vice president for news, or news administrator. She or he controls the budget, hires and fires, and has the ultimate responsibility for everything that goes into and comes out of that news operation. She or he is hired or fired by the station's general manager. The successful news director today is one who can handle the bud-

*Ibid.

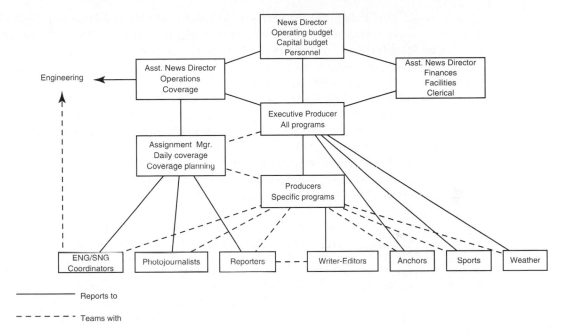

Figure 7.2. The newsroom team. This organizational structure is typical for a medium-size newsroom. While the news director and his or her assistants are in overall command, this structure puts heavy responsibilities on the assignment desk manager and the producers who plan and manage the coverage and news program production.

get, supervise the operation so that it turns out quality (and popular) news programs, lead subordinates through tricky but inevitable change (many changes prompted by equipment and technological advances), and motivate the staff. News directors today say you should study economics, business practices, technology, journalism, and especially, they say, the so-called people skills—how to get that motivation, what the coaches endlessly call "momentum." As one news director said, "Some days I think I should have majored in abnormal psychology."

Next in authority are assistant news directors, assignment managers and editors, executive producers, and producers. They are in charge of operational functions. They are expected to direct the hour-by-hour, minute-by-minute news gathering, preparation, and production. If the staff structure includes several assistant news directors, each one may be given responsibility for one key facet of the news operation, such as budget control, operational supervision, or liaison with the engineering department.

The Assignment Desk Manager

At the heart of any news operation is the assignment desk. A station's news-gathering success is keyed to the successful functioning of the assignment desk. The desk manager is the main source of coverage planning and execution. The assignment desk manager maintains elaborate files—the **futures file** or "**tickler file**" or the like—a calendar keeping track of scheduled future events, government hearings, court cases, key sources, and where these sources can be quickly located.

Another assignment desk function is to keep on the lookout for new angles on breaking stories and follow-ups on continuing stories. In sum, its personnel must know what has happened, what is happening, and what is going to happen.

The assignment manager usually relies on the station's newsroom computer system, or at least a dedicated computer, to keep track of the scores of details juggled at the assignment desk. Typically, the assignment desk software includes:

- access to all incoming press agency and network wires.

- a file to list and update all of the day's news events, assignments, and developing stories. This information is shared with key managers and supervisors, including the News Director, Assistant News Director(s), Executive Producer, Producers, ENG Coordinator, and Operations Coordinator.

- a data base which lists each assignment, with its time, location, topic, contact names and numbers, and other information, such as parking restrictions. As each assignment is filled, the names of reporters, field producers, videographers, technicians, and the designation of key equipment such as Microwave Truck Two, are added or revised. The data base can be updated to alert producers to delays or completion of the assignment.

- a file of all common contacts (the computer equivalent of a rotary card file).

- special calling lists to be used in emergencies, such as an aircraft crash, tornado, hurricane, flood, state prison riot, or commuter rail accident.

- interfaces to data bases such as Nexus®, CompuServe®, or Internet.

- on some systems, data stored on CD-ROM, such as encyclopedias.

- a futures file which lists all known upcoming events and provides the framework for each day's assignments list.

- an interface with the producer files so that the assignment editors can read program rundowns.

- e-Mail for messages.

- a fax interface.

The speed with which a station can and must react to breaking news and deliver the coverage puts a great deal of pressure on the assignment desk edi-

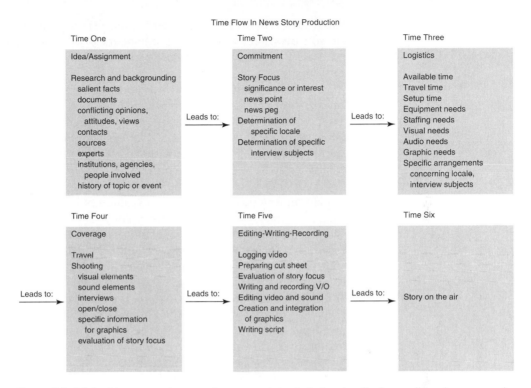

Figure 7.3. A television news story requires a great deal of planning that sometimes has as much to do with the logistics and mechanics of the medium as it does with the content of the story itself. However, all elements must be taken into consideration for the story make it to air.

tor. Yet there is more to it—the human factor. Assignment managers must have good people skills. Since they are the ones who are most frequently in direct contact with the news-gathering personnel, they have to be motivators. To get the most productivity out of the staff they must have an awareness of individual strengths and weaknesses, likes and dislikes, fears and foibles, even the personal relationships between staff members.

If your first professional assignment in broadcast news is as an assistant on the assignment desk, consider yourself fortunate. It's a good place to break in and begin your progress toward becoming a reporter or videographer or video editor, since from that desk you will get a better knowledge of the whole news operation. If you aspire to be a producer, the assignments desk is *the* place to start.

The Producers

Producers are key people in television news. The ones with the most authority and responsibility have the title **executive producer**, the person in charge of the content, order, news judgment, and production of all news programs. Then come **line producers**—the 6 P.M. newscast producer, for example. In larger operations there may be **segment producers** who have responsibility for perhaps a portion of a lengthy newscast, or for the live inserts in a newscast, or for a particular special report or department within a newscast. Then come **assistant producers** and **production assistants** and **aides** who work for producers in a wide variety of tasks.

Television news producers are commanders, directors, managers, organizers, and, above all, journalists. They make most of the news and production judgments. They have a lot to say about what stories are covered, how they are covered, and who covers them. They decide the order of the program and the amount of time allotted to each element in it. They often do a lot of the writing, particularly copy for anchors. They take or get the blame when things go wrong or wrong decisions are made. It is a truism that if the program goes well the anchors and reporters get the credit. If it goes badly, no matter what the reason, the producer gets the blame.

What every news program producer is trying to do, within the boundaries and guidelines of overall station news policy, is to provide a mix—hard news, features, consumer information, life-style elements, editorial opinion, special segments, weather, sports—that will give the audience a satisfying package of information, even a little entertainment. They want to leave the viewers with the feeling that they have seen and heard about most of the events that have happened in their community that day.

The producer is another linchpin figure in the TV newsroom. A Washington news vice president said: "I give my producers a great deal of power and responsibility. If something goes wrong I don't call the anchor, I call the producer. I expect them to have all kinds of news judgment and to be in command of everything."

A Columbus, Ohio news director: "I have a lot of arguments with my producers about news judgment. Some of them are so production oriented that they sometimes obscure the content with the production flash. That bothers me. . . . There is some truth to the claim that we have to be as clean and fast paced as the entertainment programs we compete against. But, the successful producer in the long run is the one who . . . [can] control the production elements [to] enhance the story telling, not overwhelm it. That takes judgment and it has got to be in the direction of the journalism."

A news consultant based in New York thinks the technology has given the producers a lot more power along with a heightened need to stay on top of the processing of the raw material. "They are at the end of the pipeline . . . they control what goes out . . . so they've got to be able to watch the material as it comes in, and then control what is done with it. . . . They must be there all the time shaping the content, checking it for accuracy, completeness, aptness, and deciding how it fits into the rest of the newscast."

It's both hurry up and wait. "You have to be able to wait for later developments," said the news director of a New York network-owned station, "then push for the deeper coverage ENG and SNG can provide. The producer has to be capable of directing a change to add new material 10 minutes before airtime or right in the middle of the story."

Flexible and firm in Chicago: "They've got to organize things quickly, and be flexible and firm at the same time. It's the rule now to hold off until the latest fact is in, then commit. And for the late evening news program, they've got to be able to think 'new'. What new things can we do to this story to make it better, fuller, and more satisfying for those who also saw it at 6 P.M.?"

A juggler of facts and splash in San Francisco: "They have to juggle more balls in the air at the same time. The first thing is to take care of the information content. Yet, you can have the best information in the world and if the program has a lot of production errors people will tune away. It's a tough balancing act between content and production values."

Producers are also at the center of live reports. While the most exciting live reports are those that interrupt other programming to bring the audience running coverage of a breaking story, most live reports come in regularly scheduled newscasts. These then can be called **planned live**.

For example, at the regular morning editorial staff conference a decision is made to do a live insert from City Hall, where an important council committee will be debating a major item. The best estimate is that the committee vote on the issue will come shortly before the 6 P.M. news begins. But at the editorial conference it is also decided that the live report will include pretaped material covering other angles. These include:

The impact of the decision on the area of the city most affected

How the city's action may affect a bill now going through the state legislature

The impact of the action on the political futures of city officials

Other reporters are assigned to work up material on these angles. At 6 P.M., the on-scene reporter reports live at City Hall announcing the committee decision. He or she includes the pretaped packages on the other angles within the report. This is called a **live wrap**.

Inserting these live wraps into the regularly scheduled news program challenges the skill of that program's producer. She or he may have constructed a tightly timed program that now becomes a ticking bomb. The field reporter must be able to tell the story quickly and concisely within a given time limit. Interviews may run long. Inserting the pretaped material into the live wrap requires precision and close coordination among control room staffers. If the report is to include questions and answers between the studio anchors and the field reporter, these must go back and forth crisply. No matter who goofs, the responsibility rests squarely on the producer.

What counts most is the producer's ability to keep firm control at a time when being flexible leads to either success or disaster. A Boston news director indicated just how important that ability is: "Live means less control. The producers are in charge, but someone else has that segment of the program in their hands."

In Detroit: "There is a much bigger chance to make a wrong decision when you are live. Those who make too many wrong decisions aren't producers for very long. Like quarterbacks, their pass completion average is the thing they live or die by."

In Minneapolis: "Live makes the programs really difficult to plan. No longer can they say, 'This story will be one minute thirty-three seconds with a seventeen-second lead-in!' It must be engraved in stone somewhere that no live report ever ran short. . . . Producers must be ready to rebuild the program one minute before air time or put it back together in some coherent form [if something goes wrong] during the program."

An executive producer in Los Angeles said that live inserts have made the news programs free form. "The producer knows that he or she will have some of this and some of that, but only a tentative idea about how long each of those is going to be. They've got to plan on what they can drop or add but still get everything in. . . . People who can do it and have it make some sense . . . and still come out on time . . . are gems."

Executive producers have the ultimate power because they supervise news-gathering activities, staff, content, the operations of producers and the program or segments they produce—in short, they oversee everything.

Technicians and Technical Coordinators

Technicians usually report to the head of the engineering department, not the news director, so excellent liaison between the two departments is crucial to smooth operation of the technology. Engineers are vitally interested in the technical quality of the pictures and sound going out to the audience. Journalists are vitally interested in the editorial quality of that same material, the clarity and understandability of the content of those pictures and sound.

It does no good to have fuzzy pictures that cannot be seen clearly and sound that people can't hear distinctly, just as it does no good to have stories that are so badly written and edited that the audience can't understand what the news program is trying to communicate. Both engineers and journalists must have as their primary goal the highest technical and content quality that can be achieved.

Two other variables that help explain differences in newsroom organization at different stations are station size, and union jurisdictions. In smaller, especially nonunion stations the journalists may operate cameras, video editors, and even the playback of tapes into newscasts. In larger markets union contracts may dictate that technicians run the machines while the journalists tell the technicians what content is desired.

Some of the division of labor depends on where that labor is being performed. Technicians run the machines in the station's control room and technical areas. That is their domain, and you risk sharp criticism and maybe worse if you fool around with switches, buttons, dials, knobs, and the like. It can take technicians hours to get a control room back to normal function after some curious person has wandered around idly "testing" switches by turning them on, off, up, down. Most engineers like to operate like aircraft commanders—with preflight checks and all switches in the proper position. They do not take kindly to fiddlers, and no one would want to have it any other way.

In the field, technicians operate the more sophisticated parts of the gear. While videographers record pictures and sounds and reporters get facts and report them, technicians get the mobile unit equipment up and running and keep their eyes on the readouts. Automation and computerization continue to develop at a rapid pace and thus change the technical side of the work. Technical improvements often mean much more simplified operating features for complex equipment, so with each new generation of equipment you will be apt to find gear that the typical news staffer can learn to operate.

What the engineers also do is maintain the equipment. Here their skills are vastly different from those of the journalists. The machines and computers we use are highly complex. They do break down, and except for some basic field trouble-shooting procedures anyone can learn, fixing them is an engineering job. That requires special training, thousands of dollars worth of test equipment, and a good supply of replacement parts.

Figure 7.4. Production control room. In the WTAP-TV, Parkersburg, West Virginia, production control room, the graphics/still store operator (left) and audio board operator (right), along with the director (rear) check scripts in preparation for "News at Noon." *(Courtesy of WTAP-TV. Photo by Roger Sheppard.)*

One of the most frustrating things about ENG gear is that it usually starts its decline with a partial failure—some function unexpectedly stops, but only for a split second. By the time you have said, "Hmm?" the thing is working again. That split-second failure probably will not repeat itself when you report the problem to the maintenance folks, and the equipment will operate perfectly as soon as an engineer gets it on the test bench. Then, of course, the same problem will develop the next time you are in the field.

Although it is difficult to imagine, what you and the engineers really would like is for the machine to fail. As one technically minded friend said, "What I really like is to see smoke—not a lot of smoke, but a little. When something smokes you can usually find the burned place so it is much easier to spot the problem and fix it."

Nobody really wants smoke. Most well-run stations have a preventive maintenance program designed to keep the equipment operating at peak efficiency. That will go a long way toward catching problems before they become problems. The broadcast journalist can help a lot if he or she will do three things religiously:

✔ 1. Follow the procedures set by the engineering department for operating the equipment.

✔ 2. Respect the equipment and treat it gently.

✔ 3. Report problems immediately.

The ENG Coordinator

This brings us back to teamwork. Between technicians and journalists is a still-evolving position involving staff liaison and coordination: the ENG coordinator. Coordinators provide the operational liaison between the engineering and news departments and see to it that the needed facilities are ordered from the engineering department. They plan the use of those facilities, innovate ways to use ENG and satellite technology for news gathering and production, and supervise and monitor its use when "on-line."

When news is breaking the ENG coordinator is right in the middle of the action, communicating with the station engineers and editors and producers. During less hectic times the ENG coordinator may work on such things as crew/technician scheduling, the assignment of editing rooms and equipment, the monitoring of production flow, or technical planning for future remote coverage.

STUDIO AND CONTROL ROOM PERSONNEL

We have two more places to examine on our station tour: the studio, from which the news is aired, and the control room.

Figure 7.5. A control room that puts the programs on the air. In the control room at KARE-TV, Minneapolis, Minnesota, all of the technology comes together to meld the pictures and words of the anchors in the studio with all of the videotape, microwave and satellite feeds, special effects, digital graphics, and the appropriate sounds that go with them into an on-time, high-quality, error-free production. *(Courtesy of Television/Broadcast Communications Magazine.)*

The Studio

At some TV stations, the "studio" is actually part of the newsroom itself. The anchor desk, the weather production area, and all lighting instruments may be over in one part of that newsroom. When a news program is about to go on the air, cameras and their TelePrompTer™ rigs and related equipment are wheeled in or brought out of storage and the newscast is delivered from the newsroom. Some stations that use the newsroom as a set arrange the room so that the activities of the news staff become the background of the set. In that case people in the background should be on their best behavior. Reading a newspaper or eating a bologna sandwich doesn't portray the kind of news-room intensity the audience associates with news functions.

More traditionally the studio containing the news set is in a separate location. Studio cameras and prompters, desk areas for anchors, the weather area with radar screens, keying screens, perhaps an interview area, are all permanent fixtures of the news set.

You may see more technicians. Camera operators stand behind their charges and move them, zoom, focus, pan, and tilt on command over the intercom from the director in the control room.

Larger stations certainly will have a floor director or floor manager, who provides cues and human support for the anchors. The floor director is a very important person. He or she takes commands from the control room director and relays them to the on-air talent. The relay will be made by hand signals when the studio is "live," or by terse voice commands during the playing of a tape or commercial: "A minute thirty to the end . . . commercial coming up, speed up . . . slow down . . . wipe the sweat during the next tape segment . . . calm down . . . wake up. . . ." In small-market stations the floor director function may be filled by a studio camera operator.

Automation has taken over many tasks performed by studio people. You may find that the news studio may be equipped with robotic cameras which can be controlled by one operator, or even from information written in ("embedded") in the newscast script. The prompters on the cameras are fed from the computer system which holds all the scripts and the rundown.

The studio lighting may be preprogrammed, eliminating those screeches and snaps of metal ladders being dragged or folded following a last-minute lighting change.

The net effect of such automation is to reduce the production payroll. Automation usually shifts responsibilities for planning for production functions and entering them into a computer system to reporters, writers, and producers in the newsroom.

The Control Room (or Studio Control)

Through a door, or perhaps farther down the hall, is the control room. In here are the people who get that news program on the air. A technician runs the audio board, turning microphones off and on, riding levels, playing back audio, and so on. Others run the video switcher and perhaps the character generator. Still others supervise the electronics, control the quality of the pictures from the studio cameras, play back videotape packages, switch to the microwave or the satellite.

But automation is a factor in the control room. Audio may be controlled from the script, videotapes may be played back from a tape automation system (sometimes called a **library system**) or from a digital disk storage unit, and graphics may be programmed by data entered into the script by reporters and writers.

During a newscast the star of the control room is the **director**. The director takes the program script and directs the technicians, studio crews, and on-air talent through the program. The director gives orders for any function to be carried out:

Roll opening tape . . . dissolve to camera 1 . . . cue George . . . camera on Jane . . . take 2 . . . roll VTR 18 . . . take VTR . . . stand by, remote one, we're coming to you in 5, 4, 3, 2, . . . take remote one . . . stand by, camera one . . . stand by, George, for crosstalk to remote . . . stand

by, squeeze zoom . . . stand by, Quantel . . . stand by, black . . . go to
black. . . .

On the director's shoulders rests all of the responsibility for a smooth,
clean production—one without awkward pauses while a VTR rolls through
the countdown leader; one without the wrong camera on the air; one with
everything coming up at the exact second it's needed. A director needs strong
nerves and quick reaction time.

A control room director needs to be able to read a script, watch all the
pictures, listen to the audio, watch the clock, give the studio crew and
anchors instructions, get new instructions from the producer and pass them
on, anticipate the next action, and join the network program following the
news without missing a beat.

PLANNING THE NEWSCAST

Now that you've had your tour it is time to look at how newscasts get put
together. The planning of a newscast begins long before air time. Parts of it
may be set up days before. Other segments may come from special assignment reporters or special units of the news operation that have been assigned
investigative stories, series, consumer affairs, and features. Regular weather
and sports segments have been blocked in for approximate lengths. Of
course, the newscast will contain coverage of the scheduled events and the
breaking news of that particular day. And commercials—never forget those.

The News Hole

Each newscast has its own **format**. The format is dictated by station policy. A
format is a program constant, a program's framework as distinct from its content. The program title, opening theme and visuals, anchor identifications,
headlines and the like, are examples of these constants.

Newscast planning starts by taking into account these production details
as dictated by the format and the commercials to be aired in that newscast.
The ads have been sold and scheduled. What is left, the **news hole**, is blank,
waiting to be filled in by producers. The total amount of news time in the TV
news hole varies with the length of the newscast and the number of commercials to be run. However, it is quite rigid. At the commercial networks,
the thirty-minute newscast will have about twenty-two to twenty-three minutes of news time available. For a local station with a thirty-minute newscast
the news hole can be much smaller after the time for the weather and sports
is blocked out. In an hour news program there may be about thirty-two to
thirty-five minutes of news space or quite a bit less; again it depends on the
amount of commercial time sold and regular content and production features.

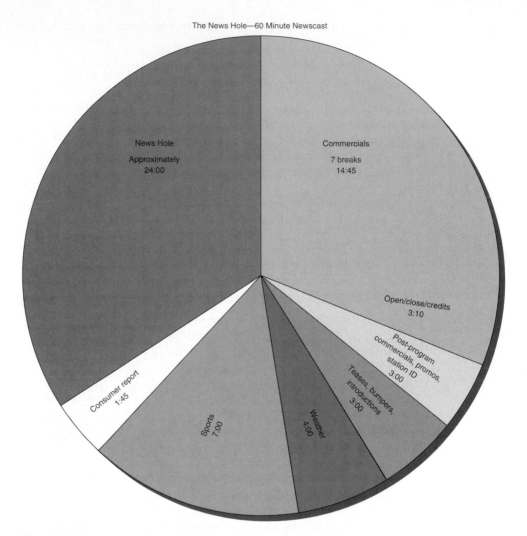

The News Hole—60 Minute Newscast

News Hole

Approximately
24:00

Commercials

7 breaks
14:45

Open/close/credits
3:10

Post-program
commercials, promos,
station ID
3:00

Teases, bumpers,
introductions
3:00

Weather
4:00

Sports
7:00

Consumer report
1:45

Figure 7.6. Every second counts in the news hole for a typical sixty-minute television newscast. After all of the production elements, such as the opening and closing, bumpers, teases, and introductions, and the commercials are subtracted from the total time, slightly more than thirty-two minutes are available for news, weather, and sports.

The Editorial Meeting

Whatever the amount of time, the specific planning usually starts early in the news day. There is an editorial conference attended by the news director, the executive producer who runs the meeting, producers, the assignment desk, reporters, ENG coordinator, and sometimes videographers. Here the previously scheduled material, the news opportunities, follow-up ideas for ongoing stories, the continuing series, and a more exact time for weather and sports

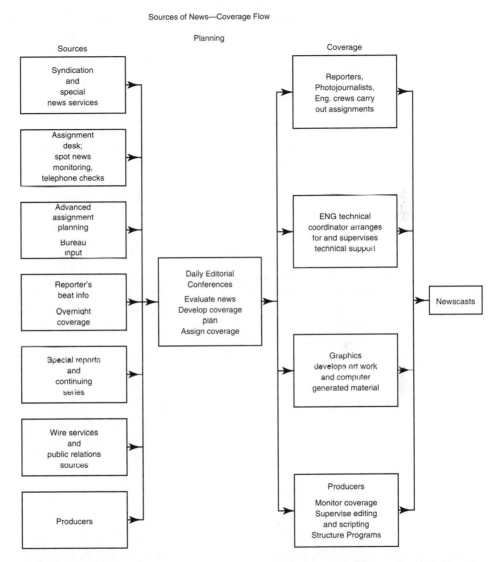

Figure 7.7. Coverage flow. Ideas for news stories and other elements in a newscast come from a wide variety of sources. In most stations these ideas flow into and out of the daily editorial conferences. Then the staff gets to work to gather and edit news items, and then produce newscasts that will contain a mixture of the most important, significant, and interesting information available.

are blocked out. Whoever runs the meeting expects the others to bring hard material—stories, segments, series that are or will be ready to run—and to contribute to general discussion of how scheduled stories and breaking news will be covered.

There usually is a good bit of give and take among producers, news managers, and assignment editors. The assignment desk has been setting up the day's activities. Its editors will have a list of story possibilities, follow-ups, new angles, and other coverage plans, in a relatively detailed form. This list is often called the **outlook report**. It grows out of the extensive advance files the assignment desk keeps—wire service reports, newspaper clippings, publicity releases, computer files, notes from beat reporters and the planning staff, and suggestions from the staff at all levels. The desk editors also watch the competition's news programs, get telephone and fax tips, viewer reactions, and brainstorms from almost anyone. They also know what coverage has already taken place overnight and during the early morning hours and who is available for assignment.

The producers will have a similar list and may also have ideas about story importance, news judgments, story length, and approach. The reporters who will be getting assignments will pitch in with other ideas and suggestions. Reporters with regular beat assignments will add comments about possibilities from their beats.

When this meeting breaks up the result should be a plan for the day's coverage and clear knowledge of who is to be where and how the coverage is to be carried out. The assignment desk manager may put this plan in writing—a detailed outlook report including proposed staffing—and then post it for all terminals, or, copies to all concerned. The producers make tentative **rundowns** for their newscasts—a list of every story, every production element, everything planned for their newscast. Reporters, videographers, and crews take off to get their jobs done.

Because there will be a number of newscasts during the broadcast day, a similar, though shorter, meeting for those involved in the late evening news may take place later on. Here staffers just coming to work go over what has been planned and look for further opportunities for coverage later in the day.

Syndicated Services

Some of the video news content may come from outside sources. Each of the national commercial television networks offers a story service to its affiliates. The idea is for the network newsrooms and bureaus to act as collecting points for video and sound coverage from the network intake and from the network affiliates' efforts. Then this material is fed to the affiliates on the network satellite links. There are a number of feeds of national and regional video stories each day at scheduled times. When there is a major story breaking the network systems can pick up affiliate coverage and send it out on a spot news basis. The satellite links can be used for unilateral coverage by or between affiliates.

Also, many stations subscribe to other syndicated services that, for a fee, provide a variety of news and features. These include special material about health, handling money, hobbies—almost anything people are interested in.

Stations that are members of broadcast groups often exchange stories among stations in the group. Others make arrangements with The Cable News Network, Conus, or similar commercial service, to take material from them and share their own coverage in return. Or stations may have their own regional or national bureaus. Satellite transmissions are a regular activity for stations. Getting a news story of interest to the local audience from some distant point via satellite is easy and economical. Satellite news gathering (SNG) is discussed in Chapter 10.

Coverage Management

Meanwhile, the assignment desk personnel are at work carrying out the coverage plans. This involves a number of activities that go on at the same time. They include liaison with the producers, reporters, editors, and the ENG coordinator or engineering department. If remote units are needed for a scheduled story the orders for those probably will have been given as soon as the need was known. There are only so many mobile units and camera crews available, so careful planning is a must.

Shaping the Coverage

As the day proceeds the time for the newscast gets closer with every tick of the clock. Now the producer's role becomes even more important. Some stories will turn out to be duds. New stories or better angles to planned stories will pop up. As the routine of getting the raw material in and processed goes on, producers will be thinking in this vein. They will be asking questions like:

1. Does this story have another angle?

2. Have we got the right approach?

3. How does this story relate to the others in the newscast?

4. Has this story changed since we started?

5. What is interesting and significant about this story, and how can we take advantage of that?

Producers are constantly working with a rundown, revising it, reordering it, and changing the program lineup as the news develops. Many producers rely on a computer system terminal and special software to keep track of and produce the rundown. The software allows the producer to

- read all wire copy, messages, internal memos, assignment lists, and specific assignments

- develop, revise, and distribute rundowns, with updated timings, revising the rundown as frequently as needed

- view and edit reporter or writer scripts

- write copy

- tap data bases and station archives

- direct or run the program from a terminal in the control room in certain instances

- share information with other staffers.

No matter what method is used, producers are constantly evaluating the components that will go into their newscast. They monitor coverage carefully by talking with the reporters and videographers and by watching coverage material as it comes in and is edited. They direct the script writing, voice-over narration, and use of special effects to enhance the meaning and production values, constantly shaping, revising. There are always questions, such as:

✔ 1. Have we got it?

✔ 2. Have we got it right?

✔ 3. Are these the important angles?

✔ 4. Is it clear? pictures? words? graphics?

✔ 5. Is anything missing?

✔ 6. What can we do about that?

✔ 7. If live coverage is involved will what we planned work?

✔ 8. If it doesn't what can we do?

✔ 9. Is what we plan to do with production elements appropriate?

✔ 10. What else can we do to make sure this is interesting, significant, *and* understandable?

✔ 11. Any legal "red flag(s)" raised by any of the above?

Because producers share so much of the responsibility for the smooth functioning of the newsroom, the stress associated with the position is apt to show in the way they look outwardly and in the way they act. Many may give the impression they are weighted down by the responsibility of their task. But don't get the idea that they are alone in this "responsibility" factor. A great deal of discussion—give and take—takes place among staffers. In fact how good the producer is in this give and take—how well the producer communicates her or his ideas and plans—is one of the important factors in personal success and getting the program on the air in its best form.

In any command situation communicating with those who carry out the orders is as important as—or even more important than—issuing the orders themselves. The end result is the program. News coverage that has been completed should provide the producer with material to make a mix of interesting, significant, informative, illuminating, well-ordered video stories, readers, special segments. That material should have crisp, clear writing, easy to understand graphics, and meaningful and appropriate production values to make the broadcast work.

ORGANIZING THE NEWSCAST

By now air time for the newscast is near and it is time to organize the material which has been prepared. You won't see neat piles of script, videocassettes, and rundowns yet. In the crunch of getting the program on the air, editing and writing may continue right up to air time, and even while the program is actually on the air. But the producer is the person who must bring order out of the hurly-burly. Scores of things have to be checked and cross-checked and more orders given and carried out. There are story angles to sharpen, story focuses to clarify, the link between words and pictures to tighten, production elements to add or discard. Through all this *timing* is never out of the producer's mind.

The Rundown

The producer has been wrestling with the rundown virtually all day. That grand plan he or she had after the editorial meeting is perhaps a shambles. Stories that seemed to be lead material may have turned out to be less important and significant. Other stories that seemed to have less strength now may have become stronger. Breaking news may have become dominant.

What the producer has in front of him or her—version 1 or version 15—is a series of news segments separated by commercial breaks. One or more of these segments will be reserved for sports. Another segment will contain the weather. Still another may contain a special department of the newscast—station editorial, sports commentary, consumer affairs report, your health, your money—a department that is a regular feature of the news program.

The Lead

Producers generally agree that choosing the lead story of the newscast is a crucial decision. The lead is generally thought to be the most important story of the day or at that hour—usually a hard news item, infrequently a dramatic development in sports or even a weather situation, something that is immediate, threatening, severe, and something that needs to be updated frequently. But, it won't work to carry "importance" thinking too far.

What if the producer arranged the newscast, start to finish, with the most

```
schwaid              Thu Sep  1 09:15   page   1

P PG  ANC   SLUG                  VISUALS     EJ TAPE        #   ED ? TIME    BCKTME
==================================================================================
 DIRECTOR: LISA SHINER                        SHOW: 6PM                         2:08
P            HEADLINES A   DOG               1  EJVO                     0:30   2:08
             HEADLINES B   SIMPSON           2  EJVO                     0:00   2:38
             OPEN                                                        0:20   2:38
P 1   GJ*   INTRO DOG FIGHTING F Q                                       0:32   2:58
   1A        INVESTIGATION ANIMAT            1  EJVOANIM                 0:00   3:30
*  1B        DOG FIGHTING FOLO/PL            2  EJPKG     VIOL JB        1:47   3:30
P 1T  PL    TAG PAT              NEWSCENTER                              0:20   5:17
             AC/ANIMATION                    3  EJVOANIM                 0:00   5:37
P 2   JG*   AC/BUS FIRE ARRESTS  ADDA        4  EJVO                     0:26   5:37
P 3   G*    AC/MACHINE GUN BUST  ADDA        1  EJVO           JK        0:23   6:03
P P4  J*    AC/GANG ROUNDUP      ADDA        2  EJVO                     0:19   6:26
P 4   J*    AC/MANNEQUIN STOLEN  ADDA        3  EJVOSOTVO      JK        0:48   6:45
P 6   G*    INTRO SIMPSON HEARIN Q                                       0:24   7:33
   6A  DK    INTRO DANIELLE       CHROMAKEY                              0:20   7:57
   6B        SIMPSON HEARING/DK              4  EJPKG     VIOL NI        1:30   8:17
P 6T  DK    TAG DANIELLE         CHROMAKEY                              0:20   9:47
P 7   G/J   TEASE 1A    UNIFORMS  TWO SHOT    1  EJVO                     0:20  10:07
             DON'T TOUCH REMOTE              ADDA                        0:00  10:27
             TEASE 1B    SMOKE               2  EJVO                     0:00  10:27
                                             V3                          0:00  10:27
P 20  G*    INTRO SCHOOL UNIFORM Q                                       0:12  10:27
* 20A        SCHOOL UNIFORMS/JS              1  EJPKG     VIOL KM        1:43  10:39
P 21  J*    GLASTONBURY SMOKE    Q           2  EJVO           JK        0:29  12:22
P 22  G/J   TEASE 2A   COMPOUNCE 2 SHOT      3  EJVO                     0:20  12:51
             BLOOD DRIVE          ADDA        4  EJVOROLL                 0:20  13:11
                                             V3                          0:00  13:31
P 30  J*    INTRO LAKE COMPOUNCE Q                                       0:23  13:31
   30A DG    INTRO DOUG           LIVE 9S                                0:20  13:54
   30B        LAKE COMPOUNCE/DG              1  EJPKG     VIOL           1:15  14:14
   30T DG    TAG DOUG             LIVE 9S                                0:20  15:29
P 31  G*    RIDE & ROCK CLASSIC              ADDA                        0:21  15:49
P 32  G/J   TEASE 3A             2 SHOT      TOWERCAM                    0:20  16:10
             PROJECT JOBS                    ADDAS                       0:05  16:30
             STOCKS YOUR DOLLAR   ADDAMUSIC                              0:15  16:35
   40        WEATHER    (5 DAY)              1  EJVO                     2:45  16:50
P 42  J/G   TEASE 4              TWO SHOT                                0:20  19:35
                                                                         0:00  19:55
P 50        SPORTS                                                       3:15  19:55
P 50A        UCONN FOOTBALL       Q UCONN    1  EJ SOT    691            0:00  23:10
P 50         PRE B - TELEPICK     DISSOLVE    ADDA                       0:00  23:10
P 50B        BASEBALL LIVE SHOT   LIVE  9B                               0:00  23:10
P 50C        US OPEN RESULTS      FULL PG     ADDA                       0:00  23:10
             HEADLINES A   DOG               EJVO                        0:00  23:10
   3   G     AC/MACHINE GUN BUST  ADDA        EJVO           JK        0:20  23:10
   6B        SIMPSON HEARING  /DK            EJPKG     VIOL NI        1:30  23:30
   20A       SCHOOL UNIFORMS  /JS            EJPKG     VIOL KM        1:45  25:00
   50        SPORTS                                                      3:15  26:45
```

Figure 7.8. A WVIT-TV, Hartford, Connecticut, producer's rundown for a 6 P.M. thirty-minute newscast. Each element of the program is listed in the order it will occur in the newscast. The rundown columns display such information as on-air talent, story slug, visuals/source, time per item and total time for backtiming. Note the extensive use of abbreviations. Some abbreviations are standard in TV news, many others are not. Writers must conform to their station's system of notation. *(Courtesy of WVIT-TV.)*

important story first, the next most important second, and all the rest of the stories arranged in descending order of importance right through the various newscast segments? The audience would soon catch on to that. Probably before the middle of the newscast half the audience would be gone.

The TV news producer is a packager. The TV viewer is not like the newspaper reader who can start anywhere and select anything throughout the paper. The viewer cannot stop the forward movement of the newscast or jump ahead or go back to something that has already been presented. Technologies under development may change this linear viewing pattern by providing news stories on-demand through interactive computers, as discussed by News Director Mark Casey at the end of Chapter 1.

The producer must construct the entire newscast with forward movement and sustaining viewer interest clearly in mind. Selection of the lead story is important because that decision does at least three things:

1. It gets the audience's attention.

2. It affects the content of the entire first segment.

3. It affects the content of subsequent segments.

Suppose, for example, that you are the producer and that you have two or even three major stories on a given day. One is a major development in the Balkans or Asia, another a major local economic story, the third the tragic death of a top rock star.

There are those producers who would say you cannot make a mistake; any one will work. There are others who will go for the rock star story every time with the rationale that such a story can happen to the star only once. Still others will say that the local economy is more important than either of the other two. There will be those who opt for the Balkans or Asia story because of peace-or-war potential, ethnic strife, or implications for American-Chinese relations. And a few will say the death of a rock star is *never* as important as other more substantive local, national, or international stories. (Yet, consider the deaths of three celebrity rock stars: Elvis Presley, John Lennon, Kurt Cobain. Each death involved tragic circumstances—a drug overdose, a murder, a suicide. Each event was given wide coverage and top play—lead story and front-page headline treatment—by national news media both broadcast and print.)

If you decided that the rock star story is your lead you certainly will get the attention of some of the audience. And you certainly will have affected the sequence of stories in the first and subsequent segments. Yet there are people in the audience who don't care about rock stars no matter what happens to them. They may say that choice amounts to pandering to the lowest common denominator of the audience. There are also thousands in the audience who do care about celebrities. They will be very interested in the rock star story. A comparable "mixed" audience reaction can result from a selection of a Balkans lead, or Asia or the local economy lead—in which cases instead of the "pandering" charge, reaction of others in the audience may be that the newscast is dull, boring, or uninteresting.

It is very dangerous to prescribe formulas, much less formats, for such producer decision making. This is because the moment a format becomes fixed policy, following it blindly can lead to poor news judgment. If the policy is that all newscasts will lead with a local story, what do you do on the day the president is shot or it looks like World War III has begun? At the least such a policy should be modified to something like: All newscasts will lead with a local story—except when something else is more important. Formulas just do not make good substitutes for sound news judgment.

News Values—News Determinants

Journalism texts give a lot of space to discussions of news values or news story ingredients that are used to judge and compare news items. Terms that are used include *timeliness, prominence, proximity, consequence, human interest, conflict, impact,* and the like.

There are as many personally held theories about what constitutes a good news story or a good lead story or the proper content of a newscast as there are producers. In his book *Newswatch: How TV Decides the News,* Av Westin, a former vice president of ABC News, said there are three parts to his formula.*

✔ 1. Is my world safe?

✔ 2. Are my city and home safe?

✔ 3. If my wife, children, and loved ones are safe, then what has happened in the past twenty-four hours to shock them, amuse them, or make them better off than they were?

Westin said that those are the questions the audience has in mind when it sits down to watch the news on television. He also said that stories in category three seldom take the lead position, though they do, he felt, belong in the newscast.

The Segments

No matter what lead story decision the producer makes, it affects the content of the rest of the first segment and the following segments. This is because the segments themselves must be structured just as the entire newscast must be structured. Each may be thought of as a small newscast within

*Av Westlin, *Newswatch—How TV Decides the News* (New York: Simon and Schuster, 1982), pp. 62–63.

the larger one, each carries the audience forward, and each makes up a part of the bigger structure of the entire program.

Although there are many variations that can be created, let's consider several commonly used segment categories:

1. National

2. International

3. Local

4. Topical

5. Geographical

What Links With What?

The first three look very much like three segments of a newscast. You could say: "Aha! I will lead with the major local story, and the first segment will be all local news." Then you could move on to the national news, then international, then sports, weather, and the closing feature.

Nothing is particularly wrong with that newscast structure. You wouldn't want to do it in the same order every day, but it certainly is much better than a random selection of stories thrown at the audience without any attention to two other important concepts: logical order and logical progression.

Your newscast should be orderly and linear. Some stories relate to each other. It is a good idea to look for and think about using these relationships even within categories as broad as national, international, and local. We know that the audience doesn't like to be bounced around through the news. Viewers become confused if the first story is about Congress, the next about the Japanese computer industry, the next about a storm in Kansas, the next about a new video game which is sweeping the country. Some of these stories may be related. Let's see what we can find. If the story about Congress has to do with raising trade barriers to the importation of Japanese computers, and the video game is made by the Japanese, then it might be good judgment to link these stories together. The story would have a *logical order,* and a good transition would provide a *logical progression.* Unless there is some wild angle to the Kansas storm story—if it destroyed the factory that manufactures the video games in the United States—it doesn't relate. And even if that unlikely angle was a part of the storm story, remember the operative word *logical.* Not all stories relate to each other no matter how hard you bend, mutilate, or twist them.

Watch out for categories that are too broad. It is often counterproductive to think of categories like national or international as boxes into which you can throw all the stories that occurred in the United States or all the stories that happened outside the country. Some of them won't fit into the box, no matter how big you make it.

So for a different perspective let's look at topical and geographical categories. Here we immediately think of "cue words" like economy, labor, weather, crime, Latin America, the Far East, Canada. Here we often find some more useful relationships. When the anchor starts a story grouping using the cue words "local economy," there is a geographical word—local—and a cue word—economy. We are setting up to use both *logical order* and *logical progression.* Stories in this group should relate to the economy, and they should be local. Not all of them will be—nor should they be—pounded and squeezed so that they do. The links must be obvious and real. And remember what we said in Chapter 5 (p. 185) about a string of stories that are very similar—lack of audience attention may blur the details.

Stories that fit into a geographic zone often work well together. Sometimes they do not. If there is a series of stories out of Latin America having to do with improved regional development there may be not only logical but also real relationships. A story or segment that brings these together and shows how the monetary policy of one country affects that of another and how United States trade policy affects them all can bring much broader understanding to the audience.

Sometimes the day's news brings a series of seemingly diverse stories from one geographic zone: an earthquake here, a flood there, crop failures elsewhere. Here geography works with less effect. The topic—broadly "nature"—may be more useful. But, beware of too much cosmic topicality.

Some stories simply stand alone and no amount of examination will result in that blinding insight you hope for. What to do with them? Try these:

✔ 1. If it is a very important story, especially if it's local, put it first, then go on to something else.

✔ 2. If it has feature possibilities it might go last.

✔ 3. If you get a tiny insight, put the story at the end of a segment.

✔ 4. If there are other "stand-alone" stories, group them.

Level of Interest

Viewers cannot choose news items to be in the newscast, so their only recourse when something uninteresting to them comes along is to "tune out." The most drastic action viewers can take is to tune out literally—change channels or turn the set off—the one reaction a producer wants most to avoid.

The problem of sustaining viewer interest is made more complex by all of the distractions that can interfere with close attention to the news. The kids are underfoot. Dinner is being prepared. The neighbor is using that electric drill again. The phone rings. The folks in the next apartment are fighting.

The TV news producer must try to arrange the order and progression of the program so that the highest level of interest is maintained throughout the program. The ideal would be that everyone paid attention all the time. That's impossible because the news program carries news some people aren't interested in, like sports, the markets, Flag Day at the elementary school, and parking problems for people who own three fancy cars. We cannot force everyone to listen to and watch everything. But producers can do things with the order and progression of the program that will at least result in renewed interest.

✔ 1. They can try to be sure that each segment begins and ends with a story that is interesting, if not significant.

✔ 2. They can take "lead-quality" stories that did not make *the* lead and use those stories to lead other segments.

✔ 3. They can make wise use of features, particularly at the end of internal segments.

✔ 4. They can look at the news value of sports, weather, and other departments and place those segments accordingly—assuming station policy permits such adjustments to format.

✔ 5. They can divide a major story, putting the primary elements at the beginning, coming back for details, sidebars, and other angles later.

✔ 6. They can update major stories later in the newscast.

Timing

One of the most important single factors in broadcast news is timing. Scheduled news programs start at a precise minute and second and end the same way. A seventy-second news update wedged into the prime-time evening schedule is just that—forty seconds of news headlines, and a thirty-second commercial. Nothing will wait for the end of that small news segment; it must begin and end precisely on time.

Filling exactly the time allotted for a thirty-minute news program is a complex and difficult task. Before anything else is done the time for commercials, the opening and the close, and "bumpers"—production transitions between news segments and commercials—must be subtracted. Other commercials, those sold adjacent to the newscast, come out of the total. For example, most news programs will be followed by—at the least—a thirty-second or one-minute commercial and a ten-second station break; that can cut the total amount of time available to 29:20 or even 28:50 right off the top.

The typical arithmetic for finding the actual amount of time available for news, weather, and sports in a thirty-minute time block looks like this:

```
  30:00

 -00:30     (adjacent commercial)

 -00:10     (station break)

 -06:00     (6 minutes of commercials)

 -01:00     (6 ten-second bumpers)

 -00:30     (length of program opening)

 -00:20     (length of program close)

  20:00
```

Without doing anything more than that, the producer has calculated that there are only twenty minutes for news, not thirty. Then, take out the time for weather and sports—let's say 3:30 for each. That totals seven minutes, so now there are only thirteen minutes left for whatever amount of news a given day may bring.

The producer works out the above arithmetic early in the day after checking the station program log to determine the number of commercials and subtracting the known length of the production elements, such as the bumpers and open and close.

If it is a heavy news day, he or she has already told the sports and weather anchors they can have only three minutes, or 2:30, and listened to their screams with tolerance and firmness. Time gained is one to two minutes.

Now the trick is to fit the news into the fourteen to fifteen minutes available. Doing that is a major, continuous, and very precise task.

First, each story is given a tentative length when it is assigned. Reporters, writers, and tape editors are given a time frame within which to work. They are told, "Your story will be a major one; you can have two minutes, or two minutes fifteen," or "Forty seconds max!" or even "Twenty seconds, firm." These times are very tentative at this point since they are based on what the producer *thinks* the story is going to be worth even before it is covered. A lot of things can change.

Second, these tentative times are written in with the story **slug** on the first rundown of the day. (A story "slug" is a one- or two-word label assigned to that item for quick story identification—fire, potholes, shooting, rescue, etc. To avoid confusion, each slug is different from all others in a newscast, no two identical.) Slugs/times are transferred to new rundowns as those are developed.

Third, all times in the first rundown are added up to see whether the total comes anywhere close to the time prescribed. If it doesn't, some preliminary but drastic reassessment has to be made. Producers develop a rather precise feeling for approximately how many stories can fit in a thirty-minute or one-hour newscast and quickly get the knack of sketching out a reasonable estimate of what is possible within the time available. New rundowns are made, adjusting story order and length, as news gathering and processing continues.

Fourth, the newsroom peacekeeping negotiations begin. As new tentative times are assigned the noise level from protests gets higher. The producer must remain firm, but must also listen to legitimate arguments from reporters, writers, and editors who are putting forth reasons why their stories can't possibly fit in the smaller time frame given them. And the producer must keep on top of the stories as they are being processed to make sure the agreed-upon times are met.

Usually everyone wants more time, but if someone figures out a way to shorten a story it is good news to the producer, who must juggle both time and information. The important and significant facts and visual material must be in the story. Unnecessary details must come out. The news hole will not get bigger.

Fifth, the final program rundown is completed. Very precise timing is required at this stage. All the completed stories and those being finished up now have actual running times. These actual running times go in the final rundown and are totaled up.

If it happens to be that one day in a year when everything goes just right, the total will match the total time available. If it isn't that day, further adjustments and fast decisions are called for:

- Stories may have to be dropped or added—or changed from a story with video and sound bite to a voice-over read by the anchor. New scripts must be prepared to reflect all changes.

- Perhaps there is time for a quick video edit to take out a second sound bite.

- Perhaps the story can be moved to a later segment to give time for such an edit.

Any of these changes alter the timing within the newscast and its total running time.

The producer can do two things to help keep accurate account of the time:

✔ 1. Get a ballpark idea about total time early. Add up the tentative time allocations as soon as a first rundown is made.

✔ 2. Revise/update as you go. As each story time changes from estimated to actual, adjust total program time by adding to or subtracting from total program time the difference between estimated and actual. Newsroom computer rundowns do the math for you, but it's wise to understand what the numbers mean in terms of producing a correctly timed newscast.

The sensible thing to do is to add or subtract two numbers and then keep track of the difference after each computation.

For example:

Story	Estimated Time	Actual Time	Difference
Mayor	1:20	1:30	+10
County Fair	2:00	2:10	+10
Brush fire	:50	:45	−05

Obviously, the difference between the estimated time and the actual time has added fifteen seconds to the time available for stories so far. If all the changes have been subtractions rather than additions, twenty-five seconds have been gained. That is nice because it doesn't take long for a few seconds saved here, and another few saved there to add up to twenty to thirty seconds, time enough for an additional story or to add more details to a scheduled story. That is why so much attention is paid to compressing and tightening stories and segments.

One other timing point the producer will want to know is the running time of the program as it plays on the air. Many stations have computer software which does all timing elements as the rundown is made, revised and updated. One column of figures shows the running time of each story, and another shows the running time of the program to that point. The producer can check off each timing point as it is met. If material has to be dropped or added, the decision can be made immediately.

One of those might look like this:

Event	Time	Running Time
Start	00:00	00:00
Open	00:20	00:20
Mayor	01:30	01:50
Fair	02:10	04:00
Fire	00:45	04:45
Bumper #1	00:10	04:55
Comml #1	00:60	05:55
Congress	01:20	07:15
U.N.	00:40	07:55
Space	02:00	09:55

And so on, through to the end of the program.

Backtiming

As a last check on the timing many producers switch to backtiming after the final program rundown is completed. This provides a security blanket that will help the producer assure that the program gets off the air on time.

Although there are many variations, the simplest backtiming method starts with determining from the station's program log the exact time the program is supposed to end—let's say 28:30 for a thirty-minute program, or 58:10 for an hour-long newscast.

With the exact end time established and with the final rundown firm, the producer begins by *subtracting* the time for each element of the newscast from the end time, moving *upward* from the bottom of the program rundown. Some producers backtime all the way to the beginning of the news program. Others pick an arbitrary point, say, the beginning of the last or next-to-last commercial break. Most newsroom computer systems include backtiming in their producer software package. Again, the point is to understand what is being done, how, and why.

Backtiming thus gives the producer a "point of no return." If she or he finds the program is running long or short at that point, the solution is to either add or delete material, or tell the anchors to speed up or slow down so that the program comes out exactly at the time prescribed on the log.

Bumpers, Teases, and Other Production Effects

Another part of the producer's mind has to focus on production elements of the program. We've already mentioned "bumpers" between the news segments and the commercial breaks. These do several things. They act to tell the audience that there is a break and they can provide information.

Bumpers are usually designed to promote upcoming stories. They can be as simple as having an anchor say, "We'll be back with more news after these messages," or the more curt, "And now this. . . ." Or they can be short segments of an upcoming taped or live story that use some or all of the special effects from that elaborate switcher in the control room.

In most stations, the bumpers are standardized: a brief headline superimposed on the screen while the anchor reads the same words. Theme music may be added. More elaborate bumpers employ rolling video or still frames and graphics that whirl or flop words or pictures about upcoming stories. Some even create a page-turning effect. Some stations use bumper time to include more information such as financial markets, farm prices, the pollen count, commuter train schedule reports—tiny visual-only stories that will not be mentioned elsewhere.

There is very little difference between a bumper and a "tease" except that the tease is just that—written and produced to arouse curiosity so that the audience will want to stay tuned in to learn what the tease was about.

Producers are usually responsible for the writing and production of bumpers and teases. Bumpers should include information and should be written so that it is clear to the audience what is coming up after the commercial. If video from an upcoming story is to be included in the bumper, the scenes shown should be carefully selected so that they show a key element or a highlight of the story. Random video scenes from the story will not whet the appetite to see more or add information. If the bumper includes words on the screen—a headline—great care should be taken to assure that the meaning is clear. For example:

"Next, the End of the World?"

That is startling, all right, but the viewer may not see the question mark in the short time the phrase is on the screen. How about:

"Next: Prices Going Up"

That's pretty routine, but if the story is about *commodity* prices going up, the headline should say so.

Cleverness, style, and taste are a part of bumper production.

"Next: Futbol and Football"
  "Coming Up: Skirts"

The first is clever, making the play on words. In Europe soccer is called, and often spelled, "futbol." So when there are both a soccer game and a football game in town and the next stories are about them, this bumper may cause a chuckle and be remembered. The second, presumably about the new fall fashions, is sexist and tacky.

Bumpers with video and production effects are often quite tricky to produce. They usually are put together as separate tape cuts and played back separately from the other video stories. Many stations purchase bumpers designed specifically for them by outside production houses. Their format is designed to link with the design of the station's news set, program intros and endings, promos, and media ads.

Assigning the Talent

Another part of the producer's job is to decide how best to assign the on-air talent. The news anchors, reporters, and weather and sports anchors represent a resource. How news anchor participation is divided—who presents which stories—within the news program is an important production factor.

A producer decision to have the anchors simply alternate stories does not take into account a number of things:

1. The way stories are linked or grouped by topical, regional, or geographic categories affects the division of stories between anchors.

2. A switch from one anchor to another can be used to change direction or topic within a newscast segment.

3. A switch from one anchor to another can be used to change the pace of the newscast.

4. Some anchors handle some kinds of stories better than others.

5. Some formats call for a certain anchor to handle certain stories.

Suppose the lead to the newscast is a roundup of major events that happened that day in the state legislature. All of that material, including the video stories by reporters on the scene, should be anchored by one person. If the next major story or group of stories within the segment moves to a major local drug crackdown, another anchor should handle it. Not only will that division give the audience a nonverbal cue that the story subject and locale are changing, the switch will keep the pace of the program moving.

Switching anchors can also be a useful way to change the subject matter completely. If the newscast contains a series of stand-alone stories, alternating the anchors will provide some nonverbal punctuation, and may even refocus the audience's attention.

Of course, the anchors should not be switched within a story or between the opening and closing of a story that includes a video report.

Sometimes the format dictates the choice of anchor. If, for example, there is a formal or informal custom that one of the anchors always reads a closing feature, members of the audience may become accustomed to that and look forward to it. The same can be said for the anchor who does a nightly "reporter's notebook," book review, or review of local entertainment—or a station editorial, or commentary.

Assigning stories to anchors for sexist reasons has gone the way of the dinosaur. We are long beyond the day when women read "women's stories" and men handled the gory stuff. Yet sometimes one or the other of the anchors should be the one to present the story because he or she has a particular interest in the story or a knack of handling the material that relates to the audience in a special way. Frequently, an anchor may have been the reporter on the story earlier in the day.

The use of reporters on the news set is another variable for the producer. Reporters appear on air routinely as part of their coverage of stories from the field. It is sometimes a good idea to bring that reporter into the studio to present portions of the story. This technique is used frequently in the presentation of investigative reports. Their studio presentation strengthens the credibility of the reporter and the report. It can also be used when the reporter has been an eyewitness to a particularly interesting breaking story, or has had an interesting experience in developing the story. It should be cautioned, however, that the practice of having a field reporter make a studio appearance may be controlled or at least affected by such things as that person's employment contract provisions.

GETTING IT ON THE AIR

Now, the big moment! It is air time. All of the work of the entire news team will come together during a sustained, high-anxiety effort that requires precise execution and professional attention.

The staff has been working all day to bring together the physical components of this complicated human-technical effort:

1. A complete script on terminal screens and reproduced on paper containing all of the words to be spoken, and all of the timing and technical cues the newscast director will need

2. A stack of videocassettes, all properly labeled or confirmation of the items and their order in digital storage

3. A rundown sheet for the tapes

4. A rundown sheet for the graphics

5. A rundown sheet for Character Generator supers, giving all the words for lower-third supers, scores, weather words, and so on

6. Anchors in the studio, director, producer, and technical staff in the control room

7. All fingers crossed

Stations have a variety of procedures for handling instructions to the director. One is to put all of the cues and timing information in the script and let the director make sure that all the elements like videotapes, graphics, and supers are ready. That puts a lot of responsibility on one person's shoulders. Because several people have to perform a variety of functions in the control room and studio during the airing of the program, another system may call for the producer to provide individual rundown sheets for each function. Computer systems are capable of providing comprehensive rundowns and breaking out specialized information.

No matter what system is used, the script must contain all necessary information. At this point it becomes the essential production tool and guide.

As you know, the script contains two columns of information—the production information the director will need to function as commander of the technology and the words the air talent will speak.

We've included a transcription of a WAVE-TV, Louisville, Kentucky, script, Figure 7-9. The director's information is in the left column, the anchor's material on the right. Words in parentheses explain the cues.

Now, let's look at this script page carefully to see what it provides as a production tool. The director would take all the pages of the completed script and mark them up with his or her own written-in reminders. The first thing in the video column is a simple indication that one of the anchors, David, is on

SCRIPT WITH ANCHOR V/O AND SOUND BITES

Video	Audio
/OC David	Contracts with four city employees' unions
[on camera, Anchor #1]	apparently will expire tonight without
	settlement.
	About 16-hundred workers are involved.
ENG #	
[tape #--]	
V/O NATSOT	
[voice-over, natural sound	
on tape]	
V/O: 12	Among those without a contract are the
[Voice-over lasts 12 seconds]	firefighters, who this afternoon resumed
	negotiations with the city.
	Early settlement is the exception in labor
	talks. Both sides were optimistic, but
	cautious about specifics:
SOT FULL: :27	(((SOT)))
[sound on tape up full, lasts	
27 sec.]	IN CUE: "IT IS HARD TO. . ."
Insert: Ron Gnagie Firefighters union	
[lower-third super]	
--- Charles Roberts	
City Negotiator	
[lower-third super]	OUT CUE: ". . .AM VERY CONFIDENT."
V/O NATSOT: :15	Also unsettled are police, firemen and oilers,
[Voice-over, natural sound on	and teamsters. All are expected to continue
tape, lasts 15 seconds]	working while negotiations go on.

Figure 7.9. WAVE-TV News, Louisville, Kentucky. A page of script with anchor voice-over and sound bites. *(Courtesy of WAVE-TV.)*

camera. In this instance, since David will be on camera 3, that notation would be written in next to the /OC command.

The command VO NATSOT means, as indicated, that David will read this part of the script as a voice-over with videotape that contains natural sound from the scenes on the tape. The director needs to know this so that he or she can tell the audio operator to open David's mic and hold the tape sound underneath the narration. The director also sees that this portion of the narration that David will read is twelve seconds long.

SOT FULL means that the sound on the tape, the sound bites, must be brought up to full volume—again a command the director gives to the audio operator. The script also shows those sound bites will run twenty-seven seconds.

The inserts below SOT FULL indicate that two lower-third supers will be inserted when the two speakers are seen and heard. The Character Generator rundown will instruct the CG operator to put those names and titles into the character generator. The director will tell the person running the switcher when to bring them up on the screen.

After the sound bites, the closing to the story is again read as a voice-over by David, and the script notes this will take fifteen seconds.

Note that the "in cue" and "out cue" are placed in the audio column of the script. This is because they are part of the *sound* that will be included in the story. This brings up another rule: All video-directing commands go in the video column; all audio-directing commands go in the audio column.

The internal time cues, such as those indicating the length of the voice-over narration and the sound bites, are put into the video column so that the director will know the length of those individual elements as well as the length of the entire story. Many directors use stopwatches that can display both elapsed time and split times. Thus, the director can keep track of both the running time of the entire program and the timing of each element of each story.

Let's look at another script page, one which includes a completely packaged tape story by a reporter, Figure 7-10.

This script serves a dual purpose. It is a "map" for both the videotape editor and the newscast director. It was written by the reporter to provide the voice-over narration that he put on audio tape before that audio was edited together with the pictures on the videotape. It also contains the in cue and out cue for the sound bites he chose for the package. And it tells the video editor where the voice-over narration should be brought up to full level. Finally, it provides video directing information—the lower-third inserts—so that the newscast director can order them put on the screen at the appropriate time.

Even though all of McConnell's story was packaged on a videocassette, the script is included in the program script so that the director and anchors can follow the packaged story as it plays. Also, there are elements of it that must be performed while the program is on the air.

SCRIPT FOR PACKAGED VIDEOTAPE STORY

Video	Audio
/OC LAURETTA	School officials are glad to get the 350-thousand dollars allocated by Fiscal Court yesterday. But even with the good news, an old problem may be made worse. Reporter Jeff McConnell says there'll be no more subsidy to anyone
ENG #8 [tape # 8]	(((SOT)))
McConnell	NARRATION UP FULL
[reporter's name]	IN CUE: "IF SCHOOL OFFICIALS. . ."
Insert: Jeff McConnell WAVE-TV	OUT CUE: ". . .TRANSPORTATION SUBSIDY."
[video McConnell standupper]	
	NARRATION UP FULL
Insert: Yesterday	Catholic school officials like D. K. Dumeyer had no
[video is scenes of	comment yesterday. And even a day later he still wasn't
yesterday's confrontation	ready to talk about where to find the 675-thousand dollars
between Dumeyer and	to transport first through eighth graders to parochial
McConnell]	schools. In fact, Dumeyer told me by phone it could be two weeks before they are prepared to talk.
[video is :10 McConnell	IN CUE: "BUT TODAY. . ."
doing this bite on camera	OUT CUE: ". . .THE FISCAL COURT."
in the field]	
	NARRATION UP FULL
[video is B-roll from scenes	Catholic school and public school relations were already
shot at Public School	less than good after the county school board came out
Headquarters]	against tuition tax credits for private schools. So what will Dumeyer's decision do to that relationship?
Insert: 4:12 Ingwersen	IN CUE: "THE PARENTS. . ."
[video, Ingwersen interview]	OUT CUE: ". . .CHANGE THE FACTS."
LIVE OC TAG	Meanwhile, county school officials still haven't decided
[Live on-cam tag by Lauretta]	which of two or three plans it will pick to get the rest of the money needed for optional busing.

Figure 7.10. A script for a package story. *(Courtesy of WAVE-TV.)*

A script for a news program must include all program elements. If a bumper and a commercial segment are to follow the story about the school system, there would be pages or at least notations after the school story indicating that the bumper and commercials are the next program elements. Those notations would indicate which bumper and which commercials are to run in that time. If McConnell had reported his story live, the program script would contain a page indicating where the live remote was to come from, the anchor's lead-in, time limits, and what videotaped segments are to be rolled in along with their in and out cues.

News departments that have newsroom computer systems may have radically different procedures and capabilities built around the script and rundown.

The writers and reporters may be required to insert (imbed) all graphic cues, tape or disk playback cues, audio cues, and even camera instructions in their scripts. These imbedded instructions may replace the director's handwritten reminders and may cause most or all production functions to be executed automatically. If this system is used, a tremendous responsibility is shifted to the reporter or writer who must remember to include every production move needed. Producers also take on added responsibility to check for accuracy and omission of needed instructions. (These instructions are frequently deleted in the prompter version of the script that the computer provides to make it easier for the anchors to read the prompter copy.)

The Videotapes

There are variations in station procedures regarding how the videotape segments are played back into the program. Some stations dub (copy) cassettes prepared by the news department onto one-inch video CARTS for playback from automated CART machines. Many stations play the cassettes directly into the program either from dedicated playback machines or from automated videocassette machines. At some stations stories are edited digitally and played back from computer disk or digital optical scanner. Whatever system is used, great care must be taken to assure that the right tape is played at the right time. An accurate videotape rundown is a necessity. Producers must be sure that changes in the tape order made during the preprogram planning are entered into that final rundown version. Producers must also know how to, and when not to, move elements while the broadcast is on the air.

Words and Effects

The same thoroughness is needed in checking video effects to be inserted into the program. Care must be taken to make sure the lower-third supers are spelled correctly, and that the right one goes in the right place. No one wants to have the wrong name appear as identification of the speaker in a sound bite. Not only sloppy, such a mistake could lead to a libel suit. Newsroom computer systems put initial responsibility for this accuracy on writers and reporters who enter supers information in their scripts.

Any other video effects to be used must also be indicated on the script at the exact point they are supposed to appear. It is up to the producer to make sure the script tells the director what is desired. Otherwise mistakes are made and the post-program review results in a lot of shouting matches. The director's job is tough enough without having to guess the intentions of the producer.

SUMMARY

To TV news personnel, the most important time of their day has arrived when the news broadcast goes on the air. No matter what else has happened that day the time has come for everyone involved to get sharp. The entire effort can come off smoothly and professionally or it can go down the tube in a flurry of missed cues, wrong tapes played, anchors looking around wildly trying to figure out what to do next, and much evil language bouncing around the control room.

Precision of execution is what is needed. In the control room, the producer and the director share the burden, but not in equal parts. The producer has brought the program to the director to execute. In the preceding six or seven hours the producer has made myriad decisions—story selection, content, and length; program order and timing; production elements to be included. Now the director takes the helm. He or she must see to it that what the producer has created gets on and off the air without a glitch.

Yet the producer may still have to make many decisions in the event of a technical or human failure—a VTR refuses to play back a tape, an anchor gets lost in the script or makes a mistake, a live report fails to come up on time. The producer must decide what to do next.

If the tape machine fails, the producer and director must keep the program going—back to the anchor quickly for an apology to the viewers. If the anchor has made a misstatement, it must be corrected as soon as possible. If the live report fails, the questions are: Will the technicians be able to get it on immediately, soon, later, or not at all? If the remote is lost completely, there's a big hole in the program that must be filled with something else. If the remote works but runs badly overtime because the news maker rambles on and on, something will have to be dropped to get the program off on time. These are producer decisions; they must be made quickly and firmly.

No matter what happens, the reality is that there will be a newscast at a certain time of day and that it will run a certain number of minutes and seconds. The larger reality is that the precision with which the producer makes news and production judgments, checks the details, anticipates problems, and has alternative plans to solve them leads to the crisp execution of a program that is clear, informative, and satisfying for the audience.

As is the case with so many other aspects of the craft of television news, producing is a trial-and-error combination of art and science, part logic, part intuition. When a broadcast comes off smoothly everyone on the team feels a huge sense of accomplishment. When it doesn't the producer must inspect everything she or he or others did that contributed to the failure. Post mortems about program failures are no fun.

PROFILE

Valerie Hyman directs the Program for Broadcast Journalists at The Poynter Institute in St. Petersburg, Florida. She created the program, which began in 1990, and organizes and teaches Institute seminars on reporting, newsroom management, producing, and ethical decision making.

Immediately before joining the Institute, Valerie was Director of News Development for the Gillett Group of network-affiliated television stations (now New World Television). She traveled to the twelve Gillett stations across the country, assessing newsroom operations and coaching newsroom managers, reporters, and producers.

She started her broadcast career as a radio and television reporter in Knoxville, Tennessee, at CBS affiliate WBIR, and later became assistant news director there. She moved to WSMV-TV in Nashville as senior reporter, doing general assignment news, documentaries, and investigations. Her work in Nashville earned Valerie two Peabody awards, the DuPont-Columbia Silver Baton, National Headliner awards, and other honors.

Valerie graduated from Indiana University with a B.A. degree and graduate work in telecommunications/news and public affairs. In 1986 she was awarded a Nieman Fellowship and spent the 1986–87 school year at Harvard University.

The Producer's Challenge

Valerie Hyman
The Poynter Institute

What a privilege it is to produce news programs, and what a challenge. To decide what goes in and what stays out, to influence reporters and photo-journalists as they work, to determine how to present stories most effectively, to shape the way news programs are promoted.

Lots of details and pressures influence those decisions on a daily basis, but at their foundation must be the principles of journalism and the role of journalists in a free society: to seek truth and report it as fully as possible, to be independent of associations that could compromise editorial integrity, and to minimize the inevitable harm reporting news causes.

It's hard to remain true to those principles in today's competitive environment. You may enter a newsroom that has chosen to do "happy, warm, fuzzy" news, perhaps to the exclusion of important, albeit unpleasant, stories. Or your first job may put you in the swirling middle of a tabloid-style approach, emphasizing high story count, violence, and sex. My advice: stay true to your principles and you'll never go wrong. In fact, you'll gain a reputation as a leader to whom others look for guidance.

Your job as a producer is to reach beyond overnight ratings to long-term success, to reach beyond glitz to substance, to reach beyond format to responsiveness—all in the service of journalism that empowers citizens by informing them. To inform audiences, you must first engage them with compelling material, presented in a form that makes sense, in a context that shows you understand not just what *happened,* but what it *means.*

Lots of journalists think they have a lock on what their audiences need and want to know, but the most recent and comprehensive research shows they don't. That isn't surprising, considering that journalists as a group are younger, whiter, wealthier, and better educated than the public as a whole. And to make matters worse, they spend most of their time talking to each other. Keep that in mind when you make decisions about which stories get covered and which don't, where to place stories in newscasts, and how much time to devote to them.

In fact, people across the country, in big cities and small, North and South, tell researchers pretty much the same thing, and it goes something like this:

I want to see stories about issues that make a difference in my life, presented in a way I can understand. Don't just show me crime after crime—tell me trends or patterns of crimes in my community so I can get a clearer sense of what the problem is. Don't just show minorities as criminals and victims—incorporate people of color throughout the news, regardless of whether the story involves race. Don't pander to what you think will draw my attention to your news program—sex and violence—show me you care about my community by spending the time and resources to explain even the most complicated issues in a clear and compelling way. And include the good things in our town as well as the bad.

It's good advice. And it's time we journalists started to follow it. Here are some ideas on how to get started:

- Write a mission statement for your news program, in keeping with the overall mission for the newsroom and the station. Include such things as your target audience, the program's general pace and style, and mix of local, national, and international news.

- Treat reporter/photographer "crews" as teams. Coach them at the front end of their day, by asking what they anticipate to be the focus of their story, and what interviews and visuals they think they'll need to tell it. Encourage them to emphasize interviews with people directly affected by the story, and play down the "talking heads" of experts and government officials.

- Encourage reporters and photographers to look for details to help describe what it was like to be in this story, the "telling tidbits" that recapture the experience for viewers.

- Be flexible with your format. When a reporter comes up with an enterprise story and it's compelling, let it run long. Break out an important element with an anchor voiceover and a graphic. Tease a sidebar to the lead story for after weather. Be open to forty-five-second packages from reporters on matters that require no more than that to make their point. Remember: let the content determine the form.

- Don't let crime stories slither into your newscast. That's how we've come to have segments full of unrelated crimes, complete with body bags, bloody sidewalks, and blacks and Latinos in handcuffs. Instead, make deliberate decisions about each story, make each meaningful, and put each in context. That could mean grouping certain crimes for a brief overview once a week, or using graphic maps to show where crimes occur over time.

- Become familiar with a wide range of computer data bases, and do your best to ensure your newsroom uses them. It's especially important to gain access to city and county government, police, and judicial public records. They can enable you to break important stories twenty-four-hours a day, seven days a week.

- Make sure your Rolodex of news sources includes lots of people of color in a variety of areas: a black pediatrician, an Asian chef, a Latina principal. Go out of your way to offer those sources to reporters at the beginning of their reporting day.

- Know what equipment your graphic artist and/or technical director has available, what it can do, and how long it takes to create the most-used graphics. Get specific ideas and photocopies of maps to them as early in the day as possible.

- Disclose your process to your audience. If a grieving family has invited you to cover the funeral of a child, tell that to your audience in the lead to the story. Make sure whenever you use pictures and sound of distraught people, that your audience knows you did not exploit them, but rather followed their wishes. And then, of course, make sure you're telling the truth!

- Be the best writer you can be. Use the active voice. Be sparing with adjectives. Eliminate clichés. Use short sentences to tell complicated stories. Remember, clarity comes from selection, not compression, so make sure everything you write is central to the focus of the story.

- Encourage creativity. Consider a regular feature written by and for teenagers from local high schools, or a photo essay to close a newscast, or a spot for guest commentators from the community, or letters/faxes to the newsroom.

- When you face a difficult decision, create options beyond, "We either use it or we don't!" For example, if you decide to run some especially sensitive or potentially harmful video, consider calling the people involved, and letting them know about your decision before the story airs. The idea is not to ask their permission, but to be sensitive to their feelings. The editorial decision is yours.

- Be generous with praise and stingy with criticism. Consider mistakes— especially your own—as learning opportunities.

- Always remember, the journalist's primary responsibility is to the public.

When you become a journalist, you answer a noble call. Nobody else does what journalists do in our society. No other professionals are responsible for revealing information, for holding the powerful accountable, for giving voice to the voiceless. Only journalists carry that burden. With it comes certain obligations and, potentially, the ability to make the world a better place.

Producing Live News

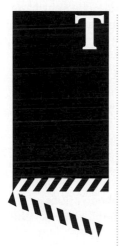

The full flowering of the technology of television news comes when news departments are called on to use it for their coverage at the scene of a news event. Reporting live is the most dramatic, most difficult, and most rewarding development to come out of the developing technology of ENG. Using the technology to bring viewers news as it happens requires the utmost in careful planning and management teamwork, and a little bit of luck.

EQUIPMENT FOR REMOTES

The electronic equipment which permits TV journalists to report live from outside the studio consists of: (1) a package of electronic equipment to perform the gathering, editing, and production of television news stories; (2) a package of equipment to transmit the TV audio and video back to the studio; and (3) a truck or van to get the equipment and personnel to and from the location of the news story.

Electronic Package

The basic equipment to acquire live pictures from the site of a live report is a stripped-down, miniaturized version of the equipment used in a television studio. It consists of one or more cameras, camera controls, a switcher, an audio board, possibly a character-generator and frequently, video and audio recording equipment. It is possible to reduce the extent of the equipment package for bare-bones coverage, or considerably expand it for multi-camera live production with special effects and graphics. The choice of equipment is determined by the station's budget for news technology, and the production demands of its TV market.

Usually at least one camera and one recorder carried in a remote unit can be used for videotaped interviews in the same way a videographer operates when taping stories to be edited at the station or a bureau. Most remote units carry lighting equipment ranging from the simple light kit to high-powered, generator-driven exterior production lights.

Transmission

There are currently three ways to transmit a television picture (with audio) from a remote site to the TV station. They are: (1) microwave, (2) satellite, (3) cable.

Microwave

Microwave is a form of "radio" transmission which can be used to send any bandwidth signal, from telephone and data to television video and audio. Much of America's long-distance telephone service continues to be sent from point to point by microwave, although telephone service also travels by satellite and fiber-optic cable. We see microwave antennas mounted on tall towers next to telephone company buildings and mounted part way up the towers of FM and TV broadcast stations. (Now you have something new to look for.)

In general, a microwave signal will travel 25 to 40 miles from its transmission point, depending on the height of the transmitting antenna, the frequency of the signal, and power of the transmitter. Hills or buildings can block the signal from arriving at its destination. Microwave works on a line-of-sight basis from point to point.

Several clever systems have been developed to expand the range of microwave-equipped remote vehicles. A mini-microwave unit can be used to transmit the signal from the actual news site, such as the twelfth floor of an office building, to the mobile vehicle. This is very helpful when the ENG vehicle can't be driven close to the site of the coverage.

In major cities, truck operators have learned how to "bounce" microwave signals off certain buildings to get around other buildings which block the line-of-sight signal path between the truck and the TV station. In some major markets, stations have established networks of "repeater" antennas which receive signals from vehicles and relay them to the station along clear signal paths. One TV station, WCTV in Tallahassee (FL)-Thomasville (GA) used its old fixed microwave tower at a downtown studio site in Tallahassee to receive signals from the portable microwave equipment and then relay the signals approximately 25 miles to the station site.

Relays are done using helicopters, which can also be the source of microwave signals for airborne coverage.

Microwave-equipped units, which are called, generically, ENG or Electronic News Gathering units, can be as small as a sedan with folding portable equipment stored in the car's trunk, to a heavy-duty diesel truck built by a company which specializes in remote unit construction. Stations tend to favor three types of vehicles, the highly flexible four-wheel drive sports vehicle which can cover difficult terrain, the van or minivan for ease of coverage in urban areas, and the larger truck-type vehicle which offers space for more production equipment but is less flexible in terms of where it can be driven.

The majority of ENG vehicles have a telescoping mast installed to allow the operator to raise the antenna to the maximum height possible.

Satellite

There are so many satellites available for civilian use that U.S. broadcasters can order short periods of satellite service on what is called an "occasional use" basis. There are communication companies which coordinate these short-term applications, making it possible to obtain satellite time almost any time a broadcaster needs it.

A satellite vehicle usually resembles a large microwave unit, and in fact, some satellite trucks can also transmit microwave signals. The truck is, in the language of the satellite communication industry, an "uplink." An **uplink** is a combination of a transmitter and antenna which can send a signal from earth to a satellite's antenna approximately 22,300 miles above the equator. The uplink is also a **downlink**, meaning it can receive signals from a satellite.

The typical satellite vehicle has a fairly large antenna mounted on a hydraulic lift which allows the operator to manipulate it to target or aim at the correct satellite. This targeting process, called **telemetry**, is done automatically using a microcomputer-driven electronic box. The truck is equipped with cellphones, two-way radios, and satellite audio links, which permit the operator to talk with the satellite control center and the TV station's satellite operations and production desks. Other circuits are available to assist reporters and producers with communications.

The truck is equipped with one or two generators to provide electric power and is completely self-contained. An experienced operator can put the typical satellite truck into service in ten to fifteen minutes.

The production equipment aboard a satellite truck, also called **SNV**, for Satellite News Vehicle, is the same as is used on a microwave truck.

Most satellite news trucks use the Ku satellite band because it utilizes a smaller antenna which can be folded and stowed on or within the truck's body.

A well-equipped satellite news vehicle could cost up to a half-million dollars for the chassis and its custom equipment. Its advantage is that the truck can be operated anywhere in the United States, thus breaking down the limitations of distance for live electronic news coverage. These vehicles are discussed in more detail in Chapter 10.

While it is possible to drive halfway across the country to do live news coverage, this is impractical for most television stations, so stations and networks form satellite news cooperatives. The idea was spawned by several Florida large-market television stations which wanted to have video originations from major stories occurring in other cities in the sprawling, 600-mile long state. The stations agreed to share on a daily basis major stories originating in their markets. In the late afternoon each station fed its contributions to the coordinating station in Jacksonville, which then relayed all of the stories in one or two feeds at set times each day.

The idea caught fire and soon other cooperatives were established. Pretty soon the three major commercial television networks—ABC, CBS, and NBC—came under pressure from affiliates to reform their traditional New York-based "news feeds" to provide better regional coverage. In time, each network established a system of regional coordinating and collecting points, and soon all affiliates had the benefit of receiving dozens of stories from around the country on their daily network feeds. The networks benefited by being able to get much needed live video from the location of breaking news stories.

In fact, the cooperative system offered so many advantages, the networks helped some affiliates pay for the cost of buying expensive satellite trucks. NBC News even set up a separate news feed operations center in Charlotte, North Carolina. The Cable News Network, and the Hubbard broadcasting interests in Minneapolis operating as **Conus**, established independent news cooperatives, to which stations could subscribe for supplemental coverage.

Cable

It is possible to connect a remote vehicle to the newsroom by cable. For years the technique was limited to very important events because of the high cost of connecting to the local and long-distance telephone circuits controlled by the Bell System of AT&T.

A small number of local or regional cable news organizations developed an inexpensive alternative for use in their own markets. When the cable company strung its lines, channels were reserved for internal use by the cable company for news and live sports coverage. The news truck could drive up to a utility pole on which the cable company had mounted a connector box, and plug into the special circuit. This was not as flexible as microwave or satellite coverage, but it worked, and it was relatively inexpensive.

The advent of digital technology, which changes audio and video signals into thin data-streams rather than capacity-gobbling "broadband" signals, makes it possible to send high-quality audio and video over fiber-optic cable, which is now in place connecting most major U.S. cities.

Fiber-optic cable is not yet available on every block, but in the near future it will be possible for TV crews to use the "information superhighway" technology to plug into cable to telecommunication circuits in buildings, and transmit live or delayed feeds to their newsrooms.

In 1994 the World Cup Soccer Championships in the United States made extensive use of fiber-optic circuits managed by AT&T and an independent carrier named Vyvx to bring live soccer coverage from nine locations around the country to a Dallas, Texas, coordination center, where the signal was routed over fiber optic lines to satellite uplink centers in California, West Virginia, and New York. Similar arrangements were developed for the 1996 Olympics and are used weekly for professional sports broadcasts.

PLANNING

The luck factor is always there but in live news reporting the luck factor can be reduced in importance by a good operational plan—one that can be applied across time and the vagaries of each individual news story.

First, you have to know what your technical resources are. Then you have to figure out a way to use those resources efficiently, economically, strategically, and logically. Major elements of the plan must deal with facilities and technical support, staffing, programming, policy and decision making, and editorial control. The components of such a live coverage plan will look something like this:

✔ 1. Facilities and technical support: What have we got to work with, where is it, who's available to run it?

✔ 2. Staffing: Who will produce, who will edit, who will report, who will supervise?

✔ 3. Programming: Will this be used in regular news programming? Will we do bulletins, special reports, one or more wrap-ups? Will there be continuing coverage, will the story last a long time? When will it be time to stop the coverage?

✔ 4. Policy and decision making: Who will call the shots? Who has the responsibility? Are the responsibility lines clear?

✔ 5. Editorial control: Who will maintain an overview of the coverage? Who will monitor the coverage? Who will provide liaison with the field? Who will check facts and keep additional information flowing to the field? Who will monitor the writing, editing, and production elements?

No single producer, writer, editor, reporter, videographer, assignment desk editor, or technician is going to be called upon to make all these decisions. The ultimate authority lies with the news director and the general manager of the station. The generalized checklist above is full of decisions only they can make. But other decisions within that checklist clearly are to be made by those farther down in the table of organization. If the news director had to make logistic and operational decisions at the same time he or she was called on to supervise, administer, and make go or no-go decisions, it would be too big a load for one person.

Thus, every station has, or should have, a "game plan" which has been worked out in advance and is well known and understood by its staff. Without such a game plan and a clear description of responsibilities, people working in the flurry of live coverage may not know when they are supposed to concentrate on their part of the team operation, when they are supposed to ask for guidance, or what to do next.

A quickly called game plan for a television news operation may sound like this: "You produce, you coordinate, you edit, you write, you report. Everyone keep me informed. Now go!"

Production of a story when using the mobile equipment can be simple or very complex. Let's take a simple case.

The Story

The assignment is to take the news van to the airport and cover the arrival of a senator returning home after a visit to Russia. The van will microwave the material back to the station for editing and use in the noon news program. A longer version and a sidebar interview with the senator's wife will be prepared later for use in the dinner-hour news.

This is relatively easy because the assignment desk has known the senator's return date and time for several days. It has ordered facilities—the van and crew and the intake of the microwaved material—and has made advance contact with the senator's press aide. The decision to microwave the report was made because the senator is arriving at 11:30 A.M. Time is too short to deliver a videotape any other way.

The reporter has known of the assignment for twenty-four hours and so has researched it and prepared a list of good questions. The producer of the noon news will monitor the feed and, with an editor-writer—and some radioed editing suggestions from the reporter—will see that the story is edited and the script written for the noon anchor.

It all goes well; the senator makes some very provocative comments on U.S.-Russian relations. The senator's wife gives interesting details about the trip. During the afternoon the reporter will recut the story for the 6 P.M. news and edit and write script for the sidebar interview with the senator's wife.

The Story Changes

The wire services also covered the senator's arrival. By 4 P.M., there is an uproar from the State Department in Washington. Spokespersons there deny what the senator has said and accuse him of upsetting some very delicate trade negotiations.

The assignment desk reacts. Where is the senator now? Can we get him to respond? The reporter drops whatever she is doing, checks her notes, and gets on the phone. Quickly she finds out the senator is in a meeting at a local hotel with party leaders, doesn't want to come out of the meeting just now . . . meeting will end at about 5:30 . . . is due at cocktail reception in the same hotel at 6 P.M. The 6 P.M. producer, the desk editor, and the reporter decide that a mobile unit will be dispatched to the hotel. The reporter will go to the hotel to set up to do either a live-delayed or live shot for the 6 P.M. news.

Remember "keep me informed"? Chances are good that the news director or executive producer has been keeping an eye on what the operational staff is doing. If someone had anticipated there would be a reaction, plans could have been made earlier. Nevertheless, something has to be done quickly, and the new plan is acceptable. Except the boss says, "Hell, everyone will be wanting reaction . . . the place will be swarming with the competition . . . anyone got any ideas?"

The assignments editor says, "Channel 10 is already setting up outside the party room and plans to go live from there."

Enterprising Reporter raises her hand. "I've got something. I know the senator well, his wife, too. They're staying in a suite. I'll bet he's going to change clothes for the party. Can we get into that suite so that I can grab him before he goes downstairs? Could we do a live shot from there?"

ENG Coordinator: "Sure, we can use the mini [short-range microwave] for a double hop—out the window to the truck, from the truck back here. But someone's got to get us in and we'd better also set up where Channel 10 is . . ."

Enterprising Reporter: "I'll get us in the suite; you set it up."

News Director: "Okay, but we better have the backup location too, otherwise we might get zilch. Put a field producer on it." He goes off mumbling about overtime.

The ENG Coordinator moves to set up the facilities. The reporter gets on the phone to the senator's aide. The aide sounds doubtful, worried about catching heat from the competitors. Enterprising Reporter calls the senator's wife. His wife says sure, and come up earlier so we can have a chat, I want to tell you more about our trip.

The gamble is on. The backup location will be installed in case the reporter has to do a live wrap around the senator's earlier remarks. But the beat in the making depends upon the success of the interview in the senator's suite.

The Team at Work

The crew, ENG Coordinator, Field Producer, and Enterprising Reporter take off. The line producer (6 P.M. telecast producer) begins to restructure his program. At the hotel, Enterprising Reporter, Field Producer, technicians, and camera operator go right to the suite. Enterprising Reporter introduces them, they start the setup procedure, and the senator's wife tells about the trip. The double-hop microwave system works just fine; soon pictures from the suite are being received back at the station. The radio coordination circuits are working. IFB is established for the reporter. The field producer says all systems are go.

Downstairs, the senator is running late. He shoots out the door of the meeting room, telling reporters he'll talk to them in a minute. He gets on an elevator and goes to his suite. He's a little startled to find his friend the reporter there, but says as long as they're all set up why not do it. He makes a mental note to talk to his wife about his need to keep all of the news media happy. His aide sputters a bit, but subsides.

So the senator and Enterprising Reporter sit down and have a nice ten-minute interview in which he comments on the Washington reaction and gives some more details on why he said what he said earlier. Enterprising Reporter's questions are incisive; the senator seems to enjoy fencing with her.

Back at the Shop

At the station the video and audio of the interview are logged as they flow in and editing decisions are made. A package of material including the senator's original comments and his reaction to the State Department's comments is put together. While the interview is going on the News Director tells the Field Producer to tell Enterprising Reporter to hustle downstairs to do a live wrap from the backup camera location outside the party meeting room door.

There, the makings of the usual buffalo stampede are in progress. The competing TV stations are set up to go live as soon as the senator shows up. But Enterprising Reporter knows something they don't. Her story will lead the program, and the tape package is ready to go.

As usual, the senator is a little late. Reporters from the competing stations lead their program with some lame material like: "The senator hasn't arrived yet, Fred . . . but he caused quite a stir when he arrived at the airport this morning and made these comments . . ."

Enterprising Reporter goes on the air at the same time as the others. But the package she cues into contains both the highlights of the material from the airport that morning and excerpts from her exclusive interview. She does a smooth opening and narration between the segments and signs off saying that the senator hasn't arrived yet but that she will stand by; She also says that if there is anything new to report she will come back and relay it to the audience during the program.

Perhaps there will be something new in what the senator has to say when he is confronted by all those microphones and a flurry of questions. Just to rub it in a little, the station does switch back. Enterprising Reporter does a quick wrap-up of the new things the senator said and reminds her audience that they can see more of the exclusive interview on the late news.

The Results

It's a big success. Lots of factors made it so. They begin with the good relationship the reporter had cultivated with the senator and his wife over a long period of time. They include her suggestion about getting into the senator's suite and the professional way she went about it. Another factor was the solid work of the technicians and ENG crew—the use of technology to get the double-hop—and the decision by the news director to spend the time and money to do it. The rewards for the news staff are in knowing they all worked together to do a superior job—and perhaps some giggles thinking about the news staffs at the other stations watching the newscasts side by side and commenting, "Jeez, look at that!"

It was also rewarding to their audience, who got a clearer, more detailed, more carefully presented story that told the basic facts and updated the story with the latest developments. Although no one called the news staff to thank them for working so hard, many people in the audience were made aware, in an indirect way, that this station could be counted upon to give them the latest news.

A final note. The station's network called later in the evening to ask for a satellite feed of the tape of the interview. It appeared on the network's morning newscasts the next day. The reporter got network notice and exposure and made a little extra money on the side.

The Post-Mortem

Now, lest we get carried away by the euphoria of the moment, we should remember that a lot of things could have gone wrong. The setup to get the pictures and sound from the hotel suite to the news van might not have worked. Other equipment might have failed. The senator could have refused to do the interview or might have been running so late it was impossible. Cues could have been missed.

Scores of things can happen in a situation like this. But the planning and coordination by the news and technical staff was good, and they gave themselves a good chance to pull it off. It is not just a case of crossing your fingers or saying a few words to the gods of electricity. Planning is the key to success.

All of the components of the operational plan were included in this coverage. The facilities were available. They were cleverly used to get the exclusive material and back up the coverage in case the hotel room remote did not work out.

The staff was in place. The reporter was able to handle both ends of the live feeds. It might have been safer to send another reporter to cover the party room location in case things got very tight for the reporter in the hotel suite, but this also would have cost quite a lot more.

The lines of responsibility were clear. Each person in the chain of command knew what was expected of him or her. The news director made the important decision to set up both live locations and activated the tentative decision to have the reporter do the live wrap.

This story did not require a decision to break into regular programming for bulletins and/or special reports. It did not need continuous coverage. It did require more than average staff and facilities, but not an inordinate amount.

Editorial control was maintained. The staff might have realized earlier that it had the makings of a good story and moved to do something about it sooner. The material was carefully monitored as it came in. A field producer was sent to the scene to coordinate the visual and aural elements and to serve as liaison with the line producer, news director, and reporter so that late decisions were quickly and properly carried out.

INFORMATION CHANNELS

One of the most important ingredients for good mobile news coverage is information. In the example above, the reporter did have time to research her story so she could get the background information needed to do a professional job on the exclusive interview. And she did have an IFB so she could get the other information she needed—cues from those recording her interview, and when she was on the air at the beginning of the newscast and during the later insert. The presence of a field producer helped make the editing of the tape material and the program production go smoothly while the reporter dashed from one location to the other.

The Spot News Information Need

When a station is covering a spot news story with mobile equipment, the need for information flowing to and from the field becomes paramount. The reporters and crews dispatched to the scene of a spot news story have to work at high speed. While the crews are setting up the video and microwave equipment reporters have to begin gathering facts. The information needs we are talking about here include:

1. Information needed to run and control the live broadcast

2. Information from other sources for the reporters and producers on the scene

Both kinds of information are distributed through a private two-way radio system, cellular phones, or specially installed telephones. In some cases computer links speed written communication between the newsroom and personnel at the story. The voice systems are aptly called **co-ord circuits**. Normally there are two separate systems, one for the technicians, the other for the editorial staff.

On the **"tech" circuits** the live unit field technicians communicate with control room engineers who monitor the technical operation. On the **"news" circuits** reporters, field producers, and videographers exchange facts, editorial decisions, and cues. It is important to separate these channels because the technicians and news people have different information needs and must be able to speak to each other at any time. These circuits are also isolated from the video and audio broadcast channels being relayed back to the station so that operational information doesn't interfere with the steady flow of news.

The major problem for a reporter at a live shot is that she or he has to be on the air and collect information at the same time. The whole point of a live spot news broadcast is to get on the air as soon as possible and stay on the air as long as is necessary.

Often good solid facts and details are at a premium. Rumors are everywhere. Various versions of what happened are circulating. Authorities who could give information are very busy. But the reporter's job is to keep reliable information flowing, avoid rumors and speculation, and stick to the facts.

That's one half of it—the half that the audience sees and hears. The other half is the flow of information *to the field.* We tend to think of ENG as being one-directional: News goes from some story location back to the station and to the audience. It must be a bidirectional system; news departments have to organize themselves during a spot news story to make it so. No matter how good the reporters and producers in the field are, the station's real news-gathering strength is in the newsroom. There the staff can get on the phone, go to other news sources, monitor radios, check the facts, dig into resource material, write scripts, prepare graphics, edit recaps, locate eyewitnesses and additional interviews, and do all the other things necessary to give shape to the story.

Management personnel can monitor what is on the air and make decisions about where the story is now, where it is headed, and what needs to be done in the next seconds, minutes, and hours to stay on top of it.

The Story Breaks

As an example, let's take a real story: the explosion of sewers in a large area of Old Town, a neighborhood of Louisville, Kentucky.

In this example, we are not going to talk about what the specific newsrooms there did with the story. We are going to look at this story to see what it tells us about the need for bidirectional information flow.

The facts are relatively simple. Faulty equipment caused material from a local industry to flow into the sewers. This material formed a gas that exploded in the early morning hours, blowing up the streets and damaging nearby buildings like a string of bombs dropped during a bombing run.

Imagine you are on the news staff of a Louisville station when the big blast occurred. You don't know much of anything at the beginning. Very quickly you have a strong hint that it's a big story. Several calls have come from people in the area. The police radio traffic on the scanners increases; more calls are coming in by the second.

The very first thing to do is to confirm the basics: Has there been an explosion of some sort? Where is it? Is it real? Is it a hoax?

The next thing to do is to get the reporters and technicians moving, the news vans out to meet them, the helicopter in the air, and at the same time get something on the air. Then inform the news director and engineering

Figure 8.1. WHAS-TV, Louisville, Kentucky, reporter Jeffrey Hutter live at the scene of one of the control points established following an early-morning explosion in the city's sewers. *(Courtesy of WHAS-TV.)*

supervisor. They may know something already, but don't count on it—more than one call on something like this is a thousand times better than none.

That's a lot of things to do. In doing them you have begun the information flow. You have also created a voracious monster. There's someone in the studio telling the audience the few facts so far available and both he or she, and the audience, desperately want more.

Now the system has to start churning out those facts. What are your resources?

1. The phone

2. Official sources

3. The reporters

4. The news staff

5. The mobile units

6. The helicopter

Note that the phone is the fastest thing you've got right at the beginning. You use it to (a) get more facts from those official sources, (b) relay that information to the on-air people, and (c) summon more help. The phone and the people to use it are all important at the beginning of a big spot news story. Those machines with all the fancy electronics in them still have to get to the story and be set up to broadcast. That's going to take some time.

So organization is all important. If your news staff is proud of its record for fast, accurate information, people will arrive quickly. Journalists instinctively head for the story or the newsroom when a big one breaks, whether they've been summoned or not. The important thing is to put these people to work in an organized way. It is game-plan time again: "You take the cops, you the sheriffs, you City Hall, you the power company, you the sanitary district, you the hospitals, you the eyewitnesses."

In rapping out those orders you have established a system that will begin to amass facts for the on-air broadcast. You have also established the inside half of the communications system that will sustain your flow of information even after the live units get on the air.

Figure 8.2. A WHAS-TV News off-air picture of destruction caused by an explosion in the sewers in Louisville, Kentucky. Careful labeling of the various streets that were damaged was important because the blast occurred just before drive time began. *(Courtesy of WHAS-TV.)*

The Live Broadcasts Begin

The mobile units start to come on-line. The helicopter is up and over the scene. One mobile unit is live from the ground. Reporters in each are describing what they see and what the audience is looking at. Another unit will come up from the police command post. A third will establish another live remote from another vantage point. Camera and reporter teams with portable videotape equipment are working other locations. Couriers are shuttling videotape to the mobile units—where it can be inserted into the live remotes—and back to the newsroom. Soon you have a good flow of facts and a lot of good interviews with eyewitnesses—the human side of the story—and with officials and experts who add depth to it.

The Bigger Story

So far, so good. But each of those live remotes is providing only a part of the overall story. The reporters and videographers are so busy at their individual locations that they cannot get a feeling of the bigger picture, the whole story.

For instance, it has been quickly established that no one was killed and the number of injured is small. Everyone at the remotes needs to know that. It has also been learned that it was a gas explosion in the sewers; the fire department says there seems to be little danger of more explosions. Nobody knows yet why it happened. That news needs to get to the field reporters as well as to the audience. Perhaps the reporters and technicians have been able to monitor the live broadcast. But don't count on that; perhaps they have been too busy to do so.

What is needed here is editorial control. Each reporter needs to be kept informed of the progress of the story. They can be kept informed through the two-way system we've been talking about. They are apt to be less effective in the field if they are in an information vacuum.

The anchorpersons in the studio have the same problem. Their role is to provide the basic early information, to keep repeating the basic facts as more viewers tune in, and to provide continuity. The anchors are starved for information at the beginning of the broadcast but may suffer information overload as it goes on. They are so busy relaying facts, leading into the live remotes, and keeping the broadcast going that they cannot get a very good sense of the big picture, either.

Then, too, the focus of the story expands. Part of the bigger picture is the impact of the event on the metropolitan community. Here is where producers, editors, and news directors come into play. The system needs people to watch the overall broadcast. Some must check the facts, making sure that inadvertent mistakes are corrected quickly and that errors of fact are not allowed to become embedded in copy, narration, or ad-lib comments. Others need to be looking at where the story is going. If few people are dead or injured, a remote at a hospital is not going to be productive after those facts are established. If the explosion has created a massive traffic jam during the morning rush hour, that, for an hour or two, may become a major element of the story.

What about school closings? Business closings? If there is no more danger of explosion, what about danger from falling walls or buildings that may collapse? What about control of people and vehicles heading toward the area? Is the sewer system still working? Is the water supply interrupted? If so, where? What other events will be canceled or postponed, and when will they be rescheduled?

Here again, the inside system is the primary mechanism for providing answers to those questions. The information it develops also enables the editors and producers to make wise decisions about where and when to move some of the reporters to new focal points of the story.

The final important decision is: When should we end the broadcast? This one lands squarely in the news director's lap. It involves a lot of considerations. Some are economic, some competitive, some editorial.

Bill McAndrew, a former president of NBC News, won fame and a lot of audience appreciation for his network with a fairly simple policy: "We will go on the air *before* the other networks, and we will go off *after* they have finished." The first part was difficult, but he spurred his troops on and they usually met the challenge. The second part was a combination of stubbornness and machismo. Both attitudes are very competitive. The audience can develop a huge appetite for more information about a major story. Portions of that audience will stay tuned as long as there is even the hope of learning anything new.

That leads to the editorial part of the decision. As long as there is new information, or even the chance of new information, the news director who decides to quit too soon runs the risk of disappointing viewers, and missing the chance to tell them something they need to know.

Another portion of that audience becomes restless. There are, after all, other programs they may want to see. They will tune away if the broadcast becomes boring and repetitive. That's part of the economic factor in the decision. The other part is that there are faithful advertisers who sponsor other programs on the station. They deserve to have their programs shown at the scheduled times unless there are good reasons to cancel those programs.

A major news event is a good reason. News directors usually have the authority to take over programming, and they do. Over the years most news directors have acted in a very responsible way in regard to preempting regular programming to bring the audience live coverage of major important events. But it's a truism of American broadcasting that they have to take the economic factor into consideration.

ALL-OUT LIVE

When a major disaster strikes, live television news can become the ultimate channel of information for everyone. No other medium, with the possible exception of radio, can be as quick. When the full resources of television are focused on the major disaster—hurricane Andrew, a devastating tornado or earthquake, or an act of terrorism such as the bomb blast at the Federal Building in Oklahoma City—TV news can equal the comprehensiveness of the print media, and also provide a viewer experience unequaled by any other news medium. ENG, run by journalists with dedication, vision, imagination, and powerful news judgment, is what does the job. We have two examples of such all-out-live efforts that demonstrate the point.

The Cloud over Dayton

WHIO-TV in Dayton, Ohio, was geared up for the 6 P.M. newscast one July afternoon when, at about 4:30 P.M., a CSX freight train derailed and caught fire near Miamisburg, a Dayton suburb. Three live interrupts between 4:50 and 6 P.M. included shots from WHIO-TV's helicopter showing a huge and growing white cloud blowing right across the Dayton metropolitan area. The live picture of that cloud would come to be an almost permanent image on Dayton TV screens during the next thirty-two hours as WHIO-TV shifted its gears into overdrive and broadcast more than six hours of live broadcasts and special reports.

At times the cloud was 1,500 feet high, 3 miles wide, and many more miles long. Its source was a 30- to-40-foot-high boiling fire from a ruptured tank car containing 1,200 gallons of white phosphorus. White phosphorus is nasty stuff; it bursts into flame when it hits air, and fighting those flames with water just makes the fire hotter.

The fire itself was not the danger, since the derailment occurred in open country near the west bank of the Greater Miami River, but the cloud, "smelling like matches" everyone said, made eyes burn, noses run, and throats sore, and could cause serious problems for people with respiratory problems. Before firefighters and chemical experts got it under control, 35,000 Dayton area residents would be evacuated, and hundreds would visit hospital emergency rooms.

The WHIO-TV assignment desk heard the original police traffic about the derailment and sent the company's leased Bell Ranger helicopter—"Chopper 7"—to have a look.

WHIO-TV News Director Skip Hapner said that it took no longer than ten or fifteen minutes for him and the staff to realize they had a complex story and that they were going to play a major information role for both the audience and area officials.

Hapner's newsroom did not have a written plan for disaster coverage. However, WHIO-TV did have a standing policy that turned out to be a key ele-

Figure 8.3. The cloud that frightened Miamisburg, Ohio. A train derailment ripped open a tank car containing 12,000 gallons of white phosphorus, which burns when it makes contact with air. Wind carried clouds of toxic fumes directly over Dayton. For the next thirty-two hours, WHIO-TV, Dayton, tracked the cloud with its helicopter and transmitted many hours of live reports from it. *(Courtesy of WHIO TV.)*

ment in its coverage. The station frequently invites police and fire officials to ride in its helicopter when covering stories these authorities might become involved in. Hapner said:

> The policy was to work very closely with police and fire authorities. Some news directors will tell you they would never let a policeman or fireman ride with them . . . but my philosophy is different. I think that having them there helps the story. . . . They can use their own radio equipment to talk to those on the ground and coordinate things, and then we can interview them and pass the information on to the audience immediately. We have an official source right there with us—what could be faster than that?
>
> Furthermore, a situation like this is as much a public service broadcast as it is a news broadcast. You are fully into public service messages as you tell people about evacuation and public health procedures . . . go here . . . don't go there . . . avoid these areas because the smoke is heavy there . . . and you have the legal authority right beside you.

Another policy decision was made on the fly. "As soon as I knew the enormity of it," Hapner said, "I called my boss, Stan Mouse. I told him what we had. The first thing he said to me was: 'Okay, you make the decisions, whatever you need to do, do it. If it means canceling prime-time programs, do it. Whatever . . . you know what the situation is, and you're in charge.'"

WHIO-TV used three live mobile units for the majority of its coverage over the next two days. Chopper 7 was in the air most of the time, stopping off only for fuel. A live microwave unit with mobile editing capabilities was parked 125 yards away from the burning tank car. A third live unit moved from point to point as needed—the Miamisburg city hall, hospitals, evacuation centers, and so on. WHIO-TV also had a live production unit parked at the NCR Country Club, location of the U.S. Women's Open Golf Tournament, which was to start on Thursday. That was used to report evacuation of practicing golfers from the course.

Hapner said that the basic policy for the live broadcasts the first two days was to keep the live helicopter picture and updates from the chopper's reporting team on the air as much as possible. "We just had to keep the information flowing . . . and since people could see the smoke cloud from almost anywhere in the area . . . we just kept that unit live as much as we could, showing where the smoke plume was headed, how big it was, how much fire there was, what was being done to try to put it out."

WHIO-TV's other major effort was in trying to sort out the facts as to exactly how dangerous it was to breathe the toxic fumes and how and where evacuations were taking place. The pictures of the cloud were frightening, and it was important to avoid panic. It was quickly established that the fumes, while toxic, were not life threatening unless someone got a heavy dose in the thick of the cloud or had respiratory problems. The major point that was made over and over again—and in as many ways as people could think to say it—was to get away from the cloud or stay indoors with the windows shut and with air conditioner vents closed so they wouldn't bring in outside air.

Regarding evacuation, WHIO-TV relied on its live units and its newsroom staff to track and relay the appropriate officials' statements and instructions and to keep in touch with the Red Cross and disaster relief authorities as the situation progressed.

WHIO-TV interrupted its live broadcast to play a videotape of the CBS Evening News with Dan Rather and to carry another kind of live broadcast—the weekly Ohio Lottery Drawing from Cleveland. But it came back again at 8 P.M. for another twenty minutes or so to recap the story and to tell the audience that the situation seemed to have stabilized and that the total evacuations so far had reached 16,000 persons. This segment included live and taped reports from a hospital, a Red Cross evacuation staging center, and both the helicopter and ground locations.

By 11:00 P.M. WHIO-TV was able to report that the fire was under control, and to follow up with a report from an evacuation center at Miamisburg High School that the people there didn't expect to get home before dawn. At 11:40

Figure 8.4. WHIO-TV used its helicopter with a reporter and a fire captain aboard to get close to the source of this toxic chemical fire caused by a train derailment. The fire captain, an expert on such fires, was able to spot changes in the nature of the fire and cloud and relay immediate orders to firefighters and the public. *(Courtesy of WHIO-TV.)*

P.M. the station again went live to cover a news conference held by Ohio Governor Richard Celeste, who had flown back from New York City to see to the situation in Dayton.

The Aftermath

By all logic and experience the following day should have been somewhat easier for WHIO-TV's staff. The state of emergency was still in effect, and fire officials and chemical fire experts had spent the day making plans to get the slowly burning phosphorus fire to a once-and-for-all finish.

But shortly after the opening of the 6 P.M. local newscast, the problem flared up again. The station again interrupted the news with a live, helicopter report that there had been another major outbreak of fire at the disaster scene.

For the next hour and ten minutes, the situation was very tense. Officials worried that the phosphorus and sulfur from an adjoining rail car would mix. In fact they did. About 7:11 P.M. another big belch of smoke erupted from the fire site.

With the fire active again, civic officials started several major evacuations to the University of Dayton Arena and then to the Dayton Convention Center when it was discovered that the Arena wasn't air conditioned. Fire and police officers drove and walked through neighborhoods announcing the evacuation on bull horns.

Dayton's major shopping mall was covered by the smoke and evacuated for the second time in twenty-four hours. This caused large traffic jams and plenty of frustrated evacuees. Some people who had gone on a shopping trip in the late afternoon weren't allowed to go back to their homes until late that night. The mayor of Moraine called WHIO-TV to say there was not going to be an evacuation there, even though one had been ordered by disaster officials. In all 35,000 Dayton area residents were moved out of their homes.

Through all this WHIO-TV's news crew kept the same cool heads they had the night before.

The Crash of Flight 191

In 1979, an American Airlines DC-10 crashed shortly after takeoff from Chicago's O'Hare Airport. All 279 people on board were killed. It became the worst aviation disaster in U.S. history.

WMAQ-TV covered the crash and its aftermath with a plan that news director Paul Beavers had designed from years of experience in Los Angeles which included coverage of the assassination of Robert Kennedy, California earthquakes, and the Symbionese Liberation Army shootout. On those earlier events, his rule of thumb for coverage was: "Go get a lot of pictures and then figure out what to do with them." As live ENG developed his rule changed to: "Get on the air—then support the air."

Beavers had a game plan with which to support the air. It called for putting control of the live broadcast into the hands of a small number of people with specific responsibilities.

✔ 1. *A field producer* goes to each live *remote unit.* That producer is the principal information relay to and from the station, and to the principal on-air reporter. Other reporters at each live remote site feed information to the field producer for relay to the live reporters or through the newsroom to the anchors.

✔ 2. *The assignment desk manager* handles logistics of the movement of mobile units and reporters.

✔ 3. *Producer of facts* is responsible for the intake of all facts and details; shaping the story, looking for angles, directing the in-house staff of reporters and researchers. Worries about supporting the content of the program, not the program itself.

✔ 4. *Producer for program* works in the control room with the ENG coordinators and live-program director to keep the program going.

✔ 5. *The news director* supervises it all.

Much of what went on the air about the crash that day was due to the way Beavers' game plan worked. The in-house staff located eyewitnesses, checked them carefully to make sure they had newsworthy information, and then passed them on to the control room and studio set phone for the anchors to interview. The anchors were briefed about what the eyewitnesses had to say. Even the small details were controlled; each time an eyewitness was put on the phone, that person's name was superimposed on the screen—and it was spelled correctly. The assignment desk managed the movements of five live units and four crews with portable tape but no live capacity.

Beavers' system and the effort it touched off produced a mountain of raw material; the first day fifty-six videotape cassettes were filled with pictures and sound by the crews—that is something like thirty to thirty-five *hours* of material. In all, the WMAQ-TV crash coverage, which continued with extended news specials for two more days, produced 136 video cassettes, easily more than seventy-five hours of outside coverage.

Many other disasters have been given comparable efforts of all-out live coverage by TV news—the Los Angeles riots of 1992, and Hurricane Andrew; the Waco, Texas, David Koresh tragedy of 1993, and widespread flooding in the Midwest; earthquakes in San Francisco, Los Angeles, Kobe, and so forth.

"All-out live" events are challenging, and exciting to cover; the experience can be professionally satisfying (depending on the outcome). One purpose of recounting the examples in this chapter—a neighborhood incident in a medium market city, a potential disaster posing a health threat to an entire metropolitan area in a medium market, a stunning tragedy in a major-market setting—is to drive home the point that each all-out live situation is unique. But, by analyzing details of how television news responds in a given situation, you can learn many tips and pointers about the competitive environment of television news and about newsroom organization and operations, in other words, about how the people who run competitive operations stay on top of spot news.

USES AND PROBLEMS OF LIVE COVERAGE

Producing a successful live news broadcast, as we have seen, calls for quick decisions, flexibility, careful control, and concentration. What you do is what the audience sees.

Elmer Lower, former president of ABC News and a veteran executive of all three television network news divisions, said a live broadcast is unique.

"We are," he said, "the only journalistic medium that does its reporting and editing right in front of the audience."

Lower said that at something like a national political convention, all of the editors and reporters from all the media do the same kinds of things. They get a report that something important may be developing. Then they go out onto the floor and into the caucuses to check it out. This is the uniqueness of live television shows. While the reporters for the newspapers and wire services are doing their checking more or less privately, the television news reporters are on the air while they are running the story down.

That has led to a number of things. A story suddenly blossoms, then wilts as the TV reporters swarm over news makers only to find that it was someone's carefully planted trial balloon that didn't fly. Other times it turns out that there really was some substance to the story. Whatever the outcome is, the TV audience is watching the *process* of journalism as well as the result.

Flashback World

When a live broadcast mixes live segments with pretaped material there is a danger that the story may move away from the linear form—beginning, middle, and end—to one that jumps around in time. This can cause discontinuity for the viewer—a loss of the time frame. Though the story gets to the viewer as a forward-moving sequence of scenes, not all time elements are in sequence. Here are a couple of examples.

Almost every fall the outlying metropolitan area of Los Angeles is beset by a seasonal outbreak of brush fires in the parched hillsides. On the network newscasts and on local newscasts elsewhere, viewers see one version of that story. Typically, it contains scenes from the fires—always more spectacular at night. They race up a hill, over the top, and down into the next valley. There are fire trucks with whirling red lights, many shots of people dazed by the sight of their burned-out homes, other shots of people trying to prevent the inevitable with a garden hose. There are lots of interviews and the victims invariably say, "We've lost everything we've got."

From television stations in Los Angeles the local audience often gets a different version in which time and place are altered by a combination of live and prerecorded scenes. One year the fires were unique in that for a time they threatened the transmitter sites of most of the Los Angeles television stations. Sometimes it was difficult to figure out who was more worried: the television people who feared they would lose their transmitters, or the viewers who feared they would lose their television programs.

Nevertheless, the stations' mobile units rushed from place to place as they fed hours of raw material back to their newsrooms. On every local newscast, and on frequent special live reports, the editors and producers selected from a tremendous volume of visual material that provided an almost continuous flow of fire stories *across* location and time.

A typical story went like this:

Scene 1:	Reporter live from some fire location.
Scene 2:	Zoom past the reporter to pick up details of whatever fire was burning near him or her.
Scene 3:	Continuation of the live camera peering around, panning slowly, zooming in on details—eyes for the audience.
Scenes 4, 5, 6, 7, 8, etc:	On tape: scene of a fire last night, burning heavily, firefighters and fire trucks; evacuees at a YMCA; scenes of other destruction earlier that day; several different locations and time frames.
Scene 9:	Reporter back live at the location of Scene 1.

The conventional wisdom is, of course, that the audience understands best those stories in which the scenes relate to each other in a linear manner—Scene 2 builds on Scene 1 and relates forward to Scene 3.

In the Los Angeles fire coverage continuity often didn't work that way. The viewer watching the example above can follow the first three scenes and is reoriented by the final scene. But in between, time and location are uncontrolled, with flashbacks and flashforwards.

Careful attention must be given to the location and time elements in both the audio and video. Sometimes the Los Angeles reporters and producers did provide this: "Earlier today here's what it looked like on Mulholland Drive . . . last night in Holmby Hills," or time and location were indicated by words superimposed on the screen. But sometimes viewers were left to figure it out for themselves. News executives, producers, editors and all those involved along the line must make sure that the pizzazz of technology doesn't get in the way of understanding.

The File Tape Curse

An even more pernicious tinkering with the time frame of a story happens when file tape is used improperly. Videotape can be archived easily, and it is of real value when editors and reporters want to review something that happened a while ago. But when the tape from the files is mixed in with tape shot today, it is only ethical to tell the audience as quickly as possible after the file scenes appear and to label the tapes properly.

It is very important that the viewers be able to sort out what they are looking at: Is this tape of troops in Haiti *new tape* or the same tape shown last week? Are these scenes of tankers going through the Persian Gulf scenes *recorded today,* or are they the ones recorded two years ago? In this montage of wrecks at the same railroad crossing, why do we see snow on the ground in only some of the scenes?

Any time the video you include in a story package raises questions like these, you have distracted the viewers and have seriously hurt their ability to comprehend. The only legitimate use for file tape is to show the viewer what happened before, like an instant replay in sports. When file tape is used as "representational pictures," we are not showing the viewers what happened today; we are showing them something that happened before that looks like what happened today. The very least we can do is admit it.

Live Means Important

The audience has become accustomed to live reports on local television stations. It has also become more sophisticated and less impressed by technology.

Neil Darrough, a former CBS executive, stated that live news broadcasts have evolved significantly. He said:

> We've all been guilty of mistakes. Hell, I can recall at the beginning we were pleased just to get a picture. Let's shoot it, we'd say, because that will give people the impression that we are there.
>
> But the audience too quickly becomes sophisticated as to whether there's news in it or not. Our research now shows that the big word is *update;* that's the element of live news reports that makes sense. If your live operation is constantly updating a story, and you're telling the audience something they couldn't get any other way, then boy, they're with you all the way and they just plain eat it up.
>
> If you are doing it just for the sake of doing it—it's not really an important story—the audience knows, and your credibility is damaged.

Dick Graf, a veteran network and Boston news executive, said live is only *one way* to cover a story. For the audience, the mere fact that the story is being covered live means that it is important. He stated, "If it isn't important they are amused and angry at the same time—amused because you are going to so much trouble to cover something that isn't important, and angry because you are wasting their time."

By no means do all uses of live coverage involve spot news. A popular news coverage technique—for local station news as well as for network news coverage—is the live, on-site, "expert interview." As noted in the Chapter 6 section on "interviewing," Ted Koppel of ABC's "Nightline"® and anchor/reporters for "The MacNeil-Lehrer News Hour"® pioneered the technique of using teleconferencing facilities—linking one or more experts into the program by satellite or other connections. Often experts are more willing to participate in a teleconference setup than they are to take the time and trouble to travel to the studio for a live appearance.

Live Trivia

A live report that is using the station's technology as a delivery system to get the story on the air makes sense when time is of the essence. But the technique can be and has been abused. Many stations learned this the hard way. Our own survey resulted in a partial list of things *not* to do live. All appeared on some TV newscast, some more than once.

2:40 on a Cub Scout talent show

A two-alarm house fire

A male go-go dancer's opening night

A senator's campaign kickoff party

A news conference that just happens to be scheduled at 6 P.M. or 11 P.M.

How to open a champagne bottle (New Year's Eve, 11 P.M. news)

Firefighters removing a cat from a tree

Asking the pope as he passes by, "What do you think of your reception so far?"

And then, claiming that the question to the pope was "an exclusive live interview"

Covering a local convention that hasn't started yet by touring the exhibit booths with the PR representative

The scene of a meeting that ended two hours earlier

A courtroom where the verdict was reached in mid-afternoon; now only the reporter and janitor are there

The airport arrival of a movie star

Especially if her plane has not yet arrived

Interviews with sports stars who are going to speak later at a local dinner

Almost all man-on-the-street "samplings of opinion"

Any time the story is over and the reporter has to say, "We don't have much to add . . ."

From the Interstate, where traffic is flowing normally

A live picture of the sky that purports to show what a stationary front looks like

Live as a Two-Edged Sword

Another level of live reports about the trivial and ridiculous raises worries about the use of the live shot as a weapon or its intrusion into the news itself.

The arrival of local live capability brought out politicians and public relations people the way robins follow a spring rain. Earlier publicists quickly learned to release stories in time to meet morning and afternoon newspaper deadlines. Now they announced important news conferences or brought out their candidates near or at the time of major newscasts in the hope they could lure live coverage.

A few stations got burned before they learned never to *promise* live coverage. Today they are much more likely to set up for a tape-delay operation if it looks like there may be some news in the event. That way they can study the material as it is fed in and make some news judgments as to whether any of it should be edited for later insertion in the newscast.

The live shot as a weapon is another facet that requires editorial judgment. There is a line from the word game I Knew It Was a Bad Day When . . . that goes, "I knew it was a bad day when I got up and looked out of the window and saw the TV crews on the front lawn . . ."

It is possible to chase and corner people with a live unit in the hope they will cave in and talk. In Milwaukee the school superintendent had been hard-nosed about closing the schools because of bad weather. One of the local stations had received a lot of phone calls from parents who complained that their children were being put in danger. The station tried all of the conventional ways to get the superintendent to state his views. Finally, they rolled their news van up in front of his house, turned on the cameras to show the deep snow drifts on his street, then sent a reporter with a microphone to the front door to call him out. The superintendent came out, said a few words about the weather situation, and a lot of harsher words about the station's methods and how much snow was blowing onto his front hall carpet.

When public employees were on strike in Pennsylvania, two stations owned by the same group set up a live report with the governor in Harrisburg. They put reporters with him in his office and also had reporters in their studios at both ends of the state to ask more questions. Many observers thought this setup had unfairly trapped the governor and that the reporters had become advocates for legislation to stop the strike. The stations defended their action by saying it was really a live news conference.

The Live Environment

Live television coverage can intrude on privacy and affect the way a story develops.

A Milwaukee station uncovered the fact that a local woman was the mother of a man about to be executed in the Bahamas after having been convicted of a capital crime. The mother had tried everything possible to get the sentence commuted. She was expecting a call from a United States senator who had agreed to try to help.

The station moved live equipment into the woman's home and went on the air from her living room at the time the call was supposed to come. The reporter and woman waited. The phone rang. The reporter said something like, "Here it is—let's listen." The woman proceeded to chat amiably for several seconds. The call turned out to be from a friend who wanted to tell her about a bargain sale at a local department store. The reporter finally had the grace to say, "I think we'd better leave."

That live report ended up with no story at all. In more significant situations the presence of the live equipment can affect the way a story develops. Most stations try to avoid getting their staffs into the middle of breaking stories.

Don Ross, a former WBZ-TV Boston news director, said he had tried hard to make sure his staff understood the environmental impact of having live equipment too close to an event, especially in civil disorders.

> We had to rethink a lot of the splash because of tensions in the city. We painted some of our news vans a plain color, and we went out to cover an event in as low a profile as possible. Then, when the information was gathered, we'd move away, put up the antennas and say something like, "Right down the street this happened, and here are pictures of that." Or we'd tape an interview, edit it and use that to lead into pictures of the event.

In Baltimore a news director talked about an incident in which a sniper had taken hostages. The sniper was a patient in a mental hospital who had taken other patients hostage and was threatening to throw them out of a window. All of them, hostages and hostage taker, needed medication. Reporters and crews were sent to the place where the police had surrounded the sniper.

> The hostage taker demanded to go on the air to vent his grievances. We agreed, through the police, that our reporter would go in, talk to him, and then come out and tell what he had on his mind.
>
> We went live for that and the reporter did a very careful paraphrase of what the man had said. We had to be extremely careful because we knew the man was listening. It all worked out fine . . . at noon, while we were live, the man came out, thanked us . . . and the police hauled him away.
>
> After the sniper had been taken, we set up with lights and edited the video we shot during the stake out. The reporter went on the air to say that the story was over, and then rolled in the video to illustrate what had happened. You just don't go out and show puddles of blood for the hell of it.

Editorial Guidelines for Live Reports

Many stations have developed written guidelines about the proper management and handling of live reports, especially those which may involve civil disorders or situations involving hostages. Such documents evolve and change with coverage experience, with changes in personnel, and the like, but examples of what they contain indicate the basic idea behind them.

Figure 8.5. WBZ-TV, Boston, Massachusetts, wanted to avoid intruding into a news story so it painted some of its microwave vans a neutral color without the station's logo or other identification. After the microwave antenna goes up almost everyone who sees it will know what it is, but before that the vehicles are much less obtrusive. *(Courtesy of WBZ-TV.)*

Example: all employees at KRON-TV, San Francisco, are provided with station guidelines. These guidelines put the responsibility for live coverage decisions in the hands of the executive producer, the assignment editor, and the news director. The decision to go live rests on three conditions:

✔ 1. The safety of all KRON-TV personnel involved

✔ 2. The potential for inflaming the situation

✔ 3. The possibility of conflict with orders of law-enforcement agencies

If the story is about a civil disorder, the KRON-TV president or station manager must give prior approval.

These guidelines require the news director to provide operational control of the coverage and to give primary consideration to the safety of the staff and general public. They call for the station to stop coverage if it appears to inflame the situation or hamper the police.

Regarding hostages, the KRON-TV policy forbids making any telephone calls to the hostage takers and bans the start of any coverage if police forbid it. It also requires the staff to follow police orders in general. If calls are coming in from hostage takers, the staff is required to inform station officials and the police.

The rules end, "Act as if your own children are being held hostage."

LET'S WRAP IT UP

One prime concept weaves through this chapter—the story of the senator's trip home, the sewer blast, the tank car fire, the airliner crash—and all of the other live broadcasts mentioned. The overriding concept is that the journalism drives the coverage. Virtually every one of the decisions that has to be made when a live story starts, rises to a climax, and subsides is a journalistic decision.

No machine yet invented has news judgment. No system goes out and covers the news by itself. No helicopter decides where to fly. Stories don't come in already reported. It is the planning, operation, and editorial control the journalist provides that get the job done.

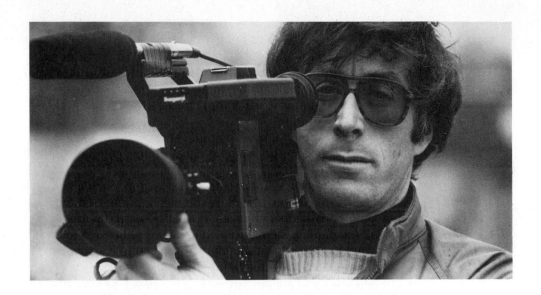

PROFILE

John Premack is one of the best-known TV photojournalists in the country. Born in Minneapolis in 1944, he started his career as a part-time dispatcher with KSTP-TV, shooting 16mm black-and-white film with a single-lens Bell and Howell wind-up camera. That led to full-time work at KSTP when that station was among the national leaders in adapting color film technology to television news.

In 1974 he became chief cameraman for WCVB-TV, Boston, one of the first stations in the country to purchase a Ku-band SNG truck. Active in the National Press Photographers Association as a director of the NPPA Television News Workshop, he also lectures and leads seminars for photographers, reporters, and editors.

While his assignments take him all over the world for an average of eight to ten weeks a year, John says he is happiest roaming New England in his four-wheel drive Blazer, which is equipped with every possible component of ENG. He adds, "While my duties as chief cameraman require a certain amount of paper shuffling, I've resisted every opportunity to move behind a desk."

Live News

John Premack

Nowhere has the impact of the electronic camera been more strongly noted than in the ability to report live from the scene of a news event. News film cameramen never had to contemplate the possibility. Electronic photojournalists must become as adept at doing a live shot as they are at covering a news conference or a three-alarm fire.

Live shots may be the most physically demanding, boring and least creative assignments a television photojournalist is likely to encounter. Pulling cables and lumping portable microwave units into buildings or atop roofs is dirty work that often seems pointless if you realize that the same report, prerecorded and edited, would probably look better on the air and require less time and effort as well. Nevertheless live shots have become a staple of today's newscasts and deserve to be approached and executed in a smooth and professional manner.

There are three basic modes of live news broadcasts that the broadcast news photographer is likely to encounter. First, the most common, is the reporter standup from the scene of an event. Adding variety to the usual fare of in-studio anchors and taped reports, the live standup allows conversation between the reporter in the field and the anchorperson in the studio.

The basic or "naked" standup is often relieved by the use of a **doughnut**, previously recorded tape and interviews, edited with a narration track, aired in the middle of the live shot.

In the basic reporter standup, the photojournalist's primary concern is to set up a shot that allows the viewer to see enough of the background to understand easily where the reporter is. This generally requires shooting at wide focal lengths and placing the reporter no more than 6 to 10 feet from the camera.

But selecting the shot primarily on the basis of the background—what's the point of being on location if people can't see it?—often creates the need for supplemental lighting. When the sun is out, it is rarely where you'd like it to be, and a reflector or fill light is required to prevent the reporter from suffering the indignities of harsh shadows or appearing in semi-silhouette.

Similar care must be taken after dark. With the reporter close to the camera, it's easy to place the lights too close to him or her. You should use only as much light as is absolutely necessary—too much light is the cardinal sin of shooting video at night. The photographer must take full advantage of the light already existing in the selected background. Too much light on the reporter results in a "limbo" shot with nothing but blackness instead of the background you chose.

The second basic live shot is a variation on the first in that the reporter does the standup and also conducts an interview. This two-person, one-camera situation differs from the ordinary interview setup because both the reporter and the interviewee must be able to face the camera, talk to each other, and still avoid being shot in profile. This is accomplished best by putting the interviewee in a fixed position and having the reporter turn away from the camera to conduct the interview.

To do this correctly a little preplanning by the reporter and photojournalist is essential. Positions are found and marked with tape if necessary. The subject should be pre-positioned, standing or seated, facing the camera. Then the reporter can begin his report on a "one shot," take a few steps as the camera widens to a two shot, and then turn to the subject while the camera zooms into a one shot of the subject (changing focus to a mark preset on the lens).

Care should be taken to insure that the reporter remains nearer the camera than the subject if you are to avoid shooting the subject in profile. An easy way to guarantee that both reporter and subject stand where they should is to briefly rehearse the blocking, where each will stand, and mark the positions with a coin or piece of gaffer's tape.

It is wise to use two lavalier microphones—one for the reporter, the other for the subject—so that the reporter doesn't have to hold a hand mic in the subject's face; the photojournalist also has more freedom to compose the shot. While two mics are nice, many live shots are done with a single hand mic. This is often a trade-off, swapping production values for convenience. Crews don't always have sufficient time or cable to run two audio lines, and there is no chance that the wrong mic will be turned on when only one is in use. Also, hand mics are technically superior in noisy locations.

Reporter cooperation is also essential. If the reporter doesn't understand what you'd like to do, there is the risk he or she will inadvertently block your shot while conducting the interview. It is one thing to interrupt a taped interview to reposition the reporter or subject, it is quite another when you are live. Preplanning cannot be overemphasized: When you are doing a live shot, there are no second takes.

The third and most infrequent live situation occurs when you actually have the opportunity to air a spot news event as it happens. While most live shots are done during newscasts, our ability to provide live coverage on short notice gives us the opportunity to break into programming whenever the news warrants.

The name of this game is: Get there fast, pan in the microwave, and locate the camera where it can command an uninterrupted view. Camera position is critical: It is disastrous if the studio switches to you when you aren't able to supply a look at the event. Elevation is generally required to see beyond the other crews and spectators. One common mistake in this type of situation is to compromise the camera position to allow the reporter to appear on camera. Not only do you sacrifice a vantage point of the action, you run the risk of being harassed by the news photographer's nemeses, known locally as the hi-moms, who appear in your shot grinning and waving just as you go on the air.

There can be conflicts in deciding what the live crew is supposed to provide. If an event is big enough to require live coverage, it should be standard operating procedure to assign a second camera crew to do the tape coverage of the story. A live crew cannot do an adequate job of covering all the angles of a story if it is restricted to the end of the coaxial cable that feeds its picture to the microwave van and back to the station. One reporter might be able to swing between the fixed camera location and the portable crew, but a single crew trying to do live shots, feed tapes, interviews, and general coverage will do none well.

BREAKING NEWS

While most live shots are generally dull and routine assignments, covering a breaking story is the most challenging and potentially frustrating assignment you can have. Don't plan on a PR person to hold the action for you if you arrive late. Shots missed while changing tapes or batteries are never available again.

Breaking news events are unique because they have a momentum of their own. We have all become used to having so many of the news events we cover prescheduled, prearranged, lit, and staged for the mutual benefit of the would-be news makers and our cameras that we sometimes lose sight of the fact that we ought to be simply observers and recorders of events rather than participants in them.

It is often said that good spot news coverage depends on simply being at the right place at the right time. It is true that you have to be there, but that isn't nearly enough. Successful coverage of breaking stories requires preparation, courage, and anticipation.

Being prepared requires a lot of things. You must be as quick and as comfortable operating your camera as a carpenter is swinging a hammer. The successful photojournalist develops his or her own habits and routines. Charged batteries here, and dead ones there. Mike cords coiled to drop open free from tangles. Color bars laid down when the fresh tape is loaded. Equipment always put away in the same order. If your checking and double-checking become an unconscious routine, you'll never arrive at an assignment and realize that the last time you saw your tripod was when the reporter picked it up and walked away.

TROUBLESHOOTING MEANS UNTROUBLED SHOOTING

Sometimes I think it would be a good idea if photojournalists could trade places with their cameras for a few days. It should go without saying that the electronic camcorders we use must be treated with respect. The camera lying on its side and bouncing around in the trunk of a car, lenses that are inadvertently used to hold open a door, and tapes left lying in the sun will all deliver images far below their potential. These overt acts are bad enough, but those that result in failures from lack of attention to the needs of the equipment are worse. Recorder heads need to be cleaned regularly. Yet at some stations this simple chore is often performed as a remedy instead of as prevention. Most other equipment failures are attributable directly to broken cables and faulty batteries.

Everyone in this business needs to learn more about the insides of the cameras and recorders. Yes, I know that there are a large number of engineering managers and maintenance technicians who in various ways perpetuate the myth that no one save an anointed few may open the covers of a camera or recorder. And yes, I know that it takes only two minutes with a little green-handled screwdriver to totally negate two hours of careful adjustment and alignment. But who is going to set up your camera at two in the morning in a motel room 600 miles from home? Only the photojournalist—if she or he knows how.

Most photojournalist's are not total idiots and with a little training and a lot of respect for the equipment can be safely trusted to operate those controls that deal with basic camera adjustments. Everyone in this business should carry a personal kit of head-cleaning materials, small tools, spare fuses, and cables.

The truth is that operating a camera goes far beyond locating the on/off switch and other external controls. Since it is your camera and your livelihood, you should learn how to use a waveform monitor to set levels and colorimetry. You should also be familiar enough with the layout and internal controls to troubleshoot and attempt to correct more serious problems with a maintenance technician talking you through the steps by telephone. Our job is to bring back the pictures. There are no good excuses.

As technology advances, our cameras and recorders will become easier to maintain and operate as well as significantly smaller and less conspicuous. Until that day comes, our goal should be to be as unobtrusive as the newspaper reporter who does his or her job competently yet quietly while seated within earshot and view of an event. We must never forget that our presence can alter the course of events. The camera tends to create its own reality. That's why there's a photojournalist operating it.

This devotion to your tools must extend to the creation of an unthinking intimacy with your camera and recorder. You've got to be able to set the controls by touch—without looking. If you have to look at the camera to see if the audio level is set for auto or manual, if your hand doesn't instinctively turn the focus ring in the proper direction, if you forget to white balance for a new lighting condition, and if you are surprised when the battery warning light comes on . . . you don't know your equipment, and you aren't going to be able to give full concentration to whatever is going on around you. The camera, despite its complexity, must become an automatic extension of the photojournalist's eyes.

The other significant skill required to cover spot news is the ability to anticipate action and to get ahead of the event. The photojournalist who has the camera rolling, waiting for the wall to fall or the bottles to break, is going to turn in well-framed and in-focus video, while the photojournalist who tries to react to actions as they happen will miss more than he or she captures. Being in the right place at the right time with the camera rolling is not a matter of luck at all. It is an acquired skill that comes only from a devotion to the small details of a craft. It is a reflection of a professional's experiences in similar situations and skill at selecting and positioning him or herself at the best possible vantage point.

There are a few basics to keep in mind when everything is going down around you. In the midst of a melee or high action of any sort, roll your recorder early, confirm that it is rolling, and don't shut it off. Leaving the recorder on prevents lost shots and insures no problems in editing scenes that would not have had sufficient lock-up time had you been starting and stopping the recorder each time you saw something to shoot.

Once you have a few cover shots, start looking for closeups. It takes courage to isolate one element of a big event. You run the risk of not being able to hold focus and are constantly afraid that being so tight will make you miss something. That's true. You also give yourself a chance to capture some dramatic tape that can be easily edited as opposed to a series of medium and long shots that, after a while, all look the same.

Hold your shots longer than seems necessary to capture the action. Novice photojournalists are often amazed to find they have most of the action, but in a series of three-second shots, once the camera movement and focus adjustments have been edited out.

Don't be afraid to stop shooting for a few seconds to look for a better vantage point. The steps of a building, the trunk of a car, or the small stepladder you carry in your own car can provide you with just enough elevation to get you over the crowd and prevent you from losing a great shot because someone got in the way. It is better to sacrifice thirty seconds shooting time than to have two minutes of unusable video as you and your camera are jostled and blocked.

If you're not wearing headphones to monitor the audio, don't forget to occasionally check the VU meter to confirm that you are recording sound. In the rush of the moment, it's possible to bump the mic volume controls or forget that the shotgun mic needs to be switched on.

It is easy to forget closeups when the action is heavy, yet the drama of an event is often best told on the faces of just a few individuals. When the action is at a distance, send someone back for the tripod. Stories where the media are kept at bay, such as hijackings and bomb-squad activity, require the longest lens you can muster and that demands a tripod. Having a 300mm lens on your shoulder is no guarantee you can make usable pictures by leaving it there.

AN ETHICAL VIEW

While the work of a television news videographer is both technical and creative, it must be remembered that the things just mentioned are simply areas of skill required to pursue our fundamental craft—journalism. The news videographer is also a *journalist,* responsible for the truthfulness of the images recorded on tape and presented on television in the same way that a reporter is responsible for the script and the manner in which a story is produced and edited.

As journalists, we can neither stage nor re-create events for our convenience, nor can we allow others to stage action that would not have occurred if cameras had not been present. It is as dishonest to single out for a cutaway the only person in an audience who has fallen asleep as it is to shoot a smoky, one-alarm fire entirely in closeups. In both instances the viewer is denied the opportunity to see in fair perspective what actually occurred.

The overriding goal of a competent photojournalist should be to show someone who wasn't at an event an accurate representation of what happened, to show the person who was there what he or she missed, and to do it without allowing the presence of the camera to affect materially what was going on in the first place.

We must recognize that a television camera tends to create its own reality. Part of our job as photojournalists is to understand that our mere presence can inflame, incite, initiate, and otherwise alter events we wish to cover.

Although we don't like it, many of the events we attend are staged to some degree in order to attract news coverage. The picket line that materializes from out of nowhere when a news van turns the corner and disappears even before the camera is back in the van, the news conference, the candidate's media event, and the incumbent's "photo opportunity" are all designed to generate publicity. As photojournalists we become quite used to participating in these "events." We think nothing of delaying them until we are ready, telling folks where to stand and how to pose during cutaways.

But we are journalists. We must not let our work habits—developed to cope with staged "news" events—extend to situations where we must be strictly uninvolved observers. Fires, riots, floods, and other stories that qualified as news before we arrived must be allowed to unfold without our assistance. We are, please remember, recorders of events. We must allow them to occur spontaneously, unimpeded by the technical restrictions of sound and light and the physical presence of the news crew.

This means giving folks a chance to get used to having us around for a few minutes instead of entering a tranquil and orderly scene with portable lights blazing. This means putting the camera in the shadows instead of under everyone's nose. This means communicating with the reporter and other crew members quietly without drawing attention from the event we are there to witness and record.

Photojournalists should also remember that they represent their station to the public and dress appropriately. While the work can occasionally be strenuous or dirty, crews should not stand out like a bagel in a Chinese restaurant. While there is no need to engage reporters in a contest for sartorial splendor, denim jeans, T-shirts, and tank tops should be saved for off-duty hours.

SATELLITE REPORTING

There are three areas of difficulty that you (and every other itinerant news crew) are likely to experience: communications, editing, and actual transmission.

Communications Problems

The most critical element in the successful airing of live reports is communications between the control room and the crew in the field. You can be doing a microwave relay through your helicopter overhead, a six-hop relay from 200 miles away, or beaming across the country via satellite, and if the reporter and cameraman don't know they are on the air or can't hear instructions from the producer, the entire live shot can fall apart—on the air.

Many crews carry a portable black-and-white receiver so that the reporter can see what is on the air. That isn't nearly as critical as the need for the crew in the field to hear off-air audio *and* cues direct from the control room. Reporters and cameramen rely on a system called IFB to receive their cues and hear the newscast. IFB (Interrupted Fold Back) refers to the delivery of off-air audio which can be interrupted by the director or producer in the control room. Many stations have a two way radio frequency assigned to this function, allowing crew members the convenience of using a walkie-talkie or other portable receiver to monitor the IFB. When the live shot originates beyond the range of a station's radio system, having the IFB is just as important. Then telephone lines are used, and the crew must be equipped with a specially modified telephone or clip leads and small amplifier to feed audio from the telephone into the reporter's earpiece.

A word of caution is in order concerning the IFB fed to the reporter who is broadcasting live through the satellite. Since the report must travel over 50,000 miles through space to reach and return from the "bird," it will take over one-third of a second for the reporter's words to reach the control room. If the incoming audio goes on the air and then is fed back via telephone to the reporter's IFB earpiece, she will hear her own words after she has spoken them. This is similar to the disorientation suffered by someone who is using the public address system in a football stadium for the first time—hearing their voice bouncing back while trying to concentrate on what is to be said next.

The solution is simple, but it must be anticipated in advance since the problem occurs only once you are actually on the air. The remote location is not fed the usual IFB mix of off-air audio and cues, but instead is supplied with what is called **mix-minus** sound. The studio audio board is set up to return all audio except the incoming report so that the remote crew need not be bothered at all by the built-in delay.

Another potentially embarrassing problem unique to satellite feeds is that you can't run over your scheduled time on the "bird" by even a few seconds. Satellite time is tightly scheduled and sometimes controlled automatically by a computer. That means that when your assigned time is over, the transponder on the satellite is automatically fed the next customer's program whether you're finished or not.

When you're on the road out of two-way radio range, it is impossible to stay in touch with your newsroom without a phone. It's hard to work a story without one, too. Many news operations have discovered that the cellular telephone is as important a news-gathering tool as the camcorder.

All SNVs are equipped with at least one *cellphone.* This is fine as long as the story you are covering is located near an interstate highway or population center big enough to support cellular service. Many SNVs also have telephone service by way of their satellite system.

Unfortunately these phones are unfailingly located in the tiny cabin that also houses the editing and transmission systems, which is convenient when there's only two or three people in the truck. This oversight can create mayhem when six people want to make calls, edit tape, and uplink live shots from the same twenty square feet of floor space.

Even when phones are available, they may be in heavy demand. Don't count on using the only phone in the truck for one of those long story conferences with the producers back home, especially when three other stations are waiting to feed tapes. If you want unlimited access to a telephone, bring your own. A portable cellular phone makes life easier for everyone.

And it doesn't hurt to toss an inexpensive one-piece telephone in your road kit either. With so little room and so much going on in an SNV, visitors may be denied access to one of the phones installed in the cabin simply because it would interfere with an editing or recording session. Connecting your own instrument across the phone line where it connects to the SNV on the outside of the truck allows for unrestrained telephone access.

Editing Problems

While communications problems can usually be resolved, difficulties in editing a video story can seriously imperil the quality of your report. There never seems to be enough time to turn out an elaborate piece when you're on the road, even when you aren't sharing an SNV's editing station.

There is rarely a traffic manager supervising and scheduling the editing sessions in a satellite news vehicle. Visitors have to line up and are at the mercy of the host station.

Since editing in an SNV is so often an act of desperation instead of creativity, one of the first "Rules of the Road" is: Don't overshoot. Shooting too much videotape wastes time twice; once when you shoot it and again when you edit it. Keep your interviews brief and to the point. Try to shoot the story in sequence. Keep a running log as you shoot the story so you won't waste time later searching for a particular shot. Every minute saved before editing pays major dividends in improving the quality of your spot.

Another time saver is recording narration tracks in advance. The well-upholstered interior of an automobile is an excellent place for a reporter to find the isolation and relative silence needed to cut audio tracks. Remember to use a separate videotape for this function so you won't have to shuttle back and forth as you switch between the reporter's voice-over and sound bites from the event.

Remember, too, that many SNVs are staffed by a transmission engineer whose duties do not include editing. You must be prepared to do the editing yourself, possibly on machines that are unlike the ones you are most familiar with. If you want to do more than bang a few sound bites together, you should be prepared to edit early. When time is short, sitting down to an editing session with too much tape, too little preparation, and jumbled, skimpy, unreadable logs is an invitation to disaster.

Being prepared also means packing a few tapes ready for use as edit masters. It's always easier to grab a tape prerecorded with control track than it is to hook up your camera and make one in the field. Always edit onto a twenty-minute cassette instead of the hour-long tape that you use at home. There's always the chance that you'll be expected to feed your edited tape from a portable recorder. While the smaller cassette can fit into any machine, most portable recorders cannot handle a full-size Beta cassette.

It is important to create a perfect sound mix as you edit. You may be used to riding levels during playback at your station, but satellite time limitations can thwart any chance to refeed a spot just because the sound mix was bad. Feed time can be precious. Make sure it is right the first time.

Another potential problem grows out of the way satellite time is scheduled. Because of cost considerations and limitations on the number of satellite uplinks and transponders available, most stations book satellite time in five-minute increments. These bookings aren't always available at exactly the time you'd like to feed tape or go live. They're often made hours in advance as producers try to anticipate the requirements of the crew in the field and where the story is likely to play in the newscast. Sometimes these preemptive bookings turn out to be strokes of genius, guaranteeing the precious "top of the hour" position for a breaking story. At other times they serve to lock you into a time slot that doesn't coincide with the latest revision of the newscast lineup, or one that requires feeding your edited story earlier than you'd like.

Most stations book two "windows," one for the live shot and an earlier one to feed the edited tape report in advance. While this allows maximum flexibility, some cost conscious stations avoid the prefeed and roll the cut spot from the SNV while on the air. This technique has the added benefit of allowing editing to continue up to the last minute but carries the major risk that if something goes wrong, nothing will get on the air.

One of the tricks to avoiding total disaster when confronted with feed times that don't mesh with your schedule is to feed a back-up open or close which can be edited into your report if it looks like your window is going to slip out of sync with either the beginning or end of the live portion of the report.

Another technique that is helpful when you're editing down to the wire is to edit both picture and audio tracks as the spot is built. Many reporters and editors are more comfortable with the **cut-and-cover** editing technique—laying down the reporter narration and other sound on blank tape and then covering the blank spots with appropriate video B-roll. While this technique assures that the story can be reassembled without major problems before too much time is invested, it doesn't consider the possibility that an editing session could be terminated before the spot is completed. Editing both audio and video as you go guarantees that an editing session terminated before the spot is fully edited will at least produce a partially edited story, one that will be airable even if it's incomplete. Stories edited with the cut-and-cover technique will always contain color bars or black holes until the last minute and thus cannot be aired uncompleted.

Transmission Problems

By the time you are ready to do the actual live shot, most of your problems should be behind you. Live broadcasts are actually the easiest part of working with an SNV. Short of technical malfunction, the only thing that is likely to give you trouble is the IFB, the system that delivers cues and off-air audio from your station's control room.

There is nothing more embarrassing than watching an anchor introduce a live report only to have the reporter stand there like a vegetable because he or she has not received a cue and doesn't know if he or she is on the air.

There are two things you can do to avoid this imbroglio if you hit your window and haven't heard word one from the folks back home. The reporter should turn his or her back to the camera while the photographer or field producer tries to reach the control room by phone. (Here's where your cellphone comes in mighty handy.) Few directors will punch up a shot of a reporter's back, and still fewer will fail to understand the message you are trying to convey. You can try to make a little sign and hold it up to explain the problem—but who has a marking pen and paper when they are needed most?

While some stations will insist on using satellite news vehicles to do the weather forecast from remote locations, the trend is to use SNVs for expanded news coverage both locally and across the nation. Whether you are working out of your own truck 100 miles from the studio or another station's SNV three times zones away from home, you're more and more likely to be covering an important story.

The responsibility of the crew in the field, photographer and reporter, is to recognize the satellite news vehicle for what it is—a tool, an expensive, high-tech tool—and to use it efficiently and effectively. A little bit of planning and anticipation can go a long way toward mastering this latest approach to electronic news gathering.

PERSONAL SURVIVAL TECHNIQUES

This essay wouldn't be complete without a brief look away from the technical and creative skills needed to be a TV news photographer toward those required for personal survival—getting along. It's important to recognize that as a videographer, you are a small cog in a big machine. A bit of perspective is necessary to endure the job without sacrificing your individuality, curtailing your initiative, or antagonizing your co-workers.

Being a photojournalist means working under constant pressure. The next story is too far away, traffic is heavy, parking nonexistent. The assignment desk has another job waiting, and lunch turns out to be the coffee and Danish you ate at ten-thirty. Your work is, of necessity, restrained by considerations of time, equipment limitations, access restrictions, and, unfortunately, internal rivalries and personality conflicts.

You are expected to be not only a camera operator but also a technician-journalist-editor-cab driver-field producer, and occasionally a reporter. This requirement to do many things, sometimes at the same time, can cause conflicts. When does one stop being the field producer and let the reporter take over? Who knows best how long it will take to get to the story and what is the best route? When does the photojournalist stand up to the assignment editor and argue the merits of an assignment, or simply accept the assignment, whatever it is, without a fuss?

Many reporters and assignment editors would voice a preference for photographers who always do what they are told, never complain, and never voice their opinions. Thankfully there are also those who recognize that the photojournalist can contribute more than framing, focus, and f-stop to a story. The videographer who recognizes that she or he is part of a team and works at getting along is a greater asset to a news organization than the individual who defines the videographer's role strictly in terms of his or her skill in operating a camera. The problem for videographers comes in recognizing when their input and contributions facilitate the coverage of the story and when they unknowingly become negative factors.

Being "on the street" instead of in the newsroom is one of the privileges unique to being a news videographer. Tied not to a desk or telephone but to a beeper or portable radio, videographers enjoy an autonomy unknown to other news staffers. They spend their work day away from the newsroom and studio, responsible only to the assignment desk and the reporter they are teamed with.

This freedom brings with it a unique problem. Working in relative isolation on only one story, the videographer is usually unaware of what else is being covered, of the priorities and problems of the day as viewed from within the newsroom. Thus the videographer often has a very limited perspective on how this assignment relates to the scope of the day's overall coverage.

While it is easy to recognize a videographer's contributions to a story, it's sometimes difficult to see that his or her commitment to "just one more shot" or reluctance to work a little faster or accept a change of assignment in the middle of a more interesting one can have a negative impact on the total news-gathering process.

We TV news photographers, of necessity, must be devoted to the assignment at hand. We usually tend to view whatever we are doing as the most important thing at any given moment. In fact there are probably at least a half-dozen stories being covered by different crews at that same moment, some of which are scheduled to run earlier in the newscast. The assignment editor must constantly reevaluate the merits of scheduled and breaking stories in response to manpower availabilities, equipment limitations, and the whims of various producers. There is a natural conflict in viewpoints and priorities between the crews in the field and the folks in the newsroom.

When the videographer is asked to drop one story in midshot and chase across town to do an interview that could have been done two hours earlier, he or she must try to understand that this means that someone with an overview of the day's events is once again changing priorities.

The photojournalist must recognize that it is the final product, not simply the news-gathering phase in which she or he is most actively involved, that is going to determine the success or failure of the station's mission. Photojournalists must recognize that time wasted on a story will be time wasted in editing, and in the time available for the other stories of the day to be shot and edited.

WORKING AS A MEMBER OF A TEAM

Ideally a news crew works in unspoken harmony. The photographer knows what the story is about and what to expect. The reporter knows what shots have been made without asking, and the cutaways get made automatically. On the way to the story, discussion includes expectations of what will happen and what the completed spot might contain. On the way back, suggestions for opening shot, sound bites, and sequences are exchanged.

This kind of relationship doesn't occur often enough. Reporters may doubt a photographer's enthusiasm for a story and attempt to direct everything from light and microphone placement to framing and length of individual shots. Photographers, wary of being told to shoot everything in sight while the reporter postpones decisions that should be made then in the field—not later in the editing room—begin to develop slow reflexes. Reporters who found critical shots missing on the last story will be uptight the next time out with that particular photojournalist. Meanwhile the photojournalist, who begins to suspect that his or her shots are going to be edited by a committee, shows even less enthusiasm for the story.

Putting a story on the air requires much teamwork. The combination of skills and efforts required is not limited to the field duo of videographer and reporter. Each story is touched in one way or another by producers, assignment editors, tape editors, and audio, program, and technical directors. Any one of these people can inadvertently cause the best efforts of the others to go down the drain. No one is entitled to give anything less than his or her best effort. There are new assignments every day for the television news photographer. You are only as good as your last story.

ENG and the Law:
An Introduction

Dwight L. Teeter, Jr., Ph.D.

Professor Richard Yoakam has an oft-retold story about the perils of instantaneous transmission via electronic media, or what used to be called "live broadcasting." His anecdote goes like this:

Not long ago, a radio talk-show host in a midwestern city was fielding phone calls about good places to eat and drink in that area.

A caller named a bar he had visited recently and said:

Caller: I found a pubic hair in my drink.

Host: What did you say?

Caller: I found a pubic hair in my drink.

Host: You can't say that on my show!

Caller: Oh? Well, maybe it was a mouse hair.

Because the host was broadcasting without a tape-delay mechanism, he had no way to cut off the caller's unhelpful contribution. Nonetheless, the station was potentially liable for defamation of the bar.

In New York City, WCBS-TV reporter Lucille Rich and a camera crew arrived unannounced at a well-known French restaurant, *Le Mistral.* Despite the objections of the restaurant's president, they barged into the establishment with cameras rolling. The station's interest was legitimate. It was doing a series of reports on restaurants that had been cited for city health-code violations. But the restaurant was private property, and the crew had no permission to enter. The restaurant sued successfully for invasion of privacy and trespass.[1]

An Ohio television station broadcast a free-lancer's film on The Great Zacchini, a "human cannonball" performing at a county fair. The fifteen-second clip showed Zacchini's 200-foot trip from takeoff to touchdown. The voice-over was entirely laudatory: "It's a thriller . . . you really need to see it in person to appreciate it." But Zacchini viewed the station's unauthorized broadcast as appropriation of his act, and the Supreme Court of the United States held that the station had no First Amendment right to broadcast the entire act.[2]

These are examples of some of the legal bear traps that await broadcasters in the age of ENG.[3]

Basically, the law as it affects ENG is not new. ENG enjoys no more or less protection than conventional broadcasting, or for that matter, print media. But the new technology has increased risks for broadcast and cable news simply because it allows them to do more things. The more thoroughly and aggressively a station covers its community, the more opportunity to get into trouble.

Second, the new technology, with its emphasis on timeliness—*instantaneous timeliness*—has sliced away much of the time that used to be available for decision making. Back in the days of film, a news director usually could expect to have an hour or so to decide whether to run a particular shot. With ENG, the time is reduced to minutes, and with live broadcasts, to zero.

The purpose of this chapter is to explore problems of defamation and invasion of privacy in the context of electronic news gathering. New information is added for this third edition on reporter-source confidentiality and on open meeting and open records statutes. Also, some attention is given to personal attacks. At this writing in mid-1995, personal attack rules are still in force, a leftover part of the Fairness Doctrine mostly repealed in 1987 by the Federal Communications Commission. Congress may resuscitate all or part of the former Fairness Doctrine, and it is assumed here that the personal attack rules will remain in force.[4]

Whether or not Congress or the FCC revives the Fairness Doctrine or retains the personal attack/political editorializing rules, responsible broadcasters and cablecasters ought to seek both the appearance and the reality of fairness in their conduct. Stations or journalists seen as predatory or generally unfair are apt to draw more than their share of lawsuits, with all the time, expense, and bad publicity litigation can bring about. Ethical concerns over balance and fairness should drive professionals' behavior, whether or not the FCC or Congress tries to make rules on what is or is not "fair." Self-generated fairness may be broadcasters' best defense, both legally and financially.

Much of this chapter is speculative, because ENG technology still is so new that it has not generated a great deal of law. Basically, this chapter looks at existing legal principles and tries to apply them to special problems created by ENG.

DEFAMATION

Defamation consists of publication of a falsehood that defames an identifiable person or corporation. Since that definition is deceptively simple, some elaboration on each of its elements is needed.

Publication includes broadcasting. The ancient distinction between slander (oral) and libel (written) has been abandoned in most broadcasting cases. Now, broadcasters generally are governed by the same libel law as newspapers.[5] Publication also includes republication, which is another way of saying that a broadcaster is responsible not only for his or her own defamatory comments (the news anchor's commentary, for example) but also for those of third persons whose words are circulated by the station in its news broadcasts (allegations spoken by an interview subject, for example).[6]

Pontius Pilate is said to have asked, "What is truth?" As a *legal* matter, a falsehood is anything the broadcaster can't prove is true. Through the 1970s, a few cases suggested that a plaintiff—the person bringing a lawsuit—bears the burden of proving that a statement is false.[7] In 1986, the Supreme Court emphasized the importance of placing the burden of proving falsity on the plaintiff in *Philadelphia Newspaper Co.* v. *Hepps*.[8] The hitch after *Hepps*, however, was that only reports of matters deemed by the courts to be of public concern are protected. In *Hepps*, a 5-4 decision, the Court held that investigative stories by the *Philadelphia Enquirer* suggesting that a businessman had undue influence on state government and ties to organized crime was of *public,* not merely private, concern. In that context, the burden of proof was on the plaintiff.[9]

Even so, "truth" may be elusive. If a plaintiff can convince a jury that a statement is false—and trial juries frequently are hostile to the media—then the broadcaster is likely to lose. Truth, of course, should be the goal at all times. But as a practical matter, truth is quite seldom used as a pivotal defense in defamation cases. If a media defendant can prove truth, chances are a lawsuit will not be started. Even if something is true, proving it in court, under rules of evidence that are labyrinthine, may not be easy. If the truth is embedded in inadmissible evidence, or if key witnesses refuse to testify, die, or disappear, the truth becomes a purely metaphysical matter. It is sad but true for libel defendants (and plaintiffs) that the only truth that matters is the one that can be proven in a court of law.

It is important to distinguish between truth and accuracy. Suppose, for example, a reporter does a standup at City Hall, reporting that a competing contractor has accused Acme Paving Company of defrauding the city. The report may be a completely accurate summary of what the contractor charged, but the defense of truth is not available unless the city—or the broadcast station—is prepared to prove that Acme Paving is in fact defrauding the city.[10] *Truth* means the truth of the underlying defamatory statement. The accuracy of the report may be important in giving the statement the benefit of *privilege* (more about this later), but it does not establish the truth.

A statement is defamatory if it tends to damage a person's reputation. Obviously it is defamatory to accuse a person of committing a crime or of engaging in immoral or dishonest activity. But it can also be defamatory to say that he or she threw a temper tantrum, is a bigot, or is a coward.[11]

Identification: Persons are identifiable if they are named or pictured, and also if they are recognizable to their acquaintances even though they are not more specifically identified. Sometimes a title can be enough. For example, a report that "an assistant vice president in the trust department" was dismissed for embezzlement could be defamatory if there is only one assistant vice president in that department and that is known to his or her acquaintances.[12]

Identification also can occur when a person who is not mentioned by name is a member of a group: the jury, the basketball team, the police force (in a small town), or even a football squad. Folklore has it that if a group is larger than twenty-five, no otherwise unidentified person within the group can be defamed.[13] Depending on the jurisdiction, however, identification has been held to take place in groups having as many as fifty-three members.[14]

PRIVILEGE

Many statements are protected even if they are published about an identifiable person and are false and defamatory. They are protected because they are privileged.

Consider, for example, a live broadcast from a trial. Some sort of photographic coverage was allowed in the early 1990s by courts in forty-five states.[15] Roughly half of the states allow cameras in trial courts.

What if the witness on the stand utters a defamatory falsehood when under oath? (Assume that this statement by the witness is *not* stricken from the record by order of the judge, for if it is, it never existed in any legal sense.) The answer is *privilege*. A fair and accurate report of the judicial proceeding is *privileged*. There are similar privileges for accurate reports of public proceedings, such as candidates' forums, the official sessions of city councils, county commissions, subcommittees, or commissions appointed by those bodies.[16]

THE FIRST AMENDMENT

Broadcasters enjoy the same First Amendment protections—in libel suits, at least—as their print competitors. So even if a broadcast is false, defames an identifiable person, and is not privileged, it still may be protected under the Federal Constitution. If the victim is a *public official*, he or she cannot recover damages unless it can be shown that the broadcaster acted with actual malice, that is, knew the report was false or had serious doubts about its truth.[17]

That same rule applies to *public figures*, although that classification was narrowed so much in the 1980s that the only persons sure to fall within it are celebrities and busybodies. Celebrities are persons so well known that their names are household words: Carol Burnett, Dolly Parton, Tom Hanks. Busybodies (sometimes called "special purpose public figures" by courts) are persons who thrust themselves into public controversies with the objective of influencing their outcome.[18]

If the person defamed is neither a public official nor a public figure, the Federal Constitution doesn't offer much protection to broadcasters. Such a person—a private plaintiff—need show only that the broadcaster was negligent with respect to the truth or falsity of the broadcast.[19] What negligence means in this context remains unclear; broadcasters probably could be found negligent for failing—where there is an opportunity to do so—to edit out defamatory matter or to take the time necessary to investigate further.

These principles of defamation law are familiar to most news directors and must be high in the consciousness of their staffs. Difficulties crop up, however, in applying those principles to ENG. Television news directors know there are potential legal problems in broadcasting "live" or "live delayed." ("Live delayed" as used here means a live setup with microwave or helicopter platform links to gather videotape or CD-ROM images, to check the images quickly, and then to get them "turned around" and on-air as quickly as possible.)

Some television news directors seem to feel they are safer (or at least that they have better excuses) when their crews are sending in live reports that go on the air *instantaneously.* They hope to be able to show that they were operating as carefully as possible, with a field producer at the scene and with producers in the control room monitoring the incoming broadcast as it proceeds onto the air. These producers are talking over the intercom system (IFB) to the on-air reporters. They can relay advice: "Watch it! You're on thin ice; change the subject now!" or "Cut it, get off it, pan away from it." The line of thinking relied on by such news directors is something like this: "Look, it happened. We used all the editorial control we had available, but we can't predict and avoid defamatory blurts a hundred percent of the time."[20]

To date, the law recognizes no such defense. In court the question in most cases will be whether the broadcaster used reasonable care to determine the truth of the statements broadcast. The plaintiff doubtless will argue that broadcasting live was unreasonable for that very consideration: It gives broadcasters no opportunity to prevent defamation or invasion of privacy. It will be up to judges and juries to decide what is reasonable in each case.[21]

Analogies provided by courts come from cases involving tape delay in the context of radio talk shows. Unfortunately, they point in different directions.

The host of a call-in show on WBOX in Bogalusa, Louisiana, was broadcasting without a tape delay when an anonymous caller named a doctor and a pharmacist and connected them with drug dealing at a local pizza restaurant. The doctor, pharmacist, and manager of the restaurant all collected damages. The court had no sympathy for the station's broadcasting live without a tape delay:

> We would have no difficulty in finding a station liable, if it received defamatory material from an anonymous source, and broadcast the

report without attempting verification. The direct broadcast of such anonymous defamatory material, without the use of any monitoring or delay device, is no less reprehensible in our judgment. The publication, in either event, is done by the station, and we find that there is the same reckless disregard for the truth in either instance.

Appellant placed itself in a position fraught with the imminent danger of broadcasting anonymous, unverified, slanderous remarks based on sheer rumor, speculation and hearsay and just such a result actually occurred. Such an eventuality was easily foreseeable and likely to occur, as in fact it did. In our judgment, the First Amendment does not protect a publisher against such utter recklessness.[22]

A Wyoming court viewed the tape delay matter quite differently. A caller to a talk show said falsely that a businessman, a former state official, "had been discharged as insurance commissioner for dishonesty." But the Wyoming Supreme Court held that the station's failure to use a tape delay was not proof of reckless disregard for the truth. If it were, the court said,

> broadcasters, to protect themselves from judgments for damages, would feel compelled to adopt and regularly use one of the tools of censorship, the electronic delay system. While using such a system a broadcaster would be charged with the responsibility of concluding that some comments should be edited or broadcast not at all. Furthermore, we might recognize the possibility that the requirement for use of such equipment might, on occasion, tempt the broadcaster to screen out the comments of those with whom the broadcaster . . . did not agree. . . .[23]

The Wyoming approach displays a far better understanding of the nature and importance of broadcasting than does the Louisiana decision, and it contains a much more persuasive analysis of the issue. However, there are not now enough cases on the "tape delay" point to tell which view will become most prevalent.

In the absence of a clear precedent, "delayed live" should be preferred over "live" at least when the speaker is someone whose judgment the station does not trust. This preference also should apply when a situation is so volatile there's a considered risk that something the station does not want to broadcast will get on the air. Where the importance of the story justifies live coverage, the reporter and the producer must be ready to change the subject instantly, to pan away, or to cut the sound when the specter of defamation appears.

If a defamatory blurt does occur, the station should act promptly to minimize the damage. The defamer *immediately* should be cut off the air to prevent him or her from making additional actionable remarks. The reporter on the scene or the anchor back in the studio should try to undo the damage that already has been done by correcting factual errors, if possible. Also, the reporter or the anchor would be well advised to dissociate the station from the defamatory remarks, and to apologize (if circumstances make that appropriate) to the person defamed.

Though these steps need to be taken promptly, they also require careful judgment. If it is not clear whether the accusation is true or false, confessing error would be a mistake. The station might want to assert the defense of truth later in court. In such a case, the reporter, anchor, or news director merely should inform viewers that the station cannot at the moment vouch for the truth of the accusation, perhaps even suggesting that viewers keep an open mind on the matter.

In deciding whether a defamatory blurt is actionable, courts probably will take into account at least two factors. One will be the urgency of the story being covered. If the story is an important one about which the public needs immediate information (such as a riot or natural disaster), courts are likely to be more protective of the broadcaster. On the other hand, a breathless live report of a one-car rollover in which judgment is offered about who is at fault is not likely to win much judicial sympathy.

The urgency of covering "hot news" long has been recognized in other contexts. For example, a generation ago, the Supreme Court allowed Georgia football coach Wally Butts to recover against *The Saturday Evening Post* for implying that he had revealed helpful secrets to arch rival Bear Bryant before a Georgia-Alabama game. Justice John Marshall Harlan then declared:

> The evidence showed that the Butts story was in no sense "hot news," and the editors of the magazine recognized the need for a thorough investigation of the serious charges. Elementary precautions were, nevertheless, ignored.[24]

In contrast, in a case decided simultaneously, the Supreme Court denied recovery to General Edwin Walker, whom the Associated Press described erroneously as having taken command of a violent crowd and having led a charge against federal marshals during a riot over the enrollment of the first black student at the University of Mississippi. Justice Harlan wrote:

> [T]he dispatch [of the AP reporter] which concerns us in *Walker* was news which required immediate dissemination. The Associated Press received the information from a correspondent who was present at the scene and gave every indication of being trustworthy and competent. . . . Considering the necessity for rapid dissemination, nothing in this series of events gives the slightest hint of a severe departure from accepted publishing standards.[25]

Although these cases had nothing to do with ENG or broadcasting, they show that the Supreme Court has expressed sympathy toward the problems of covering hot news under deadline pressure, but that not every sensational story can be treated as hot news.

Perhaps particular wariness is called for when stories take on the nature of a follow-up, even when there seems to be a good "news peg." In 1981, a South Carolina TV station was following a story about the unsolved murders of two teenaged stepbrothers more than a year earlier. It broadcast statements by the father of one victim that the other dead boy's father had not cooperated. It was said the other father refused to take a truth serum, was hiding behind the Fifth Amendment [right against self-incrimination], and had employed an attorney. Even though the plaintiff was not mentioned specifically in the 1981 broadcasts, the South Carolina Court of Appeals reversed the court's grant of summary judgment favoring the TV station. The appellate court found William C. Adams had been identified and that the language "was susceptible of the inference that Adams was either guilty of the murders of the teenagers or was withholding information relative to the commission of the crimes."[26]

A second factor courts are likely to evaluate is the foreseeability of trouble. A broadcaster who carries a live interview with someone who is notorious for his or her venomous and intemperate remarks is more likely to lose than one who gets blind-sided while interviewing an apparently responsible person on an innocuous subject. This should come as no surprise. Broadcast journalists develop an instinct for spotting and avoiding "kooks," and many news directors expect their reporters to have some idea of what a live interview subject is likely to say. While perfect clairvoyance can't be expected, the courts undoubtedly will be unsympathetic to broadcasters who ignore obvious risks.

The broadcast journalist must remember that courts will evaluate these factors from the point of view of the public, not the broadcaster. News directors' pleas that they felt compelled to broadcast live because they feared competitors would, or because competitors had beaten them on the air and they were playing catch-up, or because they were under pressure to boost sagging ratings—all are likely to fall on deaf ears. It is broadcasters whose decisions are based on the public's needs and sound journalistic judgments who will succeed in the courts.

THOSE SNEAKY AMBUSH INTERVIEWS

Sometimes the compulsion to get a story leads to "ambush interview" situations: the reporter pushing a microphone into an unwilling news source's face while the camera is on. The public seems to consider the ambush bad form. That such behavior is disliked by nonjournalists may be seen in a jury's $1.25 million "false light" privacy judgment against reporter Arnold Diaz and WCBS-TV of New York City. While investigating dumping of chemical wastes, WCBS jumped a corporation executive with a surprise interview about chemical waste on a lot adjoining his business. The interviewee's irate reaction was later broadcast, and his tearful account of the pain caused him by the broadcast clearly impressed the jury.[27]

On appeal, however, the jury's verdict was overturned by a United States Court of Appeals. It found that the broadcast's portrayal of the unwilling man as furious and evasive was borne out by the tape of the interview.[28] The conclusion that "the TV station won" should be tempered with the warning implicit in that $1.25 million jury verdict. In a general way, those jurors represent the public and its attitudes toward intrusive reporters and photographers.

WARNING LABELS FOR BROADCASTERS?

Warning labels appear on packs of cigarettes; cigarettes can be hazardous. Perhaps broadcasters should put warning labels on their own microphones and cameras. The cigarette-related defamation case of *Brown & Williamson* v. *Walter Jacobson and CBS* did not deal with ENG technology, but its fact situation contains some dos and don'ts for all journalists. To emphasize the obvious, *let facts shape the story, not vice versa.* There are reasons totaling $3 million for saying that. By refusing to hear this case, the Supreme Court in 1988 let stand a $3 million libel judgment against Jacobson and CBS. Libel lawyer Floyd Abrams said at the time that was the largest libel judgment up to that time to survive appeals.[29]

Brown & Williamson, manufacturers of tobacco products, sued TV reporter Walter Jacobson and CBS for a "Perspective" broadcast in 1982. That program accused tobacco manufacturers of aiming their ads at America's youth in a most unwholesome fashion. Jacobson said:

> Television is off-limits to [advertising of] cigarettes and so the business, the killer business, has gone to the ad business in New York for help, to the slicksters on Madison Avenue with a billion dollars a year for bigger and better ways to sell cigarettes. Go for the youth of America, go get 'em guys . . . Hook 'em while they are young. . . . Just think how many cigarettes they'll be smoking when they grow up.[30]

Jacobson was touted by CBS ads for his hard-hitting work, for being a journalist who will "make you angry." His November 11, 1982 "Perspective" broadcast made the tobacco company plenty angry.

> Get some young women, give them some samples. Pass them out on the streets, for free, to the teenagers of America. Hook 'em while they're young. . . .[31]

Although accusations before Congressional committees in 1994 about duplicity in the tobacco industry might have helped shield Jacobson and his CBS affiliate from liability in the 1990s, the fact remains that given a similar fact situation, a jury might still be hostile.[32] In any event, the broadcast at issue here was made a dozen years earlier, in 1982. Even so, lessons still can be extracted from that case. For one thing, a journalist's righteous indignation may turn out to be defamation in the eyes of a jury. Jacobson's overheated commentary had declared:

> "For the young smoker a cigarette falls into the same category with wine, beer, shaving, or wearing a bra," says the Viceroy strategy. "A declaration of independence and striving for self-identity. Therefore an attempt should be made," says Viceroy, "to present the cigarette as an initiation to the adult world, as an illicit pleasure, a basic symbol of the growing-up maturity process. An attempt should be made," say the Viceroy slicksters, "to relate the cigarette to pot, wine, beer and sex. Do not communicate health or health-related points." That's the strategy of the cigarette-slicksters, the cigarette business, which is insisting in public . . . "[W]e are not selling to children."
>   They're not slicksters. They're liars.[33]

Jacobson was commenting on a tangled fact situation, and a jury found falsity and actual malice (publication with knowing falsity or reckless disregard for the truth) in the words quoted above. Facts presented to the jury included these items:

> The advertising strategy attributed to Viceroy—even though it was written up in a report of the Federal Trade Commission—was a strategy proposed by a market research firm hired by an ad agency working for Viceroy. The cigarette manufacturer had rejected the proposed strategy and fired the ad agency, in part over displeasure with the report [34]

> A Brown & Williamson executive told "Perspective" producer and researcher Michael Radutzky of WBBM that the strategy had not been adopted and that the FTC report had been written six years earlier.[35]

> The "Perspective" report did not cite (and had not found) any Viceroy ads adopting the pot-wine-beer-sex strategy to induce children to smoke cigarettes.[36]

Broadcasters should take this to heart: if involved in a lawsuit, or if you know a lawsuit is about to begin against your station, do *not* destroy potential evidence, even evidence that might "look bad." In the Jacobson case, the Court of Appeals found that the "most compelling evidence of actual malice submitted to the jury was the intentional destruction of critical documents by Jacobson's researcher, Michael Radutzky. . . ."[37]

Radutzky destroyed a sample script and a copy of the Federal Trade Commission report on which he had written notes. The Court of Appeals concluded that Radutzky destroyed only "the parts of the documents that would have been relevant to this litigation." Radutzky's explanation that he had been "housecleaning" was not believed; the court declared that his housecleaning had been too selective.[38]

There's a footnote in this decision that carries a warning for station executives with the impulse to go for sensationalism during a "sweeps week" rating period—and producers of year-round sensationalism such as "A Current Affair" or "Hard Copy" might pay attention too. In that footnote, the Court of Appeals noted the Brown & Williamson contention that ratings pressures to do interesting stories during the November "sweeps" period might be considered "strong proof of actual malice."[39]

Reporters and others in the news process should take the above-mentioned items to heart. Journalists would be well advised to avoid behavior that asks for trouble. On air, understatement is preferable to overstatement. In the newsroom, judgmental or wiseguy notes or marginal comments are simply a bad idea. Whatever a station's policy about saving outtakes and notes—and a policy of purging such notes can be made to look suspect to a jury should a lawsuit occur—do not destroy materials once litigation is imminent or has begun.

By allowing the Seventh Circuit Court of appeals ruling to stand, the Supreme Court left in place a ruling that the "Perspective" reports on the tobacco industry contained deliberate falsehoods.[40]

SENSATIONALISM

Like it or not, the most ethical broadcasters or cablecasters have some real enemies in the forms of the sleazy, sensationalized "news programs." To John Q. or Mabel Citizen, it may be that "news is news," and that tabloid TV shows such as "Hard Copy" or "A Current Affair" seem the same as "CBS Evening News with Dan Rather."

The sensationalized tabloid programs surely cheapen the media in the eyes of the public. Jurors, who in general are not chosen for their sophistication, are unlikely to draw fine distinctions between a straight-up news program and a tabloid news show. It also should be noted that even when a station or journalist "wins" a libel or privacy case, there's often a heavy financial penalty involved in terms of lawyer fees and court costs, to say nothing of the time, effort, and distractions accompanying defending against a lawsuit.

In 1994, Professor C. Thomas Dienes said: "When publishers and broadcasters go to trial, they lose the majority of cases." Even so, it appeared that

"[T]he vast majority of libel cases are knocked out either before trial or on appeal . . . stages at which judges review the merits and apply the law."[41]

PRIVACY

ENG offers the broadcaster numerous opportunities to run afoul of the law of invasion of privacy. Some of these arise, like defamation, from the broadcast of material that harms some identifiable individual. Others arise from the methods used to gather news, irrespective of what is broadcast.

Trespass or Intrusion

The case of *Le Mistral* restaurant, mentioned earlier, is an example of a problem arising from the *method* of news gathering. This branch of invasion of privacy is similar to trespass law, but broader. A camera crew that goes into someone's home without permission would be guilty of trespass. A camera crew that goes into someone's home with permission, but while there installs a hidden microphone, would be liable for the form of invasion of privacy called intrusion, even though there might be no trespass because the entry was made with consent. The unauthorized installation of the microphone would be actionable even without trespass.[42] And in both cases there would be potential liability even if nothing were broadcast. That is, the wrong lies in the intrusion itself, rather than in anything that might be revealed to the public. (Such revelations, as will be shown, can compound the privacy problem.)

A broadcaster's assertion that the crew was engaged in news gathering at the time of a trespass or intrusion usually provides no defense. As the courts are fond of saying, the First Amendment does not give the media a license to ignore the law in the name of news gathering.

> The First Amendment never has been construed to accord to newsmen immunity from torts or crimes committed during the course of news gathering. The First Amendment is not a license to trespass, to steal, or to intrude by electronic means into the precincts of another's home or office. It does not become such a license simply because the person subject to the intrusion is reasonably suspected of committing a crime.[43]

Thus in *Oklahoma* v. *Bernstein,* a state district court ruled that reporters were guilty of criminal trespass when they followed demonstrators onto the construction site of a nuclear power plant. Even though there was substantial government involvement with the nuclear installation, the judge ruled that it was still the private property of the Public Service Company of Oklahoma, which had told the media to stay out. The judge did not doubt that the demonstrators' invasion of the plant site was a newsworthy event, but that did not excuse trespassing by a reporter.

> A weighing of respective press and government interests in the context of the total circumstances . . . indicates that the legitimate rights of the State have outweighed the arrested [person's] right of access.[44]

Similar rules seem to apply to media access to scenes where a disaster has occurred. A 1985 crash of a Midwestern Airlines flight at Milwaukee's General Mitchell Field led to a camera crew from WTMJ-TV driving through a sheriff's department roadblock, following an emergency vehicle down the only access road to the crash site. A cameraman clambered over a fence bearing "No Trespassing" signs and ran to a hill where he took pictures of the wreckage. A detective ordered the cameraman to leave; he refused and was arrested and ultimately convicted of disorderly conduct.[45]

That conviction was upheld by the Wisconsin Supreme Court, which declared that reporters have no constitutional right of access to scenes of crime or disaster from which the general public is excluded. The court's majority opinion noted that news media likewise have no right of access to meetings of official bodies gathered in "executive session" or to meetings of private organizations.[46]

On the other hand, if a camera crew can see its subjects from a public place without trespass, no liability should occur. Mr. and Mrs. James Jaubert were irritated when they returned from a trip to learn that a photograph of their home had been published on the front page of the Crowley, Louisiana, *Post-Signal,* with this caption: " 'One of Crowley's stately homes, a bit weatherworn and unkempt, stands in the shadow of a spreading oak.' " Although the Jauberts were awarded one thousand dollars in damages by the trial court, the Louisiana Supreme Court reversed. The state supreme court held that there was no invasion of privacy because the photo had been taken from the middle of the street in front of the house, duplicating the view available to any passer-by.[47]

The same kind of conditions apply for ENG crews shooting pictures from a public place into any kind of private area. The military frequently attempts to prevent the media from taking pictures of plane crashes, of the mobilization of equipment for the handling of civil disturbances, or of other kinds of "troop movements." Companies often do not want pictures of new products—such as the brand-new autos before they are formally made ready for sale—to be made before the unveiling. But if a manufacturer is careless enough to put new models outside where anyone can see them from a public place, or if the military or the police carry out their activities within public view, then they ask for exposure.

The key in cases of this sort is that the camera is recording only what viewers could see if they were present. A passer-by who just happens to look into an uncurtained window commits no wrong, but the same cannot be said of someone who stands on the street peering into someone's house with binoculars. Likewise, we can expect the courts to treat the camera operator who uses a zoom or telephoto lens, or something more elaborate like a nightscope, differently from one who merely records what is visible to the unaided eye.

In general, persons in public places may be photographed with impunity, but there are limits. If the camera is used as a weapon in the service of so-called confrontation journalism, the victim may find a remedy in the precedent established by Jacqueline Kennedy Onassis against photographer Ron Galella. Galella made a career out of stalking Mrs. Onassis and her children with his cameras. He was a *paparazzo,* which a federal judge described as a breed of photographers who "make themselves as visible to the public and as obnoxious to their photographic subjects as possible to aid in the advertisement and wide sale of their works."[48] Mrs. Onassis successfully sued for an injunction ordering Galella to stay a prescribed distance away from her and her children. Galella subsequently was found in contempt of court for violating the order.[49]

It should be taken as a general proposition that a camera crew has no right to go on private property in pursuit of a newsworthy event without the owner's consent. A famous case—*Florida Publishing Co.* v. *Fletcher*—holds out some hope for an exception to that rule if photographers are invited onto private premises by law enforcement authorities when (a) such invitations are common local practice and (b) if the owner is not present to object.

In the *Fletcher* case, a 17-year-old girl had burned to death in her home. A fire marshal and a policeman invited news media representatives to accompany them into the house, said to be a standard practice in Florida. The fire marshal wanted a clear picture of the silhouette on the floor of the house after the removal of the body, and asked a photographer from the *Florida Times-Union* to take the picture, which became part of the official investigative records but was also published by the newspaper.

Cindy Fletcher's mother, who had been out of town, first learned of the facts involved in her daughter's death by reading the newspaper story and seeing the accompanying photograph. She sued for trespass and invasion of privacy.

The Florida court ruled against her, saying that because there was no objection to the entry and because the officials and the photographer had followed common practice, there was no trespass or actionable invasion of privacy by the newspaper. (It should be kept in mind that the *Fletcher* case has been little followed outside of Florida, perhaps because other courts question the "custom and practice" reasoning.)[50]

If the tenant or owner *is* present and asks that a camera crew not enter the property, a different result can be predicted. A Rochester, New York, humane society investigator got a search warrant to enter a home, authorizing him to seize any animals found to be in unhealthy or unsanitary surroundings. The investigator alerted television stations about the "raid," and camera crews from WROC-TV and WOKR-TV followed the investigator into the house. The crews ignored the occupant's demand that they stay out of her home. Stories were broadcast on the stations' evening newscasts.

Based on that fact situation, a court held that the First Amendment does not protect news gathering on private premises without the consent of the homeowner, even though the entry was made at the invitation of a humane society investigator.[51] The distinction apparently is that law enforcement officers may have the power to consent on the owner or tenant's behalf when that person is absent, but not when an owner or tenant is present.

A 1993 lawsuit showcased multiple privacy-related claims against CBS-TV's "Street Stories" news magazine program. A TV crew entered the home of a woman who was making a domestic violence complaint. When the woman confronted TV personnel entering her home, she ordered them out. But a policeman led her to believe that " 'It's okay. They [the TV crew members] are from the DA's office. They are here to help you.' " The woman allowed them to stay. She did say, however, that she did not want to be on TV. When she called CBS in New York to protest the program before it was aired, she was told only that there was nothing she could do about it. A United States district court dismissed her trespass and intrusion claims but left plaintiff's claims of revealing private facts, fraud, and intentional infliction of mental distress intact.[52]

Content That Invades Privacy

So far we have discussed only privacy problems that arise in the course of news gathering. Once the images and information have been obtained, there are additional hazards in the selection of material to be broadcast. One of these involves a branch of privacy law often termed *appropriation,* but which adds up to commercial exploitation. This was the theory invoked by Hugo Zacchini, the "human cannonball" whose case was mentioned at the beginning of this chapter. The Zacchini case was unusual, however; not many performers have an act capable of being shown in its entirety in a fifteen-second clip.

In the normal course of news coverage, broadcasters are not likely to encounter this branch of privacy law. But they might well encounter it in their promotional efforts. If a person's name or likeness is used to promote the station or sell a product or service, the broadcaster should be sure that the person had consented to that use of his or her name or picture.[53]

False Light

Yet another branch of privacy law comes into play if the broadcaster depicts a person in a *false light.* This can happen if file footage is used to illustrate a story with which the subject has no actual connection. For example, if videotape taken of a woman at a pregnancy clinic was used later to illustrate a story on an abortion clinic, the woman's portrayal in connection with an abortion story places her in a false light in the eyes of her friends and colleagues.

Another example: If videotape made of people shopping in a supermarket is used in a story about the problems of shoplifting, it may give the impression that those people are shoplifters. Of special concern in this situation is what is being said while the video is being shown. A line of narrative saying, "Shoplifters come in all shapes, sizes and ages" that accompanies pictures of a nice little old lady taking a dress from a rack and holding it to herself to see how it fits may give the audience the idea that "This is a typical shoplifter."

The theory behind false light is similar to that behind defamation, except that the statement need not be defamatory. To say that a person favors abortion is not defamatory, but it can be embarrassing and painful to be falsely portrayed as holding those views, and the "false light" branch of privacy is the law's remedy.[54]

Sometimes, however, a broadcast can touch off lawsuits for both defamation and false light invasion of privacy. Consider *Duncan* v. *WJLA-TV,* a case that should encourage careful editing of video images. WJLA-TV, Washington, D.C., broadcast news reports in 1982 about a promising new treatment for genital herpes.

In its 6 P.M. newscast on March 30, 1982, WJLA-TV presented an "on the street" format for a story by reporter Betsy Ashton. As her report began, the camera panned down K Street and focused on pedestrians standing at a corner behind Ms. Ashton. The camera focused on one pedestrian, a private citizen named Linda K. Duncan, who turned directly toward the camera and became clearly recognizable. Then, as the camera began to focus on reporter Ashton, the voiced introduction to the report began.

Ms. Duncan sued for defamation and for invasion of privacy based on the 6 P.M. report and also on that evening's 11 P.M. newscast, which was heavily edited and presented in substantially different form. In the 11 P.M. version, anchor David Schoumacher presented the story. In the later version, plaintiff Linda K. Duncan was seen turning directly toward the camera and pausing as Schoumacher said, "[f]or the twenty million Americans who have herpes, it's not a cure." That version ended as Ms. Duncan was seen turning away from the camera and walking down the street.

A U.S. District Court ruled in 1984 that the 6 P.M. broadcast was neither defamatory nor a false light invasion of privacy. That report was said to provide viewers with sufficient context for reporter Ashton's on-the-street report, and the audio portion did not provide information from which viewers might infer that the plaintiff was a herpes victim.

The court decided, however, that the 11 P.M. report presented a different question, which should be considered by a jury. The court said:

Rather than using the K Street scene to place an "on-the-street" reporter in context, defendant [WJLA-TV] chose to have the anchor person read a shortened version of the report and to use the K street film as an illustration. To facilitate its use, the film was cropped so that what remained was the segment in which the camera zoomed in on plaintiff as she turned towards it. Thus, viewers saw a closeup of plaintiff turning directly towards the camera, pausing, and then walking away. While the scene was on the screen, Mr. Schoumacher stated that "[f]or the twenty million Americans who have herpes, it's not a cure. . . ." As plaintiff turned and walked away from the camera, the film ended; viewers did not see Ms. Ashton in the foreground as they did in the six o'clock report.[55]

Thus, the court granted a summary judgment to the television station involving the 6 P.M. newscast, in effect throwing out the libel and privacy claims for that broadcast. The court, however, denied a summary judgment involving the 11 P.M. report, saying a jury needed to consider whether the later newscast might be understood as defamatory or privacy-invading.

Private Information

The final branch of privacy law concerning broadcasters involves disclosure of purely private information. This body of law gives the individual a cause of action for the disclosure of private information that (a) would be highly offensive to a reasonable person, and (b) is of no legitimate public concern. The kinds of disclosure that most commonly fall within this definition involve medical and sexual matters. If a station should obtain and broadcast a videotape of a private person's consultation with a physician about a sexual problem, the station probably would be liable under this body of law. The same might be said of a disclosure that an individual has AIDS or has a physical deformity.[56]

The key problem, of course, is that such disclosures are sometimes matters of perfectly legitimate public concern. Suppose, for example, that a presidential assassin turns out to be a homosexual. Can it be said that the public has no legitimate concern with everything about such an individual, including his sexual orientation?[57] In a less dramatic example, suppose a city's mayor is an alcoholic, tours the bars at night, and sometimes calls for a police car to take him home in an inebriated condition. Although the mayor may claim he always gets to work on time and that his drinking is a private matter, doesn't the public have an interest in it? Also, what about the diversion of a police car and officers from what may be more important duties?

One answer is that what is a matter of public concern depends upon the circumstances. Overall, the courts have been fairly generous in determining what constitutes matters of legitimate public concern.

For example: The Iowa Supreme Court held that the name of a fifteen-year-old girl who had been sterilized involuntarily while a ward at a county home was a matter of legitimate public concern, even though her lawyer argued that the *Des Moines Register* could have told the story just as well without using her name.[58] And in Illinois, a vice squad officer sued the American Broadcasting Company's Chicago station for surreptitiously filming him while he made a case for solicitation against a model in a "deluxe modeling studio." The court said: "[T]he conduct of a policeman on duty is legitimately and necessarily an area upon which the public interest may and should be focused."[59]

News directors and reporters should keep in mind, however, that they are not the final judges of what constitutes legitimate public interest or concern. The courts make that decision themselves, based on a highly unscientific case-by-case analysis of specific fact situations. Not everything the public is interested in is a matter of legitimate public concern.[60]

For example, although the public undoubtedly was interested in *Time* magazine's photo of a "starving glutton" who lost weight despite her insatiable appetite, the court held that the woman's privacy had been invaded.[61] The public no doubt was interested in a movie that identified a respectable California housewife as a former prostitute who had been involved in a sensational murder case eight years earlier, but a court awarded the woman damages.[62]

Hustler Magazine v. Falwell

In the early 1980s, lawyers found an additional cause of action to use in lawsuits against the press: "intentional infliction of emotional distress."[63] But help for the media arrived in 1988's Supreme Court decision in *Hustler Magazine* v. *Falwell.*[64]

"Intentional infliction" added up to a kind of "end run" around the more traditional and better-known rules of defamation and privacy law (which vary quite widely from state to state). Although provable truth can be the best defense to a libel suit, truth is irrelevant in privacy cases except in the "false light" category.

That is tricky enough, but lawyers are adding in intentional infliction of emotional distress as a kind of legal wild card: There could be liability even if the material complained of was not defamatory and did not invade privacy.[65] On its way to the Supreme Court, the Falwell case caused considerable alarm among broadcasters and publishers: The circumstances of the case were so outrageous that it seemed likely a dangerous precedent could result.

This case arose when Larry Flynt's *Hustler* magazine twice published parodies of Campari liqueur ads, with the double-entendre theme of "the first time." The amorous ambience of the couples made it clear that "the first time" applied to much more than sipping Campari. *Hustler's* version, labeled in fine print "ad parody—not to be taken seriously," claimed that the first time famous evangelist Jerry Falwell had sex was in an outhouse, with his mother, while she was drunk.[66]

Giving a deposition before the trial, Flynt was asked by Reverend Falwell's attorney if he was trying to hurt the evangelist's reputation. Flynt helpfully volunteered that he was trying "to assassinate it."[67] The trial jury found that Falwell had not been libeled (no one would believe the ad) and that his privacy had not been invaded. However, the jury awarded $200,000 to Falwell to compensate for intentional infliction of emotional distress.[68]

Despite Reverend Falwell's understandable anger, he actually turned the ad parody to some advantage. He used a sanitized version of the *Hustler* parody in a mailing that raised $800,000 to help him sue Flynt.[69]

The Fourth Circuit ruled that with the intentional infliction tort, all that was needed to impose liability was a jury finding of intentional or reckless misconduct.[70] The Supreme Court reversed the judgment, yanking the $200,000 away from Falwell. Writing for an 8-0 Court (newly appointed Justice Anthony Kennedy did not take part), Chief Justice Rehnquist declared that a tougher standard of proof was needed under the First Amendment than "intentional or reckless misconduct." He wrote that what was needed was the actual malice standard from the law of defamation.[71] Where public officials or public figures are involved, liability for intentional infliction of emotional injury requires proof of publication with knowledge of falsity or with reckless disregard for the truth.

Although he expressed little tolerance for Flynt's fetid attempt at humor, the Chief Justice enunciated strong support for sharp-edged traditions of American political satire and cartooning. The Court said that even though a showing of hostile intent might be a finding of tort liability in other areas of law, breathing space was needed for comment on public officials and figures. "Were we to hold otherwise, there can be little doubt that political cartoonists and satirists would be subjected to damage awards without any showing that their work falsely defamed its subject."[72]

Despite the Supreme Court's unanimous decision in the Falwell case, the tort of intentional infliction of mental injury is still very much alive. Often, plaintiff's attorneys will add a claim for infliction of mental injury into a defamation or privacy lawsuit; sometimes, a fact situation will bring claims for all three causes of action.[73]

File Video

Use of old video poses some special problems. If the tape was defamatory or privacy-invading originally, its rebroadcast almost certainly will be actionable, too. If the statute of limitations has expired on the original use of the tape, rebroadcast will give the defamed individual another opportunity to sue. A tape that was unobjectionable when originally shown may become actionable through the passage of time. To give one example, if a person were under indictment at the time the tape was shot—and then the indictment is dropped while the tape sits on a shelf—failure to provide an update can be a problem. Or, consider the California case mentioned earlier. There, accounts of the former prostitute's role undoubtedly were newsworthy at the time.

Eight years later, however, the court felt that the public no longer had any legitimate interest in the matter. The limits of broadcasters' or cablecasters' rights to dredge up the past have not been determined. About all that can be said is that matters of continuing historical interest are probably safe, while the reopening of old wounds merely for curiosity's sake is not.

Consent

In the day-to-day operation of a television or cable news operation, the most important defense in all these branches of privacy is consent. Persons who admit the camera into their home, who agree to be interviewed, or who voluntarily disclose intimate facts about their lives have no cause of action because they have consented to what might otherwise have been an invasion of privacy.

The consent need not be in writing. It can be implied from circumstantial evidence, such as a tape showing the subject willingly cooperating. The key is to be sure the subject knew exactly what was being consented to; consent will be ineffective if obtained under false pretenses or if a subject did not understand how an interview was to be used.[74]

Camera crews should be warned not to exceed their authority in making representations to subjects. If an on-scene reporter, producer, or camera operator does not know how the film or tape ultimately will be used, no representations should be made on the matter. If a subject agrees to be interviewed, not knowing whether the depiction will be favorable or unfavorable, the subject arguably has consented to even an unfavorable treatment. But if a subject's consent is given on anyone's assurance that treatment will be favorable—and it is not—then consent is ineffective because it was based on misrepresentation.[75]

Delan v. *CBS, Inc.* is another case illustrating that considerable care needs to be exercised in seeking consents. In 1978, CBS News did a documentary at a state mental hospital in which David Delan was a patient. Bill Moyers and a camera crew went to Creedmoor State Hospital, photographing and videotaping a program later broadcast under the title of "Anyplace But Here."

David Delan signed a release, but the document had been cosigned by a doctor of psychology. A court ruled that was not the same as having a signature from an "attending physician" as required under New York law. CBS lost this case, even though Delan's image appeared for only four seconds in a sixty-minute news documentary. In 1983, however, an appellate court reversed, granting CBS a summary judgment on the ground that Delan's image was not used for purposes of advertising or trade under New York's narrowly drawn privacy statute.[76]

Consent is a troublesome concept after the 1975 decision by the Ninth Circuit Court of Appeals in *Virgil* v. *Time, Inc.* Surfer Mike Virgil had been interviewed by *Sports Illustrated*'s Curry Kirkpatrick about his bizarre antics, which included varieties of showing off such as eating spiders, extinguishing cigarettes in his mouth, and throwing himself down a flight of stairs because "there were all these chicks around." Shortly before the article was published, a *Sports Illustrated* fact-checker called Virgil's home to verify information. At that late point, Virgil "revoked all consent" for publication.

In words that frighten journalists who can foresee consents being withdrawn just before a broadcast is made, Judge Merrill said:

> Talking freely to a member of the press, knowing the listener to be a member of the press, is not then itself making it public. Such communication can be said to anticipate that what is said will be made public since making it public is a function of the press, and accordingly such communication can be construed as consent to publicize. Thus if publicity results it can be said to have been consented to. However, if consent is withdrawn prior to the act of publicization, the consequent publicity is without consent.
>
> We conclude that the voluntary disclosure to Kirkpatrick did not in itself constitute a voluntary disclosure . . .[77]

"Public" Places

In truly public places such as streets, parks and public buildings, photojournalists and television crews have broad rights of access, just as members of the general public have. But another set of problems develops when these same staff members attempt to cover news in what might be termed "semi-public" areas. In such places, including football stadiums, concert halls, and fairgrounds, the public has no general right of access, and neither does the press.

Admittance here is by ticket or press pass, and the photojournalist's rights may be limited by the rules under which he or she is obtaining access. Concert tickets, for example, often expressly forbid taping or photographing. Such restrictions are valid even though a concert or other kind of show is held in a publicly supported hall such as a civic center or memorial coliseum.

As a general rule, the photographer is bound by whatever limitations are posed as a condition of access. If he or she accepts a press pass under rules that say it entitles him or her access to the press box only, he or she has no right to go to the sidelines or into the spectator section to shoot pictures. On the other hand, if a photographer is in the press box when the end zone bleachers collapse, everyone knows that photographer is going to ignore the restriction and rush to the end zone to cover the story. There isn't much the stadium management can do about it. Technically, a photographer who ignores the conditions under which he or she is admitted becomes a trespasser, but as a practical matter the usual sanction will be revocation of the pass rather than legal action.

In the case of professional sports and some entertainment events, the rights of radio and television crews will be determined by elaborate contractual arrangements. Here again, the restrictions normally are controlling. If the promoters have given exclusive television rights to someone else, you have no right to televise the event, no matter how newsworthy it may be. If there is nothing in the contract that says local media can have access but other outside media can't, then you are stuck with it, although you can and should raise a beef about it. If your station holds the contract, then your rights are whatever the contract says, and no more.

In addition to restrictions imposed by the managers of semipublic places, broadcasters also face possible invasion of privacy actions by the performers and fans. It is here that the semipublic nature of the place can be most helpful. Even though the stadium or concert hall is not "public" in the sense that everyone has a right to be there, it is "public" in that people who go there forfeit some—but by no means all—of their privacy. Unless there are specific restrictions about photographing or recording, the performers on stage or field cannot complain when their performances are photographed or broadcast even though they may be embarrassing. If the lead guitarist falls down in a hazy stupor, if the star tight end drops a winning pass in the end zone, if the pageant queen's dress falls apart and exposes her anatomy, no complaints can prevail, even if the videotape is played over and over again. Those performers have invited people to see their acts. If they are mortified, that's tough; the acts are newsworthy. The same is true of those who perform on the sidelines, including cheerleaders and coaches or the master of ceremonies.

But suppose a television news team is assigned to shoot a feature on drunks misbehaving at the stadium. Do drunks at games have privacy? Yes and no. If the camera captures someone vomiting into the bouffant hairdo in front of him, that's something that happened in the stands, in public. But beware of voice-over comments; it might be difficult to prove that the incident happened because of booze and not the flu, should the person pictured decide to sue for invasion of privacy or defamation.

The judgment of on-site directors is critical. Care should be taken in selecting shots to be broadcast from the stands. "Honey shots" of attractive women are broadcast routinely. However sexist they may be, these shots present no legal problem as long as no actionable comments are made while the women are on camera.

Even if an individual is pictured in a humiliating way, it may not be actionable. A fan at a Pittsburgh Steelers game asked a *Sports Illustrated* photographer to take his picture; the photographer obliged. The fan was embarrassed when the picture was published because it showed his fly was open. The judge ruled that the photo had been taken in a public place, with the fan's permission and at his urging.[78]

It is one thing, however, merely to depict what happens. It is quite another to induce someone to perform for the camera. Thomas Taggart was present at the 1969 Woodstock Festival in Bethel, New York, servicing portable latrines for the "Port-O-San" company. As Taggart performed his necessary but unpleasant task, he was interviewed by filmmakers. The result was a hilarious two-minute sequence in the film *Woodstock,* featuring Taggart talking about his job as he emptied latrines.

Taggart sued the filmmakers, claiming he had been drawn involuntarily into being a performer for someone else's commercial advantage. The filmmakers replied that Taggart had been a participant in an event of public interest. With the facts in such dispute, a United States Court of Appeals overturned the trial court's summary judgment for the filmmakers and sent the case back for further proceedings.[79] There obviously is a difference between a television crew urging a group of fans to "moon" the opposing team's fans and the same crew taping "mooning" that was instigated by the fans themselves. If one of the fans later found the pictures to be embarrassing, the question might be: Who started it, and for what purpose?

Halftime activities are usually fair game. Years ago, an animal trainer whose act included dogs, ponies, and monkeys performed at halftime during a Washington Redskins-New York Giants game. A portion of Arsène Gautier's act was televised, and announcers then read commercials (then allowable) for a brand of cigarettes.

Gautier sued, claiming his name and picture were used for advertising purposes without his consent. However, the court ruled that unless there was exploitation of a name or picture in the commercial directly connected to the product being peddled, there was not "use" for advertising purposes. Therefore, Gautier's suit failed.[80] This case, however, is a reminder that no one's picture can be used in an advertisement without that person's permission.

Once the media are given access to an event, they generally have fairly broad power to depict the performances that take place. Another example from the 1969 Woodstock happening: Frank Man was a professional musician who made the scene. Man climbed up on the stage and played "mess call" for a pixilated audience of 400,000. Movie cameras also were present, and Warner Bros., Inc. included Man's performance in the film *Woodstock.* Man sued, claiming his performance was included in the film without his consent. Man's contention failed, however; a United States District Court said:

> The film depicts, without the addition of any fictional material, actual events which happened at the festival. Nothing is staged and nothing is false. . . . There can be no question that the Woodstock Festival was and is a matter of public interest.[81]

The court concluded that Man, by his own choice, had put himself into the spotlight at a sensational public event, thus making himself newsworthy and depriving himself of the ability to collect for the commercial exploitation of his performance.

OPEN MEETINGS AND OPEN RECORDS

In support of the instantaneous excitement of ENG reporting, every reporter needs to know the basics of federal and applicable state freedom of information laws covering both open meetings and open records. Successful reporting often turns upon knowledge of when you lawfully can be excluded from a meeting of a public body and when you should protest. Similarly, reporting often means overcoming the reluctance of many "public servants" to make available records of the public's business, whether those records are on paper or in computer-readable form.

Note that the phrase "public's right to know" is only a term of convenience. Like it or not, there is no general constitutional *right* to receive records of government. Reporters, however, do have some weapons at their disposal.

Open Meetings

The federal Sunshine Act[82] commands that sessions of about fifty agencies be open to the public, and thus to the news media. These agencies include those headed by boards named by the President and confirmed by the Senate. All meetings of such agencies are to be open. At least one week's public notice is required. Sometimes, when secret business is conducted, the Sunshine Act is clouded by a list of ten broad "exemptions." Such exemptions are similar to those provided under the federal Freedom of Information Act,[83] which is discussed below.

Open Records

Every state has laws governing access to meetings and records, although there is substantial variation among the states. It is incumbent upon every serious reporter to know the law in his or her state. Fortunately, the Reporters Committee on Freedom of the Press publishes guides to open records in the states and in the federal government. For assistance, contact:

The Reporters Committee for Freedom of the Press
1735 Eye Street NW
Washington, D.C. 20006
Telephone: (202) 466-6313

The federal Freedom of Information Act declares broadly that records of federal government agencies—at least those under the Executive Branch—will be open to the public. As promising as that sounds, there are nine exemptions which have been used to hide much material, and not only that which legitimately needs to be kept from public view. These nine exemptions are:

1. Records authorized to be kept secret under criteria established by a Presidential executive order. "National defense" or "foreign policy" classifications come into play here: Top Secret, Secret, and so on.

2. Matters related only to an agency's internal personnel rules and practices.

3. Matters exempt from disclosure by statute.

4. Trade secrets and commercial or financial information that is privileged or confidential.

5. Inter-agency or intra-agency communications, including "preliminary" memos on policy choices.

6. Personnel and medical files, the disclosure of which will cause a "clearly unwarranted" invasion of a person's privacy.

7. Investigative files compiled for law enforcement purposes, if investigations are ongoing, if confidential sources would be endangered, if it would interfere with a fair trial or be an unwarranted invasion of privacy.

8. Reports prepared within or for an agency regulating or supervising financial institutions.

9. Geological and geophysical information and data involving oil and gas exploration.

Using open records statutes at either the federal or state level is often a tedious process. Delays of three months are not uncommon for many state agencies when an open record request is made, and federal agencies often take longer.

CAMERAS AND MICROPHONES IN COURTROOM

Increasingly, electronic media coverage of courts is permitted, but generally under strict guidelines and under the control of the presiding judge. Keep in mind that there is no *right* to cover a courtroom electronically. If a judge decides there's to be no camera or microphone coverage, that's it! On the other hand, many judges are coming to appreciate the benefits of a citizenry that is better informed about the judicial process in both civil and criminal proceedings, thanks to the television camera.

The first rule in covering a court with cameras and microphones is to get permission. If permission is granted, ENG operation may still be out of the question. You can't expect to stride into a courtroom during legal proceedings (or leave when you jolly well feel like it). Chances are that if permission to telecast or videotape is granted, it will be done under strict rules. These rules might include having a camera in one fixed position, with one camera operator, and no coming or going while court is in session. For trials or proceedings of great newsworthiness, pool coverage may be specified by the presiding judge.

The Radio Television News Directors Association keeps track of developments involving microphones and cameras in courtrooms, updating the information frequently. For information call or write:

Radio Television News Directors Association
1000 Connecticut Ave., Suite 615
Washington, D.C. 20036-5302
Telephone: (202) 659-6510

The RTNDA's ongoing "Survey of Expanded Media Coverage of State Courtroom Proceedings" showed that camera coverage of both criminal and civil trials and appellate proceedings now is permitted in a majority—thirty-eight—of the state judicial systems. The RTNDA survey for January, 1994, showed that only the District of Columbia, Indiana, Mississippi, and South Dakota allow no electronic media coverage in courtrooms.[84]

The federal courts long have resisted admitting cameras, although there may be some softening of the posture of the United States Judicial Conference against such coverage. From 1991 to mid-1994, a Judicial Conference-approved experiment was held allowing media coverage of civil (not criminal) trials and appeals in a number of courts.

REPORTER-SOURCE CONFIDENTIALITY

If a reporter promises a source confidentiality, that may be more an ethical than a legal situation. Despite the existence of "reporter shield laws" in more than half of the states, such statutes are not absolute protection against a reporter being ordered by a judge to testify before a court or a grand jury about who the source is or what the source said. Such state statutes—there is now no federal shield statute—often fail because, after all, they are being interpreted by a judge. For example, if a judge balances a reporter's First Amendment rights against a courts's right to get the information it needs in a judicial (or grand jury) proceeding, you can understand that to the judge, the First Amendment might not be the biggest concern.

There is no First Amendment right not to testify before a court or a grand jury; in fact, it has been held that it is a citizen's duty to do so.[85] So, promises to protect a confidential source or confidential information should not be lightly given. If you stand by your word in the face of judicial demands to testify or provide information—and refuse to testify—you could wind up in jail for contempt of court.

Fortunately, not all is lost if a reporter is subpoenaed to testify about confidential matters before a court or grand jury. Basically, a series of court decisions have developed rules to protect reporters from "fishing expeditions" by lazy prosecutors or lawyers. The commonly used rules now seem to be that a reporter will not need to divulge a confidential source or confidential information unless:

1. The information sought cannot be obtained from any other source (to avoid damaging First Amendment interests in news gathering).

2. The information is centrally relevant to a claim by a party in a legal action.

3. The subject at issue involves overriding, compelling interest.[86]

Here, as always, ethics can be a practical matter. If a reporter has promised to keep a source confidential—and then does not because of unwillingness to go to jail to protect that source—then what will that do to the reporter's credibility as a respecter of confidences?

Before promising confidentiality, check with management. Management will need to know enough of what is going on to responsibly decide whether the reporter should put so much on the line. On the other hand, once confidentiality is promised, management had better not change its mind and reveal the source. The *Minneapolis Star-Tribune* broke a reporter's promise and—after the source was fired from a job—the newspaper was assessed $200,000 in damages for what amounted to a breach of a verbal contract.[87]

CONTEMPT: A LESSON FROM CNN'S NORIEGA TAPES EXPERIENCE

Early in November 1990, the Cable News Network got access to tape recordings of telephone calls between General Manuel Antonio Noriega, the Panamanian dictator, in his Florida jail cell and his attorney. After CNN declared that it had the tapes, defense attorneys sought—and U.S. District Judge William Hoeveler granted—an injunction forbidding CNN's broadcasting of the tapes. Although CNN did not broadcast conversations between Noriega and his attorneys, the cable network did broadcast portions of Noriega's calls to others. A U.S. Court of Appeals upheld the injunction as a permissible form of prior restraint, and the Supreme Court refused to hear the case.[88]

By late November, after CNN had released the tapes and Judge Hoeveler heard them, he ruled that CNN could proceed to broadcast them, which CNN chose not to do.

But the matter did not end there for CNN, which had disobeyed a judge's order. On March 30, 1994, CNN was charged with criminal contempt for willfully disobeying Judge Hoeveler's injunction; in November, 1994, Judge Hoeveler found CNN guilty of criminal contempt for disobeying his order. CNN received a tongue lashing in which the judge invoked the "thin bright line between anarchy and order." The judge declared that defiance of court orders cannot be justified or tolerated. CNN escaped with an apology and with payment of $85,000—the amount it cost to employ a special prosecutor to pursue the contempt matter against the network.[89] The lesson should be clear. A judge's order may be appealed to a higher court. But if that order is upheld (or if no appeal is pursued), it can be defied only at the peril of the broadcaster or cablecaster.

THE FAIRNESS DOCTRINE AND PERSONAL ATTACK

Regulations of the Federal Communications Commission are beyond the scope of this chapter. It can only be urged that you be sure to know about them *if* they are in existence. Deregulation has been the FCC buzzword for years, but the FCC—once called the "leaning tower of Jell-O" by former CBS producer Fred Friendly—was showing signs of increased activity in the mid-1990s.

Tied to the FCC's stance as a reluctant regulator is an increased concern for the First Amendment. Back in August, 1987, the Commission drew cheers from most broadcasters and flak from citizens' groups by repealing its own thirty-eight-year-old Fairness Doctrine.[90] Not *all* of the Fairness Doctrine was repealed, however. The personal attack and political editorializing requirements of the Fairness Doctrine were left in force, although they *might* at some time also be eliminated by the FCC.

The Fairness Doctrine's demise had been proposed to Congress as early as 1981 by Mark Fowler, who chaired the FCC during most of the presidency of Ronald Reagan. His argument—enthusiastically seconded by believers in "market forces regulation"—ran that the scarcity of broadcast frequencies had been alleviated if not in effect wiped out by the increasing number of broadcast and cable voices available.

Although the Fairness Doctrine was little enforced in the 1980s, it took a 1987 United States Court of Appeals decision to embolden the FCC sufficiently into actually declaring the end of a big chunk of that doctrine.[91] Many broadcasters and civil libertarians hated the Fairness Doctrine, which had added up to broadcasters at times being ordered to make response time available to spokespersons on "controversial issues of public importance" if the station had broadcast only one side of an issue. Broadcasters, understandably, took the position that this infringed upon their First Amendment rights, and that they were denied equal protection of the laws because no such requirements were laid on print media.

In the so-called TRAC case—*Telecommunications Research Action Center (TRAC)* v. *FCC*—the court held that the FCC did have the authority to repeal its own doctrine and that a 1958 reworking of the Communications Act by Congress that made reference to the Fairness Doctrine had not placed the doctrine beyond Commission authority.[92]

Although the controversial public issues portion of the Fairness Doctrine has been declared dead by the FCC, that section could be revived later on in the 1990s. Although a large majority of members of the House of Representatives and the Senate evidently favor legislation to codify the doctrine in statutory language, the Reagan and Bush presidencies used the veto power to head off a Fairness Doctrine statute.[93] The Clinton presidency, or its successor, may someday see such a codification.

One part of the Fairness Doctrine remaining in effect in the middle of 1988 will be mentioned, mainly because it is so closely related to the defamation of privacy torts discussed earlier. It is called the "personal attack rule" and it reads as follows:

(a) When during the presentation of views on a controversial issue of public importance, an attack is made upon the honesty, character, integrity or like personal qualities of an identifiable person or group, the licensee shall, within a reasonable time and in no event later than one week after the attack, transmit to the person or group attacked (1) notification of the date, time and identification of the broadcast; (2) a script or tape (or accurate summary if a script or tape is not available) of the attack; and (3) an offer of a reasonable opportunity to respond over the licensee's facilities.

(b) The provisions of paragraph (a) of this section shall not be applicable (1) to attacks on foreign groups or foreign public figures; (2) to personal attacks which are made on legally qualified candidates, their authorized spokesmen, or those associated with them in the campaign; and (3) to bona fide newscasts, bona fide news interviews, and on-the-spot coverage of a bona fide news event (including commentary or analysis contained in the foregoing programs) but the provisions of the paragraph (a) of this section shall be applicable to editorials of the licensee.[94]

Because of the exception in section (b) (3), the personal attack rule normally will not apply to live news situations, but it does apply to documentaries, talk shows, and other kinds of public-issue programming. The distinction between editorials and commentary contained in news programs should be noted: Commentary is exempt (unless the commentator has been authorized by the management to speak for the station) but editorials *are* subject to the rule.[95]

There is no personal attack unless someone's honesty, integrity or morality is impugned. Thus, it is not a personal attack to criticize a public official's performance of his or her job, or to question a person's professional competence.[96] On the other hand, it is a personal attack to call someone a coward or to accuse him or her of undertaking a smear campaign.[97]

Although the rule speaks of an "identifiable person *or* group," the Commission has declined to apply the rule to attacks on large groups. Thus, it is not a personal attack to accuse all the "men of the Roman Church" of being hypocritical and immoral, because the group is too large for identification to take place.[98]

When the personal attack rule is triggered, the station can avoid trouble with the FCC by complying promptly with the requirements stated in the rule for offering the victim an opportunity to respond. If this is done, the FCC ordinarily will take no further action.[99]

SECTION 315

Just in case broadcasters needed a reminder in 1988 that Section 315 of the Federal Communications Act (providing "equal opportunity" for candidates' use of broadcast time) was still in effect, consider the case of William H. Branch. An on-air reporter for KOVR-TV, Sacramento, California, Branch petitioned the FCC in 1984 for a ruling that Section 315 was unconstitutional.

Branch wished to run for town council of Loomis, a municipality just northeast of Sacramento. Told by his bosses that he would have to take an unpaid leave of absence if he ran for the Loomis post, Branch then sought the ruling from the FCC. He argued not only that Section 315 was unconstitutional but also that it effectively meant he could not continue to work and run for office.[100] Branch's employers calculated that his candidacy could obligate the station to provide about thirty-three hours of time to Branch's opponents if he continued to work there during the campaign period. Faced with the choice of an unpaid leave or remaining employed, Branch left the race.[101]

The FCC turned down Branch's petition and was upheld by a three-judge panel of the Court of Appeals, District of Columbia Circuit, in July 1987.[102] And in 1988, the Supreme Court declined to review the case, leaving Section 315 in force.

CONCLUSION

Most of the problems discussed in this chapter can be avoided in two ways. First, by maintaining a heightened awareness of the problems themselves, and second, by vigilantly exercising sound and ethical journalistic judgment.

Most of the time, ethical sensibilities will go a long way toward keeping a broadcast or cable news team out of trouble. But one spectacular lapse in ethics cost NBS News dearly, in reputation if not in money. Late in 1992, a "Dateline NBC" telecast charged that some General Motors-made pickup trucks were unsafe because of susceptibility to gas tank explosions in collisions. The NBC broadcast showed a pickup truck bursting into flames after a staged crash, but the flames were helped along by rigged "sparking devices" to make sure a fire occurred for the camera. After the subterfuge was revealed, General Motors brought a libel suit against NBC, soon settling for an apology from the network.[103]

Unfortunately, in the context of ENG, that awareness and judgment frequently must be put to work at the scene of a breaking news event, instantaneously and without benefit of consultation. Such pressure-packed situations obviously increase the risk of making a wrong judgment.

The legal problems raised by ENG can best be dealt with in the same way as many other problems created by the immediacy of the new technology: by careful planning.[104] Because there simply isn't time to devise a solution after a problem arises, contingency plans must be worked out in advance. Producers, reporters and anchors should be given guidelines dealing with such matters as when to use delay systems, what to watch out for when viewing tape for a quick turnaround, how to screen interview subjects, what to do if a speaker defames someone, and what to do when access to a news site is denied or in question.

These are matters each station should work out for itself in consultation with its own lawyers, in the light of its own state law. The guidelines should address the most common situations and provide station personnel with specific guidance for handling problems that are readily foreseeable.

Such guidelines will not cover every situation. Part of ENG's excitement is that every situation offers new perils and opportunities. For that reason, each station ultimately must depend on the professional skill and judgment of its news personnel.

NOTES

David A. Anderson, J.D., Thompson and Knight Professor of Law at The University of Texas at Austin, was the original co-author of this chapter when *ENG: Television News and the New Technology* appeared in its first edition in 1985. Much of the substance and form of this chapter owes its strength to Professor Anderson. Dwight Teeter wishes to make clear that Professor Anderson should not be held accountable for any materials added since 1985. Specific additions by Professor Teeter for the 1989 edition included material on ambush interviews, the $3.2 million libel verdict in *Brown and Williamson* v. *Walter Jacobson and CBS,* information on intentional infliction of mental injury and on FCC regulations. For this edition, Teeter has updated that information as needed and has added new material including speculation about the impact of tabloid television on libel and privacy litigation; access to information; cameras and microphones in courtrooms, and reporter-source confidentiality.

1. Le Mistral, Inc. v. CBS, Inc., 61 A.D.2d 491, 492 (1st Dept. 1978); *TV Guide,* May 3, 1980, p. 6.
2. Zacchini v. Scripps-Howard Broadcasting Co., 433 U.S. 562 (1977).

3. For a predictive early look at new technology and its impact on television news, see Richard D. Yoakam, "ENG: Electronic News Gathering in Local Television Stations," Research Report No. 12, School of Journalism, Indiana University (November, 1981).

4. The personal attack rule—along with the political editorial rule where a station favors an individual candidate—survived the FCC's repeal of its own Fairness Doctrine in 1987. If a broadcast attacks the character or integrity of a person or group, the person or persons attacked must be notified promptly by the station and offered air time to respond. Political editorials favoring or opposing a candidate are treated similarly. See Don R. Le Duc's discussion of this in Teeter and Le Duc, *Law of Mass Communications,* 7th ed. (Westbury, N.Y.: Foundation Press, 1992), pp. 397–398.

5. See Wilson v. Scripps-Howard Broadcasting Co., 642 F.2d 371 (6th Cir. 1981), cert. den. 102 S.Ct. 984. See Annot. Defamation by Radio and Television, 50 A.L.R.3d 1311. The major exception is California, which long has treated broadcast defamation as slander. See Cal. Civ. Code S46, 48.5 (West, 1982, 1995).

6. See, e.g., Snowden v. Pearl River Broadcasting Corp., 251 So.2d 405 (La.App. 1971).

7. Garrison v. Louisiana, 379 U.S. 64 (1964); Wilson v. Scripps-Howard Broadcasting, supra note 5; cf. Cox Broadcasting v. Cohn, 420 U.S. 469, 490 (1975).

8. 106 S.Ct. 1559 (1986).

9. Ibid., 1563.

10. See, e.g., Dickey v. CBS, Inc., 583 F.2d 1221 (3rd Cir. 1978).

11. See, e.g., Vitteck v. Washington Broadcasting Co., 256 Pa. Super 427, 389 A.D.2d 1197 (1978); Afro-American Publishing Co. v. Jaffe, 366 F.2d 649 (D.C. Cir. 1966); Ladany v. William Morrow & Co., 465 F.2d 870 (S.D.N.Y. 1978).

12. See, e.g., Harwood Pharmaceutical Co. v. NBC, 9 N.Y.S. 460, 214 N.E.2d 602 (1961).

13. The folklore seems to come from careless readings of the famous case of Neiman-Marcus v. Lait, 107 F.Supp. 96 (S.D.N.Y. 1952), 13 F.R.D. 311 (1952). There, members of a group of nine models termed prostitutes were found to have been identified. Also, members of the group of twenty-five men's store salesmen (a group termed "the nucleus of the Dallas fairy colony") also were held to have been identified and thus had the ability to sue for defamation. Members of a group of 382 "salesgirls"—also termed prostitutes—had their lawsuits dismissed. The court held that 382 simply was too large a group to allow identification.

14. Brady v. Ottaway Newspapers, Inc., 84 A.D.2d 226, 445 N.Y.S.2d 786 (1981), in which one of fifty-three unnamed members of a police force was told he was not barred by lack of identification from suing. In another jurisdiction, however, a newspaper was held not to have identified individual members of a twenty-one-person police force in an article that was the subject of a libel suit.

15. Teeter and Le Duc, op. cit., p. 648.

16. E.g., Holy Spirit Association for the Unification of World Christianity v. New York Times Co., 49 N.Y.S. 63, 414 N.Y.S.2d 165 (1979) (report of Congressional investigation); Phoenix Newspapers v. Choisser, 82 Ariz. 271, 312 P.2d 150 (1957) (report of public candidates' forum).

17. See New York Times v. Sullivan, 376 U.S. 254 (1964); St. Amant v. Thompson, 390 U.S. 727 (1968).

18. Gertz v. Robert Welch, 418 U.S. 323 (1974).

19. Ibid.

20. Material used here was adapted from Professor Richard D. Yoakam's interviews with news directors as referred to in the note at the beginning of this chapter.

21. A number of states have special statutes, passed years ago at the behest of the National Association of Broadcasters, shielding stations from liability for defamatory remarks of third persons unless the plaintiff proves that the station failed to use due care to prevent the statement from being broadcast. See, e.g. 1 Wyo. Stat. 872, and Art. 5433a. Vernon's Ann. Tex. Stats. These statutes were enacted to protect broadcasters from strict liability before the United States Supreme Court began imposing restrictions on state libel law, as in Gertz v. Welch, 418 U.S. 323 (1974). Whether these statutes will now be used against broadcasters, on the theory that they imply that broadcasters are liable for failing to keep third party defamers off the air, is an open question. With that last sentence's cautionary note in mind, see Robert L. Hughes's "Radio Libel Law: Relics That May Have Answers for Reform Needed Today," *Journalism Quarterly,* Vol. 63, No. 2 (Summer, 1986), pp. 288–293 f.

22. Snowden v. Pearl River Broadcasting Corp., 251 So.2d 405 (La. App. 1971). See also Holter v. WLCY-TV, 366 So.2d 440, 454, citing Snowden and saying that broadcasting a defamatory allegation from an anonymous source without further checking was the same as using no tape delay.

23. Adams v. Frontier Broadcasting Corp., 555 P.2d 556, 565 (Wyo. 1976). See also Pacella v. Milford Radio Corp., 462 N.E.2d 355, 360 (Mass. App. 1984), saying failure to take advantage of a seven-second tape delay was not "actual malice" (publication of a defamatory falsehood with knowledge of falsity or with reckless disregard for the truth).

24. Curtis Publishing Co. v. Butts, 388 U.S. 139, 157 (1968).

25. Walker v. Associated Press, 388 U.S. 130, 158 (1968).

26. Adams v. Daily Telegraph Printing Co., 13 Med.L.Rptr. 2034, 2037 (S.C. Ct. of App., Dec. 8, 1986).

27. Machleder v. Diaz, 538 F.Supp. 1364 (S.D.N.Y. 1985).

28. Machleder v. Diaz, 801 F.2d 46 (2d Cir. 1986).

29. Stuart A. Taylor, Jr., "Justices Uphold $3 Million Libel Award on CBS," *The New York Times* (national ed.), April 5, 1988, p. 11; The Supreme Court of the United States was affirming Brown & Williamson v. Jacobson, 827 F.2d 1119, 1122–1123 (7th Cir. 1987).

30. Brown & Williamson v. Jacobson, 827 F.2d 1119, 1122–1123 (7th Cir. 1987).

31. Ibid., 1123.

32. For examples of 1994 articles covering Food and Drug Administration attacks on the tobacco industry, Congressional hearings, and tough reporting on that industry see three articles in *The New York Times* by Philip J. Hilts, "Cigarette Makers Debated the Risks They Denied," June 16, 1994, p. A1; "Tobacco Company Chief Denies Nicotine Scheme in Testimony," June 14, 1994, p. A1, and "Ban on Cigarettes Could Be Avoided, F.D.A. Chief Says," June 29, 1994, p. A1. See also Warren E. Leary, "Surgeon General Urges Banning Cigarette Ads Aimed at the Young," *The New York Times,* February 25, 1994, p. A1.

33. Brown & Williamson v. Jacobson, 827 F.2d 1119, 1123 (7th Cir. 1987).

34. Ibid.

35. Ibid, 1134.

36. Ibid.

37. Ibid., 1137–1138.

38. Ibid.

39. Ibid., 1137–1138.

40. Ibid., 1134.

41. Milo Geyelin, "Libel Defendants Fare Well on Appeal," *The Wall Street Journal,* May 31, 1994, p. B11, quoting Professor Dienes of the George Washington University National Law Center.

42. Cf. Billings v. Adkinson, 489 S.W.2d 858 (Tex. 1973).

43. Dietemann v. Time, Inc., 449 F.2d 245, 250 (9th Cir. 1971).

44. Oklahoma v. Bernstein, 5 Med.L.Rptr. 2313, 2323–2324 (Okla. D.C. Rogers County, Jan. 21, 1980), aff'd *sub nom.* Stahl v. Oklahoma, 9 Med.L.Rptr. (Okla. Ct. Crim. App. 1983).

45. City of Oak Creek v. Peter Ah King, 436 N.W.2d 285, 286–287 (Wis. S. Ct. 1989).

46. Ibid., pp. 292–293, quoting Branzburg v. Hayes, 408 U.S. 665, 684–685 (1972).

47. Jaubert v. Crowley Post-Sentinel, 375 So.2d 1386 (La. 1979).

48. Galella v. Onassis, 487 F.2d 986 (2d Cir. 1973).

49. Galella v. Onassis, 8 Med.L.Rptr. (D.C.S.D.N.Y., March 2, 1982).

50. Florida Publishing Co. v. Fletcher, 340 So.2d 914, 915–916 (Fla. 1977). See discussion of this case in Marc Franklin and David A. Anderson, *Mass Media Law: Cases and Materials,* 4th ed. (Westbury, N.Y.: Foundation Press, 1989), pp. 675–676.

51. Anderson v. WROC-TV, 109 Misc.2d 905, 441 N.Y.S.2d 220 (N.Y. Sup. Ct. 1981). See also Negri v. Schering Corp., 333 F. Supp. 101 (S.D.N.Y. 1971). See also Ayeni v. CBS Inc., 22 Med.L.Rptr. 1466, 1470 (U.S.D.C., E.N.Y., March 17, 1944), in which a television network videotaped federal agents' going into a private home with a search warrant. The TV crew was invited into the house by the agents despite the objection of Mrs. Ayeni. The court held this videotaping to be unlawful, saying: "CBS had no greater right than a thief to be in the home, to take pictures, and to remove the photographic record [the videotaped images]."

52. Baugh v. CBS, Inc., 21 Med.L.Rptr. 2065, 2067, 2074–2075 (U.S.D.C. N.D. Cal. 1993).

53. The inclusion of brief clips of newsworthy matters in station promotional materials probably is protected as long as the promotional use is merely incidental to the original newsworthy use. See Namath v. Sports Illustrated, 39 N.Y.2d 897, 386 N.Y.S.2d 397, 352 N.E.2d 584 (1976).

54. Cf. Raible v. Newsweek, Inc., 341 F.Supp. 804 W.D. Pa. 1972); Arrington v. New York Times Co., 8 Med.L.Rptr. 1351 (N.Y. 1982); Peay v. Curtis Publishing Co., 78 F.Supp. 305 (D.C.D.C. 1948).

55. Duncan v. WJLA-TV, 10 Med.L.Rptr. 1395, 1398 (D.C.D.C., Feb. 17, 1984).

56. E.g. Clayman v. Bernstein, 38 Pa. D&C 543 (1940); Justice v. Belo Broadcasting Corp., 472 F.Supp. 145 (1979).

57. Cf. Sipple v. Chronicle Publishing Co., 82 Cal. App. 143, 147 Cal. Rptr. 59 (1978), where a hero who foiled an attempt on President Ford's life was identified as gay by the news media yet was held to have no cause of action when he sued for "private facts" invasion of privacy.

58. Howard v. Des Moines Register and Tribune Co., 283 N.W.2d 289 (Iowa, 1979), cer. den. 445 U.S. 904.

59. Cassidy v. ABC, 60 Ill. App.3d 831, 17 Ill. Dec. 936, 377 N.E.2d 126 (1978).

60. See, e.g., Virgil v. Time, Inc., 527 F.2d 1122, 1129 (9th Cir. 1975), quoting the *Restatement (Second) of Torts:* "In determining what is a matter of legitimate public interest, account must be taken of the customs and conventions of the community, and in the last analysis what is proper becomes a matter of community

mores. The line is to be drawn when the publicity ceases to be the giving of information to which the public is entitled, and becomes a morbid and sensational prying into public lives for its own sake, with which a reasonable member of the public, with decent standards, would say that he had no concern. . . ."

61. See Barber v. Time, Inc., 348 Mo. 1199, 159 S.W.2d 291 (1942).
62. See Melvin v. Reid, 112 Cal. App. 285, 297 P.91 (1931).
63. This "infliction of emotional distress" tort can be pursued as either "intentional" or "negligent." See Robert Drechsel, "Negligent Infliction of Emotional Distress: New Tort Problem for the Mass Media," 12 *Pepperdine Law Review* 989 (1985).
64. 14 Med.L.Rptr. 2281 (1988).
65. David Margolick, "Some See Threat in Non-Libel Verdict of Falwell," *The New York Times,* Dec. 10, 1984, p. 6.
66. Falwell v. Flynt, 797 F.2d 1270, 13 Med.L.Rptr. 1145 (4th Cir. 1986).
67. Ibid.
68. Ibid.
69. Ibid.
70. 14 Med.L.Rptr. at 2285 (1988).
71. Ibid., at 2284.
72. Ibid., at 2284.
73. Baugh v. CBS, Inc., 21 Med.L.Rptr. 20675 (D.C.N.D. Cal., 1993); Kolegaas v. Heftel Broadcasting Co., 20 Med.L.Rptr. 2105 (Ill. Sup. Ct. 1992).
74. Raible v. Newsweek, Inc., 341 F.Supp. 804, 806, 809 (W.D. Pa. 1972); Metzger v. Dell Publishing Co., 207 Misc.2d 166 182, 136 N.Y.S.2d 888 (1955); Russell v. Marboro Books, 18 Misc.2d 8 (1955).
75. Cher v. Forum International, 7 Med.L.Rptr. 2593 (C.D.Cal. 1982).
76. Delan v. CBS, 7 Med.L.Rptr. 2453 (N.Y.Sup.Ct. App. Div., 2d Dept., Jan. 24, 1983).
77. Virgil v. Time, Inc., 527 F.2d 1112, 1127 (9th Cir. 1975), cert. den. 425 U.S. 998 (1976).
78. Neff v. Time, Inc., 406 F.Supp. 858 (E.D. Pa. 1976). See also Harrison v. Washington Post, 391 A.2d 781 (D.C.App. 1978), which arose when a photographer, who was standing on a public sidewalk, took pictures of a man being led away by police officers. No liability was found.
79. Taggart v. Wadleigh-Maurice Ltd. & Warner Bros., 489 F.2d 435, 437 (3rd Cir. 1973).
80. Gautier v. Pro-Football, Inc., 271 App. Div. (1951), aff'd 107 N.E.2d 485, 304 N.Y. 354 (1952).
81. Man v. Warner Bros., Inc., 317 F.Supp. 51, 53 (D.C.N.Y. 1970). The Zacchini case, supra note 2, constitutes a narrow exception to this rule. It merely holds that if a state wants to allow a performer to recover damages for the broadcast of an entire act, the First Amendment is no bar. But state law generally protects the depiction of events of public interest, as the Man case illustrates.
82. 5 U.S.S. A. Sec. 552b.
83. 5 U.S.C.A. Sec. 552a.
84. RTNDA, *News Media Coverage of Judicial Proceedings With Cameras and Micro-Phones* (Washington, D.C.: RTNDA, 1994 ed.).
85. Branzburg v. Hayes, 408 U.S. 665 (1972).
86. Teeter and LeDuc, op.cit., pp. 559–560.
87. Cohen v. Cowles Media, 111 S.Ct. 2519–2520 (1991).
88. "Tales of the Tape," *Newsweek,* Dec. 17, 1990, p. 29; U.S. v. Noriega, 18 Med.L.Rptr. 1348, 1349 (D.C.S.D. Fla., Nov. 8 & 9, 1990).

89. "CNN to Delay Playing of Noriega Tapes," *The New York Times,* Nov. 13, 1990, p. A12; Judge Hoeveler's decision, U.S. v. Cable News Network, Case No. 94–154—CR-Hoeveler, pp. 1–2, 35–37; "CNN Found Guilty in Contempt for Tapes Broadcast," *The New York Times,* Nov. 2, 1994, p. A8; News Notes, 23 Med.L.Rptr. No. 1, Jan. 3, 1995; The Associated Press, "CNN agrees to air admission of error in contempt sentence," The Knoxville *News Sentinel,* Dec. 20, 1994, p. A1.

90. In re Complaint of Syracuse Peace Council Against WTVH, Syracuse, Memorandum Opinion and Order, 63 R.R.2d 5452 (1987).

91. Telecommunications Research Action Center (TRAC) v. FCC, 61 R.R.2d 330 (1987). See also Public Law 274, 86th Congress (1959), amending equal opportunities provisions of Sec. 315 of the Communications Act. Although Sec. 315 applies only to bona fide candidates for political office, with the 1959 amendment Congress stated that broadcasters had obligations "under this Act to operate in the public interest and to afford reasonable opportunity for the discussion of conflicting views on issues of public importance." But in the TRAC case, the Court of Appeals said in effect that the 1959 amendment did not forbid the FCC from repealing the Fairness Doctrine. Adapted from Don R. Le Duc, Chapter 9, "Regulating Broadcasting," pp. 392–399, in Teeter and Le Duc, *Law of Mass Communications,* 7th ed. (Westbury, N.Y.: Foundation Press, 1992).

92. Ibid.

93. Le Duc, op. cit., 396–397.

94. 74 C.F.R. Sec. 73.123, discussed in Le Duc, op. cit., at 397–399.

95. See Let's Help Florida Committee, 74 F.C.C.2d S84, 46 R.R.2d 919 (1979).

96. See Mayor Henry W. Maier, 50 R.R.2d 73 (Bd. Bur. 1981); Rev. Lester Kinsolving, 67 F.C.C.2d 158 (Bd. Bur. 1977).

97. See Straus Communications, Inc. v. FCC, 530 F.2d 1001 (D.C.Cir. 1976); Red Lion Broadcasting Co. v. FCC, 395 U.S. 367 (1969).

98. Diocese of Rockville Centre, 50 F.C.C.2d 330, 32 R.R.2d 376 (1973).

99. See Anti-Defamation League of B'nai B'rith v. FCC, 403 F.2d 169 (D.C.Cir. 1968), cert. den. 394 U.S. 930.

100. Branch v. FCC, 14 Med.L.Rptr. 1465, 1467, 1473, 1475 (7th Cir. 1987).

101. Ibid., 1465–1466.

102. Ibid.

103. Elizabeth Kolbert, "In NBC's Truck Crash Test, Law and Journalism Collided," *The New York Times*, Feb. 10, 1993, p. A7; and Ken Auletta, "Changing Channels," *The New Yorker*, March 15, 1993, p. 38.

104. See Yoakam, supra note 3, at pp. 5–6.

"And Still To Come . . ."

I ts time now for our look over the horizon.

What new tools will television journalists acquire in the next decade?

Where is television news headed?

How can I best position myself for career opportunities?

NEW TOOLS

Digital Technology

To understand **digital** technology we must first describe the original technology of television, which is **analog**. In the invention and development of television, internal television signals that move around the TV station, from camera to switcher to transmitter, flow through wire just like an electric current. These signals take up a lot of electronic "space" and require fairly heavy wire, so if you have to handle a lot of signals, you end up with a very thick cable made up of several wires bundled together or a lot of smaller cables running under the floor and behind the equipment.

The flow of the signal through a video cable cannot be interrupted if you want to have a picture. It is a continuous stream like water flowing through a garden hose.

There's nothing wrong with the analog system for moving TV signals from one place to another. However, the convergence of other new technologies offer scientists and engineers opportunities to move more signals with better quality over equal-sized or smaller cables.

One of these technologies is the **computer**. The basic idea of processing data by computer is to convert the data into combinations of 1's (numeral 1) and 0's (numeral 0) into a sort of space-age Morse Code. A computer's central processor accomplishes this conversion of data into strings of 1's and 0's at fantastically high speeds, one of the advantages of the technology. Computer processing also conserves precious electronic "space" which is another of its crucial advantages.

Digital signals are a lot like picking up a dry garden hose, only instead of having a continuous flow of water through it, let's hold the hose up and pour sand through it. Those little grains of sand are like the little "bursts" of digital information that are moving through advance communication cables.

Because digital signals can be divided up into little clusters or bursts of energy—the bursts are called "packets"—the signal can be interrupted, or two or more signals can even be sent over the same channel, each within its own little set of "packets." Of course, it takes some pretty clever technology to convert a TV picture into digital packets and then at the other end, find those packets, sort them out, and recreate the TV picture 300 miles away.

From a practical standpoint, digital technology allows us to: make equipment smaller and lighter; stuff more TV signals (channels) in a cable (or satellite beam); and use computers in conjunction with audio and video. It can mean moving 100 TV signals over one cable, rather than one signal, using the same relative amount of space.

Scientists have learned to make TV cable out of fine strands of glass. The "code" then becomes a matter of turning a light source off and on very rapidly. We call this cable **fiber-optic**. Its main virtue is that we can stuff a lot more high-quality video signals into a fiber cable of equivalent size to its predecessor, the copper wire cable. Fiber-optic cables are bringing cable TV into homes, they connect major ballparks with production centers a thousand miles away, they make up the backbone of the U.S. long-distance telephone networks, and they carry telephone calls, data, and video beneath the Atlantic and Pacific oceans.

Digital Technology: What It Means

As we have noted, digital technology helps manufacturers make the equipment we use much smaller and lighter. Not so long ago field reporting crews went to assignments carrying 75 pounds of equipment. This included the camera, the videotape recorder, a small spotlight, and a battery belt to power all these units.

Digital technology has helped reduce the size of the video recorder, so it can now be attached to (or "docked" with) the camera. No more toting around 20 to 30 pounds of recorder on the end of a long shoulder strap! The weight of batteries is down, too, because digital technology draws less power.

Digital technology even allows CNN and other networks and stations to broadcast amateur video shots by viewers who just happened to be in the right place at the right time to capture some action on videotape. Digital devices enhance these pictures shot by amateurs to meet government and professional requirements.

The next transition is from videotape to computer or **optical disks** as the field recording medium. The camcorder (camera/recorder) will be made even lighter. Also, the disks from the field recorders will be compatible with the new **nonlinear** editing machines, so you can begin to edit as soon as the disk is inserted in the edit machine's disk drive. If you use videotape in digital non-linear editing, you first have to copy the videotape in "real time" (regular speed) onto a disk in order to edit.

Digital technology opens up new vistas in graphic creation, in fact some news programs are being broadcast without having an actual set for the anchorperson. The "apparent" background is really an electronically generated visual, and the anchor is "inserted" into this picture.

Digital technology permits you to bring data (stories), still video, and moving video into a desktop computer, which means a writer or reporter can write and edit a story right at her or his desk.

Digital technology also permits producers to build broadcasts in a computer, so that very little studio time is needed. Continuous news services like CNN Headline News can have anchors prerecord their on-camera bits for the producer to insert in the broadcast. The anchors then do other tasks (such as anchoring segments for the Airport Channel) until they are needed to record the next portion of the news.

News can also be replayed, and re-edited without having to do the actual broadcast over. Similarly, tape from stories can be stored in its "as-shot" form in a computer's memory, and then it can be called up by several writers or producers at the same time, who can use it in different ways for different time periods.

Digital technology also helps organizations such as NEWSCHANNEL 8, an all-news cable channel in the Washington, D.C., area, split some of its segments into three simultaneous feeds that feature news of particular interest to viewers in Virginia, Maryland, or the District of Columbia. Digital technology also moves video from government buildings to Washington news bureaus.

Digital technology makes it possible to plug the camcorder output into a telephone outlet, and send video around the world. The Associated Press has built a television news service on the premise that you can slow down a digital video feed in order to send it over low-quality telephone or data circuits, and then play this slow-speed transmission at regular speed during its scheduled worldwide distribution of news video. If the pictures don't have to be used live, this method of transmitting TV pictures overcomes many communication problems found in less developed parts of the world.

Other Applications

Some of the new tools for television journalism include: ultralight camcorders; video transmission over telephone wires; better and more creative editing; multipurpose work stations where writing, editing, and graphics can be produced by one person.

Automation will cut down on studio production jobs, and allow newsrooms to distribute news broadcasts to a variety of outlets.

ENG and SNV vehicles won't disappear, but they will get either (1) smaller, or (2) more versatile by carrying more equipment in the same space. These vehicles may decrease in numbers over time as alternative means of transmitting video back to the newsroom become readily available.

Portable satellite uplinks will multiply and become smaller. Portable uplinks have been used extensively to cover major news events like the Gulf War and the invasion of Haiti, but they still require a dozen or so cases of equipment, accessories, and power generation equipment.

Reporters will switch to **PCS telephones**, small personal telephones that they will carry with them all the time. Eventually, video will be transmitted back to the newsroom from these phones. Video is already being transmitted via cellular telephones.

Message relaying and portable computing equipment will get smaller and more efficient, making each reporter a walking (or driving) news bureau. It is possible that someday reporters will carry all the equipment now available in SNG and SNV trucks in personal automobiles.

Imagine grabbing your briefcase (containing ALL of your technical equipment), suitcase and plane tickets, and flying off to Uzbekistan to cover a civil war for the network!

WHITHER VIDEO JOURNALISM?

Today's video journalism hasn't changed the traditional internal structure of newsrooms too much. It requires: reporters, videographers, writers, technicians, editors, producers, anchors, and managers. A few specialized occupations have been created by ENG and SNG technology and computers, but the way a television broadcast is prepared differs little whether it is transmitted over the air, via cable, or over a satellite transponder. Most of these traditional positions will exist for a long time to come. What may change is the emphasis on a particular job category.

"Video On Demand"

One of the concepts offered by futurists suggests if we use digital and compression technology to massively expand the number of TV channels we can deliver to a home, we won't be able to fill all those channels with programming.

What will the media industries do with the added capacity? They will use it to provide movies, programs, information and news "on-demand." This concept is similar to the services offered by Home Box Office (HBO) or a closed-circuit sports event. Instead of calling and ordering a special program (for an added fee), viewers will use their remote controls to "buy" programming they want. The content will be held in computers, and will be played to individual subscribers "on-demand" at the time the viewers select.

Early experiments with this technique, such as those by Time-Warner Corp. in Orlando, Florida, would have viewers ordering whole news broadcasts. This is the same as **time-shifting**, when you tape a program and view it later.

The long-term idea is to be able to put menus on the screen, and let viewers select what segments, and even what news items, they want to look at. Theoretically, the viewer would be "producing" his or her own news broadcast.

How would "news stories on demand" affect journalists?

Some analysts predict the focus will swing toward reporters, who may produce their own finished stories, perhaps without a producer's oversight. This view could mean the reporter does the research, shoots the video, conducts the interviews, does the writing, edits the piece, and then sends it to a computer.

This raises serious questions. Among them: How many skills should one person be expected to have? How is "editorial balance" achieved if editorial oversight is removed? What about the legal liability individual reporters might face for defamation or invasion of privacy?

In the mid-1990s, a rapid expansion in the number of broadcast newsrooms due to the growth of the Fox Network and the addition of regional cable news channels, created a shortage of producers. The news-on-demand scenario we just described suggests that eventually, there might be fewer rather than more producers.

Writers who can edit video may find they have more to do as more organizations reprocess their inventory of news video to fit different uses.

Anchorpeople will be needed, but they will have to offer additional skills, such as writing and editing. They will work harder, in terms of time spent actually reading copy on-camera, and the number of "star" anchors with the seven-figure salaries may go lower.

Technical personnel will have to perform more tasks, but are likely to be asked to do the more complicated tasks, leaving simpler duties to others who will use "foolproof" devices.

In fact, while there will probably be traditional newsrooms, the question is—how many?

News-on-demand suggests that the news selected might be commercial-free. This and fractionalization of news outlets might diminish the traditional advertising support of most news broadcasts.

No one knows whether we will actually have a "video-on-demand" world. The basic question is: do consumers want to select and shape their viewing (in micro segments), or do they prefer to have some help or guidance in organizing the information? It's a "couch potato" question. Will the majority of viewers sit on the couch and watch established channels?

PREPARING FOR A CAREER

There are some truths we should remember, however, as the new world of cascading channels of information flowing into homes develops.

- Communication and journalism skills will be needed, probably more communicators will be needed, not less. So far, no one has built a robot which can go to City Hall, find a legal parking space, work the building to collect news, and then attend the city council meeting and come up with a story twenty minutes before airtime!

- Careful preparation now can pay tremendous dividends in the future. Students who learn as much as possible about all the skill areas, and practice enough to demonstrate professional abilities in several areas will be best prepared to meet the challenges.

- We all like to think technology, and in fact the world itself, will remain pretty much the same as it was when we were in college. That just won't happen. Nothing ever stays the same, and our world seems to change ever more quickly. Don't fight change, adapt!

- Take advantage of fellowships, scholarships, courses, advanced degrees. Education has become a lifelong task. Make if fun and useful, by planning.

- Special skills, such as advanced computer knowledge, graphic arts skills, second or third language ability, can lead to exciting new opportunities.

- Special knowledge can be marketed. Business, finance, science, medical, education and other specialized reporters will find challenges.

- Americans are becoming more "internationalist." Our nation has been labeled as "isolationist" by some since its founding, but modern communications technology and better transportation are changing trade, politics and business, and we must know more about the rest of the world. University overseas programs, foreign scholarships and fellowships, and personal travel offer opportunities to jump on the international information superhighway.

- Consume information. Read a wide range of "trade" publications, including the ones that address technology. Read and view sources of daily news other than your local media. Find out as much as you can about what other people are doing. Journalism is about what goes on in the world, not what goes on in one newsroom. Every time you go to the reading room or library, read a publication you have never looked at before.

- Belong to professional organizations and create a network of friends and acquaintances. You need constant input when an industry is changing, and it never hurts to know people who can explain changes, or help you refocus your career.

STILL WORKING . . . AND CHANGING:
THE HELICOPTER

Eye in the Sky

Of all the things technology has brought to local TV news, the arrival of the helicopter—"Skycam," "Skyeye," "Flycam,"—has brought controversy, booming promotion, and a whole set of costs, opportunities, and worries to the television newsroom staff.

The use of helicopters in broadcasting is not a recent development. Radio news reporters have used helicopters for years to cover traffic during rush hour. ENG and portable microwave equipment made possible the coverage of television news by helicopter. Management discovered that television news and the helicopter were made for each other. The uniqueness of the chopper in the pursuit of breaking news is well established. Certainly it was a prime tool in the skies over Los Angeles in coverage of the O. J. Simpson chase and arrest following Nicole Simpson's death. No fewer than seven news helicopters followed the Simpson vehicle along Los Angeles freeways and streets—a spectacle in TV news annals that will be examined and debated by social scientists, TV industry critics, and journalism commentators for years to come.

A helicopter equipped with elaborate radio communication systems and a microwave receiver and transmitter can be used as a platform in the sky that can deliver live pictures and from-the-air commentary. It can also relay pictures and sound from the news story on the ground back to the station's receiving antennas. A fully equipped helicopter can cost a million dollars or more. It provides room for a pilot and a videographer, and for up to four persons in larger models. Helicopter pilots require special training and licensing, and they operate under stringent rules regarding health and safety requirements. Pilots by necessity are more concerned with rules of the Federal Aviation Administration than they are about the broadcasting rules of the Federal Communications Commission.

Problems with Helicopters

Choppers have good uses and bad uses. The cost is stiff; at a Louisville station, the helicopter budget allocation for six months was spent in the first six weeks of use. Most stations learned quickly that the worst use of a helicopter is to send it up in the morning looking for some news. The "it's-a-dull-day-maybe-the-eye-in-the-sky-will-find-something" syndrome faded rapidly as the bills came in.

Beyond that, the helicopter can't fly in bad weather. It can't fly just anywhere you want; flight paths are regulated around airports and in controlled airspace. Even though the bird is tethered to a landing pad on the roof of the station or in the backyard, a flight plan and permission from air traffic control is required.

When important people or big crowds are on the ground, no helicopter is allowed to fly directly overhead. The Secret Service does not allow helicopters to twirl down for a closeup when the president is attending an event.

Use of a chopper for news coverage may stir up other controversy. A news account quoted a Union Carbide official at a company plant in Charleston, West Virginia, as recommending that air space in areas affected by chemical leaks be restricted. The recommendation came following an incident involving a chemical leak at the plant, and a TV station's helicopter coverage of it. The company complained that the chopper's hovering over the plant site was blowing fumes around. The helicopter pilot responded that he kept his craft at a safe distance and added he thought the real motive of the company proposal was to keep media away from news potentially damaging to the company.

San Francisco harbor authorities accused a San Francisco station's chopper crew of causing the Coast Guard difficulty in recovering the body of a woman who had jumped from the Bay Bridge. The Coast Guard said the wash from the helicopter blades forced the body under the surface just as a crewman was about to retrieve it with a grappling pole. The station's manager denied the charge, adding coldly that a review of the tape showed the woman was dead anyway.

Helicopters are more dangerous than other kinds of aircraft. Stations and networks have had fatal accidents. If the engine fails the helicopter is supposed to "spiral down" like a maple seed, but if it is too low in the first place, the landing is much more like a crash than what is called an "auto-rotate descent." In densely populated areas or crowds, a crash could be disastrous. Add to ownership cost the hefty liability insurance policy premiums.

Shooting pictures from a helicopter is not easy. Even with the latest stabilizing gyroscopes, there is some vibration from the helicopter blades. It is relatively easy to get stable wide shots but it is quite difficult to get good closeups with the zoom lens fully extended because the vibration is magnified along with the rest of the picture. Even wide shots present problems. A lot of moving wide shots, with the major point of interest disappearing under the ship, or even slow circles that change the aspect of the scene as the ship moves around, do not provide a good visual reference point for the viewer. Such scenes also do not provide the closeups and details that make a story visually interesting.

STILL WORKING . . . AND CHANGING: THE SATELLITE

A satellite news-gathering system is the space-age equivalent of a ground-based microwave system. Twenty-two thousand, three hundred miles above the earth's equator is a parking lot for geostationary communications satellites.

Satellites come in various shapes and sizes. Some look like giant helicopter blades. Others are spherical—about the same size as a big above-ground outdoor swimming pool—with a fan-shaped antenna on top. All are covered with solar power cells. All are draped with other antennas of all kinds.

Let's review a few terms:

Geostationary satellite: This is a satellite that is placed into orbit about 22,300 miles above the earth's equator. It flies in the same direction as the earth turns and at a speed that, at that altitude, is the same as that of the earth's rotation. Therefore in effect it stands still.

Communications satellite: This satellite contains receiver-transmitters that can receive signals transmitted from the ground and retransmit the

Figure 10.1. A satellite ground station. The large dish antennas can send or receive signals from geostationary satellites located about 22,300 miles above the equator. A large installation such as this one is sometimes called a satellite farm. *(Courtesy of GTE Spacenet Corporation.)*

signals back to the ground. It is powered by batteries charged by solar cells.

Uplink: A transmitter on the ground that sends signals to the satellite.

Downlink: A receiver on the ground that receives signals from a satellite.

Transponder: The receiver-transmitter in the satellite that receives the signals from the uplink and retransmits them on the downlink.

C-band: That part of the electromagnetic spectrum between 3.7 and 4.2 gigahertz assigned for United States satellite use.

Ku-band: That part of the electromagnetic spectrum between 11.7 and 12.7 gigahertz assigned for United States satellite use.

Footprint: The area on the ground covered by the satellite downlink transmission.

Figure 10.2. A tornado that television viewers were able to watch. The KARE-TV, Minneapolis, Minnesota, helicopter flew around this tornado in northern Minneapolis for more than an hour, feeding live shots of the twister as it developed, ripped through a manufacturing and storage complex, and dissipated in a suburban forest area. *(Courtesy of KARE-TV.)*

The satellite is an electronic backboard in space. It can be used to "bounce" radio frequencies between two points that are a great distance apart at ground level. In the United States, most of the satellites used for SNG have a footprint large enough to cover the entire continental United States. As with ground-based microwave systems, the super-high-frequency signals do not bend, so the antennas must be aimed carefully and must have line-of-sight between the earth station and the satellite in space.

In 1965 just one geostationary satellite, called Early Bird, flew above the Atlantic Ocean. It provided 240 telephone circuits and one quite fuzzy black-and-white television channel between Europe and the United States. By 1969 a global system operated by the International Telecommunications Satellite Organization—**Intelsat** for short—was in place. Today Intelsat is a consortium of over 100 nations that supervises a globe-girdling system of satellites providing much of the international telephone and data traffic and a majority of all international television exchanges as well as domestic telecommunications for many member nations. Other systems are INTERSPUTNIK (a Russian consortium); INMARSAT (used to link land-based telephone and Telex with ships at sea); a raft of regional satellite systems with names like EUTELSAT (for Europe), ARABSAT (for the Arab League countries); and domestic sys-

Figure 10.3. AT&T's Telstar 4 Satellite. Communications satellites can simultaneously receive and retransmit multiple paths of traffic. SNG trucks lease time on satellites to send and receive pictures and sound of news reports and special live broadcasts, and to exchange news stories. *(Courtesy of AT&T.)*

tems that serve Australia, Brazil, Canada, China, India, Indonesia, Japan, Mexico, and Russia.

In the United States, the C-band satellites came first. PBS was the first to deliver all its programs to its affiliates by satellite. CNN, the Cable News Network, went heavily into C-band satellites to set up its twenty-four-hour news network and is the granddaddy of the satellite news systems. Using the Turner Broadcasting Service antenna farm in Atlanta, CNN gained simultaneous access to as many as eleven satellites, including both C- and Ku-bands.

For a while C-band was all that was available. C-band was reliable and sturdy, and overcame interference from storms. Its disadvantage was that the satellites shared frequencies with ground-based microwave systems. The FCC required anyone setting up a C-band ground station to make an exhaustive survey to be sure its transmissions would not interfere with others in the same area. The FCC required the same information to be filed when a portable C-band link was set up. It was difficult to come sweeping up on a spot news story with such restrictions.

Ku-band offered the answer for news operations. It did not share frequencies with anything else. Therefore higher-power amplifiers and smaller dishes could be used to uplink to the satellites from any location, and the satellite's antenna could concentrate its return signal into a narrower beam; thus smaller antennas were okay on the receiving end, thus making portability much less of a problem.

A Satellite Culture

Initially the daily use of satellites to deliver raw videotape, story packages, and live broadcasts was thought of as a "network" kind of activity. ABC, CBS, and NBC had the facilities and the world-wide news coverage organizations. They used satellites to cover world news and to ship material back to their New York headquarters. Then CNN came along and built its cable news services with satellites as the basic foundation.

It is possible to fix a single date when the use of satellites for news gathering by local stations made a deep and lasting impression on these stations and their audiences. That was Tuesday, January 20, 1981, the day President Ronald Reagan was inaugurated. That was also the day Iran released the fifty-two Americans who had been held hostage in Iran for 444 days.

Never before had communication satellites been so important. In place were the networks' inaugural coverage plans. More stations than ever before would cover the local angles of the ceremonies with their own reporters in Washington.

During the weekend before the inauguration a break in the hostage story had been strongly indicated. The networks' long-standing contingency plans for covering the hostage return went into high gear. These included not only coverage from the Middle East and Europe but also coverage of the hostages' families in their home towns all over the country. Elaborate plans to dispatch network correspondents to "stake out" the hostage families were made. Sometimes that wasn't so easy; many small towns were difficult to reach and had no satellite facilities, let alone land lines that could be used to transmit videotape of family reactions. A number of hostage families didn't want the publicity. The mother of one hostage retreated to the family summer home in a remote mountain location and told a nosy network correspondent she wouldn't come down until she heard something official.

As the hostage story got hotter so did the interest of local stations. It became even more important that they have their own people in the nation's capital. On January 19, Iran announced it had reached an agreement through Algerian diplomats to release the hostages in return for U.S. concessions. By the time of the inauguration the next day—noon in Washington—almost everyone was sure both things would happen at the same time. They almost did except for one final irony: The Iranians waited to let the hostages' plane take off from Tehran until just a few minutes after President Carter stepped down and handed the leadership over to President Reagan.

That evening the whole world watched as the Algerian airliner carrying the hostages landed in Algeria. Network correspondents in the United States (one of whom had spent weeks memorizing the faces of the hostages from

Figure 10.4. The Americans held hostage in Iran on their return to the United States. On the day the hostages were released and President Reagan was inaugurated, and on the days that followed, satellite use by American networks and individual stations was at the highest level in history. *(AP/Wide World Photos.)*

still picture files) did a flawless play-by-play narration as live pictures of the hostages coming down the plane's steps flowed in, by satellite, from Algerian television. For the first time we knew that all fifty-two had been released. They were counted, live, as everyone watched. A few moments later then-Assistant Secretary of State Warren Christopher took charge, and United States military planes flew the hostages to Frankfurt, Germany, on their way home at last.

American television and its viewers were thankful the Algerians had the satellite connection on January 20, 1981. One top network television executive suggested that RTA, the Algerian television network, should get an Emmy for its coverage of a major world news story.

The hostage return story didn't remain a "network story" for very long. Scores of local TV stations sent crews to Frankfurt to get the first interviews with hostages from their areas. Hundreds were on hand when the hostages landed at West Point and later when they arrived in Washington.

From that day on the local television stations around the nation looked at satellites in another way—as local reporting tools and ways to deliver information.

The Satellite As Delivery Service

Satellite downlinks are being used as delivery systems. Both American wire services, AP and UPI, use satellites to deliver their services. Both CNN and CNN II Headline News are delivered by satellite to cable systems and to stations that are affiliated with them. PBS and NPR deliver all of their programs by satellite. Group-owned stations have combined to share satellite costs so that they can get same-day and/or live news feeds from their Washington bureaus.

Satellites are being used to share news on an informal basis and to form new networks. Those stations that have both downlink and uplink facilities have the world at their fingertips. By having the ability to send and receive, stations can make permanent or temporary arrangements with other stations in other parts of the country to get news of local interest.

Satellites are being used for special coverage by the station's own anchors, reporters, and videographers. We are not talking here about the once-every-few-years trip to Washington to interview a homestate senator or to a national political convention where a homestate politician is a candidate for high office. Nor are we talking about the occasional coverage of a national story with strong local ties, like the return of the American hostages from Iran in 1981. We are talking about how satellite technology changed the definition of what local news is.

IT'S NOT JUST A TRUCK ANYMORE

Another technical step for local stations came with the development of the Ku-band technology and the satellite ground station on wheels. Station news managers were familiar with an ENG van. It was a basic tool and the way to get to the news within 40 or 50 miles of the station. When an uplink and receiver were mounted on a truck, a station could go virtually anywhere and send back live pictures and sound by satellite.

A satellite live shot is much like a microwave live shot. While the reporter and videographer chase the news, a technician gets the truck ready and lines up the signals.

All SNVs must operate through a satellite control center. The SNV's satellite dish is retractable and steerable. After the vehicle is parked, an engineer raises, tilts and pans the dish to aim it at a specific satellite. A small amount of power is then supplied to the antenna. The SNV operator talks to the satellite control center to fine-tune the signal to the transponder and then to receive final clearance to transmit.

When the uplink connection is made with the satellite that also establishes the downlink transmission from the satellite. Since the footprint is very wide, that downlink signal is being seen by both the satellite control center and the SNV's home station.

Two-way voice communication between the truck and its station is estab-

Figure 10.5. A SNG news-gathering unit. A vehicle of this size can carry everything needed for anything from a live insert in a newscast to an all-out special broadcast. Cameras, VCRs, videotape editing equipment, portable microwave links, and on-board computers can make this a mobile newsroom. Either microwave or satellite connections can link it to its affiliate network, to its home station, or to other SNG units covering other angles of a major story. *(Courtesy of Conus Communications.)*

Figure 10.6. Inside an SNG van. SNG coordinators can receive and send satellite signals, take in video and audio from a number of sources, edit videotape, originate a live broadcast, or feed back on-the-spot material within minutes of arriving at a news story. Communications to coordinate such activities are often just as important as the satellite link itself, so the vans are equipped with telephones, two-way radios, and mobile and cellular phones, along with the more exotic satellite gear. *(Courtesy of Centro Corporation.)*

lished either as a signal carried on the band edge of a video transponder or with the use of another transponder dedicated solely to voice circuits. Technical matters completed, the broadcast of pictures and sound from the SNV to the station can begin.

Okay, We're Saturated . . .

That's what the SNV engineer says to the reporter when he or she is ready to begin a satellite feed.

SNVs differ in many ways making it difficult to generalize about them. They can be built as just an uplink with a satellite dish to transmit, or they can be equipped with production equipment for editing and dubbing. Prices vary accordingly. An uplink model can cost anywhere from $250,000 to $300,000. A truck equipped to edit can cost $500,000 or more depending on remote needs. Maintenance may add another $75,000 to $100,000 per year to the cost of ownership.

Many satellite trucks have what is called *redundancy,* which means they are equipped with two of everything necessary to transmit. If the primary system fails, the backup system is switched on. All but the smallest SNVs need

Figure 10.7. A smaller version of an SNG van. Getting to the news can be difficult for larger semi-trailer-type SNG vehicles. So some stations are equipping themselves with smaller units like this as a versatile alternative to the larger versions. *(Courtesy of Conus Communications.)*

ICC (Interstate Commerce Commission) licensing. The driver must have a commercial driver's license (**CDL**) and follow over-the-road regulations. Repairs of delicate equipment that breaks from being bounced over a corduroy road can add up to many thousands of dollars.

Yet most SNV owners say buying a vehicle is a sound investment and that they cannot do without one (or two!) in a competitive local market.

It Depends on What You Do with It . . .

Almost unanimously news directors whose stations own SNVs said they used them to put their newscasts on the road when they first got them. This was akin to the kind of promotional showmanship that accompanied the introduction of ENG. But most say it didn't last as long, and many felt that there were real benefits to moving their newscasts out of the studio and to the scene of major news from time to time. Many said they continue to use their SNVs to produce live stories about the scenery, culture, and unique areas of their states.

Most everyone agrees that SNV's primary use should be to cover spot news. A Texas news director: "I don't worry so much if the truck sits out back for a day or two, but I do get worried if it gets too far away from the station. We would never hear the end of it if we had another plane crash in Dallas, and the truck was in Amarillo."

In Baton Rouge: "The live truck on the scene is worth everything. Our market research shows that when the big story hits, people turn to us. We had five hurricanes within ninety days of buying that truck, and we covered them all . . . live. . . . The governor was put on trial twice in New Orleans eighty miles away . . . We covered teachers striking—not here, in the same old place, but in places we'd never have gone to before."

In Phoenix: "Spot news is more accessible now; you can focus attention on the place and the story in a more concentrated, attention-getting manner. And you can stay with a story longer, be less hit-and-run, making second-day angles and 'why it happened' a lot clearer."

In Pittsburgh: "It has saved us a number of times on spot news stories. Our terrain is hilly. The farther East we get, the more mountainous it becomes and the less effective the microwave [ENG] becomes."

SNG/SNV Factors

Controlling Costs

If there is an SNV owner who doesn't worry about the cost factors in owning one, he or she hasn't been found. It is not so much the purchase price or even the operational costs that matter. As with other elements of news coverage, logistics can damage the budget the most.

Transportation, housing, and feeding of staff costs more than transponder time. Special combinations of satellite hookups, ground-based microwave and communications packages can run the bill off the graph. Nobody sends the truck out in the hope it will find some news. Editors and assignment desk personnel must be cost conscious in dealing with SNVs.

SNV use by local stations has raised viewer expectations the same way ENG did. Once the audience learns that a station can use satellite technology, it assumes this will be done from that point on. Nobody wants to figure the cost in station prestige and, ultimately, lost viewers if their expectations for news coverage are not met.

Network-Local Relations

A major impact of SNG has been on the traditional relationships between the commercial networks and their affiliates. It has been popular to speculate about the "Death of Network News."

No longer does the local affiliate have to jump when the network makes demands. Independent SNG systems, such as Conus, CNN, and group co-ops, give the local stations many new avenues and partners to work with. "Old-boy networks," influenced by geography or composed of news directors and managers who know each other from previous jobs, journalism schools, or other professional contacts, have sprung up throughout the country and operate on a daily basis.

This has led to something that almost never happened before satellites: an ABC affiliate sharing material with an NBC affiliate, or a CBS station borrowing something from CNN. Not in the same city, mind you—not that much fraternizing! But the informal networks, the groups, and the independent SNG systems have ABC affiliates in Denver sharing videotape with CBS affiliates in Pittsburgh—or any other kind of cross-affiliation intercourse that you can imagine. And none of those involved apologize to anyone, except when, through a mistake or a slip in communication, something someone ships out to a friend shows up on a rival station in the same market.

All these new venues demand loyalties that siphon off the power of the national commercial networks to make their affiliates toe the line. In fact the affiliates have found that *they* can make the demands, and the networks have made moves to appease them. The current elaborate satellite-delivered news feeds, network cost sharing on the purchase of SNVs, and increased transponder time availability for affiliates followed heavy pressure from the networks' members.

Crowding on Interstate Skyways

Although a Ku truck can operate independently, it must observe some electronic manners. Satellites are lined up along the equator at 2-degree intervals. Therefore the truck's electronics must be able to operate within that 2-degree spacing. This calls for precision and careful maintenance to keep that precision. The trucks are also supposed to identify themselves in the material they are beaming up.

A more difficult issue is piracy. Nothing except signal scrambling prevents anyone from grabbing anything out of the air as it comes back down from a satellite. Entertainment channels such as HBO have resorted to scrambling. News people don't really support such scrambling. Yet everyone involved in SNG has a war story about material they developed that showed up on someone else's feed. There is no question that copyright and content-ownership laws apply. Yet the ease of use the systems bring means it's also easier for some to conduct themselves illegally or unethically.

A SNG Crunch

As the number of SNVs increases, transponder use goes up. Everyone wants to use the satellites for live feeds during the dinner hour and late news. And if it's a major breaking story, everyone wants to lead with it. This puts a premium on producers to make decisions and satellite coordinators to know how to get the signals from there to here the quickest way possible. Furthermore if a producer can't get a "window" at the top of the program, the story must be produced so that live material can be worked in whenever the window becomes available.

Reporters have had to learn to be even more careful about timing. When the satellite window opens, the reporter has got to be ready; when the window closes, it does so with the finality of a bank vault.

Watch Out for the News Drought

One element of SNG's great flexibility and outreach is frightening: the crunch that can develop almost instantly when even a fairly good story breaks on a slow news day. The stations in the market jump quickly to begin their coverage. And almost as quickly the phone starts to ring with calls from out-of-town stations wanting some coverage.

In the days before SNG, a station could spend a lot of precious time making dubs of videotaped material and getting the tapes to the airport. Now, stations can simply put their live coverage up on a satellite transponder and let everyone interested know where it is. Or they can edit a package of material and send it up at a certain time.

But the problems multiply when out-of-town stations want to send their own crews and use the local station's SNV to uplink. Or the out-of-town stations want the local station's already stretched-out staff to do feeds, including especially tailored throws to out-of-town anchors.

Lastly—and this bears repeating—we continue to see indications that news judgments may get twisted simply because a live satellite shot is possible. Many SNG news operations report that stories can almost take on a life of their own with SNG. Because the SNV is on the scene, a report will be filed, and another, and another. Pretty soon the truck—not the event it went to cover—is the story, and the technology is running the journalism.

Co-opting the Traditional News System

The year 1994 was marked by yet another milestone in the brief history of satellite news gathering. In July of that year, Conus Communications of Minneapolis-St. Paul, observed its tenth anniversary. Stanley S. Hubbard II, owner of KSTP-TV and other communications interests, formed Conus in July, 1984, thus becoming a pioneer of Ku-band satellite news gathering, becoming the first—it is still the largest—cooperative of local U.S. television broadcasters and international news organizations.

Hubbard got a group of television broadcasters in other cities to join Conus in a SNG cooperative. Members using trucks equipped with Ku-band satellite uplinks connected through Conus Master Control in Minneapolis-St. Paul via satellite transponders, to achieve coordination of live television coverage of news from virtually anywhere in the United States. Hubbard's venture included a subsidiary company that manufactured the trucks and equipped them with the satellite uplinks and TV news production equipment so they became newsrooms on wheels.

Hubbard even brokered the news product. The functional idea was simplicity itself. A station bought into the Conus Cooperative and became a limited partner. It bought a truck—although that is not a requirement for membership—and started covering news anywhere it wanted to go. When the station wanted to send that news back to its home studio, the crew in the truck fired up its satellite uplink and called Conus in Minneapolis-St. Paul. There, Master Control set up time on the transponders, helped the truck fine-tune its uplink (it takes about thirty seconds), and then relayed the story by way of another transponder back to the home station. If a live report was wanted, a specific time on a transponder was set, and the reporter did it on cue, just as if he or she were down at city hall.

Since Conus was a cooperative and not connected to a commercial network, all members could share news or have access to any other member's news simply by recording it or taking it live as it was returned to earth on the downlink. The independence from network affiliation meant that stations dealt with each other through Conus, not through the affiliate relations setup of the network in New York.

Networks traditionally, and by contract, demanded loyalty from their affiliates. They were to broadcast the networks' news programs and provide coverage and facilities in their area if asked. In return the networks provided a news feed of national and international stories once or twice a day.

By September of 1984 Conus was ready to start its news service providing daily feeds to a handful of stations across the country. The feeds were made up of stories covered by its members, cooperative stories contributed by ad hoc groups formed to cover regional news in a given region, and from other sources both domestically and abroad.

To member broadcasters Hubbard's setup seemed an idea whose time had come. The cooperative was in business only because it had members, so a new loyalty developed—to Conus first and then perhaps the network. And stations could deal with anyone they wanted to deal with in another city.

Today Conus, Tomorrow the World?

As it grew, Conus took on larger aspirations reflecting the ambitions and inspirations of its owner and the impact of satellite news-gathering technology.

In 1985 it established a bureau in Washington, D.C., to provide coverage of the nation's capital to its members, and a year later it began producing TV Direct, a concise news service that localized national news by delivering events and issues in Washington to member stations. TVDirect steadily expanded its reach to include live coverage of such events as presidential news conferences; and White House, State Department, and Pentagon briefings.

By 1988, the cooperative having grown to nearly eighty members, its international reach was extended when Fuji-TV, Japan's largest commercial broadcaster, became a Conus participant. By 1989 Conus had ninety-three members in six countries, including Network 10 of Australia. It signed on seven more stations toward the end of that year, marking the 100-member milestone. It was also 1989 when Conus began producing the *All News Channel* in a joint venture with Viacom Satellite News Inc.

From the start, Conus took a leadership role in developing regional inter-

Figure 10.8. The Conus nerve center, Minneapolis-St. Paul, Minnesota. The nerve center links a member station's SNG van at a news event through a communications satellite to the van's home station. This control center handles many paths of traffic simultaneously, but 1500–1930 Hours EMT (Eastern Military Time) is busiest. *(Courtesy of Conus Communications.)*

est. The cooperative was quick to jump on a live story and to hook into a member station's live coverage to provide it for all members via satellite. In February of 1991, the company divided the operation into regions. Nine regional feeds were added daily, hub stations were established in each region, and a regional manager was assigned to each region to coordinate coverage. It was also in 1991 that Conus signed a ten-year agreement for satellite capacity, assuring its operations into the twenty-first century. International expansion included deals with GATS—Global Access Telecommunications Services—to create an international satellite system, and with News Network in Budapest, Hungary to establish a fixed uplink.

Founder Hubbard from the beginning has been evangelistic about his satellite news cooperative. His view is that his business gives individual local stations independence from their network and lets them cover breaking news anywhere in the country. "It has," he said, "returned to local station management the ability to decide how a national story should be covered in order to be most meaningful for the viewers in the local market."

Charles Dutcher III, President and General Manager of Conus, has been equally forceful in his analysis of Conus impact. Reviewing the first decade of the cooperative, Dutcher said:

What started out as a good idea using advanced technology has turned into a company that has revolutionized television news. We have forced the networks and CNN to develop news sources in response to stations needs, yet we have remained the force providing local stations the improved ability to cover national news. We have become the service-oriented news organization stations have deserved for many years. Even in uncertain times, our members know they can count on us to be there for them.

Group Organizations

Another set of players in the SNG game are group-owned stations. These consist of stations with a common ownership located in markets around the country. One of the most organized is the group of stations owned by the Gannett Company.

This big newspaper chain was very aggressive in the 1980s in developing its broadcast division. With stations in Washington, D.C., Minneapolis-St. Paul, Oklahoma City, Denver, Atlanta, Boston, Jacksonville, Greensboro, Austin, and Phoenix, it established its own Washington-based broadcast bureau and a policy of group loyalty among its station news operations.

Here again, sharing facilities and coverage worked as a multiplier. Gannett newspapers long supported the Gannett News Service (GNS) to cover major stories for its papers and to share stories among its papers. It also established a broadcast arm of GNS in Washington, D.C., to provide coverage for its stations. That service then expanded to include a number of reporter-videographer crews to cover the federal government on a regular basis and be on call for special assignments, including a flying squad ready to go anywhere in the world to provide coverage for the group.

Each of the Gannett-owned stations got a SNV, and since the policy is to share, the group can mount a major effort on a story in a hurry.

Traditional network affiliate loyalty has been superseded by a loyalty to a closer and more dominant influence: the company that issues the paychecks. But it is also clear that the Gannett stations see their horizons broadened by satellite technology, giving their stations the ability to work together on stories of national as well as local interest.

AN SNG WATERSHED: THE POPE'S 1987 AMERICAN VISIT

Just as the release of the American hostages held in Iran marks a significant date in the history of ENG, the trip of Pope John Paul II to the United States in the fall of 1987 was a watershed event in the history of SNG.

For the first time on such a large scale, local television news operations took over from the commercial networks the primary responsibility for continuing coverage of a major running story as the pope moved through nine cities in ten days. While the networks covered the story for their own news programs and provided aid and counsel through their affiliate satellite news systems, the major coverage was planned and carried out by local stations and local pools. For the first time it really didn't matter how the national networks covered the story. ENG/SNG technology, network affiliate exchange systems, syndicate co-ops, such as Conus, and ad hoc networks made extensive live coverage possible. Satellite transmission of the stories from station reporters and pool pictures from each city made hours of material on the story available to anyone with a downlink. Even if a station was not involved in any of these, the Roman Catholic Church picked up the pool signals and made them available by satellite to anyone who wanted them, free of charge.

Long-Range Planning

It would be expected that the TV stations in the cities the pope was going to visit would plan and carry out extensive coverage. They've done so each time the pontiff has visited the United States. They did it again this time. In Miami, the Carolinas, New Orleans, San Antonio, Phoenix, Los Angeles, Monterey, San Francisco, and Detroit, planning began six and even eight months in advance, usually with the local Catholic diocese.

Stations in Miami, New Orleans, and Los Angeles, which compete intensely every year to provide the "best-most-widest-longest" coverage of football bowl festivals, had blueprints and plans they could dust off and adapt. Yet local pools and production and technical committees worked for months to set up the coverage. The Florida News Network provided SNG vans and personnel. Some Miami stations broadcast as many as sixteen hours of programs about the pope's stay there. WSVN-TV said it produced the most extensive single-story coverage in its history. It used six microwave links and ten live cameras for its own coverage. At one point just staying on the air was a problem as a wild thunderstorm over Miami forced the pope to stop an open-air Mass, and several technicians were slightly injured by a lightning strike.

The New Orleans and Los Angeles stations did fourteen-hour stints, and at the end of the trip, a Detroit station stayed on the air throughout the night the pope stayed in suburban Hamtramck.

For WIS-TV in Columbia, South Carolina, the six hours the pope spent there called for a maximum effort that brought in WBTV, Charlotte, North Carolina, WYFF-TV, Greenville, South Carolina, and WCSC-TV, Charleston, South Carolina, to pool people and equipment. The result was live coverage at each local papal stop.

Sharing was the name of the game at most locations. Some of it got pretty complicated: WYOU-TV, Scranton, Pennsylvania, a CBS affiliate and a member of CBS's syndicated affiliate news service, sent its satellite truck to Colum-

Figure 10.9. When the pope travels, the media are close by. The pontiff travels in a special van dubbed the "Popemobile." That vehicle not only provides security and visibility. It is also a mobile studio. It can generate a close-up TV picture of the pope, which can be microwaved so that it can be inserted into local broadcasts. *(Reuters/Bettmann Newsphotos.)*

bia, South Carolina, to serve as the network's syndicate facility there. WYOU anchor Russ Spencer went to Miami for the pope's arrival; weekend anchor Beth Powers went to Columbia. Spencer's and Powers' reports with interviews of Scrantonites who were meeting the pope ran live and back-to-back in the station's major newscasts—all accomplished by the satellite setups in three different cities.

Other examples:

WOTV-TV Grand Rapids, Michigan, used its membership in the Michigan News Exchange Cooperative to get help from WDIV-TV Detroit to set up a motor home at the Pontiac Silverdome as an editing base, and used the Group W Satellite truck to get its stories from the papal Mass at the Silverdome back to Grand Rapids.

KIRO-TV, Seattle, Washington, used its network satellite links and cooperative friends in Los Angeles to cover both Masses the pope celebrated while he was in Los Angeles.

Many stations from medium and even small markets sent reporters to cover some or all of the pope's stops. At each point these reporters usually lined up with their network affiliate services to use editing equipment or plug in their own, and to uplink their reports back to the stations. Most affiliates had high praise for the help provided by their networks. Conus established a special extra-cost papal trip unit, feeding very frequent update reports during most days and providing extra windows for members' coverage and virtually round-the-clock uplinking of the various pool pictures.

Coverage Closeups

WBRZ-TV, Baton Rouge, Louisiana, was a part of the New Orleans pool; it ran more than ten hours of its own broadcasts and fed the ABC-TV and affiliate satellite network all at the same time. It accomplished this with a simple but subtle plan that was—and is—instructive because, despite heavy security around the pope, it used all the advantages of a large high-tech facilities pool while allowing the station to maintain its own identity.

In New Orleans the ground rules worked out by the pool forbade the building of anchor sets along the parade routes and also ruled out microwave or satellite transmissions from any of the event sites. Therefore the pool provided video coverage from ten event locations, while open coverage was allowed from just four spots.

WBRZ-TV set up its satellite truck and cameras across the street from the New Orleans cathedral and then moved to another location for the next day's parades and events. Using an anchor team in the home studio in Baton Rouge, the incoming pool signal, roving camera/reporter teams, and the satellite truck as a remote broadcast point at New Orleans' Jackson Square, the station was able to mix its own coverage with the pool and anchor the whole thing with its own personnel.

Skip Haley, then WBRZ-TV assistant news director, said that it was important to highlight the station's presence in a broadcast that contained a lot of pool material and ran for many hours. He said, "We concentrated on the people who were there, not so much on the ceremonies that were going on—'Why are you standing here for four hours to see this man who you'll never see again?' We also carried ten hours of the events. It is important that you provide the whole thing, but put your own reportorial stamp on it."

And they used the station's computer system to manage the coverage. They carved a video editing room from a suite of hotel rooms and wired the computer system back to the station and to the satellite truck. That enabled them to see all scripts from any location, to create scripts and other "on-air words" for all on-air staff, and to manage the flow of dozens of videotape packages they created.

Haley said that the broadcast could have been done without SNG, but that it would have been much more expensive, and the station would have been much more limited, and much less flexible, in its coverage. He said:

> The truck probably cost two thousand dollars for a thing like that; hard-wiring the circuits through the telephone company instead of using the satellite would have run it up to between eight and ten thousand dollars just for the lines. And, of course, the pool and our own

roving camera/reporter teams gave us a huge amount of interesting program material to choose from.

In Phoenix, where among other events the pope met with Native American tribal leaders, a lot of advance planning and a history of cooperation among broadcasters seem to have been crucial to what one news director called "an incredible amount of work, incredibly expensive, and incredibly fun television."

KTSP-TV News Director David Howell said the event was the biggest challenge that any of the local stations had ever faced: "We couldn't have done it without the pool—we each could not have covered all the elements of the story—and so the pool gave us a chance to go all out together."

Behind it, however, is an interesting connection to another issue in broadcast news—coverage of courtrooms. Howell explained: "Arizona is one of the states that has pioneered cameras in the courtroom, so there's this pattern of pooling together to get one camera in a courtroom and share the video."

Unlike the New Orleans situation, the local arrangements in Phoenix allowed for anchor locations to be established and built along parade routes, and the stations made good use of the press box at Sun Devil Stadium to cover a papal Mass.

Touchdown to Take-off

In Detroit, the pope's last stop, WDIV-TV provided all-out coverage of the visit along with an advance build-up to it that began months before. This included trips by a WDIV-TV documentary team to cover the pope's spring trip to Poland and to the Vatican in Rome to gather other material.

The WDIV-TV executive producer of news specials, Terry Oprea, developed a plan that was unique in its scope, depth, and creativity—a textbook example of the way local special-events producers can use satellite technology to expand and innovate elements for a local station broadcast that only networks would have attempted in the past.

"Without the satellites," Oprea said, "we would not have done it. Without satellites we would have had to piggyback on some of the network feeds, and that wouldn't have carried it through. The way we worked—signing up with a bunch of Group W stations for satellite time—we could get the time at a reasonable cost and when we needed it."

Oprea also felt the need to work up to the pope's visit over a period of time. He did this for two reasons. First, the audience needed to know much more about the pope; second, the news staff needed to become more familiar with the technology before it launched into heavy use under pressure.

"It was incremental," Oprea said. "First a trip to the Vatican with eight satellite feeds through NBC's facilities in four days. Then we went to Poland, gathered material for the documentary, and covered the hard news as the pope braced the Polish government over human rights. We were the only crew there when a demonstration became somewhat violent."

As the pope traveled across the country, a five-person WDIV-TV reporting team followed him. That team fed or went live by satellite fifty-four times in those nine days, providing fresh material for each major newscast and much of the content for nightly fifteen-to-thirty-minute news specials that followed the 11 P.M. news. The hour-long documentary, "The Polish Pope," played in prime time three days before the pope's arrival.

Preparations for WDIV-TV's broadcasts while the pope was in Detroit were just as extensive. Other reporter/camera/producer teams prepared more than forty packages for use during that time. Because that included Saturday morning, WDIV-TV even produced a series of packages about the pope that were prepared by children and aimed at the child audience on Saturday morning.

It's safe to say that both WDIV-TV and its audience were ready for the pope. Oprea then hauled out his final touch—the station would stay on all night while the pope slept in Hamtramck, a heavily Catholic Detroit suburb. WDIV-TV reporters gave live reports throughout the night as the station repeated some of its earlier coverage of the pope's arrival and its documentary.

The next day the pope met with the people of Hamtramck and with Catholic leaders and lay people, made a speech in Hart Plaza in downtown Detroit, said Mass in the Pontiac Silverdome, and left the United States in mid-evening.

The Detroit pool setup was elaborate. Thirty-five cameras were set up in thirteen different live locations. WDIV-TV helped out in the pool and in addition had six of its own live locations plus a roving ENG van to supplement the live pool coverage and prepackaged material.

Was it a success? Was it wise to devote that much time and so many resources to such an event? Oprea said "Yes":

> We proved a number of things. First: You can budget for such a series of events; our budget was in six figures, and we came quite close to those numbers.
>
> Second: The audience will be with you and will grow with the extension of your coverage. The ratings showed that at times we doubled the combined ratings of the other stations. The public reaction, based on the mail, was very strong and very positive.
>
> Third: We had about two hundred of the WDIV-TV staff of two hundred forty involved in this thing. A lot of our people who don't normally have much contact with the news department—advertising, public relations, promotion, community relations, administrators—were called in to help out with various parts of the preparations. They got caught up in it. . . . There was a very warm feeling throughout the station in the days that followed.
>
> Fourth: Sometimes I think we news people need to think about our own demographics. . . . A number of times I heard, "People don't care

about the pope," but 28 percent of the Detroit population is Catholic. . . . And it's clear they care about the pope, and that the non-Catholics in the audience will follow it as a story if you make it interesting and understandable to everyone.

MANAGING THE NEW TECHNOLOGY

From the very beginning of this book we have emphasized the need for the human mind, intelligence, judgment, and creativity to be brought to bear on technology. Nothing in the future of television news is more important than that.

Let's turn then to a discussion of how that can be done from operational, organizational, and philosophical points of view. The first step is to get the operational matters of the daily news function under tighter control.

The Tale of Two Newsrooms

There is a big difference in the size of newsroom staffs as you go from major-market, to medium, to small-market stations. That is due in large part to over-all station budgets and revenues—the cost of operation versus profit bottom line. To make this point more vividly, we compared the rosters of two newsrooms, WSET-TV, Lynchburg, Virginia, a small market (market rank in the 70–80 bracket) and KRON-TV, San Francisco, a top-ten market. The Lynchburg station news staff under News Director Rog Wellman consists of:

1 assignment editor

1 producer (who was the second anchor)

1 anchor

1 sports director

1 meteorologist

4 reporters

1 chief photographer

2 photographers

1 part-time photo editor

At the time of this comparison, the station had five full-time stringers, two of whom would come in on Sunday night to present the weather and sports segments for those programs. WSET-TV also had a full-time bureau in Roanoke staffed by a bureau chief, a reporter, and a photographer.

The newsroom table of organization:

| | | News Director | | |
Assignment Editor	Producer	Bureau Chiefs	Chief Photographer	Anchors
Assignments	Writing,	All bureau	Equipment,	Air work
Reporters	producing	matters	photographers	
Interns	the news			
Trainees				

This amounted to an easily understood setup that could handle the job of presenting the several thirty-minute WSET-TV daily broadcasts. In a setup such as this, a lot of responsibility falls on each staffer because everyone is required to do several parts of the news-gathering and producing job.

Contrast that with KRON-TV in San Francisco. At that same time the KRON staff included a news director, four associate news directors, a news editor, two ENG/SNG supervisors, seven people to work on the assignment desk, producers for each of the station's newscasts, and two coordinating producers. Other staff members:

16 editors

8 writers

23 ENG crews totaling 27 persons

An SNG technical crew and vehicle supervisors

32 reporters

In the station's bureaus:

San Jose Bureau: 3 reporters, 4 crews, 1 producer

Sacramento Bureau: 1 reporter, 5 photojournalists, 2 producers

East Bay Bureau: 2 reporters, 1 photojournalist, 1 editor

Washington Bureau: 2 reporters, 3 crews, a bureau chief (two other stations shared this bureau)

Including support personnel, four field producers assigned full time to the station's "Target 4" investigative unit, and five or six part-time employees, that made more than 130 people to keep track of.

KRON-TV produced nearly four hours of news daily, and hours of other news-related programs each week. This was by no means the largest television news staff in the country. In even larger cities like Los Angeles and Chicago, let alone New York City, the staff size and work volume are bigger, though the trend to downsizing throughout the industry has reduced some staffs significantly.

Newsroom Organization Ideas

It is time for a closer look at what is happening to news staff organization. We need to look at the ways television station news staff positions are being modified to help bring about product improvement and to help gain greater control over the technology that improves it. We have already made clear the impact of ENG/SNG on the news and the people who produce it. While it is true that newsroom organizational changes designed to cope with that impact have been slower to appear, changes to news staff organization nevertheless continue to occur.

TV newsrooms historically have been understaffed at the news management level. So the easy answer would be to hire more people. But where and to do what? More reporters and crews certainly are needed to cover the bigger menu of news opportunities, but the parallel need to bring more people into the management command chain is just as crucial. Seasoned professionals have come up with some ideas about that. These, in turn, should prompt beginners to study how the changes can become career opportunities. The following are career opportunities in this evolving picture:

More Assistant News Directors

Before ENG came to television news, if a station had one assistant news director you asked about featherbedding. Now often several persons have these jobs, each with specific duties.

One may be a business manager and budget supervisor. Another may handle such things as close contact with the newsroom staff, carrying out and enforcing editorial and operational policy. A third may deal solely with liaison with the technical staff. Another may be in charge of the increasingly important nonregular-news production. However the jobs are parceled out, someone near the top-management level is the in-house technical expert. Since there is so much technology to manage it requires people with special technical expertise and a feeling for the journalism to become the systems management leaders.

Director of News Operations

Besides assistant news directors, another management staff member may be in charge of the logistics and coordination of the technical functions and the news-gathering functions. That person probably commands the ENG/SNG coordinators and video producers who supervise the minute-by-minute use of technology to bring in and digest news stories.

A news director who developed this system said, "The director of news

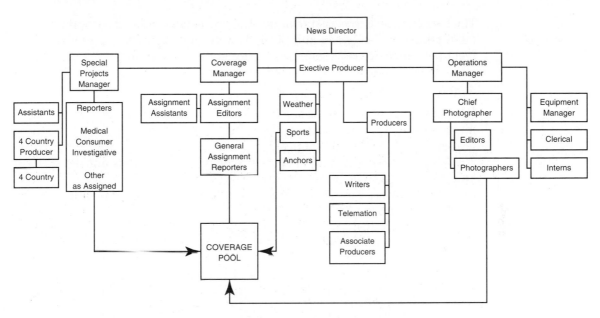

Figure 10.10. The newsroom table of organization at KDFW-TV, Dallas-Fort Worth, Texas. This structure was designed to provide a clearer chain of command, better technology management, and better management of the wide variety of news and public affairs programs the station produces. *(Courtesy of KDFW-TV.)*

operations handles before the fact, the producers and editors handle the facts, and the business manager handles after the fact."

Coproducers with Stepped Seniority

This structure is fairly common. One producer is "senior," the other is "associate." The associate producer handles all of the video, scripts, teasers, and bumpers, and also supervises the writing. The senior producer is in charge of the program order, reads the script carefully, edits it, changes it, times it, and makes sure the program gets on and off the air on time.

With these responsibilities clear, the executive producer then has the time to supervise all of this activity. He or she circulates, reads, makes suggestions, talks, cajoles, and orders things to be done with the focus on quality control and getting everyone to work as a team.

Since the news gathering of most TV stations is only as good as its (1) advance planning and (2) ability to react to a breaking story, there has been much tinkering with assignment-desk operation. Most of this tinkering is aimed at a sharper division of responsibilities.

An Assignment Manager

This person is in charge of day-to-day coverage. Ideas for stories are funneled to her or him from all directions: executives, producers, reporters, and crews.

The tactical operations that produce this coverage are the duty of the assignment manager—assigning and placing crews and reporters, moving them to meet new developments, and setting up technical support.

Assignment Editors

Note the word *editors*. It has significance because these people work on both immediate and future coverage, and their thoughts and actions have to be more journalistic than in the past.

Editors working on immediate items keep coverage going and get support and information to the reporters and crews in the field. They locate and identify additional sources or new angles and provide close liaison with the technical coordinators.

Editors who work on future planning are downstream in the news flow. They identify, consider, and evaluate stories for the following day or days and plan special coverage. As they do this, they identify both tactical and logistical problems—how to cover a story, and who and what to cover it with. They serve as an "early warning system" to identify news that should be covered and how best to do it.

A Los Angeles news director reflected on the importance of assignment planning and coordination in his newsroom:

> In the old days the assignment desk got everyone working as early as possible, and then drove them to get the visual material shot as early as possible.
>
> A lot of assignment desk guys ran it as if they were taxi dispatchers; get everyone where they were supposed to be, and then nag them to go faster.
>
> Now the technology allows you to work later, get later angles and use it to get the material back quickly or go live into the program. That takes a more journalistic person in the slot, and more planning behind it.

News executives say they are fighting a mindset that the traditional assignment system itself seems to generate. A former Los Angeles news director said a tyranny is built into the traditional assignment desk operation.

> In Los Angeles we would start out the day with thirty-five to forty-five stories assigned. Up on the wall was a big chart filled with the slug of each story, the crews and reporters assigned, and the time they started to work. Imagine, thirty-five to forty-five stories—because we had a three-hour dinnertime news program to fill.
>
> Well if you take that list seriously you've got yourself on a wheel. It's turning and you can't get off. The hardest thing to do is to break out of that locked-up schedule and meet the breaking news head on. The list on the wall becomes a work ethic; there are so many chores to perform and they all must get done.

A Boston executive producer called the assignment list "a security blanket."

> You have to plan to cover the obligatory news—the things that are important that you know are going to happen. You can't just come in in the morning with a happy face and say, "Gee, I wonder what's going to happen today." But we've got to find better ways to break loose from the routine and follow a story to its conclusion. Too many times I hear our desk personnel saying things like "Yeah, that would be fine, but I've got three other things for you to do then."

Beefing up the personnel on the assignment desk and setting short-term and long-term responsibilities for them will go a long way toward strengthening their essential function.

Reporter-Writer-Editor Teams

In most local TV newsrooms, reporters write the scripts for the stories they cover. Many times they edit these stories, too, or work with a technician to edit them. Because of the speed and volume of material ENG provides, local news executives are recognizing the need for more journalistic attention to what is said and shown, more editorial control.

Some news operations have reacted by installing writer-editors to work with the reporters on the material they have collected. Writer-editors may be in charge of the actual editing of the material, with the reporter on hand as a team member helping to shape the story into its final form. They often are called on to edit the story from notes dictated by the reporter still in the field. They serve as another pair of journalistic eyes on the production of the story. They ask about missing facts, unclear meaning, or the appropriateness of the visual material and the words that go with it. They help bring focus to the story. They provide another angle of thinking about the news judgment of the reporter, who was there and saw the story develop, and the news judgment of the producers, who have their own notions about how the story should be put together.

Quality Control

Most of these organizational changes are aimed at solving the news director's chief editorial concern: content quality control. News directors say that it is the editorial control of the words and pictures that suffers the most and is the biggest problem at a time of day when they have precious little time to make more reasoned judgments.

The producers, who are responsible for the entire program, want to come up with that mix of hard news, features, services, revelations, and illuminations that will be the most appealing and valuable to the audience. They want production elements, a high story count, and a sense of completeness. In Milwaukee, a TV managing editor said:

The system is almost too easy to use, and we've developed some people who are more interested in the TV side of it—the pictures—than they are about the facts, carefully and properly put into perspective. A major problem, because of the speed with which we can work, is that things get on the air before they have been looked at. We often have available more relevant pictures and facts. But we don't have a system that makes sure that someone takes a hard look at how the words and pictures go together and what their combined meaning is.

In Columbus, Ohio, a news director said he is *really* worried about the words. He put it this way:

We've got an awful lot of pretty newscasts in this country, and we have fewer that are informative. I didn't anticipate that when we went into ENG.

He added he thinks pictures can be addictive.

The staff spends all of its time looking at the pictures—"Let's see what the video has to offer"—and then they start worrying about writing the story. That slows down the whole process . . . and my problem is that I'm afraid we have left out the information in a lot of cases.

My producers keep telling me that we must be competitive with the production smoothness and visual impact of entertainment programs. But I'm worried about what we're saying, not what we're showing. If slickness and flash are the only way to bring the audience to your channel, it isn't going to last. Once you get the viewers there, you've got to make sure they understand it. If you don't, you're not going to keep them very long.

Toward an Information Department

Many competitors and potential competitors fight for television stations' news audiences. All-news cable channels operate twenty-four hours a day on a rotating schedule that provides for frequent repetition of major news stories. They emphasize spot news and will break into their regular pattern to go live at almost any moment. They keep on top of breaking sports stories, the markets, and the weather. They have regional bureaus. To cover other regional stories they make reciprocal arrangements with stations around the country to provide some of their coverage for the cable service.

Although the all-news cable services are aimed primarily to compete with the national commercial television networks, some local cable channels also carry some local information services. It might be a remote cablecast of city council proceedings or a high school sports event; it might be volunteer programming by civic, charitable or religious organizations using the cable local access channel; it might be coverage of special community events; it might be the cable's own highly local newscasts; or it might be local news inserts into special time blocks programmed into the cable's regular-fare menu of all-news services.

News directors and station managers closely watch cable and satellite-to-home systems even as they continue to respond to market forces and adjust their own product.

For example, it is not unusual for major regional stations to produce twenty to twenty-five hours of regular news programs per week. In addition some similar size stations are producing twenty-five to thirty hours a week of informational programming outside of their regular newscast schedule. This may include regular programs aimed at farmers and people living in rural areas. The stations also produce consumer information, "gripeline" material, public affairs, a magazine program, and sports. Some are even producing a separate newscast for other stations in their market that do not have news-rooms of their own. A producer said:

> [Before ENG] we wouldn't have dreamed of doing that much, but ENG and now satellite news gathering can help you do it, and do it rela-tively easily. There is an enormous amount of material out there that needs to be reported on . . . Some cries for the hard news approach . . . Other events are not so easy to pin down because you can't put a "this happened today" label on them. Some of it calls for longer, more sensitive treatment; some of it even falls into the soft entertainment sort of thing, but it is all informational.
>
> What we have to do is to begin to erase some of the traditional boundary lines in station organization and to revise our philosophy about what is news, what is entertainment, and what is public affairs. Our present organization has different units spread all over the build-ing . . . Some are in news, some in sports, some in production. All use the same equipment and all produce programs that are news related.

He referred to public affairs as an example. Broadcasters have always had a difficult time defining just what public-affairs programming is and how it dif-fers from news. The broadcasters do know they should do some of it and are happy to brag about it when license-renewal time comes around.

> For years now public affairs has been in the closet. They produced the Saturday afternoon panel show with the minister, the rabbi, the priest, and the black leader sitting around a table in the studio. That was about it.
>
> But ENG has taken public affairs out of the closet and into the neighborhoods and streets where it always should have been.
>
> With ENG they can do about anything they want to do, but it sure looks like more news, and it uses the same technology and resources.

Sports programming has also expanded.

Sports is all over the place. It used to be just the reports in the regular newscasts, or the games, and they had to fight for a camera crew to do interviews. Now they're all over the lot—at the stadium with live reports during the news, or producing specials about games and athletes from the area. They have much more flexibility, and that means more programs, more time, and more people.

What we need to do is form an information department that will stimulate, coordinate, and think of new things to do to meet new audience needs. This department would have overall responsibility for all information and would make sure that this unit and that unit were working in the same general direction.

Such a reorganization would, he said, do two important things. It would be more cost effective. And, it would tear down the walls now preventing creative people from thinking about the broader implications of, and needs for, information and using ENG to provide it.

THE LAST WORDS

. . . Let's thirteen it back to the truck, and two-gig it via Diablo for turnaround and wrap. The Washington site and wrap will be on K-2, Transponder 21.

Translation: Send it to the mobile van using a 13-gigahertz portable microwave transmitter and send it from the truck using the 2-gigahertz "dish" on top of the truck by way of the microwave receiver-transmitter on top of Diablo Mountain to the studio, where it will be edited into a package for the live reporter to include as part of his live report. The material from Washington bureau will be on Transponder 21 of the K-2 satellite.

That's the way some news people talk these days in local television newsrooms all over the country as they use ENG and all of its related marvels to gather and report the news. Everyday use of the new technology for local news gathering and broadcast is routine. It makes it possible to reach out farther and think bigger. The helicopter and the regional bureau lengthen the technological arm. The satellite makes the reach even longer.

As broadcast journalists ponder what is happening to TV news, one central question stays at the top: How can we use technology to do a better job?

Content Power

It is time for us to reaffirm and to restate our belief in the power of the content of the news. Television broadcasting is a very trendy business. News appetites get dull, then some development or dramatic event comes along and the audience turns back to the news. People come along with new formats, new production gimmicks, new "research" about air personalities. "Action News," "Eyewitness News," "Happy Talk" became all the rage because someone tried new formats and had new rating success. So a big part of the industry goes racing off in this or that direction—until someone discovers another idea—the tabloid format, for example—that gives them quick response in the all-important fall and spring ratings "books."

But we are in a craft that can broadcast live from the moon, replay repeatedly in slow motion the Super Bowl winning touchdown, freeze a face at the moment of victory or defeat, show the exact split second a bullet enters the president's chest. We can use a satellite to follow a story with a local angle anywhere in the world. We can show, in color and with fantastic clarity—and *live*—a Cruise missile attack on Baghdad, a close-up view of the fury of an approaching tornado, red-hot lava eruptions of a Hawaiian volcano, the fiery detonations of Scud/Patriot missile intercepts high in the night sky, or the ugly dome of a mine bobbing in the Persian Gulf. We can create and animate graphics and effects that can be of real help in explaining even the most complicated concepts.

Clearer policy standards are needed to ensure higher quality of content. The components of content quality are simple:

the right pictures

with the right words

and the right sounds

at the right time

Then those elements have to be organized—edited, if you will—for the audience so that it can receive the information accurately and clearly. Unless this is done, the most complex and wonderful technology cannot possibly hide the fact that content is disorganized or missing. In fact, sometimes the technology acts even to emphasize this.

John Corporon, a veteran executive of Independent Television News, voiced fear that if standards are not set, bad news will drive out good.

I mean lesser news, news of less significance and importance—news that may be of less interest, by the way.

When you see a producer trying to lure in more viewers by playing the lesser story over the more significant story—a more interesting story, he thinks, simply because it happened later or has stronger visual values—you can see the problem clearly.

There are some things that are of overriding importance, and it doesn't matter at what time they occur or what raw material you have to work with. If you are trying to give people a rounded picture of what happened in their world today, you can trivialize the whole thing if you ride the technology too far.

It's very slick, it's very late. But where's the analysis on the economy and where are the earlier angles that gave insight, and where's the piece you did about the long-range impact of X?

It's just like your favorite dinner. You've got to have the turkey and the potatoes. You add the piquant touches later. But don't replace the turkey with the sauce.

Let's strive for standards needed to assure that the power of the content will come through as the strongest element of the news program no matter what other elements are included:

Technology: Technology provides journalism with tools. Technological decisions are fundamentally journalistic decisions. Understanding the implications of technology is essential to good TV journalism.

Storytelling: Videographers, reporters, editors, and producers must accept the idea that complete stories are wanted, structured so that the words and pictures work together quickly for the highest possible level of audience understanding.

Editing: Strong editorial control of the processing of raw material must be maintained. Viewers need coherent stories—the right mix of words, pictures, and sounds—edited economically. Accuracy, brevity, and clarity are still the hallmarks of television journalism.

Writing: Writing will always be central to the craft, so learning to write well will continue to be essential as it always has been.

Production: The purpose of the use of production elements is to make the news easier to understand. Rely on production values less for entertainment and more for focusing and highlighting content.

Operation: Operational standards must encompass the entire spectrum of news: both professional standards and ethical considerations of the craft; both planning and execution—before as well as after the fact of coverage. Adequate time must be devoted to this continuous self-evaluation process.

The quality of the content of local television news is *the* key factor for success in whatever goals the television newsroom sets for itself.

Technological changes will continue to make an impact on the television news industry, in whatever form it evolves. The television news profession will continue to be a highly competitive and challenging arena offering great opportunities and rewards to those who are masters of its craft, responsive to its professional norms and ethical standards, and mindful of its traditions.

CODE OF BROADCAST NEWS ETHICS
RADIO-TELEVISION NEWS DIRECTORS ASSOCIATION

The responsibility of radio and television journalists is to gather and report information of importance and interest to the public accurately, honestly and impartially.

The members of the Radio-Television News Directors Association accept these standards and will:

1. Strive to present the source or nature of broadcast news material in a way that is balanced, accurate and fair.

    A. They will evaluate information solely on its merits as news, rejecting sensationalism or misleading emphasis in any form.

    B. They will guard against using audio or video material in a way that deceives the audience.

    C. They will not mislead the public by presenting as spontaneous news any material which is staged or rehearsed.

    D. They will identify people by race, creed, nationality or prior status only when it is relevant.

    E. They will clearly label opinion and commentary.

    F. They will promptly acknowledge and correct errors.

2. Strive to conduct themselves in a manner that protects them from conflicts of interest, real or perceived. They will decline gifts or favors which would influence or appear to influence their judgments.

3. Respect the dignity, privacy and well-being of people with whom they deal.

4. Recognize the need to protect confidential sources. They will promise confidentiality only with the intention of keeping that promise.

5. Respect everyone's right to a fair trial.

6. Broadcast the private transmissions of other broadcasters only with permission.

7. Actively encourage observance of this Code by all journalists, whether members of the Radio-Television News Directors Association or not.

CODE OF ETHICS
NATIONAL PRESS PHOTOGRAPHERS ASSOCIATION

The National Press Photographers Association, a professional society dedicated to the advancement of photojournalism, acknowledges concern and respect for the public's natural-law right to freedom in searching for the truth and the right to be informed truthfully and completely about public events and the world in which we live.

We believe that no report can be complete if it is not possible to enhance and clarify the meaning of words. We believe that pictures, whether used to depict news events as they actually happen, illustrate news that has happened or to help explain anything of public interest, are an indispensable means of keeping people accurately informed; that they help all people, young and old, to better understand any subject in the public domain.

Believing the foregoing we recognize and acknowledge that photojournalists should at all times maintain the highest standards of ethical conduct in serving the public interest. To that end the National Press Photographers Association sets forth the following Code of Ethics which is subscribed to by all of its members:

1. The practice of photojournalism, both as a science and art, is worthy of the very best thought and effort of those who enter into it as a profession.

2. Photojournalism affords an opportunity to serve the public that is equalled by few other vocations and all members of the profession should strive by example and influence to maintain high standards of ethical conduct free of mercenary considerations of any kind.

3. It is the individual responsibility of every photojournalist at all times to strive for pictures that report truthfully, honestly and objectively.

4. Business promotion in its many forms is essential, but untrue statements of any nature are not worthy of a professional photojournalist and we severely condemn any such practice.

5. It is our duty to encourage and assist all members of our profession, individually and collectively, so that the quality of photojournalism may constantly be raised to higher standards.

6. It is the duty of every photojournalist to work to preserve all freedom-of-the-press rights recognized by law and to work to protect and expand freedom-of-access to all sources of news and visual information.

7. Our standards of business dealings, ambitions and relations shall have in them a note of sympathy for our common humanity and shall always require us to take into consideration our highest duties as members of society. In every situation in our business life, in every responsibility that comes before us, our chief thought shall be to fulfill that responsibility and discharge that duty so that when each of us is finished we shall have endeavored to lift the level of human ideals and achievement higher than we found it.

8. No Code of Ethics can prejudge every situation, thus common sense and good judgment are required in applying ethical principles.

Acronyms and Abbreviations

AAE   automatic assemble editing
ABC   American Broadcasting Company
AC   alternating current
ACEJMC   Accrediting Council on Education in Journalism and Mass Communications
ADI   area of dominant influence
AEJMC   Association for Education in Journalism and Mass Communication
AERho   Alpha Epsilon Rho
AFTRA   American Federation of Television and Radio Artists
AGC   automatic gain control
AM   amplitude modulation
AP   Associated Press
ASCAP   American Society of Composers, Authors and Publishers
ATR   audio tape recorder
auto   automatic
AWRT   American Women in Radio and Television
BBC   British Broadcasting Corporation
BEA   Broadcast Education Association
BG   background
cart   cartridge
CATV   community antenna television
CAV   component analog video
CBC   Canadian Broadcasting Corporation
CBS   Columbia Broadcasting System
CC   closed captioning
CCD   charged-coupled device
CCTV   closed circuit television
CCU   camera control unit
CD   compact disk (computer disk)

CDL   commercial driver license
CD-ROM   compact disc-read only memory
CE   computer editing
CG   character generator
ch   channel
CNN   Cable News Network
coax   coaxial
COMSAT   Communications Satellite Corporation
CPB   Corporation for Public Broadcasting
CRT   cathode ray tube
C-SPAN   Cable-Satellite Public Affairs Network
CT   cartridge tape
CU   closeup
CVE   component video effects
CWA   Communications Workers of America
DB   decibel
DBS   direct broadcast satellite
DVE   digital video effects
DVTR   digital videotape recorder
ECU   extreme closeup. See *XCU*
EFP   electronic field production
EJ   electronic journalism
ELS   extreme long shot. See *XLS*
EM   electronic mail
ENG   electronic news gathering
ENP   electronic news processing
EMT   eastern military time
ESPN   Entertainment and Sports Programming Network
ETV   educational television
EVF   electronic viewfinder
FAA   Federal Aviation Administration
FCC   Federal Communications Commission
FF   fast forward
FM   frequency modulation
GATS   global access telecommunications system
gHz   gigahertz
GMT   Greenwich Mean Time
HDTV   high definition television
Hz   hertz
IBEW   International Brotherhood of Electrical Workers
ICC   Interstate Commerce Commission
IFB   interrupted foldback (casually, interrupted feedback)
INN   Independent Network News
INTELSAT   International Telecommunications Satellite Organization
INTRO   introductory

IPS   inches per second
ISDN   integrated services digital network
ITNA   Independent Television News Association
ITV   instructional television
JOB   *Journal of Broadcasting & Electronic Media*
JQ   *Journalism & Mass Communication Quarterly*
K   Kelvin
kHz   kilohertz
lav   lavalier
LCD   liquid crystal display
LED   light-emitting diode
LO   local origination
LPTV   low-power television
LV   laser video
LS   long shot
man   manual
MBS   Mutual Broadcasting System
MCU   medium closeup
MDS   multipoint distribution service
mHz   megahertz
MIC   microphone
MS   medium shot
MSO   multiple systems owner (operator)
NAB   National Association of Broadcasters
NABET   National Association of Broadcast Employees and Technicians
NABJ   National Association of Black Journalists
NACB   National Association of College Broadcasters
NAEB   National Association of Educational Broadcasters
NAHJ   National Association of Hispanic Journalists
NAJA   Native American Journalists Association
NASA   National Aeronautics and Space Administration
NATSOT   natural sound on tape
NBC   National Broadcasting Company
NI-CAD   nickel/cadmium
NPPA   National Press Photographers Association
NPR   National Public Radio
NTSC   National Television Systems Committee, the U.S. television broadcast standard
OC   on camera
PAL   phase alternation line, television broadcast standard widely used in Europe
PBS   Public Broadcasting Service
pic   still picture
preamp   preamplifier
promo   promotion, promotional announcement

PSA public service announcement

PTV Public Television

PUP portable uplink

rec record (verb)

repro reproduce

rew rewind

RF radio frequency

RNA Reuters News Agency

RPM revolutions per minute

RTNDA Radio Television News Directors Association

RTNDF Radio Television News Directors Foundation

SECAM *sequentiel couleur à memoire,* television broadcast standard used in Europe and other parts of the world

secs seconds

SEG special effects generator

SMATV satellite master antenna television

SMPTE Society of Motion Picture and Television Engineers

SNG satellite news gathering

SNV satellite news vehicle

SOT sound on tape

SPJ Society of Professional Journalists

STV subscription television

super superimpose

TBC time base corrector

TVRO television receive-only

UHF ultra high frequency

UPI United Press International

VCR video cassette recorder

VG videographics

VHF very high frequency

VHS video home system

V/O voice-over

VOA Voice of America

VTR videotape recorder

VU volume unit

WB white balance

XCU extreme closeup. See *ECU*

XLS extreme long shot. See *ELS*

Terms

A-Roll A separately recorded videocassette containing some of the material (frequently sync-sound portions) to be used when editing various recorded elements into the final (air) version of the story. Also the main edited story, usually containing lip-sync shots.

actuality   The voice and remarks of a newsmaker or eyewitness recorded as part of the coverage of a news event. See *sound bite*.

alignment   The correct electronic balance of a unit or units of equipment; the correct positioning of a steerable unit.

ambient sound   Sound that surrounds and encompasses the environment of a news scene. Also called "background" sound, "indigenous" sound, "natural" sound, or "wild" sound.

amplifier   An electronic component to increase a signal's power, current, or voltage without drawing power from the signal.

analog   Refers to the direct physical transfer of variables, for example, electrical voltages or shaft rotations. See *digital*.

anchor   A major air personality in a television newscast.

anchor lead   Narration read by a news anchor in the studio to introduce another person on the news set, a report from a reporter in the field, a package prerecorded by the reporter, etc.

angle   A viewpoint; in videotape recording, it is the location of the camera relative to what is being recorded.

aperture   The size of the opening controlling the amount of light passing through a lens; in photography/videography expressed numerically as an f-stop. See *iris*.

artificial light   Light produced by artificial sources such as incandescent, quartz, fluorescent bulbs, etc. Opposite of sunlight, moonlight.

assemble editing   The assembling of video and/or audio and including control track onto a blank videocassette.

assignment editor   A person who assigns personnel to news coverage, monitors the progress of the coverage, and directs shifting of assignments as a response to the ebb and flow of news events.

audio   Sound.

audio mixer   A unit for receiving sounds from various sources so that they can be combined and blended into a unified whole.

audio track   Those portions of the videotape that store the sound recordings.

automatic gain control   An electronic device that automatically regulates the levels of audio and video intensities within prescribed limits.

available light   The amount of existing light (ambient, whether natural or artificial) without additional illumination.

back light   Illumination from behind the object of interest.

background sound   See *ambient sound*.

backtiming   The precise timing of the final two or three items of a newscast or segment, designed to help control overall timing of the production, to help the crew and talent end the newscast on time.

barn door   A set of hinged flaps attached to the housing of a lighting instrument, allowing some control over where the light will fall.

bearding   See *overdeviation*.

beta   Home video system; video camera-recorder system.

bite   See *sound bite*.

blanking   The interval during which the electronic scanning beam of the television camera or receiver tube is turned off for return to begin the next scan.

bridge   A transition; usually refers to audio material.

B-Roll   Separately recorded video containing some of the material (frequently picture sequences that illustrate sound portions) to be used when editing the various recorded elements into the final (air) version of the story. Also called "cover material." See *A-Roll*.

bumper   A piece of visual material (slide, still frame, etc.), sometimes with accompanying bumper music, inserted at the end of one newscast segment to allow for a smooth transition to another segment or commercial break.

burst   A portion of the synchronizing signal that includes a timing reference for the color sub carrier. The color sub carrier is that portion of the video signal that carries the color information. It is called a burst because it occurs for only a short amount of time as it is inserted at the beginning of each TV line.

camcorder   A videotape camera/recorder unit in which the recorder is built into the camera housing, thus reducing unit size, weight, cable and other wiring, etc.

capstan   An electrically driven roller that rotates and transports the videotape moving past it at a precise and fixed speed.

capstan servo   A videotape editing deck feature that automatically controls tape transport speed.

cassette   An enclosed container with two reels, one holding a supply of audio tape or videotape and the other acting as a takeup. The sealed container is designed to be inserted directly into a record or playback machine, thus eliminating the need for hand threading.

C-band   A section of the electromagnetic spectrum between 3.7 and 4.2 gigahertz assigned for United States satellite use. See also Ku-band.

cellular telephone   A mobile radio-telephone service. Also called *cellphone*.

character generator   An electronic device to create words or graphics that may then be electronically inserted into a television picture.

chroma   The purity of a color, determined by its degree of freedom from white or gray.

Chromakey™   The electronic combining of two video sources into a composite picture, creating the illusion that the two sources are physically together. A matting technique whereby all of a primary color (usually blue or green so as to not affect flesh tones) is removed from the foreground scene and a background scene substituted. Key utilizes black in the same way that Chromakey™ uses a primary color.

closed captioning   A service for hearing-impaired television viewers in which text information is transmitted in the TV signal's vertical interval. The TV receiver must have a decoder to display the text with the TV picture.

closeup   A picture showing only the object of interest in detail, with little or no visible background or setting in which the object is situated.

cold   Refers to a presentation without the benefit of rehearsal or preparation.

communications satellite   A satellite containing receivers and transmitters that can receive signals from the earth and then retransmit them back to earth.

compression   Electronic reduction of audio and video signal levels to prevent distortion.

computer-based video   See *digital video.*

computer graphics   Graphics created entirely by a computer, or existing graphics modified by a computer, using electronic "pens," "pencils," and "painting palette." Can appear to be three dimensional. Can be animated. Can be stored for reuse.

condenser microphone   A very high quality but also extremely delicate microphone; it uses its own battery power supply.

contrast ratio   A comparison of the difference between the brightest and the darkest areas of a scene.

control track   That portion of the videotape containing the electromagnetic information required for synchronization of elements in playback.

co-ord circuits   Two-way voice radio systems linking station personnel with field reporting crews. See also *news circuit* and *tech circuit.*

copy   A news story, commercial, or other announcement. Traditionally, the piece of paper on which the material to be read is typed.

countdown leader   Numbered images recorded at one-second intervals immediately ahead of the first video on a videotape, used for cuing and precision timing. The seconds count backward from an arbitrary number, for example from 10 to 2, providing the precise number of seconds to first video.

cover shot   Sometimes referred to as a "protection" shot, meaning an extra shot recorded by the videographer just in case it wasn't done right the first time. The term "cover" is also used by some people as a synonym for establishing shot. See *establishing shot.*

cross scripting   A script intended for reading aloud with accompanying video (voice-over), but one in which the words are not well integrated with the pictures (see *keying, direct narrative, indirect narrative*).

crosstalk   Unwanted signal interference; leakage of one signal into another. Also used by some to indicate questions and answers between an anchor in the studio and a reporter in the field.

cue (noun)   Notification to begin (or cease) action; an alerting signal for smooth collaboration in production.

cue (verb)   To pre-position recorded material (audio or video tape, phonograph record, CD) in a playback unit at a precise point for precision timing in the insertion of the recorded material into the program.

cut (noun)   An excerpt from recorded video or audio.

cut (verb)   To end, cease, delete.

cut-and-cover   A video news story editing technique in which the reporter's narration is laid down on the master tape first, to which B-Roll video is added to visually "cover" the audio. The technique is quick, thus saving edit time when time is critical.

cutaway   A shot that looks away from the central action being shown and into the periphery or immediate vicinity of the action. See *reaction shot.*

cut-in   A shot that looks in (tightly) to the central action being shown, to show fine detail and exclude everything else surrounding that detail. Also called *insert shot.* An insert into a broadcast, also called *live cut-in.*

cut sheet   A list of those scenes selected from videotaped material that will be edited into the final (air) version of the story.

cuts only   Videotape editing technique in which excerpts (cuts) are compiled without manipulating the picture to create transitions.

decibel   A unit of measurement of the apparent loudness of a sound.

definition   The clarity of the detail of a television picture.

depth of field   The distance (from near to far) within which all objects are in focus. The smaller the lens opening, the greater the size of the depth of field. The shorter the focal length, the longer the depth of field.

desktop video   Video images manipulated by personal computer.

dichroic filter   A filter that allows only certain light wavelengths to pass through it.

digital   Refers to transfer of variables—such as electrical voltages—into discrete numerical units, zeros (0) and ones (1), which allows for the electronic processing of that information with fidelity. See *analog.*

digital compression   A technique allowing for expansion of cable and satellite capacity. Compression works by "squeezing" digital data (streams of 0 and 1) reducing the amount of data required in the recording or transmission of a TV image without visible loss of detail.

digital video   Video images in computer form. (See also *computer-based video, desktop video, disk-based video, nonlinear editing.*)

direct narrative   A voice-over scripting technique in which the text is correlated directly with the pictures. See also *cross scripting, indirect narrative, keying.*

directional microphone   A microphone with a very narrow pickup pattern, one which picks up sound from only one direction.

director   The person who commands the studio and control room personnel during the airing of the newscast.

disk-based video   Video and sound on computer or optical disk.

dissolve   The coordinated fading out of one picture from the screen as a new picture establishes itself, creating a gradual change of image.

dope sheet   When prepared by the assignment editor, it is background information on the assignment; when prepared by the videographer or reporter, it is information from the assignment or about the coverage.

doughnut   Previously recorded video and interviews, edited with a narration track, aired in the middle of a live shot. See also *live wrap.*

down time A period of time when equipment is not in use, usually meant to refer to broken or malfunctioning equipment on the "to be repaired" list.

downlink A ground receiver that receives signals transmitted from a satellite.

dropout Loss of picture signal, a visual blank spot.

drum servo The part of a videotape recorder that automatically controls the speed of rotation of the head drums.

dub (noun) A duplicate of a videotape.

dub (verb) To copy, make a duplicate. To add audio track to the videotape by editing.

dynamic microphone Of somewhat lower quality than the condenser type, but considerably more rugged and durable; it is a widely used general-purpose microphone in television news work.

echo effect See *parroting.*

editing The process of selecting portions of picture and sound recordings, including their timing and sequence, and the piecing together of these elements into a finished news story.

establishing shot A segment designed to orient the viewer by showing the story's location or time, or the surroundings within which the story happened or is happening. See *cover shot.*

eyewash Filed (library) video of generic scenes, pictures that can be used to cover a current news story, as for example, supermarket aisles (to go with a food costs story), grain being stored at an elevator, loaded at dockside (to go with a commodities exports story), etc.

fade A graduated change in picture or sound; a gradual fade-out or fade-in at the beginning or end of a scene, segment, or program.

field The scanning lines in one-half of one video frame. These scanning lines create the video picture in that frame by converting light values into electronic values one line at a time. In the U.S. video system (NTSC) there are 525 scanning lines in each frame. Each of the two fields in that frame creates 262.5 of those scanning lines. In videotape recording, each of the two recording heads on the head drum lays down one field alternately across the frame to create a picture meeting the 525-line standard.

filler Extra programming material, for example, news copy, used for flexibility in timing; if time permits, the copy is presented; if time is short it is not. Also called "pad copy."

fill light Additional illumination to soften shadows.

flat angle Refers to a shot made head-on at eye level.

flood light General or overall illumination.

floor director The person in charge of television studio floor activity who is linked by headset to the director in the control room and who executes the director's orders. In smaller television station operations the duties may be performed by a studio camera operator.

fluorescent light A tubular electronic discharge lamp in which light is produced by the glowing of the phosphorus coating on the inside of the tube.

footprint   That portion of the earth's surface covered by the retransmitted signal from a communications satellite.

format   A term used widely in broadcasting to indicate some sort of constant. "Program format" refers to the production's framework as distinct from its content, a videotape recorder's "format" refers to the size of the videotape it uses, for example, quarter-inch, half-inch, etc. "Format" can also refer to an electronic system, e.g., beta, VHS, M, etc.

frame   The smallest unit of videotape picture measurement, a complete picture unit.

frame store   Graphics, designs, words, and still pictures stored in a memory unit one frame at a time for instant recall. A *still store.*

from the top   Refers to doing something over from the beginning.

futures file   A listing or computer file of upcoming news events. See *tickler file.*

gaffer   An electrician.

gaffer tape   A heavy-duty press-apply (contact) adhesive tape used to hold lighting and other electrical gear in place temporarily. Sold in retail stores as *duct tape.*

gain   In audio, the amplification (apparent loudness); in video, the contrast ratio.

generation   The number of duplications (dubs) away from an original videotape recording. The "first generation" is the original; a "second generation" is a duplicate of the original; a "third generation" is a duplicate of the second generation, etc. Some signal quality may be lost with each succeeding videotape generation.

geostationary satellite   A satellite in orbit approximately 22,300 miles above earth, positioned along earth's equator, moving in the direction of and at the same speed as the earth's rotation; in effect, the satellite remains stationary relative to the earth.

glitch   Technically, a kind of picture distortion, but also used casually to indicate something that went wrong with the production.

happy talk   Banter between or among anchors during a newscast.

hard copy   Typewritten copy printed on paper. Also, the original copy in a multicopy set.

helical scan   A term to describe a process of recording visual information on a videotape. As the videotape moves horizontally, the spinning recording head crosses it diagonally. Signal information is recorded in these parallel, slanted lines, the three-dimensional effect of which would be a helix-like spiral.

hertz   Unit measure of cycles per second.

hi mom   Videographer's reference to people who, when aware that the camera is aimed at them, wave energetically or make rude gestures.

high angle   Refers to a shot looking down on the action below.

hot   Refers to an area with too much light. Also used to describe something that is turned on, as in "hot mike." See *live.*

incandescent   A lamp that emits light due to the glowing of a heated material enclosed in the bulb, as a filament.

indigenous sound   See *ambient sound.*

indirect narrative   A voice-over scripting technique in which the text is well correlated with but not directly linked to the pictures being watched while the narration is being delivered. See *cross scripting, direct narrative, keying.*

insert   A synonym for *cut-in.*

insert editing   The inserting of new video and/or audio onto a videotape that already has control track recorded on it.

into-frame, out-of-frame   With video being recorded and camera held motionless, subject of interest (a) enters picture and is centered to become the visual center of attention, or (b) moves from the visual center and departs the frame.

iris   The adjustable component of a camera lens system that allows for the control of the amount of light passing through the lens.

jitter   Picture instability in VTR playback.

jump cut   Adjoining scenes of the same content, size, and angle, that do not visually match; the "cut" occurs at the point where the two scenes join; the "jump" is an unnatural break in the action at that point, thus interrupting the flow of the visual story line.

Kelvin   A unit of the measurement of the color temperature of a lighting source.

key   See *Chromakey.*™

keying (production)   Using the color spectrum to insert pictures on top of other pictures electronically.

keying (script writing)   A voice-over scripting technique in which text is correlated with the visual so that certain words or phrases are delivered at key locations in the picture story, for example, a name identification delivered at about the time the face of the person appears on the screen. See *cross scripting, direct narrative, indirect narrative.*

key light   A focused light aimed directly at the object of interest; the main source of illumination.

Ku-band   Similar to C-band, but in the 11.7–12.7 gHz portion of the electromagnetic spectrum. See *C-band.*

lavalier microphone   A small, unobtrusive microphone; may be worn around the neck with a neckstrap much like a necklace; smaller and miniature models may be clipped to a lapel or similar part of a garment in the chest area, with good pick-up results.

lead (pronounced LEED)   Normally considered to be the first sentence or paragraph of a news story; the first story of a newscast.

lead-in   That part of the story text that introduces a sound bite.

library   Filed video from prior news coverage.

library system   An automated system in which a computer controls recording and playback of videotape or digital disk.

line-up   A listing in chronological order of each item in a newscast and including various pieces of production information; also, variously, the "rundown."

lip flap   Occurs when a speaker's lips are shown moving but out of synchronization with the sound track, or the speaker's lips move but no sound is heard.

lip sync   The situation in which lip movement matches the sound track of the words being spoken.

live   A broadcasting term that is used with a variety of meanings. A camera or microphone that is turned on is said to be "live." Programming that is not recorded is "live." The term may also be used to describe the acoustical properties of a studio or room.

live wrap   A live report that includes one or more packages. See *doughnut*.

long shot   A shot taken from a distance that is sufficiently wide so as to show the object of interest and at least some of its setting.

low angle   Refers to a shot looking up to the action above.

lower thirds   Graphics that use the bottom portion of the television picture to add information to the picture, for example, captions, identifications, etc.

medium shot   A shot showing a view of the object of interest that is somewhere between a long shot and a closeup; a "medium medium" is thought of by some photographers as a top-to-bottom shot, for example, a building framed from ground level to the roof or a person shown head to foot.

minicam   A video camera much smaller than a studio model, thus much lighter and more portable; used for news gathering in the field.

mix-minus   Program audio fed to talent via IFB but minus the talent's own voice.

montage   An editing technique in which a number of scenes of very short duration (a second or less) are edited together for a "rapid-succession" visual effect.

mooz   Describes the action of zooming out from a closeup view to a medium- or long-shot view. See *zoom*.

mult box   A portable box housing with multiple audio outlets.

multiple split   A number of pictures put on the screen at the same time in almost any pattern.

natural light   Direct sunlight, moonlight, or such light filtered by overcast.

natural sound   See ambient sound.

neutral density filter   A filter that cuts down the amount of light passing through the camera lens without altering any of the other qualities of that light.

news circuit   A two-way radio channel linking the TV station and a reporting crew in the field. See *co-ord circuits*.

news hole   The net amount of newscast time available for news, the amount of time to be filled with news.

nickel-cadmium (Ni-Cad) battery   A heavy-duty, multipurpose, portable, rechargeable battery used in the field to power a videotape camera-recorder ensemble.

noise   Random, unwanted sound or picture interference; heavy picture noise is called "snow."

nonlinear editing   Technique in which scenes, once selected, are retrieved by computer from a storage medium and assembled in order with production effects.

outlook report   A preliminary written estimate of the budget of items in a day's coverage of news.

outtakes   Shots that are edited out of the final (air) videotape of a news story; discarded, unused video scenes.

overdeviation   A black fringing effect in an overly bright picture or overly saturated color, caused by an excess of chroma or video level that is too high for the tape to handle. Also called *bearding*.

package   A self-contained field report of a news event, complete with its own introduction and conclusion. All the studio anchor has to do is introduce it.

pad copy   See filler.

panning   The horizontal movement of the camera, left to right, right to left, or both.

parroting   A scripted lead-in to a sound bite in which the lead-in text uses some of the exact words—key words—contained in the opening of the sound bite; also called "echo effect."

planned live   A live report inserted into a regularly scheduled news program.

preroll   The number of frames between the cue point and the edit point, essential to the synchronization of linked VTRs.

producer   The person in overall command and with overall responsibility for all elements of an entire story, segment, series, newscast.

protection shot   See *cover shot*.

pull focus   An on-air camera focusing adjustment technique involving the foreground and background of the scene whereby sharp focus is shifted, in view, from one to the other.

pumping   An automatic gain control (AGC) audio effect in which during intervals of very low sound level, the AGC compensates by automatically turning up the sensitivity (increasing the volume) of the microphone.

quadruplex   A videotape recording technique that uses four recording heads.

quick study   In theatre, a performer who memorizes lines quickly and effortlessly.

rack-focus   A camera focusing adjustment technique to prepare the focus for a zoom shot.

reaction shot   A shot showing the facial expression or other actions of a person or persons witnessing a news event. See *cutaway*.

reel-to-reel   Refers to a recorder whose supply reel and takeup reel must be inserted and threaded manually.

reflector   A lighting accessory to direct and control light.

remote   Broadcasting live from the field.

reproduce   To play back recorded material.

reverse angle shot   A shot taken from exactly opposite the previous one; the reverse angle shows a scene "from the other side."

ringing   The secondary edge or ghost edge, usually on the right side of objects in the picture, caused by excessive enhancement.

roll back   A videotape reversing action that occurs when the recorder (camcorder) is cycled from "record" to "stop." A small portion of the recorded videotape is rewound onto the supply spool and gets erased when recording is resumed.

rotary wipe   An on-screen visual effect that looks like pages are being turned in a book, or pictures that are made to rotate or tumble from the sides, top, bottom, background to foreground, etc.

rundown   See *line-up*.

running time   The interval of time (either estimated or actual) that it takes for material being timed to be completed.

safe area   In picture composition, the peripheral boundaries of a picture, set up as a guide so that important action or titles within those boundaries will not be lost in the transmission process.

scene   See *shot*.

scene count   See *shot list*.

scrim   An accessory mounted on a lighting instrument to reduce the amount of light coming from the unit. A gauze material may be used with a scrim to diffuse the light.

sequence   A group of shots in series.

servo system   Those components of a videotape editing system that use tracking and sync pulse to regulate tape speed and head drum rotation.

shooting ratio   The amount of video actually used expressed as a percentage of the amount recorded.

shot   The amount of video recorded from the instant the camera is triggered to run to the instant it is triggered to stop or pause. Several shots make a sequence. The word "shot" is often used interchangeably with the terms "scene" and "take."

shotgun microphone   A highly directional microphone that can be aimed directly at a sound source, thus picking up the desired sound at a fairly good distance (up to several hundred feet) while excluding surrounding extraneous noise.

shot list   A chronological list of each shot of raw (original) video together with notations of its content, and running time. The term may also apply to a listing of natural sounds recorded with the video.

side bar   An offshoot of the main story, an oddity, something offbeat, a story within a story.

signal-to-noise ratio   The amount of noise as a percentage of the transmission. Also called *noise, snow*.

slant track   Another term for *helical scan*.

slug A one- or two-word label for quick identification of individual news stories; also, more broadly, identifying information put on each news story, such as the date, the newscast the story is for, the writer's name or initials, and the like.

snow See *noise*.

solid-state Refers to electronic equipment in which vacuum tubes are replaced by transistors. For instance, CCDs—silicon chips—are solid-state elements that are replacing pick-up tubes in ENG cameras.

sound bed Background sound that is loud enough to be barely audible but not so loud as to intrude on the main sound.

sound bite A sound-on-tape (SOT) statement by a person in the news. See *actuality*.

split edit A type of edit whereby either audio or video to be added from a source (original) tape is held back and kept out of the editing process for a given amount of time.

spot A commercial. Also a type of lighting unit. See *spotlight*.

spotlight A lighting unit capable of being focused.

squeeze frame An electronic video effect that begins with a full frame of picture and squeezes the image until it occupies only a portion of the screen, with the rest of the screen space being given to other visual material.

Squeeze Zoom™ The electronic placement of any portion of picture into any portion of the screen. It may be moved to any other part of the screen, brought to full screen, or made to disappear entirely.

standup A reporting technique in which the reporter on the news scene delivers a monologue while facing the camera, either as an opener, or a transition, or a closer, or some combination of these. Also called "standupper." The standup is almost always delivered from a standing position (hence the term) but may also be delivered while seated. A variation is the walking standup, in which the reporter walks (usually toward the camera, less frequently away from it) as he or she delivers the monologue; or the reporter may walk at right angles to the camera while the camera moves with the reporter in a trucking movement.

still store See *frame store*.

Super Motion™ A Sony Corporation slow-motion technique achieved by increasing the field rate of the picture from 60 per second to 180.

swish pan Horizontal movement of a videocamera (a pan) done so swiftly that the result when viewed is a blur of motion across the screen.

sync The synchronizing portion of the video signal. It provides a timing system that synchronizes the scanning of all related equipment such as cameras and video monitors.

take See *shot*.

talent Those people who appear before the camera. See *anchor*.

talking head Video of a person talking. The phrase is often used in a derogatory sense to indicate boring video, lacking action and visual interest.

tally light   An indicator light, usually red, giving visual confirmation that a camera is "on." The light at the front of the camera alerts the talent, and the light behind the camera (for example, within the viewfinder) alerts the camera operator.

teaser   A headline or other brief reference to an upcoming news story, purposely vague, perhaps titillating and designed to arouse viewer interest and anticipation.

tech circuit   A two-way radio channel linking technicians at the station with technicians in the field. See *co-ord circuits*.

tickler file   A newsroom listing or computer file for keeping date/time/place reminders of future events, items to be followed up on later. See *futures file*.

tight shot   See *closeup*.

tilt   Camera movement in the vertical plane.

time code   Electronic technique for consecutive numbering of each individual frame of recorded video.

time shifting   Recording a program off-air for later viewing.

transponder   The receiver-transmitter device in a communications satellite that receives signals from the uplink and retransmits them on the downlink.

truck   Camera movement that is lateral, at right angles to the scene being shot.

two shot   A videotaped scene in which two subjects or objects appear in frame together, i.e., two people sitting together, two differently styled clocks arranged side by side on a table, etc. The standard shot for a one-person (reporter/guest) interview.

unrestricted keying   An electronic on-screen effect in which multiple layers of pictures are placed one atop another.

update   New information about a previously reported story.

uplink   A ground transmitter that sends signals to a satellite.

voice-over   Narration delivered in conjunction with visuals, in which the person delivering the narration is not seen in the picture.

walking standup   See *standup*.

wash light   A floodlight or spotlight placed so that its light falls on a background to provide separation of the subject from that background.

white balance   The adjustment of a camera so that it will reproduce colors accurately in a given lighting condition. Each time the lighting condition changes, the camera must be white balanced again.

wild sound   See *ambient sound*.

window   The time when a satellite transponder becomes available, thus: The window will open at 01:45:30 and will close at 05:45:30. Also, a portion of a computer screen. Also, an area in a news set in which computer-generated graphics may be inserted into the program being broadcast.

wind screen   A protective foam covering on a microphone to reduce or eliminate the sound of wind rushing over the microphone.

wipe   An electronic visual effect in which a picture is gradually changed right to left or left to right across the video screen.

wireless microphone   A microphone with a built-in miniature transmitter that can transmit sound to a distant (up to several hundred feet) receiver. (In some models the transmitter is an accompanying unit.)

wrap   To end.

wrap-around   Material such as narration preceding and following an audio or video segment, the former to introduce the segment, the latter to conclude it.

zoof   An out-of-focus zoom.

zoom   Describes the action of changing a shot by changing the lens focal length, moving in from a long-shot view to a closeup view, or out from a close view to a long view.

BIBLIOGRAPHY

General

Abramson, Albert. *The History of Television, 1880–1941.* Jefferson, NC: McFarland, 1987.

Archer, Gleason L. *History of Radio to 1926.* New York: American Historical Society, 1938. Reprint. New York: Arno Press, 1971.

Auletta, Ken. *Three Blind Mice: How the TV Networks Lost Their Way.* New York: Random House, 1991.

Barnouw, Erik A. *A Tower in Babel: A History of Broadcasting in the United States.* Vol. 1, To 1933. New York: Oxford University Press, 1966.

———. *The Golden Web: A History of Broadcasting in the United States.* Vol. 2, 1933–53. New York: Oxford University Press, 1970.

———. *The Image Empire: A History of Broadcasting in the United States.* Vol. 3, 1953–. New York: Oxford University Press, 1970.

———. *Tube of Plenty: The Evolution of American Television.* New York: Oxford University Press, 1975.

Benjamin, Burton. *The CBS Benjamin Report: CBS Reports "The Uncounted Enemy: A Vietnam Deception," An Examination.* Washington, DC: Media Institute, 1984.

———. *Fair Play: CBS, General Westmoreland, and How a Television Documentary Went Wrong.* New York: Harper & Row, 1988.

Broadcasting magazine. *The First Fifty Years of Broadcasting: The Running Story of the Fifth Estate.* Washington, DC: Broadcasting Publications, 1982.

———. *Broadcasting & Cable Yearbook.* Washington, DC: Cahners Publishing/Reed Publishing (USA) (annual).

Brown, Les. *Les Brown's Encyclopedia of Television.* New York: Zoetrope, 1982.

Crosby, John. *Out of the Blue.* New York: Simon and Schuster, 1952.

Head, Sydney W., Sterling, Christopher, and Wimmer, Roger D. *Broadcasting in America: A Survey of Television, Radio and New Technologies.* 6th ed. Boston: Houghton Mifflin, 1990.

Hill, Susan M., ed. *Broadcasting Bibliography: A Guide to the Literature of Radio & Television.* Hillsdale, NJ: Lawrence Erlbaum Associates, 1989.

Keirstead, Phillip, and Keirstead, Sonia-Kay. *The World of Telecommunication: Introduction to Broadcasting, Cable, and New Technologies.* Boston: Focal Press, 1990.

Lewis, Tom. *Empire of the Air: The Men Who Made Radio.* New York: Harper Collins, 1991.

Lichty, Lawrence W., and Topping, Malachi C., compilers. *American Broadcasting: A Source Book on the History of Radio and Television.* New York: Hastings House, 1975.

Metz, Robert. *CBS: Reflections in a Bloodshot Eye.* New York: Signet, 1976.

Newman, Edwin. *Strictly Speaking.* New York: Warner, 1975.

———. *A Civil Tongue.* Indianapolis: Bobbs-Merrill, 1976.

Paley, William. *As It Happened: A Memoir.* New York: Doubleday, 1979.

Paper, Lewis J. *Empire: William S. Paley and the Making of CBS.* New York: St. Martin's, 1987.

Persico, Joseph E. *Edward R. Murrow: An American Original.* New York: McGraw-Hill, 1988.

Quinlan, Sterling. *Inside ABC.* New York: Hastings House, 1979.

Smith, F. Leslie. *Perspectives on Radio and Television: Telecommunications in the United States.* 2nd ed. New York: Harper & Row, 1985.

Smith, Sally Bedell. *In All His Glory: William S. Paley the Legendary Tycoon and His Brilliant Circle.* New York: Simon & Schuster, 1990.

Sterling, Christopher H., and Kittross, John M. *Stay Tuned: A Concise History of American Broadcasting.* 2nd ed. Belmont, CA: Wadsworth, 1990.

Whittemore, Hank. *CNN: The Inside Story.* Boston: Little, Brown & Co., 1990.

Media Law and Ethics

Bittner, John R. *Law and Regulation of Electronic Media.* 2nd ed. Englewood Cliffs, NJ: Prentice-Hall, 1994.

Carter, T. Barton, Franklin, Marc A., and Wright, Jay B. *The First Amendment and the Fifth Estate: Regulation of Electronic Mass Media.* 3rd ed. Westbury, NY: Foundation Press, 1993.

Christians, Clifford C., Rotzoll, Kim B., and Fackler, Mark. *Media Ethics.* 3rd ed. White Plains, NY: Longman, 1991.

Day, Louis A. *Ethics in Media Communications: Cases and Controversies.* Belmont, CA: Wadsworth, 1991.

François, William C. *Mass Media Law and Regulation.* 6th ed. Prospect Heights, IL: Waveland Press, 1994.

Goodwin, Gene, and Smith, Ron F. *Groping for Ethics in Journalism.* 3rd ed. Ames: Iowa State University Press, 1994.

Holsinger, Ralph L., and Dilts, Jon Paul. *Media Law.* 3rd ed. New York: McGraw-Hill, 1994.

Matelski, Marilyn J. *TV News Ethics.* Boston: Focal Press, 1991.

Middleton, Kent R., and Chamberlin, Bill F. *The Law of Public Communication.* 3rd ed. White Plains, NY: Longman, 1994.

Minow, Newton N. *Equal Time: The Private Broadcaster and the Public Interest.* New York: Atheneum, 1964.

Moore, Roy L. *Mass Communication Law and Ethics.* Hillsdale, NJ: Lawrence Erlbaum Associates, 1993.

Overbeck, Wayne, and Pullen, Rick D. *Major Principles of Media Law.* Annual ed. Fort Worth, TX: Harcourt Brace, 1994.

Pember, Don R. *Mass Media Law.* 6th ed. Dubuque, IA: William C. Brown, 1993.

Ray, William B. *The Ups and Downs of Radio-TV Regulation.* Ames: Iowa State University Press, 1990.

Teeter, Dwight L., Jr., and Le Duc, Don. *Law of Mass Communications: Freedom and Control of Print and Broadcast Media.* 7th ed. Westbury, NY: Foundation Press, 1992.

Zelezny, John D. *Communication Law: Liberties, Restraints, and the Modern Media.* Belmont, CA: Wadsworth, 1993.

Journalism Commentary and Analysis

Barrett, Marvin, ed. *The Alfred I. duPont/Columbia University Survey of Broadcast Journalism 1968–69.* New York: Grosset & Dunlap, 1969.

———, ed. *Year of Challenge, Year of Crisis: The Alfred I. duPont/Columbia University Survey of Broadcast Journalism, 1969–70.* New York: Grosset & Dunlap, 1970.

———, ed. *Stage of Siege: The Alfred I. duPont/Columbia University Survey of Broadcast Journalism, 1970–71.* New York: Grosset & Dunlap, 1971.

———, ed. *The Politics of Broadcasting: The Fourth Alfred I. duPont/Columbia University Survey of Broadcast Journalism.* New York: Thomas Y. Crowell, 1973.

———, ed. *Moments of Truth? The Fifth Alfred I. duPont/Columbia University Survey of Broadcast Journalism.* New York: Thomas Y. Crowell, 1975.

———, ed. *Rich News, Poor News: The Sixth Alfred I. duPont/Columbia University Survey of Broadcast Journalism.* New York: Thomas Y. Crowell, 1978.

———, and Zachary Sklar. *The Eye of the Storm: The Seventh Alfred I. duPont/Columbia University Survey of Broadcast Journalism.* New York: Lippincott & Crowell, 1980.

———. *Broadcast Journalism, 1979–81: The Eighth Alfred I. DuPont/Columbia University Survey of Broadcast Journalism.* New York: Everett House, Dodd Publishing, 1982.

Bliss, Edward, Jr. *Now the News: The Story of Broadcast Journalism.* New York: Columbia University Press, 1991.

Boyer, Peter. *Who Killed CBS: The Undoing of America's Number One News Network.* New York: Random House, 1988.

Brinkley, David. *Washington Goes to War.* New York: Knopf, 1988.

Craft, Christine. *An Anchorwoman's Story.* Santa Barbara, CA: Capra, 1986.

Chancellor, John, and Mears, Walter R. *The News Business.* New York: Harper & Row, 1983.

Donaldson, Sam. *Hold On, Mr. President!* New York: Random House, 1987.

Ellerbee, Linda. *And So It Goes: Adventures in Television.* New York: G. P. Putnam, 1986.

Frank, Reuven. *Out of Thin Air: The Brief Wonderful Life of Network News.* New York: Simon & Schuster, 1991.

Friendly, Fred W. *Due to Circumstances Beyond Our Control.* New York: Random House, 1967.

Gates, Gary Paul. *Air Time: The Inside Story of CBS News.* New York: Harper & Row, 1978.

Gelfman, Judith. *Women in Television News.* New York: Columbia University Press, 1976.

Graham, Fred. *Happy Talk: Confessions of a TV Newsman.* New York: W. W. Norton, 1990.

Hewitt, Don. *Minute by Minute.* New York: Random House, 1985.

Hosley, David H., and Yamada, Gayle K. *Hard News: Women in Broadcast Journalism.* Westport, CT: Greenwood Press, 1987.

Joyce, Ed. *Prime Times, Bad Times: A Personal Drama of Network Television.* New York: Doubleday, 1988.

Kendrick, Alexander. *Prime Time: The Life of Edward R. Murrow.* Boston: Little, Brown, 1979.

Kuralt, Charles. *On the Road with Charles Kuralt.* New York: G. P. Putnam, 1985.

Leonard, Bill. *In the Storm of the Eye: A Lifetime at CBS.* New York: G. P. Putnam, 1987.

Lower, Elmer. *Broadcasting and the 1984 Presidential Election.* Syracuse: Newhouse School, Syracuse University, 1984.

MacNeil, Robert. *The Right Place at the Right Time.* Boston: Little, Brown, 1982.

Madsen, Axel. *Sixty Minutes: The Power and the Politics.* New York: Dodd, Mead, 1984.

Matusow, Barbara. *The Evening Stars: The Rise of Network News Anchors.* Boston: Houghton Mifflin, 1983.

McCabe, Peter. *Bad News at Black Rock: The Sell-Out of CBS News.* New York: Arbor House, 1987.

Mickelson, Sig. *From Whistle Stop to Sound Bite: Four Decades of Politics and Television.* New York: Praeger, 1989.

Rather, Dan, and Herskowitz, Mickey. *The Camera Never Blinks Twice.* New York: William Morrow, 1994.

Reasoner, Harry. *Before the Colors Fade.* New York: Knopf, 1981.

Robinson, John P., and Levy, Mark R., with Davis, Dennis K. *The Main Source: Learning from Television News.* Beverly Hills, CA: Sage, 1986.

Rooney, Andrew A. *Pieces of My Mind.* New York: Atheneum, 1984.

Savitch, Jessica. *Anchor Woman.* New York: G. P. Putnam, 1982.

Schorr, Daniel. *Clearing the Air.* Boston: Houghton Mifflin, 1977.

Small, William. *To Kill a Messenger: Television News and the Real World.* New York: Hastings House, 1970.

Sperber, A. M. *Murrow: His Life and Times.* New York: Bantam, 1987.

Stamberg, Susan. *Every Night at Five.* New York: Pantheon, 1982.

Stephens, Mitchell. *A History of News: From the Drum to the Satellite.* New York: Viking, 1988.

Wallace, Mike, and Gates, Gary Paul. *Close Encounters.* New York: William Morrow, 1984.

Walters, Barbara. *How to Talk with Practically Anybody About Practically Anything.* 2nd ed. New York: Doubleday, 1970.

Westin, Av. *Newswatch: How TV Decides the News.* New York: Simon and Schuster, 1982.

Woodruff, Judy, and Maxa, Kathy. *This Is Judy Woodruff at the White House.* Reading, Mass.: Addison-Wesley, 1982.

Zousmer, Steven. *TV News Off-Camera.* Ann Arbor: The University of Michigan Press, 1987.

Shooting, Reporting, Interviewing, Writing, Editing

Biagi, Shirley. *Interviews That Work: A Practical Guide for Journalists.* 2nd ed. Belmont, CA: Wadsworth, 1992.

Bliss, Edward, Jr., and Hoyt, James L. *Writing for News Broadcast.* 3rd ed. New York: Columbia University Press, 1994.

Block, Mervin. *Writing Broadcast News.* Chicago: Bonus Books, 1987.

———. *Rewriting Network News: Word Watching Tips from 345 TV and Radio Scripts.* Chicago: Bonus Books, 1990.

Brady, John. *The Craft of Interviewing.* Cincinnati: Writer's Digest, 1976.

Dondis, Donis A. *A Primer of Visual Literacy.* Boston: MIT Press, 1973.

Fang, Irving. *Television News, Radio News.* 4th ed. St. Paul, MN: Rada, 1985.

Gaines, William. *Investigative Reporting for Print and Broadcast.* Chicago: Nelson-Hall, 1994.

Gaskill, Arthur L., and Englander, David A. *How to Shoot a Movie and Video Story: The Technique of Pictorial Continuity.* Dobbs Ferry, NY: Morgan & Morgan, 1985.

Gibson, Roy. *Radio and TV Reporting.* Needham Heights, MA: Allyn & Bacon, 1991.

Hausman, Carl. *Crafting the News for Electronic Media: Reporting, Writing and Producing.* Belmont, CA: Wadsworth, 1992.

Hood, James R., and Kalbfeld, Brad, compilers and editors. *The Associated Press Broadcast News Handbook.* New York: Associated Press, 1982.

Keirstead, Phillip. *The Complete Guide to Newsroom Computers.* Prairie Village, KS: Globecom Publishing, 1982 (2nd ed., 1984).

Lewis, Carolyn D. *Reporting for Television.* New York: Columbia University Press, 1984.

Lindekugel, D. M. *Shooters: TV News Photographers and their Work.* Westport, CT: Praeger Publishers, 1994.

Macdonald, R. H. *A Broadcast News Manual of Style.* 2nd ed. White Plains, NY: Longman, 1994.

Mayeux, Peter E. *Broadcast News: Writing & Reporting.* Dubuque: Brown & Benchmark, 1991.

Merton, Robert K., et al. *The Focused Interview.* Glencoe, IL: Free Press, 1956.

Musberger, Robert B. *Electronic News Gathering.* Stoneham, MA: Focal Press, 1992.

O'Donnell, Lewis B., Hausman, Carl, and Benoit, Philip. *Announcing: Broadcast Communicating Today.* Belmont, CA: Wadsworth, 1992.

Ohanian, Thomas A. *Digital Nonlinear Editing.* Boston: Focal Press, 1993.

Radio-Television News Directors Association and Time-Life. *The Newsroom and the Newscast.* New York: Time-Life Books, 1966.

Shetter, Michael D. *Videotape Editing: Communicating with Pictures and Sound.* Elk Grove Village, IL: Swiderski Electronics.

Shook, Frederick. *Television Field Production and Reporting.* White Plains, NY: Longman, 1989.

———. *Television Newswriting.* White Plains, NY: Longman, 1994.

Smeyak, G. Paul. *Broadcast News Writing.* 2nd ed. Columbus, OH: Grid, 1983.

Stephens, Mitchell. *Broadcast News.* 2nd ed. New York: Holt, Rinehart and Winston, 1986.

Stone, Vernon. *Let's Talk Pay In Television and Radio News.* Chicago: Bonus Books, 1993.

Strunk, William, and White, E. B. *The Elements of Style.* 3rd ed. New York: Macmillan, 1979.

United Press International. *The UPI Broadcast Stylebook: A Handbook for Writing and Preparing Broadcast News.* New York: United Press International, 1979.

Utterback, Ann S. *Broadcast Voice Handbook.* Chicago: Bonus Books, 1993.

Watkinson, John. *The Art of Digital Video.* 2nd ed. Boston: Focal Press, 1994.

White, Paul W. *News on the Air.* New York: Harcourt, Brace, 1947.

White, Ray. *TV News: Building a Career in Broadcast Journalism.* Boston: Focal Press, 1990.

Willette, Leo. *So You're Gonna Shoot Newsfilm.* Ashville, NC: Inland Press, 1960.

Wulfemeyer, K. Tim. *Beginning Broadcast Newswriting: A Self-Instructional Learning Experience.* 3rd ed. Ames: Iowa State University Press, 1993.

Zettl, Herbert. *Television Production Handbook.* 5th ed. Belmont, CA: Wadsworth, 1992.

Magnetic Media/Film Products

The Anchor. PBS Video, 1984.

Best of 60 Minutes (2 vols.). CBS/Fox Video, 1984, 1985.

Big Name . . . Fair Game? PBS Video, 1981.

Diary of a News Story. New Dimensions Media, Inc., 1990.

Ethics. New Dimensions Media, Inc., 1990.

Express Yourself: The First Amendment. ACLU of Northern California, 1992. (ACLU computer program)

Forty Years of Television Broadcast Journalism. Legacy Home Video, 1988.

If It Bleeds, It Leads. Cinema Guild, 1986.

MacNeil-Lehrer NewsHour. PBS Video, 1990.

Making the News. Simon & Schuster, 1986.

Making the News Fit. Cinema Guild, 1986.

News Travels Fast: All About TV Newscasting. Rainbow Educational Video, 1988.

The On Camera Series (4 programs). BBC, 1984.

The Power of TV News. New Dimensions Media, 1990.

Powerful Writing. The Poynter Institute, 1992.

The Reel World of News. PBS Video, 1982.

Six O'Clock News and All's Well. Cinema Guild, 1980.

The Television Newsman. Pyramid Film & Video, 1976.

TV News: Behind the Scene. Kentucky Educational Television, 1985.

TV News: Behind the Scenes. Encyclopedia Britannica, 1973.

TV News: Measure of the Medium. Phoenix/BFA, Inc., 1971.

A TV News Story. Luminance Films, 1991.

I N D E X